The Monster

'Attempting to stab – Liverpool', *Illustrated Police News*, 27 September 1884. Reproduced with the permission of the British Library, Colindale Newspaper Library.

The Monster Evil

Policing and Violence in Victorian Liverpool

John E. Archer

LIVERPOOL UNIVERSITY PRESS

First published 2011 by
Liverpool University Press
4 Cambridge Street
Liverpool L69 7ZU

British Library Cataloguing-in-Publication data
A British Library CIP record is available

ISBN 978-1-84631-657-9 (hardback)
ISBN 978-1-84631-683-8 (paperback)

Typeset in Warnock by R. J. Footring Ltd, Derby
Printed and bound in the UK by Bell and Bain Ltd, Glasgow

For my Mother
and in memory
of my Father

Contents

List of illustrations, figures and tables

Preface

British society has over the last generation expressed growing concerns about gang violence, gun crime, hooded youths, racist assaults and, most frightening of all, paedophiles. Liverpool, along with other major cities, has occupied a place in the pantheon of public fears. The Toxteth riots, the murder of James Bulger in 1993 and of Anthony Walker in 2005 and Rhys Jones in 2007 brought unwelcome attention to the city. These incidents and crimes are seen as 'new' or 'unprecedented' by some sections of the press, signifying to some that society is in the process of disintegration. The term 'broken Britain' was even used during the 2010 general election. Historians interested in violent crime, while mindful of the present, need to look back and discover the histories of such crimes and their locations. This book is an attempt to understand violent crime in the context of Liverpool. The city, a world port and second city of the British Empire, gained a unique and notorious reputation during the second half of the nineteenth century for being an abnormally violent and criminal place.

The Monster Evil explores the historical foundations of Liverpool's stigmatization and, in the process, examines whether the fears of violence were real or an invention of the Victorian newspapers. As we know only too well today, perceptions of violence and the reality of violent crime can lead separate and independent existences from each other. Attempting to gauge the 'reality' of crime is a notoriously difficult, if not impossible, business. One way to attempt some kind of estimation is through the interpretation of criminal statistics and, nowadays, the British Crime Survey (BCS). However, historians working on the nineteenth century do not have the luxury of being able to use the BCS figures; they have, instead, the annual statistics collected by the local police forces. These were flawed, so much so that historians bent on simply counting crimes face enormous methodological difficulties. This has not prevented eminent historians from forming judgements, most notably Vic Gatrell (see bibliography), who concluded that there was an extraordinary decline in crimes of violence between 1850 and 1914. Such a conclusion is examined here in the light of Liverpool's experience up to 1900.

In addition to a quantitative approach, I have chosen to examine and analyse in a more qualitative fashion all forms of reported everyday violence and the more unusual and notorious acts of brutality. By attempting to discover the social dynamics contained within the acts of violence, and by locating and contextualizing these crimes in relation to Liverpool, I hope to present readers with the first significant account of nineteenth-century violence in any English city. Many of the themes, such as age, class, ethnicity and gender, are not unique to Liverpool but the pressures acting on the borough's population were distinctive and contributed to how the town (it gained city status only in 1880) and some its population reacted to social and economic pressures and tensions. In attempting to understand the violence experienced within the borough it is necessary to understand how the town was policed and whether the behaviour and presence of this constabulary force contributed either directly or indirectly to the violence. This will lead to a consideration of how violence was perceived by the majority of the population.

In pursuing this study of Liverpool, I have found a number of historical interpretations and debates of past violent behaviour informative, instructive and thought provoking. The findings and conclusions of other scholars have implicitly and explicitly informed this study. Recent historical studies have examined and analysed criminal violence in relation to class and gender. Notably, three historians, Clive Emsley, Martin Wiener and J. Carter Wood (see bibliography), have examined male violence, both towards other men and towards women. They have argued that violence was increasingly condemned and prosecuted during the nineteenth century. Customary forms of fighting, such as the 'fair fight', which had traditionally been regarded as 'English' and an expression of manliness, were increasingly regarded by the police and the courts as illegal and punishable. Violence, whether in the home or on the streets, was deemed unmanly, vicious and brutal behaviour, and those who partook in such practices were regarded as little better than savages and brutes. Violence took on new meanings and was tolerated less and punished more. Traditional male behaviour, albeit brutal to modern eyes, such as beating one's wife, became subject to heavier punishments, although, as Wiener showed in his 2006 work *Men of Blood*, the 'moral worth' of the wife continued to be taken into account by judges and juries. That is, wives who fulfilled the Victorian ideals of domesticity and femininity were regarded with sympathy when victims of their male partners' drunken assaults, whereas female victims who were classed as idle drunkards or adulteresses did not command the same kind of sympathy in court, which meant their male attackers were treated more leniently and even had their cases dismissed. This book thus intends to examine the changes in attitude towards violence and its policing over the second half of the nineteenth century.

This book has arisen from an Economic and Social Research Council project I undertook between 1998 and 2001 on violence in the north-west of England between 1850 and 1914. In undertaking that study and the writing of this book on Liverpool between 1850 and 1900 I have consulted the *Liverpool Mercury* over the course of the 50-year period. Begun in 1811, this newspaper was chosen because of its continuous run, its moderate tone when it came to the reporting of crime, and its excellent 'police court' column. Given my time constraints, it was not possible to examine every edition of the paper and so I chose to examine a three-monthly random sample for each year. If a crime was unresolved within the sample period, I followed it up, where possible, as far as the month in which the case was settled in court. This allowed me to gather a wealth of information on reported violent crime within the borough, whether it occurred within the home or workplace or on the street. Details of what was said, who the victim was, what weapons (if any) were used and the attitudes of both the police and the neighbourhood to the violence sometimes emerge in these reports. A number of other national and local newspapers and journals were consulted, foremost among them the *Porcupine*, Hugh Shimmin's highly critical and readable liberal paper, which began life in 1860. All these papers provided different insights into interpersonal violence, especially in relation to people's attitudes towards it. Unfortunately, it was often difficult to find evidence from the people most directly involved in the violence, as either victims or perpetrators, although what in the court proceedings was reported to have been said does offer some indication. I have quoted some press reports at length in the book. This gives an immediacy to the events being reported which the reader would not gain from an indirect and abbreviated report written by me. The language of the reports and where the emphasis was placed within the news items allow readers to form judgements and offer them insights into the Victorian era.

Other source material also provided interesting insights. Depositions from witnesses held at The National Archive at Kew in London occasionally added to the detailed press reports of assize trials. The annual registers of Liverpool coroner's court for the 1850s and early 1860s were particularly useful in identifying possible infanticides. The Liverpool police have a few surviving records, among which are the unusual daily report books for the latter years of the nineteenth century. These give historians a view of violence that went unprosecuted, particularly fights between policemen within the confines of the police station. In addition, the Liverpool Record Office (LvRO) holds an almost complete run of the head constable's annual reports, as well as reports to the borough watch committee. Some records belonging to the Liverpool Society for the Prevention of Cruelty to Children are also held at the LvRO and these document a large number of cases of violence to young children.

An act of violence, whether a punch or a stab, whether to a partner, to a stranger in the street or to a child, contains a story. In their time, such incidents were briefly news items and now, 150 years or so later, they are being turned into history. The historian has to look for the significance hidden in such anti-social acts and try to explain them to later generations. Sometimes there may be no significance: they are just random acts of brutality that can strike in unpredictable ways during any decade, in any town or city. That is why it is dangerous to impart too much significance to one particular act of violence and draw conclusions that the society in which the violence occurred is, or was, 'broken'. Politicians are often quick to read too much into individual events and it might be helpful to people nowadays to learn what reactions were generated in the nineteenth century to particularly gruesome crimes. The story or narrative is, therefore, not just about the act of violence, how it was dealt with and punished, but also about how it was regarded. Was there a panic, did it set off general fears about being a possible victim of violence? *The Monster Evil* examines violence in all its many facets, from murder to minor assaults, in one town over a 50-year period; in doing so it will provide the reader with insights into the level of violence in years gone by and how that society responded.

The book is divided into three parts: chapters 1 and 2 form an introductory section. In chapter 1 the aims of the book are set out. These are, namely: to examine Liverpool's criminal reputation in the second half of the nineteenth century; to establish how the borough was policed; and to analyse and describe all forms of everyday violence which occurred within the borough. The chapter also examines the increasing stigmatization of the port as a place of violence during the second half of the century. Newspapers, both local and national, identified and labelled the town, particularly in the 1870s, as brutal and dangerous. Moreover, its inhabitants were branded as drunken and debauched and Victorians were able to deploy criminal statistics to support their views. In chapter 2, Liverpool's distinctive dock-based economy and the society on which it was built are examined. The areas and streets regarded as 'rough' and dangerous by Victorians are identified and the role of alcohol in interpersonal violence is considered.

Part II of the book, chapters 3 and 4, is concerned with the Liverpool borough police. Chapter 3 examines the rise of the 'new police', which in Liverpool was the biggest force outside London, making it the most heavily policed town in provincial England. This fact had inevitable consequences for the amount of reported violence in the town. Contemporary Liverpool journalist Hugh Shimmin gave a detailed eyewitness account of night duty, during the mid-1850s. His series of articles, from which extended extracts are reproduced in the appendix to the book, provides one of the most detailed and authentic accounts of what it was like to police a large town at night. His obvious sympathy and support for the force, which is so evident in 1857, is dispelled in chapter 4, which examines police–community relations over the 50 years. Shimmin, along with many others, came to be suspicious of the force and challenged its increasingly dictatorial ways. Accusations of police violence to members of the public are examined, as are the anti-police attitudes which were so evident in certain neighbourhoods.

Part III deals with crimes of interpersonal violence under the headings of ethnicity, gender and age. Chapter 5 deals with the large influx of poor Irish immigrants, who were soon regarded as being responsible for half the town's crime while making up only about a quarter of the borough's population. The question of their criminality and their violence, especially when associated with heavy drinking, is considered. There was, in addition, considerable anti-Irish and sectarian prejudice against Roman Catholics from the local population and from members of the police. This led to riots and a clear-out of the police force in the 1850s. Everyday sectarian tensions never really dissipated for the remainder of the century but they tended to rise and fall with the politics of Home Rule and Fenianism. Chapters 6 and 7 deal with the main instigators of violent crime: men. The former chapter begins with a case study of a fatal fight at Aintree in 1875 which brings into sharp relief Victorian working-class values associated with the 'fair fight', male culture and the attributes of masculinity. Increasingly during the nineteenth century there was a clash between Victorian middle-class notions of masculine respectability and working-class manliness. However, did the reality of working-class violence match traditional beliefs of English fair play, in which weapons were not used? The chapter examines numerous examples of violence in public houses, knife fighting and racist violence directed against black sailors and the local black community. In chapter 7, the notorious Tithebarn Street murder of 1874 is examined in the context of both the national press reaction and the 'cornerman' phenomenon. The latter came to prominence in the 1860s; cornermen were also known as 'roughs', and this labelling process continued through to the 1890s. During the 1880s a supposedly new problem, the High Rip gang, terrorized the city, but was it just a case of a new label being placed on a group of young men who had long been identified as problematic and dangerous?

Chapters 8 and 9 deal with women as perpetrators and victims of violence. The former chapter considers the reputation of Liverpool women, who were regarded as some of the most violent in the country. The realities of living in overcrowded slums meant that many poor women failed to conform to the Victorian ideals of womanhood; moreover, because they were women they were stigmatized more than men when they committed acts of violence. Some violence was peculiarly specific to women, such as the killing of infants and very young children; these crimes were associated with poverty. Women were thought by contemporaries to use underhand and surreptitious methods in the killing of their victims, such as poison. Flanagan and Higgins' notorious poisonings clearly fall into this category but an examination of how women fought or killed, and what weapons they used, suggests that this sensational case was untypical.

Most studies have viewed women as victims of male violence and chapter 9 begins with such a case, the murder of Dinah Quigley in 1867. This incident is used to illustrate contemporary attitudes towards domestic violence both in Liverpool and across the nation. Despite increasingly tough laws against domestic violence, popular attitudes could be complex and ambivalent towards such incidents. News reports tended to label the victims as either good wives, and thus worthy of the reader's sympathy, or drunken slovenly women, who clearly attracted a harsher range of emotions. The courts, too, might assign blame to the woman victim if she failed to measure up to stereotypes of female respectability. The chapter concludes with a brief examination of sex crimes and, in keeping with modern-day conventions, victim anonymity is maintained.

Chapter 10 begins with the infamous matricide of 1873 in which a son 'danced' on the unconscious body of his mother in the then notorious Chisenhale Street. This murder was regarded with horror by contemporaries and attracted large crowds of sightseers to the scene of the killing. This chapter lays bare the casual brutality that family members inflicted upon one another, in what were often hidden crimes. Although these familial crimes shared many of the features of domestic violence – victims were often female, for example – this kind of violence could display notable differences, inasmuch as daughters and mothers also fought with one another and the assailants were not invariably male.

Attitudes towards violent children have changed greatly over the centuries. In chapter 11, two separate murders, in 1855 and 1891, in which both the victims and the assailants were under 10 years of age, are examined in detail. How the Victorians viewed and dealt with these two killings may seem surprising when set against the murder of James Bulger in 1993. In neither of the two nineteenth-century cases was there a suggestion that society was broken or in terminal decline. However, when a teenage killing on Christmas Eve occurred in 1883, closely followed by another killing by teenagers early in the new year, public discussion about youth social policy was generated. This was soon followed up with the formation of youth clubs and institutions in the city.

Children were more commonly the victims of adult brutality but the dividing line between legal chastisement and criminal violence was not always clear, either to parents or to teachers, or even to the courts. It was considered acceptable for children to be routinely disciplined for minor acts of disobedience but as the century progressed children were increasingly seen as vulnerable and in need of protection. Liverpool became the first town in England to establish a society for the protection of children, predating the National Society for the Prevention of Cruelty to Children by six years. As a result, more cases of child abuse came to the notice of the authorities. Chapter 12 concludes with a brief study of the sexual abuse of children. Details were not published in the papers but it has been possible to draw conclusions regarding popular reactions to such incidents. Public anger and popular fears of paedophilia were, by present-day standards, muted.

The book concludes by returning to the question posed in chapter 1: did Liverpool deserve its reputation? Other questions, such as whether Liverpool conformed to the national pattern of declining violence by the end of the century and what continuities and changes over time were experienced by the city, will also be addressed. While this study is not exhaustive in its coverage, and is not necessarily the only approach, I hope it offers some insights into the violence experienced by the people of Liverpool in the second half of the nineteenth century.

Acknowledgements

The history of violence has attracted enormous scholarly interest over the last two decades. While not being one of the original 'gang of violence' historians, I was soon recruited from rural East Anglia, where my investigations into arson, poaching and horse ripping were coming to an end. Ever since being drawn into the world of violence, I have met and been inspired by many fellow colleagues in crime. Not all were historians, for Professor Betsy Stanko, formerly of Royal Holloway, University of London, and now at the Metropolitan Police, gave me the opportunity to study the history of violence in the north-west of England between 1850 and 1914, as part of the Violence Research Programme, funded by the Economic and Social Research Council (ESRC) (award number L133251004), out of which this study of violence in Liverpool between 1850 and 1900 arose. She was an inspiring colleague who provided great leadership to the ambitious and successful violence project. To her and the other project leaders I owe a debt of gratitude. In undertaking my project I had considerable help from researchers – David Orr, Carol Lewis-Roylance and Jo Jones – who undertook a lot of the retrieval work in record offices and archives throughout the north-west. To Jo a special word of thanks for her enthusiasm, computer skills and unfailing cheerfulness during her two years with the project.

I would also like to thank the staff at the record offices and libraries at Liverpool, Manchester, the Merseyside Police at Canning Place, The National Archive in London and the British Library and Colindale for their help, advice, service and permission to reproduce images from the *Illustrated Police News*. The British Library should be given enormous credit for the digitalization of nineteenth-century newspapers, which provides an incredible fund of information for students and academics. This resource came on stream during the writing of this book, and I thank Edge Hill's Learning Resources for allowing me access to it. My thanks also go to cartographer Sandra Mather for her excellent map of Liverpool in the 1880s (p. xix) and to Alison Welsby of Liverpool University Press, who has been a most supportive and helpful editor.

As I said at the beginning, there are many historians now working in the field of crime, policing and violence. I suppose the 'Godfather' – I hope he does not mind me calling him that – is Clive Emsley, whose leadership in these fields and encouragement to us juniors have been greatly appreciated. Other colleagues and friends, over the course of years and at conferences, have been especially helpful to me: Alyson Brown, Carolyn Conley, Shani D'Cruze, Barry Godfrey, Louise Jackson, Peter King, the late Eric Monkkonen, Frank Neal, Judith Rowbotham, Jim Sharpe, Bob Storch, Howard Taylor, John Walton, Martin Wiener, Chris Williams and John Carter Wood. To them and the many others, too numerous to mention, I extend my thanks. My gratitude finally extends to two close colleagues and friends: first, to Laurie Feehan, who, as a colleague in the history department at Edge Hill University, introduced me to Hugh Shimmin and the history of Liverpool; and second, to Andy Davies, who, more than any other friend, has been so encouraging, critical in the most supportive way, and generous in his advice from the years before, during and after the ESRC project. His intelligent and, at times, critical responses to much of this book when it was in the drafting stage were helpful beyond measure. My thanks go to all those mentioned above. Needless to say, none of them is responsible for my errors of judgement or interpretation, or any mistakes which may have found their way into the text.

Last but not least, I wish to thank my family: my two sons, James and Tom, for reminding me of my fallibilities in the nicest possible way, and James for providing me with crucial IT advice, and my wife, Helen, who has patiently lived with this project and with me all these years. Her encouragement, her love and patience during a few bleak years of poor health, and her intelligent and close scrutiny of my work, have been more generous than anyone, least of all me, could expect or hope for.

Abbreviations

BPP	British parliamentary papers
IPN	*Illustrated Police News*
LM	*Liverpool Mercury*
LR	*Liverpool Review*
LSPCC	Liverpool Society for the Prevention of Cruelty to Children
LvRO	Liverpool Record Office
MC	*Manchester Courier*
NSPCC	National Society for the Prevention of Cruelty to Children
PC	police constable
PMG	*Pall Mall Gazette*
TNA	The National Archives

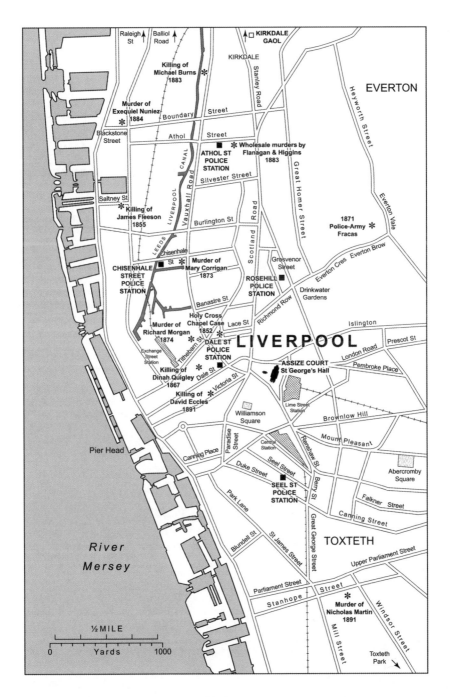

Street map of Liverpool in the 1880s, showing the locations of the more notorious murders discussed in the text.

Part I
Liverpool

Chapter 1

Liverpool and the taint of criminality

Crimes of violence and disorder were the monster evil....[1]

DURING THE COURSE of the nineteenth century Liverpool was stigma-tized as being abnormally violent and criminal. No other British town or city was regarded in quite the same way as Liverpool. Violence was, acknowledged the town's professional magistrate, Mr Thomas S. Raffles, 'the monster evil'. He had, after all, to deal with violent crime on a daily basis in the police court. It is a reputation which Liverpool has had trouble shaking off even to this day. In the decades following 1850 the taint of criminality increasingly stained the town's reputation.

This book attempts to establish the origins of this criminal stigma through an examination of everyday violent crime within the town during the Victorian period and how it was reported in the regional and national press. In doing so, it has to be asked how far the borough's infamy was founded on fact, prejudice or press exaggeration. In answering such difficult questions we need to sift through early-Victorian statistical data. Such data collection was in its infancy and was, and is, full of bear traps for the unwary and uncritical observer. The claim, allegedly made by Disraeli, of 'Lies, damned lies and statistics' needs to be kept firmly in the forefront of the historian's mind when pouring over the seemingly useful pages of 'facts' so carefully collected and documented by utilitarian empiricists, who believed the statistics equalled useful knowledge that would improve society and move civilization forward.

Liverpool was subject to many forces and pressures that were absent in other British towns and cities. While it escaped the hot-house forces of industrialization and factory mechanization which were occurring just down the road, canal and railway line, Liverpool was nonetheless supplying this enormous expansion by virtue of being Britain's, if not the world's, premier port. Not only did vast supplies of raw cotton get dropped off there but so also did large numbers of immigrants, particularly Irish people, who arrived in their tens of thousands even before the 'Great Hunger' of the 1840s. Their poverty and their willingness to work in hard manual labour, combined with their enthusiasm to drink, brought many and pressing social problems, not least overcrowding, underemployment at the docks and drunkenness on the streets. At any one time the port itself was a temporary home for 30,000 sailors who, on landing, were paid off. They were all men and did what many men did when away from home: they drank, sought out prostitutes and fought one another. Liverpool was, it should be emphasized, an overwhelmingly male-dominated town in which masculine pastimes predominated. This inevitably contributed to Liverpool's unsavoury reputation as a violent and unpredictable town. The book examines crimes of violence in particular, from mundane street assaults (often perpetrated by and on drunken men) to domestic violence within the home and between neighbours and violent children. The behaviour of the police, whose job it was to control this 'savagery', is also examined critically.

When looking at these crimes of interpersonal violence we have to ask how different in character and context this violence was from that seen nowadays. Were weapons used? What were the prevailing attitudes towards the use of weapons in fights? Was some violence deemed legitimate and acceptable by those involved? If so, in what circumstances and by whom was the violence not regarded as criminal and prosecutable? And finally, did attitudes towards violent behaviour alter over the second half of the nineteenth century? By looking at Liverpool it is possible to gain some kind of insight into the manner and ways violent crime, through the medium of the newspaper press, affected British society during the nineteenth century.

Liverpool and the rise of its disrepute

IDENTIFYING AND DATING Liverpool's poor reputation is a difficult task. By examining newspapers, regional and national, and government reports from the 1830s we are able to spot the slow and irresistible rise of Liverpool as a town of danger, crime and 'evil'. Liverpool was in many ways no different from other large towns and cities then emerging in the frenzied period of the industrial revolution. Urban centres were perceived as the corrupting heart of nineteenth-century society, in which crime was perceived as a kind of barometer of the nation's well-being. If crime rose, then society was immoral and vice ridden; conversely, if it declined, then those in authority were able to congratulate themselves for having implemented enlightened and morally improving legislation.

Amid the slums, alleys and courts where contagious diseases spread with the same rapidity as contagious vice, a new breed of people was thought to be emerging, namely the 'criminal classes'. They came to dominate government enquiries, social discourses on crime, prisons and even literature, if *Oliver Twist* is taken as representative of the period. One of the predominant 'instincts' of members of the criminal classes – apart, that is, from their desire to steal, their love of alcohol and their disinclination to work – was to migrate. It was thought in the late 1830s that these people moved from the policed towns to the unpoliced countryside, where they were able to rob and steal with impunity before returning to the anonymity of the town. The urban criminal became the rural hinterland's bogeyman.

Liverpool was the second largest conurbation in the country, with a population of 376,000 in 1851. Manchester, by comparison, numbered 303,000 and was the nation's third largest city. The port dwarfed neighbouring towns and dominated southern Lancashire to such an extent it was regarded by the mid-1830s as the centre for criminals. When asked about the state of local crime, one south Lancastrian's reply to Edwin Chadwick, who was then in the process of collecting information on rural policing, stated, 'County crime is not generally committed by rural residents but people from Liverpool'. Liverpool's criminal reputation grew with the advent of the Lancashire constabulary's war with criminal poaching gangs in the early 1840s, particularly the Long Gang, half of whom hailed from Liverpool. One must remember how (unlike today) the town suddenly became countryside; just a short walk from Boundary Street brought one out into the fields and game covers owned by Lord Derby and the Blundell and Molyneux families. In 1851, during a spate of armed robberies on farms north of the town, it was reported that the perpetrators made good their escape 'across the fields to Liverpool'.[2]

By 1860 the *Morning Chronicle*, in a news item headed 'CRIME IN LIVERPOOL', reported that in the past week there had been at least seven stabbings, three of which were likely to prove fatal. It continued, 'In respect to tragedies Liverpool can scarcely be surpassed by London, with a population eight times as great'.[3]

Liverpool's infamy as place of unremitting criminal activity and barbarity surfaced again in the wake of the Tithebarn Street murder of 1874, in which a respectable working man, Richard Morgan, was kicked to death on a busy thoroughfare by a group of roughs, known as 'cornermen', in front of a large crowd which evidently relished the sight of a fight. The murder of Morgan came to symbolize all that was wrong and bad with the port. Hugh Shimmin, one of Liverpool's proudest advocates and leading journalists, wrote:

> In the midst of the evidences of Liverpool's proud pre-eminence as the great centre of the world's commerce, we are now and then – alas! Sadly too often – reminded that Liverpool has a world-wide notoriety as the harbour and refuge of the most desperate ruffians unhung.... The riverside streets of New York have an ominous reputation for deeds of sudden violence. People think but little comparatively, so frequent is the occurrence of revolver shots along the East River, and the finding subsequently of floating forms, decomposed beyond recognition, but with a bullet or bowie-knife stab near the heart. Along the levees of New Orleans, by the quays of San Francisco, behind the wharves of Shanghae and Calcutta, scenes of desperate outrage for the sake of plunder often occur which sailors recount with a shudder. But for examples of

unmitigated ruffianism, unexplained (as in other and more southern ports) by
unpremeditated outbreaks of national fierceness, the lower streets of Liverpool
remain unrivalled.[4]

Even allowing for exaggeration, when one of Liverpool's most pre-eminent
journalists talks of the town's infamy in such terms it would seem reasonable to conclude that crime was a significant social problem and that
'cornermen' were its source. Their involvement and presence in numbers in
Liverpool came to signify the lawlessness of the place. Headlines in national
newspapers after the Tithebarn Street incident included 'LAWLESSNESS IN
LIVERPOOL', 'CRIME IN LIVERPOOL' and 'THE ROUGH TERROR'. Under the
last, the *Pall Mall Gazette* went on to claim: 'In Lancashire, for example,
the rough maims or murders as it suits his fancy, the victim being as often
a man as a woman; the only requirement in the former case being that he
shall be old, and, consequently, not likely to strike or kick in return, or that
the assailants shall outnumber the assaulted in the proportion of at least
three to one.' This latter comment was a direct reference to the Tithebarn
Street murder. In some cases Liverpool's own press gave credence to this
reputation. The *Liverpool Albion* reported:

> In returning once more to the discussion of crimes of violence in Liverpool,
> our excuse must be the pressing importance of the subject in the minds of all
> respectable and orderly people, and the prominence that has been given to it in
> the columns of *The Times*. The revelations of horrible brutality at the last and
> several recent Assizes have so sullied the fair name of Liverpool in the sight of
> the whole country that, though we may not be sinners above all the towns of
> the North West of England, our reputation is fast becoming unpleasant. Wigan,
> St. Helens, Bolton, Burnley, and other notorious Lancashire towns have long
> been recognized centres of brutality, but Liverpool has hitherto been content
> to know itself as the most drunken town in England; now, however, it has not
> only added a propensity to commit barbarous violence to its reputation....

The *Albion*'s comments, initially read by a small provincial readership, were
reprinted in full by the *Times* and thus guaranteed further revulsion by a
wide and important national readership.[5] Newspapers labelled the borough
firmly in the reading public's consciousness as dangerous and inhabited by
northern brutes, who became the 'folk devils' of the time. This 1874 murder
created a moral panic, which, unusually, was not London-inspired like the
garrotting panic of 1862, the 1864 rail murder, or the Whitechapel or Jack
the Ripper murders of the late 1880s. Government enquiries on violent
crime were called for and initiated, although to no great effect.

Lancashire as a whole was sucked into this panic by virtue of being
notorious for a form of fighting considered by observers to be unique
to the county, namely 'purring' or kicking; it also witnessed a number of
particularly brutal crimes in 1874. One Manchester newspaper reported
that 'the common tendency to substitute the clog for the fist in Lancashire
has no parallel in any other county in the kingdom'. Such sentiments had

earlier been aired by deputy judge Mr Higgin QC at the summer Liverpool assizes when he spoke of purring being 'peculiar to Lancashire', especially in colliery districts, where men used 'their feet more freely than their fists'. The assize court case-load for south Lancashire was not only heavy but also featured many serious crimes. The cases included four charges of murder, two of manslaughter, 10 of cutting and wounding, one of conceal-ment of birth and six of rape. In all, there were 60 prisoners brought to trial. Its notoriety led to the sobriquet of the 'black assizes' because four of those charged were sentenced to death. The *Liverpool Mercury*'s headline 'LANCASHIRE BRUTALITY' and the *Times*' 'THE LAST ATROCITY IN LANCASHIRE' emphasized the county's criminality. In February 1875 *Punch* magazine observed that a newly published book on the vocabulary and grammar of the Romany language referred to Lancashire as the 'kicking country', or 'Peero-dillin-tem' in their dialect.[6] The magazine blurred the distinction between the county as a whole and the port of Liverpool in particular in its depiction of 'roughs'. In one cartoon published the previous January, the 'rough' expresses surprise and disgust that a man was actually hanged for the seemingly unimportant crime of kicking his wife to death. While the accompanying poem referred to Lancashire and 'brass-tipped clogs', the cartoon explicitly refers to a 'Liverpool Ruffian'. Later that month *Punch* carried the words to a satirical 'new national song', 'The British Boot', which again refers to the Lancashire clog, while a cartoon depicts two Liverpool roughs discussing the possible penalty one of them would be receiving for beating his wife to 'within an inch of her life'.[7]

Thus, Liverpool had by the mid-1870s gained its notorious reputation for being the criminal capital of Britain. Many newspapers around the country published extracts from the town's annual head constable's reports, with his observations on the crimes committed during the previous 12 months. Such coverage suggested that Liverpool had become a benchmark for crime by which other towns and cities measured their own criminality. Moreover, its citizens were, according to the *Pall Mall Gazette*, 'negligent of their duties' in allowing both an exceedingly high mortality rate and crimes of violence, 'which are almost daily done in Liverpool'.[8]

The town's press accepted its notoriety; however, there was a subtle and important variant to the local newspaper headlines, in which they identified particular neighbourhoods as being rough and dangerous. By implication this helped middle-class readers steer clear of certain slum areas and streets such as Scotland Road. For those who lived there, Liverpool became a town composed of 'good and safe' streets and 'dangerous' roads and courts. This notion was taken to extremes by what can only be described as a moral map of Liverpool, drawn up in 1858 by the Rev. A. Hume. The streets of the town were shaded in different ways to denote moral and immoral repute. More recently, the *Liverpool Echo* ran a story identifying Liverpool's present-day 'streets of danger'.[9]

Within five years of the Tithebarn tragedy, both Liverpool and Lancashire were again making the headlines. The Manchester press, generally quick to identify and name Liverpool as a criminal and violent place, carried the headlines 'BRUTAL VIOLENCE IN LIVERPOOL' and 'LANCASHIRE KICKING', and the *Manchester Courier* carried an editorial on crimes of violence in Lancashire.[10] Was all this press attention towards Lancashire and Liverpool justified, or were the newspapers contributing to the region's previously established violent reputation? Certainly the writer of a letter to the *Liverpool Mercury* thought the press exaggerated the amount and effects of crime. To modern readers this seems a familiar criticism of the so-called 'red tops' or popular tabloids but such newspaper treatment of crime stories dates back to the growth of the popular press and cheap newspapers in the 1850s and '60s. Moreover, this coincided with the rise and popularity of the sensational novel, in which crime or sexual misconduct, albeit heavily clothed and disguised, titillated and thrilled readers with forbidden pleasurable feelings. A murder or some other serious crime contains a narrative in which the story has a beginning, middle and end; thus it lends itself to both fiction and news reporting. There is no doubt that Liverpool was subjected in 1874 to what was termed by Victorians 'loud writing': hyperbolic and, at times, hysterical news coverage. Liverpool's head constable, Major Greig, certainly thought so; in 1875, in a speech to police on parade at Rosehill station on 'the recent comments of the press relative to Liverpool lawlessness', he said that, 'during his 20 years' experience in Liverpool he had never seen anything beyond a brawl that might occur in any town of even the smallest population'. He asserted that what had been said and written about the dangers of the town's streets was the product of 'heated imaginations'.[11] Such comments by the head constable indicated a level of indifference bordering on the blasé, which did not endear him to the town council, which, in its own words, had to 'do something' to combat cornermen.

How criminal was Liverpool?
Victorian statistics and their interpretation

HOW CRIMINAL AND VIOLENT was Liverpool, and how did it compare with other major British cities? Indeed, how were such comparisons made and what, if any, dangers are there in making such comparisons now? Normally, the number of criminal acts is counted, and the total is compared with the totals for other towns or previous years. It was, and still is in certain quarters, argued that the true state of a town's criminality can be accurately assessed in this way. Prior to the start of the nineteenth century there was no way of knowing the prevalence of criminality in Britain, as no statistics were collected; nor did the authorities think it important to know. However, there was a sea change in attitudes in the years leading up to 1850.

Reformers brought change to the Poor Law, registration of births, deaths and marriages, the police, the prisons, and the publication of national statistics, which included the national census from 1801 and crime figures from 1810. The tabulated crime figures initially reported only the number of men and women committed for serious indictable offences. More meaningful and fuller data emerged in 1834, with the classification of criminal offences under six headings, including the most pertinent one for this particular study, offences against the person. This category covered indictable crimes of violence, from murder and other forms of homicide to simple assault. Further changes were introduced in 1856 and 1893, which allowed the reporting of more detailed statistics, for instance the number of indictable offences reported to the police (i.e. including those which did not result in a prosecution). These later improvements in data collection finally brought to light the figures for lesser crimes, notably those heard in magistrates' courts. Thus historians are able to glimpse the more mundane and everyday crimes of common assault and violence that occupied the attention of both the police and local neighbourhoods.[12] Do all these tables and figures tell us anything, though, of relevance to this study? Was Liverpool particularly criminal compared with, say, Manchester? Were there significant rises and falls in crimes of violence over the period within the borough? Was the past more violent than today?

Before any answers can be provided, let us inspect some of these crime tables for Liverpool and examine the amounts of criminal activity which were either prosecuted or known to the police, because that it is what these data represent – known crime. There is the 'dark figure' of unreported and unknown crime, whose numbers probably far exceeded the known total of reported crime, but historians have no way of knowing how large this figure was. However, there is one serious crime which experts believe was widely reported, thus narrowing the gap between reported crime and actual crime, and that is murder. Various studies have shown an overall national decline in murder during the past 500 years; that decline reflects a growing civility and an intolerance of violent behaviour in general. Nonetheless, recent research has questioned whether there really was a national decline in murder during the 100 or so years before the late twentieth century. Taylor, the historian, has suggested that murder charges in Britain between 1880 and 1966 were 'rationed' to about 150 per year because of budgetary constraints with regard to investigating and prosecuting them. The logical conclusion to his study is that some murders go uninvestigated and unrecorded. Evidence from nineteenth-century Liverpool will be put forward to support this conclusion.[13]

Whatever the drawbacks to the statistics on homicide, it is perhaps significant that one of the leading American historians on homicide has frequently compared historical data from New York with data from Liverpool. The latter, he argued, shared similarities with the former in terms of possessing

Table 1 The numbers of homicides in Liverpool, 1858–1901

Year	Murder	Manslaughter	Concealment
1858	3	9	3
1863	7	18	3
1864	9	17	1
1865	13	21	2
1866	8	25	0
1867	6	25	1
1868	27	30	2
1869	20	15	1
1870	10	21	1
1871	10	22	1
1872	5	19	0
1873	2	11	1
1874	8	10	1
1875	4	18	1
1876	3	14	1
1877	8	8	2
1878	1 + 3*	17	0
1879	4	9	2
1880	2 + 2*	10	3
1881	2 + 3*	15	0
1882	1 + 3*	4	0
1883	1 + 2*	13	0
1884	7	11	0
1885	1	9	0
1886	1 + 1*	6	2
1887	3 + 1*	6	1
1888	2	11	3
1889	4	13	3
1890	0	0	0
1891	4 + 2*	7	2
1892	2 + 1*	17	2
1893	2 + 1*	11	2
1894	2 + 1*	5	2
1896	3 + 1*	14	0
1898	3	6	4
1899	1 + 2*	8	4
1901	1	6	0

*Denotes murder of infants aged one year and under.
These figures have been taken from the head constable's annual reports bound in the annual *Proceedings of the Council*, Liverpool Record Office, H352 cou, Liverpool head constable's annual reports to the Liverpool watch committee. Figures for the years 1859–62, 1895, 1897 and 1900 were not available.

high numbers of immigrants, and the two cities had similar economies based on their ports. Moreover, Liverpool had a higher homicide rate than London and even displayed similar murder trends and rates to those of New York around the mid-nineteenth century. Thereafter, New York's homicide rate eclipsed Liverpool's, which began to mirror the national rate.[14] Can Liverpool's murder figures tell us anything significant about the port? Was it an unusually dangerous place, deserving its infamous reputation? Table 1 presents the annual numbers of homicides, classified as murder, manslaughter or 'concealment of birth' (on which see chapter 8).

Several conclusions can be drawn from table 1, not least that the numbers of homicides are relatively small for a port with a population of some half a million. No pattern is discernible in figures for the concealment of birth, which are partly complicated by the inclusion of a new heading for murder of children under one year old from 1878. This new statistical entry suggests a growing concern for children and infants rather than signifying an increasing rate of infant homicide. The manslaughter data likewise are difficult to interpret; however, there is a noticeable build-up in the 1860s, with a significant peak in 1868. The murder figures display a similar peak when, in 1868, 27 were known to the police. Translated into a murder rate per 100,000 of the population, Liverpool reached 5.65 in that year; by contrast the rate in New York was 5.8 and in London a mere 0.41 in 1868. Ten years later the Liverpool homicide rate had declined to 0.19 and London to 0.11, while New York remained at around 5 per 100,000. For one brief moment Liverpool appears to have been as violent and murderous as New York. Liverpool in the 1860s would appear, if the figures are correct, to have been caught up in a wave of homicidal violence. This is where crude statistics mislead. According to the head constable's report for 1867/68, of the 27 reported murders, 23 'were verdicts against persons unknown for the murder of infants found exposed'. The killing of infants, while morally indefensible, has occupied a curious position within English law; whatever the rights or wrongs of the system, English justice has tended to regard infanticide as much less serious than the murder of adults and children above two years old. The murder figures for Liverpool were, in other words, inflated enormously in the 1860s, and especially in 1868, because of bureaucratic and moral concerns in the coroners' courts over the high numbers of infant inquests coming before them.[15] As can be seen from table 1, the murder of infants under one year of age was separated out and given its own heading from 1878. Liverpool's reputation as a murderous city must therefore be heavily qualified. Infanticide was its defining characteristic when it comes to discussing nineteenth-century homicide (see table 2). We will examine in chapter 12 some of the reasons why, in the latter half of the 1890s, Liverpool occupied its unenviable position in possessing, allegedly, the worst record for the murder of children under one year of age, cruelty to children and abandoning children under two years of age. Presented in such

Table 2 Rates of murder of children under one year old, and of cruelty and abandonment of children under two years old, selected towns, 1895–99

Town	Number in the five-year period per 100,000 population
Liverpool	103.48
Bootle	77.11
Wigan	58.18
Warrington	53.49
Wolverhampton	47.8
St Helens	38.81
Manchester	32.31
London	8.94
Southport	5.21

British parliamentary papers, 1901, LXXXIX, *Criminal Statistics for 1899* (Cd 659), p. 45. The difference in prosecution rates was described as 'striking'. It was thought that the presence of societies for the protection of children may have raised the rates in the areas where they operated.

a stark way Liverpool, and to a lesser but equally shocking extent Bootle, appears to be deserving of its infamous reputation. But it will be shown that complex matters cannot be simplified to a table of statistics.

Do the criminal statistics harm or hinder Liverpool's reputation in other areas of incivility and anti-social behaviour? What of the figures for drunkenness, a misdemeanour which is very relevant to any study of crimes of violence? Again, Liverpool's reputation was national and infamous. In 1866 Verner White, in a letter to the *Liverpool Mercury*, posed the question, 'Is Liverpool The Most Drunken Town In England, Is There No Cure?'[16] He presented tables of summary prosecutions for drunkenness, and the ratio of drunks to the populations of certain towns and cities. The figures for Liverpool did not make good reading, for there was one summarily convicted drunk to every 33 of the town's population. The average for commercial ports in England and Wales, excluding Liverpool, was one to every 116¼. Manufacturing towns such as Manchester and Salford returned a very similar ratio, of one to 116½. Ten years later, Father Nugent, the first Roman Catholic prison chaplain and scourge of alcohol in the port, told the Select Committee of the House of Lords on Intemperance that 'Liverpool has an unenviable notoriety as regards its drunkenness'.[17] Pamphlets with titles such as *The Slain in Liverpool During 1864 by Drink* by the Rev. John Jones of Kirkdale, in which readers were regaled with extracts from newspapers reporting drunks, their violence and their untimely deaths, were widely distributed. By way of introduction to his pamphlet, Jones wrote:

> How unwelcome is [its] theme to the feelings both of the writer and the reader. By its very nature it is depressing and saddening in its influence. So have we

felt it while engaged in its preparation. Throwing oneself for the time into the very midst, as it were, of those horrible scenes of life and death enacted by the drunken, the eye loathes at the sight of their bloated and withering forms – the ear turns away from their maddened shouts or expiring groans, the imagination sickens as it dwells on their moral destiny, for there is no life that man can live, no death that man can die, more appalling to the spectator.[18]

There followed, as one can imagine, lurid descriptions of 'the killed and wounded' through drink in the town of Liverpool.

The official statistics are ambiguous and difficult to interpret. Whether a person was 'drunk' was a subjective decision which an individual constable on his beat was permitted to make. But then there was drunk and incapable, and drunk and disorderly, which again lay within the remit of the arresting policeman. On arrest he would take the offending party to the bridewell, where the desk sergeant would either charge the person with an offence or 'refuse the charge', that is, not book the individual, who nonetheless might be permitted to stay overnight in the cells to sober up. The police were even known to escort drunks home for their own safety and well-being. Where the charge was refused, the arrest of the drunk was not entered into the official statistics, even though police time had been spent on the case. As many as 2844 cases were entered into the 'refused charge' book between October 1868 and 1869, and a total of 18,000 were charged for drunk and disorderly behaviour.[19] The head constable at that time, Major Greig, was aggrieved that Liverpool's figures for drunkenness were high in comparison with other towns because of the method of discharging individuals. In Liverpool only magistrates could discharge people once they had been entered into the police's charge book, whereas in other places it was claimed that charges were simply dropped, and as a consequence the person was not entered into the annual statistics for drunkenness. Criminal statistical information for individual towns and cities was, as a result, difficult to use for comparative purposes.[20] All this sounds like special pleading, for Liverpool did have an unusually high number of drunk and disorderly cases, and the official figures, whatever their drawbacks, show an inexorable rise, from just 9832 cases in 1860 to 21,113 prosecutions in 1870. This enormous rise, partly as a result of a police crackdown, led to record-breaking Monday morning case-loads for the magistrates' courts. In October 1869, one weekend's case-load amounted to 325 prisoners being seen before the Liverpool magistrates, of whom 227 were charged with drunkenness.[21]

Conclusion

NINETEENTH-CENTURY Liverpool, in keeping with other major English towns and cities, was subject to a number of crimogenic forces. What made Liverpool different was that these forces were exaggerated or more pronounced. The poverty, the overcrowding, the unemployment and under-employment, the alcohol, the disease, the newcomers and those who were just passing through were elements in a complex matrix that made for a higher than average crime rate and a notorious profile with the surrounding towns and villages, and, on occasion, with the rest of the country. Contemporaries were well aware of these special features. The violence and the crime which appear in the following chapters were reported in the local press, especially the *Liverpool Mercury*. It was a reliable and sympathetic observer of Liverpool life and rarely resorted to sensationalism. One of its reporters, Hugh Shimmin, left to start his own satirical paper, the *Porcupine*, which was a more political and opinionated journal than the *Mercury*. While these two papers form the major sources for this study of the history of violence in Liverpool, other local and national papers have been consulted and these provide an often contrary and, at times, more unflattering picture of the borough. Whether viewed from London or Lancashire, contemporaries considered Liverpool to be an unusual, if not unique, city. An examination of its nineteenth-century profile and character, both social and economic, is particularly helpful in providing us with a deeper understanding of its relationship with crimes of violence.

CHAPTER 2

Liverpool:
'The most immoral of all immoral places'[1]

Liverpool was 'the easiest place to go to the devil in'.[2]

LIVERPOOL WAS, by the Victorian era, one of the world's major ports. As such, the volume and weight of shipping entering and leaving, bringing in raw materials and carrying away finished goods from Britain's industrial heartland, was staggering. In a 12-month period between 1884 and 1885 over 21,000 ships, a mixture of sail and steam, docked in Liverpool. Not surprisingly, during the course of the nineteenth century the town's docks grew and spread, especially northwards, to accommodate this ever-expanding traffic. In their wake, new and vast cargo sheds and warehouses sprang up and, close by, densely built working-class housing was constructed for the workers associated with the port.

The town itself was a place of contrasts and extremes. Opposite the newly built Lime Street train station stood the imposing temple to justice and social and economic inequality, St George's Hall. This fine classical building was eventually completed in 1854, 12 years after its foundation stone was laid. Equally imposing civic buildings were constructed along the short length of William Brown Street. The central library and museum opened in 1860, the Walker Art Gallery in 1876 and the Picton reading room in 1879. All these buildings, monuments to the wealth and success of the port, lay in the midst of slum housing. Dale Street, with its municipal offices and central police station and magistrates' courts, lay within the business district of the town, from which Tithebarn Street, scene of an infamous murder in 1874, radiated out towards the north end courts and slums of Vauxhall Road. The middle classes, on the other hand, tended to congregate away from the centre and up the hill around Abercromby Square, Rodney Street and later around Prince's and Sefton Parks.[3]

The population grew fast in the second half of the nineteenth century. The port more than doubled its population between 1841 and 1891, from 286,000 to 617,000. The largest increase occurred between 1841 and 1851, when tens of thousands poor and starving Irish people made the town their permanent home. This was to have a lasting and significant impact on its culture and character. The Irish, who had already been present in Liverpool for decades, were not the only migrant group to settle. The Welsh, too, had been present for many decades prior to 1841 and the town also had a black community which dated back to the eighteenth century. Liverpool, being a major international port, was a cosmopolitan community and the docks were its life force.[4]

Each dock was, by the 1880s, associated with particular commodities and cargoes. A series of fascinating articles by 'a dock labourer' described how the waterfront was organized. An example from December 1882 reads as follows:

> Beginning at the extreme north – at the new docks devoted to the Atlantic trade – we may here see any day enormous piles of wheat from Chicago, bacon from Cincinnati, cotton from Pennsylvania, tobacco from Virginia and Baltimore, corn, leather, lard, cheese, staves. Tallow, treacle, butter, and manufactured goods, from pitchforks to clothes-pegs, from perambulators to pianos. Further south, at the Huskisson, Sandon, and Nelson Docks may be seen the luscious fruits of the Mediterranean, the oranges of Seville, the wines of Portugal, the mohair of Syria, the gum of Arabia, the opium and caster oil of Calcutta, the tobacco and cigars of Manilla, together with the sugar and rum of Jamaica, the indiarubber of Para, the logwood of Hayti, and the coffee of Cuba. Again, the Victoria, Waterloo, and other docks disclose to us the grand staple of Liverpool commerce ... the cotton of the United States. The Clarence and Trafalgar docks are chiefly devoted to the Irish and Scotch coasting trades.... Continuing our survey along the line, we come to the miscellaneous docks, where we discover all sorts of importations, from Welsh slates to paving stones, beeswax and borax, Egyptian cotton, and Bombay cotton, and Sea Island cotton, sulphur and sumac, hemp, and hickory – pitchpine, oak, mahogany, maple, walnut, and all the finer descriptions of wood, to say nothing of the endless variety of useful and superfluous articles 'too numerous to mention' – from the carved idol in ivory of Japan to the ready made doors, window frames, and even coffins of Boston and New York.[5]

The docks defined Liverpool's economy and gave to its vast workforce the peculiar working style that, for many commentators and social enquirers, contributed to the distinctiveness of the port's social character. They were, according to the *Morning Chronicle*, the town's 'glory and shame'. Dock labour – unloading or packing a cargo – though often referred to as unskilled, did require experience and skill. However, because the basic attribute required of a dock labourer was his strength, men in their hundreds flocked to the docks early each morning, or to the 'stands', where they waited to be hired for the day. So competitive was this scrimmage for work that many were left unemployed for that particular day or half day. This was the defining characteristic of dock labour: it was casual and precarious, and many men rarely had a full week's work. By the early 1880s four days' labour would bring in about 18 shillings, at 4s 6d a day, for basic dock labouring, whereas the more skilled and more permanently employed stevedores earned about 5 shillings a day. There was, therefore, close to the docks a large pool of poor, comprising unskilled and underemployed men. Often their wives and young adult children had enormous problems finding permanent employment too. The comparative lack of factory employment meant that most working women took up service-industry jobs such as domestic service, cleaning, laundry and needlework. None of these paid anything like a living wage. Thus the problems of poverty were compounded.[6]

The slums of Liverpool

LIVING CONDITIONS for many of the labouring poor were, even by the standards of the day, appalling. Initially Liverpool gained a notorious reputation for its squalid, overcrowded and damp cellars, where entire families nestled underground in the dark. Soon identified as breeding grounds of disease by the enlightened Dr Duncan, England's first medical officer of health, these cellars were gradually boarded up. However, as Liverpool began to expand rapidly out beyond Boundary Street, cellar dwellings were replaced with high-density court housing. It was estimated that, in the 1870s, 150,000 people lived in just one room for each family. The description in the *Liverpool Mercury* from 1882 could apply to any decade in the second half of the nineteenth century.

> Taking at random a typical street leading off Vauxhall-road, we have a fair sample of a dock labourer's 'home'. This is a long narrow street, flanked at either end – at the corners – and fortified at many other intersecting corners throughout its length by showy public-houses. Each side of this street, at short intervals, discloses a court or narrow alley, the first prominent feature of which is a pair of waterclosets, abutting in the foreground like two unsavoury gate pillars, beyond which is seen a double row of from six to eight houses, facing each other so closely that a whispered conversation may easily be carried across from door to door.... A house in this court contains four rooms, 'straight up and down' – no back doors nor windows for immediately against it stands another similar house in the next court, and the rent is four shillings a week, 'free of taxes' – about the only objectionable thing it is 'free' of; but it may be added that it is also free of fresh air, free of drainage, free of cleanliness, free of wholesome wall paper or whitewash, free of sweetness or light or comfort, free, in short, of everything which goes to make up a happy or a comfortable home.[7]

Cramped, fetid and noisy these courts may have been but outward appearances could sometimes be deceptive. Journalists often noted that standards of cleanliness and the amount of furniture contained in these slums could vary from house to house. Some were described as 'cheerful' and well maintained by 'smart and tidy' wives, whereas others barely contained a stick of furniture and had no wood in the hearth or straw on the floor for bedding. Common to both types of home was that life was often lived outside, on the doorstep, in the street or down at the many corner ale houses.

When describing the streets or 'rookeries' of Liverpool, journalists often adopted a style of writing and description familiar to Victorian readers of books on exploration and foreign travel. Take Hugh Shimmin, the radical and sympathetic reporter and owner of the *Porcupine*, whose description of 'Sunday Evening at the North End', was typical of the genre:

> ... we proceeded northward, by way of Vauxhall-road. There is nothing cheerful or hopeful to be met with in this locality. Turn down any of the streets which abut on this trunk line, and men's folly as well as women's ignorance and sin, stare at you grimly.... Whether in Chartres-street or Paul-street – in Oriel-street or Ford-street – yes, even in Maguire-street, which is a slight improvement on these others – the same features are met with, – total indifference of parents to the habits or manners of their offspring. Any one who will go to see these streets, and will venture to any of the houses, will readily understand what faith, and hope, and strong perseverance in well-doing, it would require on the part of parents to keep children within any reasonable bounds and free from pollution.[8]

The pollution so evident in the surroundings of these courts – upturned troughs of night-soil, middens, foul air, smoking chimneys – and lack of sunlight appeared, in turn, according to these writers and social commentators, to affect and infect the people morally and physically. They thought that the children were tainted and that future generations would degenerate still further, unless some improvements in both the spiritual and the physical welfare of the present generation were undertaken. It was a bleak and depressing prognosis. Such filthy surroundings allowed for an easy identification, so many Victorians thought, of the criminal, dangerous and violent streets and areas of the town. In fact, the court style of working-class street design was, in the opinion of the Liverpool police, conducive to fighting. These cul-de-sacs were, after all, amphitheatres in which warring neighbours could settle their differences comparatively easily, without the intervention of the beat constable. Their gradual demolition from the end of the 1890s led, in the opinion of the head constable, to a decline in knife fights.[9]

Streets of danger

THE IDENTITY AND GEOGRAPHY of Liverpool's mean streets did alter over the Victorian period. In the mid-1850s, when the town was comparatively compact, the dangerous streets were identified as being close to the centre. In Lace Street the people 'lived more like savages than human beings', while in nearby Banastre Street brothels were identified as the infectors of morality. However, the courts and streets running between Vauxhall Road and Scotland Road were consistently named in press reports for their drunkenness, brutality and poverty. The north end did not have a monopoly on unsafe streets. In the town centre the area around the Sailors'

Home, namely Cooper's Row, Paradise Street and Canning Place (site of the present police headquarters) were considered the 'Rowdies' Haunt'. Close to the hostel where sailors were often paid off, groups of 'dirty ruffians, sneaks, crimps, and their abettors' were often seen, waiting 'to half-strangle, strip, or rob' the unwary or drunks staggering back to their beds. Within a 200-yard radius of the Sailors' Home there were, reported Father Nugent, 46 pubs and numerous brothels. By the end of the century this radius had been reduced to 150 yards by temperance supporters. Williamson Square, too, was the scene of much debauchery, illegal betting and drunken fighting.[10]

To the south of the centre, close to where the present Anglican Cathedral now stands, was an area considered to be unruly. Windsor Street, Falkner Street, Wolfe Street and Mill Street were all identified by the *Liverpool Mercury* between 1850 and 1900 as being the homes of roughs. In an article headed 'A Nice Neighbourhood' the newspaper reported how Blundell Street, Toxteth Park, was once called Bell-street but had had to change its name because of the roughness of the neighbourhood. Toxteth Park in general gained a reputation for being a tough area.[11]

The north end of town was, however, identified by the police as the locality for a large part of Liverpool's violent crime and much else besides. Richmond Row and Drinkwater Gardens were described as squalid as late as 1895, while Athol Street, Stockdale Street and Chisenhale Street vied with each other for the title of the most demoralized, lowest street in town. The street which was most frequently cited in news reports on crimes of violence and disorder was Chisenhale Street. This short street, which was bisected by the Leeds–Liverpool canal, gives little indication of its fearsome reputation when portrayed on a map. There is little to suggest that it was different from the other streets which ran off the Vauxhall Road. When Canon Hume, who later drew up a moral map of Liverpool, conducted his own survey of the town's parishes in 1850 he discovered there were 1539 persons crammed into Chisenhale Street. Not only was it one of the mostly densely populated in the town, but it also had the highest Irish population. Nearly 83% were Irish-born in 1850. Nearby streets with similar high concentrations of Irish-born were Pownall Square (78%), Smithfield Street (69%), Chartres Street (68%) and Milk Street (67%). The high Irish concentration of the street did not automatically make Chisenhale Street criminal and dangerous; it was, rather, the poverty of its inhabitants that did so. A survey conducted in 1842, before the Irish Famine, and covering a sample of 147 heads of household in the street had revealed that only 33 heads of household were in regular work, 54 were completely unemployed and 41 were employed between one and four days per week.[12]

Chisenhale Street had great difficulty shaking off its reputation as the meanest street in Liverpool, becoming the benchmark by which other streets were judged. The 'stroller' writing in the *Porcupine* observed that Saltney Street 'has recently become almost as noted as Chisenhale-street' on account of one brother-in-law killing another. Shimmin's paper had been somewhat premature in its assessment of the latter street back in 1861, when, in the article 'Sunday Evening at the North End', it fearlessly reported:

> A walk down Chisenhale-street revealed a state of society of which the great bulk of our populace happily know nothing; and yet the street, bad as it was, is better now than it has been for years! Close by the Canal-bridge there is a beer house, and in this were carousing a set of ruffians, the like of which could not be excelled. Women, without shoes and very few garments on, were their companions; whilst brawny loafers skulked about, and vicious cripples stuttered blasphemy at the door. The street was sloppy and strewed with decaying vegetables, and yet, amidst all, young children tried to gambol about; and old people sat at court entrances, at windows, or on door-steps, with their elbows resting on their knees, in every stage of dirt and disorder. But the blear eyes – the wolfish glance – the tawny skins and stunted forms of youth seen around, – indicated the life-struggle in which they were engaged, and the result of it could be clearly seen.[13]

Twelve years later it was noted in the same journal that, 'If, in the process of the town's improvements, the whole of that populous hive [i.e. Chisenhale Street] were swept away, Liverpool would be relieved of a pestilential and crime-haunted den, the like of which no city in the world can parallel in moral and sanitary foulness'. Clearly, any improvements noted in the

Illustration 1 The bridge by Chisenhale Street over the Leeds–Liverpool canal, *c.* 1900. Courtesy Liverpool Record Office, Liverpool Libraries.

early 1860s had not continued. A particularly heinous murder in 1873 guaranteed both the street's notoriety and its status as a place to visit for gawpers who wanted to experience the vicarious thrill of seeing and being close to the scene of the killing. What lent the street a distinctive, and some thought dangerous, character was the beer house close by the canal bridge (illustration 1). The bridge marked the first crossing point over the Leeds–Liverpool canal after the basin in Leeds Street. As such, Chisenhale Street allowed pedestrians a direct route up from the northern docks via Oil and Chadwick Streets, and as such this was the route sailors, new to the town, were directed to take. Judging by the reports of court cases in the press this was, at times, a perilous undertaking.

ROBBERY WITH VIOLENCE IN CHISENHALE-STREET

This street particularly is, and probably has been since the property has been occupied by the class of people who make a livelihood in a very questionable way, infested by a gang of roughs, who it is to be hoped, will be dealt with most severely when they fall into the hands of justice, and whose greatest fear seems to be of that whip, 'the cat.' Two of these vagabonds, named Michael Rafferty and Michael Kelly, were charged with having stolen 15s., a knife, and a pocket handkerchief from the person of John Robinson, and also with assaulting him. The prosecutor ... stated that on Sunday morning about one o'clock he was passing over Chisenhale-street canal bridge, when the prisoners came up and stood in front of him; Kelly struck him in the neck, and the other prisoner put his hand into prosecutor's pocket.... There was a young man standing on the other side of the street, and prosecutor told him to go for a policeman and he would pay him, but this fellow refused to comply....[14]

In later chapters the name Chisenhale Street will regularly occur. It seems that the pub close to the bridge was the haunt of a particularly rough set of men who took it upon themselves to charge strangers an unofficial toll for crossing the bridge late at night. Refusal to comply led to assaults, robbery and, in a few cases, being pitched over the side of the bridge. On one occasion a body was found on the canal path. James Boylan, a cattleman from Newry, who had recently arrived from Baltimore on the steamer *Templemore*, was found unconscious on the bank of the canal below the bridge. It was known that he was making his drunken way to his lodgings in Circus Street but had, somehow, fallen 25 feet over the bridge parapet. He died shortly after being admitted to the Northern Hospital. Was he pushed or had he simply toppled over? The inquest returned an open verdict, thus leaving his death 'mysterious'.[15]

As the Victorian era moved towards the twentieth century and Liverpool's docks expanded, so streets to the north, towards Bootle, became the poorest and, some would argue, meanest. According to the *Porcupine*, in an article entitled 'BOOTLE BLACKGUARDISM', the spread of the docks northwards and the removal of the timber trade from the southern docks led to the migration of 'the most degraded and immoral – that part whose constituents figured often in the criminal calendar – that part which made Toxteth Park a worthy simile for Pandemonium'. Very rapidly Balliol Terrace and Raleigh Street gained reputations to match the worst slums off Vauxhall and Scotland Roads. Crowds of swearing children playing in the dirt and women, 'too drunk to stand erect', lounging in the streets were described by the correspondent in his terror-filled account. 'Here, in the broad sunlight', he continued, 'lazy men loaf about and chaff and jostle passers-by for amusement. Here, they drink and thieve and murder – ay murder. Night comes on....' This theme was continued 15 years later in the *Liverpool Review*, headed 'Brutal Bootle: Lucky to Get Out Alive'. The streets of danger included the narrow streets running off Derby Road from Bankhall. Raleigh Street is again singled out for special mention, for being 'as bad' as Chisenhale Street or the slums of Toxteth Park. Here resided the 'lowest class of sailors, fishermen, scalers and labourers as well as bullies and rowdies' and other 'flotsam and jetsam'. The picture he paints is of a largely lawless society, where the police let the 'ruffians' and 'loafers' fight among themselves, since these people were beyond reforming. Such exaggeration excited local readers, especially those who never had to set foot in such neighbourhoods; moreover, such descriptions were vital propaganda to the various social and political groups whose central agenda was the restriction of alcohol.[16]

Alcohol and crime

> The appalling moral and social condition of Liverpool was *mainly* due to the dominance of the public-house.[17]

L IVERPOOL CAN BE BEST understood and explained through a glass of Cain's or Walker's ale. It used to be said that the shortest way out of Manchester was a bottle of Gordon's gin. The shortest way into Liverpool was to drink. Its whole social fabric was dependent on the consumption of alcohol. Dock labourers were invariably paid in the many pubs that lined the streets by the dock gates. There was a culture of standing 'treats' with mates and colleagues; male honour and manliness were based, in part, on drink and standing turns. Conviviality had an egalitarian dimension and, when funds were low, many men were able to get drink 'on tick' with the neighbourhood corner pub. 'Nothing is more disastrous', wrote 'A Working Man', than the 'tick' shop.

> It is there he loses everything he possesses worth having, and obtains what is dangerous and ruinous. 'Tick' shops are numerous and spread all over the town. They are near the working-man's home and close to his workshop. They are in the big streets and up the back 'slums.' The publican may disavow this;

it may be a matter entirely left to the discretion of the barman or manager; but the 'tick' shops are there all the same. Working-men obtain beer on credit, they get it for themselves, and they get it for others.[18]

As William Booth, no lover of alcohol, wrote, 'Many a man takes to beer, not from the love of beer, but from a natural craving for the light, warmth, company, and comfort which is thrown in along with the beer, and which he cannot get excepting by buying beer'.[19]

When the incoming sailors (100,000 of whom were paid off in 1876 when they docked at the port) are added to the local people, then it comes as no surprise to learn that Liverpool had an enormous number of licensed establishments. These ranged from small corner beer houses to the large gin palaces in the centre of town, where live music was part of the entertainment. There were, in addition, an unknown number of illicit stills in the back streets. By the 1850s there were 1493 pubs and 897 beer houses in the town. Shimmin claimed that, standing in Vauxhall Road, close to the bridewell, he could see, 'without moving', 27 pubs and beer houses. By 1874, at the height of the moral panic about violent crime, the town's pubs had increased in number to 1929, but the beer houses had declined to 383. By the turn of the century, when drink was a huge political question and watched closely by the city's vigilance committee, the numbers of pubs had declined to 1783. This, in the opinion of the Lord Chief Justice, Baron Russell, speaking at the 1895 spring assize, was one of the reasons for the large decrease in drunkenness in the city.[20]

What so concerned contemporaries was the relationship between excessive consumption of alcohol and violence. This formula found its results displayed daily in the magistrates' courts. For, as the *Porcupine* observed, 'the transition from a coarse word or a ribald jest to a kick, from a poker to a knife, are made with alarming rapidity' as the drink took its effect during the course of an evening. Inevitably, illegal drunkenness figured greatly in Liverpool's judicial annual returns. The number of people proceeded against for drunk and disorderly behaviour did, though, fluctuate greatly over the Victorian period. In 1857, for example, 11,439 were prosecuted and this figure rose gradually throughout the 1860s, eventually peaking in 1870 at a total of 21,113, and another peak in 1875, at 21,694. Thereafter, numbers declined fitfully until the 1890s, when the figure consistently dropped below 10,000. While these figures tell us very little about the actual level of drunkenness in the town, the peaks and troughs signify revivals and reverses in economic prosperity: drunkenness tended to increase when times were good. The figures also indicate various changes to the licensing laws and crackdowns on drunk and disorderly behaviour. The early 1870s, for example, were a period of political and public concern regarding 'the drink question'. Opening hours were drastically reduced in 1872, from 4.00 a.m.–1.00 a.m. to 6.00 a.m.–11.00 p.m. on weekdays, whereas on Sundays pubs were allowed to open only between 6 and 9.00 p.m., later extended to 10.00 p.m.[21]

Many of those arrested for assault of their partners, policemen or strangers in the street were drunk. Father Nugent, who was the Catholic chaplain of Liverpool borough gaol, told an 1877 select committee that nine out of ten inmates in the gaol were in prison 'directly or indirectly [due] to drink'. In an article headed 'DRUNKEN LIVERPOOL', the *Times* argued that the increase in violent crime was linked 'to the prevailing intemperance of the people'. Judges, in their assize addresses, frequently spoke of their conviction that drink was largely to blame for the heaviness of the trial calendar. Mr Justice Mellor, in 1866, told the grand jury: 'There were no fewer than seven persons charged with murder and nine with manslaughter; and it appeared to him from reading the depositions, that nearly every one of the cases of manslaughter was to be distinctly traced to drunkenness'. Baron Martin at the following assize said that 'nine-tenths of all the crime that was committed' arose from drunkenness. A year later, Justice Mellor spoke out again: 'In the cases tried in Liverpool he found more resulting from drunkenness than in any other place'. That drink was a cause of violent crime was to many Victorians self-evident and, as such, it was within the power of the local authority to control.[22]

It is, therefore, not surprising to find that the question of alcohol's easy availability was of enormous political importance to Liverpool's local politicians. Brewers were traditionally Conservatives in Victorian England, and Liverpool was no exception. Both Andrew Walker and Robert Cain were heavily involved in the politics of the town, against the Liberals, who wanted greater police control and oversight of the licensed premises. The police were to some extent pawns in this political struggle, which culminated in the vigilance committee's campaign of the late 1880s and 1890s, which called on the police to close down brothels and inspect pubs more closely. To Liberal and radical critics it seemed perverse and immoral that traditional Conservatives, through their economic interests, were willing to encourage drinking, even though it might lead to violent crime. The police, under William Nott-Bower, were caught between these two groups and could be accused of being either too lenient or too harsh with regard to public drunkenness and vice. During the 1890s they were, however, able to initiate stricter enforcement and inspection of pubs. Whether these reforms led to the apparent decrease in arrests for drunkenness is a moot point, for, by this time, more and more people were drinking at home, especially women.

Thus, the geography and the economy of Liverpool, together with its predominant pastime, drinking alcohol, combined to make a potent brew of drunkenness and violence. Attempting to combat this was Liverpool's newly reformed police force.

Part II
Policing the borough

CHAPTER 3

'An army to check barbarism': the policing of Liverpool

The coming of the new police

A T THE BEGINNING OF 1836, the watch committee for the borough of Liverpool organized and appointed a constabulary force or 'new police' along the lines of the Metropolitan force, which had been existence since 1829. However, it would be wrong to believe that Liverpool was unpoliced before 1836. On the contrary, the town had had a large force, or more correctly forces. For Liverpool used to have three separate police forces, namely, the dock, day and night police forces. However, under a parliamentary act of 1835 the day and night forces were amalgamated, as in turn was the dock force, in 1841. The stated objectives of the new force were 'preserving the peace by day and by night, preventing robberies and other felonies, and apprehending offenders against the peace'.[1] 'The prevention of crime' was to be achieved by keeping under constant observation receivers of stolen goods, who were the mainspring and life blood of the 'criminal classes', by watching closely public houses – 'these dens of infamy' – and by procuring 'information as to the number of thieves and prostitutes at present infesting this town'.[2]

Prior to 29 February 1836, when the new police took up duty, Liverpool had over 60 day police officers, the dock trustees had a private police force of 144 men and the Select Vestry ran 166 night police. The last figure is substantially more than the 50 nightwatchmen cited by the head constable in his 1900 review of Liverpool police history. Whatever the total, these men were expected to protect the borough's 240,000 citizens and their property. It is impossible to judge how successful, or conversely how inept, these men were. Much propaganda and doctored evidence has come down to us bemoaning the ineptitude of the 'old police'. Reformers in favour of new styles of policing, usually based on the Metropolitan model of a heavily centralized force controlled by the Home Secretary, made it their task to belittle and rubbish existing forms of policing. Consequently, the Liverpool nightwatchmen were, for example, said to be 'corrupt, many of them drunken, most of them old or crippled, and all of them useless for almost anything beyond calling the hours of the night'.[3] Shimmin, the journalist, was even more damning in his recollections:

> Many of our readers will recollect [the] disorderly period when Liverpool had no police force worthy of the name, and when the safety of the town and its inhabitants was in the custody of some thirty or forty old watchmen, who were a terror to nobody, an amusement only to mischievously disposed lads. These venerable Dogberries, as they rise up now in fancy before the mind, appear more like a memory of the medieval ages than [an] institution actually in existence in modern times. We see them in the mind's eye now, muffled up in their great coats, with a raffle in one hand, a lantern in the other, a truncheon in the pocket, and parading with slow steps the dirty and dimly lighted streets (for we had no gas then), and crying out the hour and state of the weather, 'Half past twelve, a fine frosty morning.' The cry of course always served to acquaint thieves with their particular whereabouts, but in any case, their depredators had very little to fear, for the poor old fellows were very infirm, and somehow or other generally lame. They dozed the greater part of the night in their little sentry boxes, after the fashion of their predecessors in *Much Ado about Nothing*, 'who knew the duties of a watch,' and so 'sat upon the church bench till two, and then all to bed.' In the eyes of the very juvenile perhaps there was something very dread in that awful symbol of majesty 'G.R.' [George Rex]; but to plague and thrash the 'trusty guardians of the night' was the chivalric feat of the fast young men of that interesting age; to bonnet them and steal their lanterns was a piece of wit; to knock them down, house and all, a more exquisite joke still. Gangs of disorderly fellows would frequently take possession of the town for hours together, insulting every well-dressed person whom they met. In Liverpool, the 'roughs' amongst the ship carpenters were resistless then, and throughout England the disorderly were only kept in check by frequent appeals to the bayonets of the soldiery.[4]

Shimmin would have been only 17 years old when the new force was established; therefore his recollections were probably based on hearsay rather than direct experience.

The years before 1836, as can be seen, were regarded as some kind of 'dark age' of anarchy and debauchery. The new police were therefore expected to usher in a 'golden age' of civilized and law-abiding peace on the streets of Liverpool, 'an army to check barbarism'.[5] How true this was will be seen, but the rapidity of the Liverpool force's expansion over the remainder of the nineteenth century does not suggest a city of civil tranquillity. In 1836 the force consisted of 390 men, about one policeman for every 631 of the population. A year later the force was increased to 585, by 1845 it had reached 702 and it was 1002 strong by 1859. After one or two decreases in the latter years of the century the force consisted of 1804 men in 1900. Liverpool was, for much of the century, the most heavily policed town in Britain outside Metropolitan London, possessing one policeman to 466 of the population by the mid-1850s. Comparable figures for other towns and cities in the middle of the century are shown in table 3.

Table 3 Ratios of police to population in selected areas in the mid-nineteenth century

Borough	Year	No. of police officers	Population served per police officer
London	1856	5813	455
Liverpool	1856	956	466
Manchester	1848	447	633
Birmingham	1848	314	694
Newcastle upon Tyne	1848	115	718
Leeds	1848	137	1213
Lancashire County	1852	614	1700

Taken from F. C. Mather, *Public Order in the Age of the Chartists* (Manchester, 1959; reprinted Westport, CT: Greenwood Press, 1984), appendix 1, pp. 239–41.

The Liverpool police force expanded for a variety of reasons, not least the changes to the city boundary in 1895, when it swallowed up neighbouring parishes and suburbs, but also the host of new duties and responsibilities which its officers were expected to fulfil. Rising crime, or more pertinently perceived rising crime, may have led to the initial expansion in force numbers. Decreasing reported crime led to a drop in police numbers between 1895 and 1900. However, the relationship between police strength and the level of crime is difficult to measure, let alone evaluate. It is, and was, usual for an increase in police numbers to lead to an initial increase in reported crime, for the simple reason that more people are involved in discovering and investigating criminal activities. Over time, an increase in police numbers may lead to a decrease in crime but it is difficult to find a causal connection.

Crimes of violence are associated with vibrant economies. Police chiefs in Liverpool were under no illusions on this score. The boom years led to full employment, which led to an increase in alcohol consumption, which in turn led to more male-on-male fights and domestic disputes. Other factors, one surprising one in particular, also had a bearing on criminal behaviour in Liverpool in the days before steam ships were the norm. '*Crime in Liverpool*', wrote Shimmin, '*is dependent upon the direction of the wind!* An easterly wind prevailing for a week will carry off from 10,000 to 15,000 seamen; a westerly wind will in a day or two cast that number, with replenished pockets, again upon our shore; and the bridewells, which had been doing slack "business", speedily become filled again.' This observation is not entirely fanciful and is probably an indirect reference to the winter of 1855, when an easterly wind was partly responsible for the food shortages which led to bread riots.[6]

Becoming a policeman

REFORMERS HAD COMPLAINED in the 1820s and early 1830s that the men then 'policing' towns and cities were of such poor quality in terms of their age, strength, physical health and moral well-being that it was imperative that a new organized and disciplined body of men be formed. This new group would look the part, being tall, uniformed and disciplined. The questions are: what were the new recruits like, where did they come from, what were their previous occupations, did they remain in the police and what rules did they themselves have to endure as members of the 'new police'?

A new recruit had to meet a set of requirements and criteria in order to join the new force after 1836. Constables had to be between 22 and 35 years of age and at least 5 feet 8 inches tall. This height requirement led Shimmin to enthuse 'it is to this restriction no doubt that we owe the fine physical appearance of the men, which nobody would be inclined to dispute; indeed, as a body, they would favourably contrast in that respect with many of our crack regiments'.[7] They had to be able to read and write well, or so the claim went. Theoretically, such skills were essential, as new appointees were immediately handed a 'Book of Instructions', a dense book of duties, by-laws and instructions, covering some 800 points. New constables were expected to read and understand this book in their first few weeks of working. The question of police literacy is a difficult one to unpick. In the 1850s it was hoped and indeed expected that recruits would possess basic numeracy and literacy skills; however, police work was viewed as unskilled and poorly remunerated; to many, it was only a possible job in times of economic recession. The force was probably not, therefore, attracting particularly high-calibre recruits. This is borne out by the comments in the head constable's report of 1899:

> Fifteen years ago, the majority of the Force were very illiterate, many even of the higher officers being quite unable to write, much less spell, a short report so as to be reasonably intelligible. Now all recruits (whose education before joining the police may be slightly better than it was fifteen years ago) are instructed by a Chief Inspector, not only in writing, spelling, arithmetic, the making of reports, &c., but also in the theory of police duty; and none are sent out for duty in a Division until they are passed as qualified.[8]

Evidence from the police courts similarly suggests that constables were not well educated. Some magistrates took a cruel pleasure, as indeed did the local newspapers, in highlighting and mocking the ignorance of some constables when they gave their evidence.

Every new applicant, in the 1850s, had to write his own letter of application and submit it with testimonials from referees to the head constable, who conducted interviews every Thursday. If successful, a medical examination took place and then the successful applicant was sworn in and given his uniform. This consisted of a great coat, an oilskin cape, two pairs of boots and trousers, a hat and two pairs of gloves. In addition, a whistle, a rattle rather like the old football rattle and a truncheon were also supplied to the probationer, who, over the next two or three weeks, attended the magistrates' or police court. Here he learnt how to present evidence and conduct himself before the magistrates, some of whom could be quite prickly and pernickety. While on probation, constables were graded as third class and received in the mid-1850s about 18 shillings a week, a wage little different from a docker or general labourer.

The turnover of new recruits was notoriously high and bears witness to the difficulties new constables had in obeying all the rules. In the early years of the force the notion of having a career in the police would have been entirely alien to most recruits. Joining the police was often regarded as a fall-back job when trade was slack. Once the local economy picked up, many constables resigned and applications went down. This actually remained an issue with the Liverpool force well into the second half of nineteenth century. Head constable Major Greig, for example, had to present a report to the watch committee on 1 May 1865 on the large numbers of young officers who left the force after only a short term of service. Among the reasons listed were:

> First the large number of young men, many of them of an unsettled disposition who come to Liverpool in search of employment, and failing to obtain it, join the Police as a temporary means of subsistence still looking out for any other situation which may present itself. This especially refers to those belonging to the Artizan Class, and skilled labourers.
>
> Secondly the nature of and character of police duty, which requires intelligence, energy and a certain aptitude, and necessitating a strict discipline and a constant and close supervision to ensure its proper discharge. This new occupation to young men, coming from various employments and who are impatient of restraint is at first very irksome; whilst exposure to the weather night and day (Sunday not excepted) together with the personal risk involved in the performance of their duty, contribute no doubt largely to a distaste for the service, and a desire to leave it on the first favourable opportunity.[9]

More problematic for new recruits were the long hours, the abuse from members of the public, working on holidays and Sundays, and resisting the temptations of the many beer houses and pubs which they were expected to police. The last proved too much for many. As one superintendent observed, 'the men must first learn to control themselves before they can attempt to control others'.[10]

It was estimated in 1857 that 'not one out of ten taken on is kept for two years; not one out of a thousand ten years'. Although this appears an exaggeration when one examines the police discipline books and personnel records, the documents do not make particularly encouraging reading. In 1838, a total of 73 officers resigned and 101 were dismissed. Some of the reasons cited for dismissal included: drunk on duty (25 officers); being the worse for liquor and being in a public house when on duty (19); absent from beats and neglect of duty (15); asleep on beats (3); absent from duty without permission and late for duty (5); being drunk or the worse for drink when off duty (3); and other offences (23). These sackings were just the tip of police indiscipline, for in the same year 160 were fined or reduced in rank for being drunk on duty, 396 for being in a public house or the worse for liquor when on duty, a massive 550 for being absent from beats and 107 for being asleep on beats, presumably in doorways. With a total police strength of 574 at the end of 1838, these figures suggest that the head constable could not afford to sack every officer found guilty of some minor transgression against the police rule book. Moreover, these figures indicate that the new officers found it difficult, if not impossible, to adjust to the new professional constraints placed upon them, particularly those relating to alcohol. To the surprise of William Nott-Bower, the head constable at the end of the century, Michael Whitty, his predecessor in 1838, was able to report to his watch committee that 'the Police Force has progressively improved'. Nott-Bower went onto boast that the 1899 figures showed 'that the Force is nearly 60 times as well conducted as it was in 1838'.[11] Liverpool's record of police indiscipline was by no means unique in Britain during the nineteenth century: every county and borough force recorded high percentages of resignations and dismissals, especially in the years immediately after formation. A quarter of Lancashire's county constabulary, for instance, had changed within the first six months of its formation in 1839, and even as late as 1870 one-third of all new recruits did not last one year.[12] For Liverpool, the early 1850s witnessed the largest clear-out of constables when the newly appointed head constable, Major Greig, was shocked at the force's poor discipline and morale.

Third-class constables who survived the first year without being disciplined or demoralized could expect promotion to second-class constable and receive a weekly wage of 20 shillings in the 1850s. Longer-serving and more intelligent officers gained promotion to first class, which attracted a weekly wage of 22 shillings. Firemen officers received an extra shilling a week for their additional duties. The post of sergeant only came in later in the century and was attained by passing 'a searching examination'. For much of the century, inspectors, of whom there were 44 in 1857, carried out duties which are nowadays fulfilled by sergeants. In addition, there were 31 bridewell keepers, who looked after the police cells, and some of these were considered to carry serious responsibilities. By the 1850s there was a separate detective office, with 17 men attached to it. Long service and retirement from the police brought a pension, which the men had partly financed with a shilling a week from their wages. The pension was, by Victorian standards, quite generous and was considered one of the perks of the job.[13]

While most recruits came from 'a class of unskilled labourers', their nationalities reflected in part the people they were policing. In 1858, of the 973 men in the force, 581 were English (60%), 234 were Irish (24%), 94 Scottish (10%) and 61 Welsh (6%).[14] The high Irish presence injected a possible sectarian dimension into the Liverpool force, which had unfortunate but predictable consequences. Some of these men were not neutral when it came to policing the Irish community in the town, as we shall see. It is enough to say that many of the English officers were Protestant and Orange in their religious and political affiliations, especially before the mid-1850s, even though they were deprived of the franchise under the 1856 Police Act, while many of the community were Roman Catholic and from the southern counties of Ireland.

Police organization and duties

WHAT WERE THE DUTIES of the new police and how was the force organized? Liverpool was divided up into two divisions, north and south. This applied also to the docks. The boundary within the town ran west to east, through the centre of the town, up Water Street, along Dale Street, Shaw's Brow, London Road, Prescot Street and Kensington. The dividing line for the docks lay at George's Basin, close to the present-day Pier Head. Within each division there was a superintendent and a number of inspectors, who each commanded a section of 15 men. By the 1850s, the force had about 12 sections. Eight of these were on night duty, that being the busier period for the police, and four on day duty. The shift times were from 9 p.m. till 5 a.m. during the summer, or till 6 a.m. during the winter months. The remaining four sections worked a complicated pattern of shifts whereby some began at 3 p.m. and finished at 9 p.m. while others went on warehouse patrol from 6 p.m. to 3 a.m. The more experienced constables were 'posted' in the busier main streets, where they had 'the exclusive duty of watching'. Others were sent out on beat duty, in which they walked a set route and became acquainted with the local residents and shopkeepers.[15] In this way they would, it was thought, get to know the 'characters' and ne're-do-wells on their beats. Surveillance was the key concept of Victorian policing, for it was argued that prevention, rather than detection, was the best way to stop crime and that could be achieved only by watching over the working-class areas of the city. This did little for the popularity of police officers, as we will see.

Policing duties expanded exponentially after 1836, for they were expected, beyond the obvious tasks of detecting crime and arresting criminals, to fulfil a multitude of various tasks. In addition to the warehouse patrol, a sizeable number of constables were primarily firemen, who could be called up in times of rioting. The average beat policeman was expected to see that all public houses and beer houses closed at the correct times and that they were not 'run in a disorderly manner'. This latter phrase covered unseemly and repeated drunkenness and the harbouring of prostitutes. Many of their duties would seem to us, nowadays, relatively minor but at the time they were no doubt time-consuming. Shimmin lists these additional tasks in 1857:

> They are to see to the removal of all obstructions to traffic in the streets; to report all nuisances which exist upon their walks; to see that cellar grids are fast; that no chimneys be set on fire to save the cost of a sweep; to make periodical visits to lodging houses and cellars; to see that no excavations be left without protection or proper signal of danger; that water is nowhere run to waste; that the public lamps are in good order, and that they are duly lighted at the appointed minute.... Everything likely to occasion an accident, whether it be an awkward projection or a piece of defective flagging, has immediately to be reported; and that they have also to bring all cases before the magistrates of cruelty to animals, whether that cruelty consist in working a horse with a sore shoulder, whipping him mercilessly, or putting upon him a greater load than he can bear. They have to see that no dogs run at large in the month when, according to popular superstition, the canine race are more likely than at any other period to go mad ... they must adopt for the time all children lost upon the streets; and that this particular duty is no sinecure may perhaps be inferred from the fact that in the first nine months of last year, 680 children found wandering the streets were restored by their agency to their parents ... to suppress vagrancy; to see that none perish from pure destitution. They have to be ever foremost in procuring prompt medical aid in all cases of accident upon the streets; nay, their tyranny is such that they will not even allow a poor wretch to drown himself without fishing him out.[16]

The Liverpool police were also the borough's fire brigade. In 1856 about 60 of the 314 dock police acted in that capacity for both the quayside and the town itself.[17] With the passing of time, increasing bureaucracy became one of the head constable's complaints. In 1899, for example, one of the 'latest additions' to a constable's list of duties was the 'Children trading in the streets' Act, which now 'required the entire time of three Constables, and a large portion of the time of very many more'. Increased wealth among the middle and upper classes of the city brought further demands on the police, as they were expected to police 'theatres, concerts, balls, weddings, private parties, &c., &c., as well as at shops during busy times'. Such an observation implies a change in emphasis had occurred between 1856 and 1900. In the earlier period, in fact from the force's inception in 1836, the police were expected to watch over the densely populated back streets and slum courts close to the docks and off Scotland and Vauxhall Roads; towards the end of the century, in contrast, the police increasingly came to be regarded as a private force established for the well-being and comfort of the middle classes when out at play.[18] Obviously, the need to keep the working-class roughs in order was still a priority. Their threatening presence made shoppers uncomfortable, for public expectations had, by 1900, become increasingly intolerant of violence and physical threat. The police had, by the turn of the century, become street ornaments, directing traffic, helping the lost and providing security in the same way that street lighting comforted the nervous.

By the 1850s, a fairly complex rota system had evolved in which a constable on town duty might come to work at 8.45 for a 9 p.m. start. This would end at 5 or 6 a.m., depending on the time of year. This shift would be repeated the following day but on the third day he would start at 3 p.m. and continue to 9 p.m. After a free night he would again be on duty at 6 a.m. until 10 a.m. Day shift patterns varied between 5 or 6 a.m. starts with 10 a.m. or 3 p.m. finishes, and the early evening shift went from 3 or 6 p.m. to 9 p.m. Dock policing was considered lighter, more pleasant and popular with the men, as they followed a simple three-shift pattern over nine days. Their work comprised mainly watching and guarding the quays and warehouses. Until the dock wall was completed, the quays literally swarmed with 'landsharks', emigrants and immigrants, carters and cab drivers, some of whom were keen to make off with unguarded goods lying on the quays. It was estimated that there was a police officer for every 88 yards of quay space. By modern standards this was heavy policing.[19]

Policing the borough

WERE THE STREETS of Liverpool as heavily policed as the docks? By 1856, the total mileage of streets within the borough traversed by the police was 191 miles, over an area of 7¾ square miles. As the century progressed, so Liverpool and its police force grew. In 1895, with the extension of the city boundaries to include the neighbourhoods of Wavertree, Walton and much of West Derby, the force was expected to patrol 399 miles of street; this was more than a doubling of the area. The practical details of patrolling and beat duty, which usually escape historical attention, were described by Shimmin after he had visited the two town stations, Rosehill in the northern division and Seel Street in the southern. At the start of the 9 p.m. shift the 'men received the word to "march," and then went, accompanied by their inspectors, to be dropped at their beats through all the northern part of town'. They must have appeared like an occupying army marching through the streets of Scotland Road and other working-class quarters. The Irish particularly must have looked on them with fear and loathing, since the police were, where they came from, a paramilitary force, created especially to oppress the native people. The paramilitarism of the Liverpool police must have created two contradictory impressions for onlookers, depending on who they were. The sight of uniformed men responding to orders, marching in step and carrying their accoutrements of cape and truncheon in an orderly fashion was, to many, suggestive of English orderliness and discipline. To others, not least the Irish, it suggested servility and brutality.

As the men marched towards their beats, constables would peel off at their respective street corner. Each man had a number of streets designated to him to watch over and patrol. It was reported that the 'biggest and best men' were sent to the 'worst' neighbourhoods and experienced officers were given the major thoroughfares to stand on. Shimmin explained the night beat system for Liverpool thus:

> For the better understanding of the system, we must take two officers as acting [in] conjunction. Having met for night duty in the principal or most disorderly thoroughfare abutting their respective walks, they stay together probably till eleven o'clock; then one remains in the main thoroughfare while the other goes [on] his round, and he is expected to traverse it within half an-hour. That time expired, he takes his station in the principal street, where he remains the second half hour, whilst the other, knowing the time, and without any necessity of communication with him, sets off on his own beat, which he accomplishes in like time; and this system of rotation goes on until one o'clock in the morning.... At one o'clock the main street is abandoned, so far as special watching is concerned, but included in the rounds of both men, who from that period confine themselves to a constant traverse of their rounds till the time of relief arrives, when other officers take their place, and they are released from duty.[20]

This tiring and dull pattern of beat policing would have been enlivened by an arrest, when the constable would then have to walk with the prisoner back to the bridewell, assuming that she or he was willing to go quietly. If the officer had to leave his walk, he was meant to tell the other officers on the adjoining beats that he would be absent; these neighbouring officers then divided up his beat and incorporated it into theirs until he returned. The beat system also allowed the inspectors to find the constables at any given time of the day or night. If, for whatever reason, the constable was not at the appointed spot when the inspector arrived, the latter would beat his stick on the flags and the constables would come running. But, as we have seen from the disciplinary records, the practice did not always match with the rule book.

Conclusion

As a result of the 1856 Police Act, county and borough constabulary forces had to be inspected in order to receive a government grant as part of their funding. Colonel Woodford, the constabulary inspector who cast his eye over the Liverpool force, concluded that it was 'The model force of the Kingdom'.[21] Praise did not come much higher than that. The borough force had, by this time (1857), under the leadership of Major Greig – head constable from 1852 to 1880 and a stern disciplinarian – become strongly imbued with military practices and attitudes. This paramilitarism, initially so widely admired, including by Shimmin in the 1850s (see appendix), was mercilessly parodied by him by the 1870s, as the following chapter shows.

CHAPTER 4

The community and the police: evidence, lies and violence

Poor Bobby gets fearfully knocked and kicked about sometimes, and nobody minds. It is all part of his business: what else does he receive his twenty shillings a-week for? You may see a policeman in the midst of a crowd struggling with a 'rough.' He is knocked down; he scrambles up again; goes down again; is kicked savagely in the head, in the face, on the shins, on the abdomen; has to fight for his very life a single combat to him as momentous and desperate as ever gladiator fought in a Pagan arena; and all the time the crowd looks on cheering, laughing, delighted, as if it were a fight between two dogs, or a sham combat in a melo-dramatic drama.[1]

… the policeman's truncheon … has for him a wonderfully soothing power. But for the workingman quite otherwise.[2]

W HILE THE MAIN TASK of the new police was the prevention of crime, they also had the important objective of policing by consent, but how far was this achievable in nineteenth-century Liverpool? To what extent were the truncheon and nightstick resorted to as weapons of offence and defence? Police brutality to innocent members of the public, on the one hand, and anti-police violence, on the other, were different sides of the same coin. The years between the new police's formation in the 1830s and the turn of the twentieth century witnessed an often tense standoff between the Liverpool force and the working classes of the borough. Both were fighting for control of the streets; the former because they were gradually trying to impose what the Victorians took to be decorum and civilized behaviour. This led one historian, Storch, to describe the police as 'moral missionaries' but, given the moral shortcomings of many policemen, one wonders if they were up to the task. The working classes, on the other hand, were attempting to retain control of their neighbourhoods, of their ways of doing things. The English criminal justice system was not seen as relevant or even necessary by many people who inhabited the slum courts when dealing with their warring neighbours or settling domestic fallouts. Such matters did not require official intervention or 'interference'.[3]

Thus there was an inherent tension at the heart of the relationship between the police and the policed. In many ways this was eventually resolved through negotiation, compromise and common sense on both sides. Policing by consent was, after all, about achieving what was practicable rather than about some middle-class-inspired drive to achieve zero tolerance towards, for example, drunken misbehaviour or prostitution. The temperance and purity campaigns of the 1890s directed at eradicating the twin 'vices' of excessive alcohol consumption and prostitution were doomed to failure in Liverpool. Consensual policing for the constable on the beat was about having to weigh up the options of intervening, or not, in breaking up a street fight. Was the watching crowd large? What kind of neighbourhood was he in? Would he be able to summon other constables and was anyone likely to get seriously hurt? Such questions were vital to the beat policeman. The ability to assess situations well would have been better the longer he had been assigned to a particular beat, which could in fact be many years.[4] The officers came to know the people on their rounds, to gain their trust to some extent and to identify the rougher elements. It was said that some constables resorted to the fist or the truncheon at night rather than make an arrest, as the latter entailed a hazardous journey to the bridewell with the accused and a time-sapping visit to the magistrates' court the following day, for which they would have been given inadequate compensation in terms of time off. A fight with a local 'rough' had the added virtue of bestowing a 'hard man' reputation on a constable. Street respect was something to be valued by both sides.

The other problem with policing in nineteenth-century England was that it was local, and so tied up with the politics of the borough. The police in that sense were servants of a solidly middle-class plutocracy of local merchants and businessmen and, as a result, were deployed to fight whatever worried their masters. This inevitably meant that policing was directed at particular social groups in specific neighbourhoods. There used to be a saying among the London Metropolitan Police that in order to protect St James the police had to watch St Giles – a neighbouring parish containing a notorious rookery. The thinking that the criminals who were centred in a poor neigh-bourhood would spill out into more salubrious districts, such as the West End, to commit their crimes was also applicable to other towns and cities by the 1830s. In Liverpool's case the Irish slums and the courts and streets close to the north and south docks were where the police were stationed in heavy numbers. The constant scrutiny under which these communities came led to tensions, fights and accusations on both sides of violence and brutality. Historically it is very difficult to determine the truth or establish the facts of these clashes, even of cases that came before the magistrates. Both sides were given to bearing false witness and perverting the course of justice. The magistrates for their part had to judge whose testimony was more reliable. Not surprisingly, they tended to favour the police evidence and this, too, brought justice into disrepute in a number of instances.[5]

'Instances of police terrorism are as plentiful as blackberries'

THE LEVEL AND FREQUENCY of police violence directed towards the public are unknowable, partly because the police were in the best position to leave such matters unreported, unrecorded and unprosecuted, and partly because they possessed the authority to use legitimate violence, which made members of the public reluctant to report violent incidents. Just occasionally there were times when the police force's poor reputation was difficult to ignore. The nadir of the Liverpool constabulary's repute was around the early 1850s. Accusations of unprovoked police brutality and their overzealous misuse of weapons were made in the assize and magistrates' courts. Two officers, Sheridan and Page, were found guilty of using their sticks and a cutlass against a drunken timber dealer, John Kilshaw, of Banfield Terrace, Kirkdale. Both men were found guilty and sentenced to 12 months' imprisonment.[6] Later in the same month another officer was suspended from duty for the unnecessary use of his stick as opposed to the truncheon. Matters came to a head in 1852 during a wave of sectarian conflict and tension between the Catholic Irish in the north end of town and the largely Protestant police, which brought about the premature 'retirement' of head constable Mathew Dowling.

During the summer of that year a pregnant woman named Margaret Baines was killed in her house in No. 6 Court, Grosvenor Street. Her death, witnesses claimed, came at the hands of police who were running amok in the neighbourhood. Ellen Baines, a cousin by marriage to the deceased, told the coroner's court how one constable came up to her and her husband and said, 'Paddy just go into your house or I will just run your eye out with this stick'. Other occupants of the court were struck and beaten to the ground by the police, all of whom were in the fire division of the force. Hannah Herrity, an occupant in the same house as Margaret Baines, alleged that one constable – witnesses identified Police Constable (PC) 175 – came in and beat a man and woman before turning on Margaret, who had cried out that her mother was killed. 'The officer then raised his hand and struck the deceased on the head with his stick. She fell from the blow. When she was lying on the floor the officer struck the deceased with his foot on the body, and then with both his hands gave her a punch with his stick on the body.'

The police, on the other hand, maintained that they were attempting to quell a disturbance at the Wheat Sheaf public house in Scotland Road, where a pistol had been fired. Inhabitants from Grosvenor Street, it was claimed, were throwing bricks and stones at them, and one particularly active participant, Gallagher by name, was seen running into No. 6 Court. All this was denied by the inhabitants, Ellen Baines going so far as to say, 'There was not a single word of an argument going on. There was no fighting, no throwing bricks or stones, all quite peaceable. No row at all there was no fighting.' Her testimony has to be doubted to some extent, as she admitted in cross-examination that she 'saw three lads run along our street and the police after them. The lads had been doing some mischief.'[7]

There followed further instances of police indiscipline, culminating in December 1852 with a scandal that suggested police morale was rock bottom. It arose out of a case in which two policemen, PCs 170 and 392, issued a summons against James Mullins, who in turn issued a cross-summons against the constables. Surprisingly, one of the principal prosecution witnesses was another constable, PC 287, Edward Harvey, who told the court that he saw the officers 'abusing' James Mullins on their way to the bridewell. Others stated that Mullins was also seen sober shortly before his arrest.[8] This case, which was initially adjourned, appears to be the incident referred to in head constable Greig's flurry of instructions and orders which were sent down to his men in mid to late December of that year. One such order, of 14 December, began:

> The Head Constable regrets beyond measure being compelled to draw the attention of the officers and men of the Force, to the reckless and unjustifiable use of the stick as shown in the case of Brunskill and Strong, whose conduct was as cowardly at it was cruel, repeated acts of violence having been committed by them on their inferior Prisoner whilst in Custody, who was unarmed and much their inferior in size and strength, which was in direct violation of their orders as Police Constables and revolting to any of common feeling.[9]

What made matters worse for Greig was the fact that the two constables were supported by their fellow officers, who had, in fact, raised money for them 'under pretext of paying legal expenses for their defence'. The two officers, however, had then absconded with the cash. It had come to the head constable's attention that a placard had been placed on the pay-table the previous Friday advertising for subscriptions to the constables' defence fund and that none of the inspectors had seen fit to bring this matter to the attention of their superiors. This episode had left a 'stain' of 'cowardice and cruelty' upon the entire force. To counter this desperate reputation, Greig ordered that all police constables, when on duty, were not allowed to carry their sticks. However, they were allowed to carry 'small light canes', which had to be inspected by the superintendent for his approval. In future, truncheons and rattles – to sound the alarm for fires or assistance – were to be used. On 22 December, Greig issued a further order:

> so as to secure ... the goodwill and confidence of the Authorities, and all classes of the Community, [the head constable] is anxious to impress on the officers and men the great importance at all times, when in discharge of their duty, of exercising the greatest tolerance to every one, never, under any circumstances, using more force than is absolutely necessary for the safe custody of their Prisoners, for which purpose the belts may be used in strapping the legs and arms of refractory persons, any improper use of the stick will be followed by instant dismissal.[10]

He went on to remind his men of their 'bounden' duty to stop any ill treatment on the part of their 'less discreet comrades' and to report what they had witnessed to their superiors. Later orders were issued telling the men not to drink on duty, nor to accept Christmas boxes.[11] Head constable Greig's tightening up of discipline and other attempts to improve the quality of the force may have had some positive results. Shortly after the 1855 'bread riots', 400 of the police force were called to parade at the Seel Street station. Here they received profuse thanks from Mr Mansfield, the stipendiary magistrate, and Mr Gregson, the chair of the watch committee. The chief magistrate reminded the parade how Major Greig 'had been at considerable pains in bringing the men into their present state of efficiency' and that it had clearly brought results during the recent riots, when the men conducted themselves with 'good temper and discretion'. He had, he continued, noted a diminution of complaints against them and he consequently had 'every reason to believe a marked improvement had taken place'.[12] While it is undoubtedly true that Greig had improved the police's conduct, it is hard to judge how much of an improvement had taken place, since he ensured that he dealt with all disciplinary matters internally. The watch committee rarely got to know what and how many breaches of indiscipline occurred within the force. There also began what nowadays would be called a public relations drive, which attempted to put the force in a more positive light. It is in this context that we have to understand and place Hugh Shimmin's masterful eyewitness account, in the appendix, of the Liverpool police in 1857.

Whenever a case or accusation of police brutality came before the magistrates' court, two contrasting stories of what occurred were put forward. Generally, the police's version of events was taken as the truth by the magistrates. A correspondent to the *Mercury* in 1866 wrote:

> There is, in truth, no disputing the fact that the general public stand in the police court at a great disadvantage in charges made against them by the police, and this disadvantage is sought to be increased in every way by the connivance nay, positive assistance of the authorities. It is notorious that some justices of the Shallow species, Major Greig, and not a few members of the watch committee seem to be possessed with the notion that a policeman can do no wrong.[13]

Just occasionally this was not the case. One of those exceptions involved the case of James Cullen, who in 1867 was accused of disorderly conduct and assault by PCs 470 (Butler) and 646. The prosecution argued that Cullen, with others, was creating a disturbance in Islington at 12.30 a.m. and that PC Butler had struck Cullen on the head in self-defence. Constable 646, who saw nothing of the original assault, helped his fellow officer in taking the prisoner to the bridewell. He claimed that no violence was used along the way. The case for the police fell down partly because of the respectability of the witnesses brought forward by Cullen. One, an accountant named Simm, spoke of seeing PC 470 striking Cullen on his head with a truncheon for no apparent reason. The same scene had been witnessed by an inspector of nuisances, who told the court that where St Anne Street and Rose Place met, PC 470 struck Cullen in the ribs several times and then kicked his legs from under him. 'I could lick a hundred like you', the officer reportedly said to the prone body of Cullen. Mr Raffles, the stipendiary magistrate, ordered PC 470's immediate dismissal from the force, while PC 646, for the slightly less serious crime of lying in court, was suspended until further orders.[14]

It is very difficult for a modern-day reader to know where the truth really lay in these cases. One is often left with a sense that some injustice had been perpetrated. Take the case of James Hooker, a labourer living in Hornby Street, who summoned two constables, PCs 738 (Throup) and 928 (Walker), for having assaulted him on 12 September 1871. In his evidence Hooker explained that he walked with friends to Burlington Bridge around midnight and then as he returned, alone, via Vauxhall Road he heard a woman screaming. Shortly after, a woman and a man ran past and a voice from a window cried, 'You murdering villains! Do you want to kill the man?' As he neared his home he heard someone following him and as he turned to see who it was, he was struck in the stomach by a policeman, who swore at him to get up. Another officer then punched him in the face and left him 'completely stunned'. Naturally aggrieved, he took his complaint to Rosehill bridewell and then to the head constable, who, after investigation, advised him to take out a summons against the constables. During the subsequent court case, Hooker was able to identify Throup as one of the men who had hit him. Another Hornby Street resident, William Blair, told the court that he had heard both a woman's cry and witnessed a constable assault Hooker. There was 'thud after thud' but he was not sure whether the sound was from the officer's baton or from Hooker's head being repeatedly bumped on the pavement. He shouted to the two officers; 'You murdering hounds! Are you going to kill the man? I am watching you.' Under cross-examination he admitted he had not actually seen the assault, nor was he able to identify Throup when being questioned by Major Greig during the initial investigation. However, he had seen the two officers following Hooker immediately before the assault and had heard his cries for mercy. Another witness, John Lyons, a baker, saw the assault and could identify one of the assailants, Throup. One other witness failed to identify PC 928, Walker, and so the case against him was dismissed. In Throup's defence it was stated that he had been in the force for 17 years, much of that time being spent in the Hornby Street neighbourhood.

Constable Walker was then brought as a defence witness and he told the court that he and Throup had heard a woman screaming and gone to investigate. They had found three men trying to pull her up a court when they had intervened. One man was caught without being assaulted and then released when she refused to press charges. One other witness for Throup, Charles Trowler of Burlington Street, saw a man trip and fall while being followed by an officer. The two magistrates hearing the case felt that although the evidence was confused, they believed Hooker had been assaulted 'by somebody'. However, the evidence with regard to the officer's identity was so conflicting they could not convict Throup. In dismissing the case they added, 'it was a grievous thing that a man should be assaulted in this way in the public street'.

This case contains many issues that can be found in other instances where accusations of police violence to members of the public were made. First came the apparently fair treatment of the prosecutor at the police station where his complaints were heard, in this case by the head constable, who then advised him to take out a summons against the two officers concerned. This seemingly helpful advice was meant to be a hurdle for the potential prosecutor, since time and money were required to do so. Then came the police denials of what was said and obfuscation as to the identity of the possible culprit. There followed a further muddying of the waters as to what actually took place: did Hooker trip or was he beaten? In this particular case the second officer, Walker, was never convincingly identified; however, Throup appears to have been seen by almost everyone and was fortunate to be let off. It is obvious what the magistrates thought: Hooker had indeed been assaulted by a policeman, and by Throup in particular, but the evidence was not conclusive enough for a successful conviction. Even when magistrates felt 'unnecessary violence' had been employed by constables in this and similar cases, the police officers often received no more than a 'strong caution ... as to their future behaviour'.[15]

Hugh Shimmin, as we have seen in earlier chapters, was initially an uncritical supporter of the Liverpool police but it is interesting to note his growing disillusionment with the force in his articles. Their military style, formerly so attractive and emblematic of discipline, now became, to the reporter at least, threatening and overbearing. 'Before teaching the police how to use military arms', he wrote, 'it would be well to instruct them how to employ civil tongues'. By 1867 he was complaining that their 'coarseness and disposition to override authority' were inseparable from their possession of a truncheon. This seems to imply that the police were able to do as they liked, that the police officer had become 'master of the street'.[16] In one *Liverpool Mercury* article from 1861 headlined 'A PUGNACIOUS POLICEMAN', a correspondent reported that:

> his attention was arrested by the conduct of a man (subsequently stated at Rose-hill Station to be P-c 356) labouring under some excitement, and who insulted nearly every one he met. Without any provocation he knocked down a girl, about seven-years-old, who was carrying an infant in her arms; and when remonstrated with for his unmanly conduct by a lady who was passing, he attempted to kick her. To escape from his violence the lady sought the protection of a publican standing at his door; and he also was upset while protecting the lady.

After assaulting some others inside the pub he was given into the charge of two other constables, who took him down to the station. Here the mother of the seven-year-old girl tried to book a charge of assault against him but was refused; furthermore, she was 'grossly insulted' by the police inspector and ordered out by the bridewell keeper.[17]

By the end of the 1860s Shimmin could barely contain his outrage. The public, he contended, needed to be 'properly protected from the insolence, brutality, and lying' of the police. Adopting a cruelly ironic and sarcastic tone, Shimmin now referred to the Liverpool force as Major Greig's 'lambs'. This was partly an allusion to the nursery rhyme 'Mary had a little lamb' (everywhere the Major went the lambs were sure to go). The force was, in other words, totally obedient to the major. It was also a sarcastic reference to the fact that lambs were seen as essentially passive and unaggressive creatures, which the officers of the Liverpool force were most definitely not. In future articles, whenever Shimmin referred to 'playful lambs', he was in fact alluding to police violence, which had become so bad by October 1869 that he advocated the 'formation of a Vigilance committee in order that the public might be, in some degree, protected from the ferocity and violence of the police'. To back up his case, Shimmin gave a detailed description of an unprovoked assault on a woman by two plain-clothes constables, an event which was subsequently covered up by two other colleagues.[18]

This incident had been witnessed by an acquaintance of Shimmin, who took the matter to the watch committee's disciplinary board. The acquaintance was outraged when the board decided to reduce the officers' wages by just one shilling a week. Only two months earlier, in a similar case, PC 135 was brought up on a charge of assaulting 'a respectable-looking woman', who, on feeling ill, had sat down but had been ordered to move on. When she refused, PC 135 set upon her. In the court case which arose from this assault, PC 135 was found guilty of 'misconducting himself to a certain extent' and was discharged with only a caution, on account of his alleged good character and police record.[19] The magistrate's leniency, according to Shimmin, only encouraged further insolence on the part of the police; 'It is known now', he wrote, 'that no one dare speak to a police man ... without being exposed to the charge of drunkenness, if not something worse. So general is this feeling that it amounts to terrorism; and, so far from the police force being gradually more and more respected, the very name "Bobby" has become in Liverpool a by word and a reproach'. In a case in which PC Clingan was summoned for assaulting Henry Cotton, it transpired that, while some officers were making an arrest, someone in the crowd called out to them, 'whereupon the defendant [Clingan] turned upon Cotton and struck him a violent blow on the jaw'. The constable in his defence argued that 'the complainant had called out "Bobby Blue, Bobby Blue", and with an oath told the police to let the woman alone'.[20]

Reported cases of police assaults actually increased in the 1870s, leading Shimmin to write, 'the arbitrary despotism of the Liverpool police is

progressing at a most rapid and cheerful rate thanks to the natural pro-
clivities of the men themselves and the apparent encouragement which is
given to them by the magistrates and watch committee. Instances of police
terrorism are as plentiful as blackberries.' Four months after these strong
words he reported on yet another case in which 'a playful lamb had grossly
insulted a woman'. Not only had a 'police-officer, or a ruffian disguised in
the garb of one', insulted and insinuated that a respectable woman walking
home with her husband was a prostitute, he also arrested the husband;
'the lamb's knuckles were pressed skilfully into his neck' as he was taken to
the bridewell. He was eventually discharged by Mr Raffles, the stipendiary
magistrate, who advised him to take out a summons against the officer.[21]
Herein lay a danger, for the police, 'by sticking together', were determined
to help a fellow officer in trouble. They made investigations against the man,
a respectable civil servant; 'not a stone was left unturned to find out the
antecedents of him who dared to summon a police-officer'. Unsuccessful in
the pursuit of evidence against the complainant, the police quietly let the
case drop by offering an apology out of court. In this way the case never
received a public airing except through the pages of the *Porcupine*.

Shimmin's comments were, no doubt, prejudiced and reflected the
opinion of a minority, albeit a substantial one, of the liberal radical middle
classes within the borough. However, there exists evidence from other
sources which supports the notion of police brutality. The recorder at
the 1877 winter sessions, for example, was critical of the police and their
behaviour in one particular case. A magistrate, in finding a constable
guilty of assault when he pushed a sober shoemaker down the steps of
St George's Hall, said the officer had acted 'indiscriminately'. The very fact
that the watch committee, in a practice which echoed assize court customs,
presented the chair of their committee with a pair of white gloves if 'not a
single complaint has been made against any guardian of the peace' in the
past week, suggested a high level of police irregularity. In another case, the
stipendiary magistrate was highly critical of PC 235, William Mills, for a
'cowardly and dastardly' assault on George McKenzie (who had originally
called for police assistance when he was being robbed in the street) and
the magistrate commented that he had 'recently sent another constable for
trial who, without the least provocation, attacked a man in a tender part
and ruined him for life'. He was, he continued, 'sorry to say that within the
last 12 months cases had come before him where officers [had] behaved
extremely disgraceful[ly]'.[22]

There is, therefore, evidence to suggest that, from the mid-1850s,
elements within the middle classes, and not just radical journalists, found
the 'soothing powers of the truncheon' unacceptable, or even reprehensible.
This growing condemnation, while not universal, probably coincided with
the establishment of, or evolution of, a quasi-independent, informal, unofficial and unmonitored police way of going about their business. There

was, in other words, an unwritten code of being a policeman, a camaraderie of supporting your mates, of getting in the first punch in difficult situations, of lying in court to back up colleagues' evidence, of being disciplined behind closed doors and so on, as opposed to following the police manual, with its emphasis on minimal force, the deployment of the truncheon only in self-defence and of prosecution in open court, or a full disciplinary hearing before a properly constituted watch committee. Such camaraderie got PC 324 (Gradwell) the sack and PC 687 suspended. The former had initially assaulted a rigger, Joseph Rodick, of Upper Mann Street, and had then involved four or five colleagues in a further assault on and arrest of Rodick. In an attempt to get the subsequent summons against Gradwell quietly dropped, PC 687, in plain clothes, visited Rodick and offered him £2 to 'square' the case. The officer was suspended from duty while Gradwell was fined 40 shillings and dismissed from the force.[23]

The present study brought to light 90 instances of violence between 1850 and 1895 on the part of the Liverpool police reported in the *Porcupine* and the *Mercury*. The question is then, what kinds of assault were the most common? Where it has been possible to discover details, a surprisingly high 54% can be described as unprovoked police assaults, in which the officer threw the first punch. In a not untypical example, PC 719 approached a Mrs Hogg, who, while she was waiting by her door for her husband's return, was seized by the neck and arm, dragged across the street and thrown to the ground, whereupon the returning husband protested and was himself arrested by another officer. In court it transpired that PC 719 had been in the force for only five months and this fact alone saved him from dismissal after he was found guilty. In another case, involving a brother and sister by the name of Stone, PC 605, whom they had passed in the street several times on their way home, suddenly rushed up to Miss Stone and said he would teach her to laugh at him, and proceeded to manhandle them roughly. A witness to the struggle told the court that PC 605 was drunk, an accusation not totally denied by the inspector, who confirmed that the policeman had had some drink 'but was not reportable'. The officer was not dismissed after the guilty verdict because he had a 'clean book'. He had in fact been twice before Major Greig for taking drink.[24]

In nearly a third of cases the violence had been committed during an arrest. Such instances appeared to have been the most contentious in the courts, and they are, for the historian, the hardest to evaluate. Many of the examples involved an accusation that false charges had been laid against members of the public, drunk and disorderly behaviour and assaulting the police being the most common. Constable Hickey, for example, was found guilty of using unnecessary violence to an abusive and inebriated Mrs Leech, whom he dragged along the street by her hair. In another case Alfred Moritz, who was saying good night to his partner, was ordered to move on by PC Carson. On refusing he was arrested and charged with drunk and disorderly behaviour; he was dragged reluctantly to the bridewell, where the keeper refused to book the prisoner in (otherwise known as a 'refused charge'). Moritz as a consequence was then able to bring a successful prosecution against Carson.[25]

In cases of violence in custody, the role and character of the bridewell keeper were crucial, as he was very often an important witness, in a position of considerable authority and influence when it came to allegations of police assaults on prisoners. For example, his refusal to receive a charge, as in the Moritz case above, when the beat constables brought arrested individuals to the bridewell was often deemed significant by magistrates. In 1859, for example, bridewell keeper McInnes was fined by the head constable for refusing to charge two men, but in the court case which followed, the stipendiary magistrate dismissed the case, which suggested the arresting officers had been lying. The keeper was thus vindicated. In another case the bridewell keeper refused to book a prisoner for assaulting the arresting officer, and as a consequence the officer was found guilty of assault.[26]

However, if the bridewell keeper was less than honest he was well placed not only to turn a blind eye to any assaults committed by other officers which took place within the station but also, if he so desired, to initiate his own brand of instant justice. One such officer was William Bennett, who was prosecuted for using unnecessary violence in the bridewell towards a Margaret Williams, who had been charged with soliciting. She claimed that Bennett 'took her by the arm and led her until she was out of sight; then he got her by the scruff of the neck and struck her in the face. She then refused to go with him. They struggled, and he threw a can of water over her. He again struck her in the face, knocked her down, kicked her, and threw more water on her.' Bennett defended himself by claiming she was violent and uncooperative, and had torn his vest; moreover, he claimed to have remained friendly towards her. His avuncular attitude – 'What's to do with you, lass.... Come this way, lass' – was witnessed by another female prisoner, who said 'she had never seen more partiality than Bennett showed to Williams, to whom the "hoight of laniensy" was also extended'. The evidence from the two prosecution witnesses, a magistrates' clerk and a prosecuting solicitor, ensured his conviction, as they had both seen his actions from a window overlooking the bridewell yard. Bennett, it appears, had been in the force since 1870 and after five years had been appointed the keeper. In the previous 22 months he had twice been summoned for assaulting prisoners, in one case breaking a prisoner's jaw with a key. In his summing up, the stipendiary magistrate said a bridewell keeper 'was really under no supervision in a great deal of the work he had to do, and therefore should be a person to be trusted, and should not be more overbearing in solitude than if a dozen persons were looking on'. Bennett was fined 40 shillings and dismissed from the force.[27]

Police officers tended to feel less inhibited when dealing with certain social groups and they were more likely to evade prosecution and conviction where their victims lacked respectability, if no respectable witnesses were present, or if the assault had taken place in an area with a reputation for roughness. People on the margins, especially prostitutes, were vulnerable to both physical and sexual assault. In 1853, for example, Sarah Gill of Glover Street claimed she was assaulted in her own home by two constables. She had, she told the court, met PC 610 at five past midnight in the street, who had said to her that it was payday and that he was going to treat her. Having invited the two officers into her house – it was a brothel – and having broken up a fight between them and a drunken sailor, she asked them 'what they were going to treat her with'. One officer replied, suggestively, 'I think you have had enough of drink'. After more words, PC 610 struck her several times and PC 331 dragged her into the street, where witnesses claimed to see the two men abusing her. Minutes later, another officer, PC 61, answering the cries of 'murder', came running and found Sarah Gill leaning against a wall with head wounds. At an identity parade the next day, Gill and other witnesses picked out the officers concerned. The policemen denied having ever been in Glover Street and claimed that they had made their way home up Hill Street. The fact that neither had met any other officers on the way appeared 'very strange, if not impossible' to Mr Clough, the magistrate.[28]

Forty per cent of all victims of alleged police assaults reported in the Liverpool press were female. Even where the primary victim of an alleged police assault was male there could be an issue relating to police attitudes towards women. In a case involving John Campbell, an iron-founder of Burlington Street, and his wife and daughter, who were arrested by PC 473 (George Sowerby) for assaulting him, the circumstances surrounding the assault which came to light in court highlighted the male culture of the force. The officer claimed he was sending away a group of prostitutes when Mrs Campbell opened an upstairs window and shouted at him. She then threw a jug of water over him and continued shouting that it would be better to chase the 'girls' away and 'not let them make such a disturbance that people could not sleep in their beds'. Meanwhile, her husband had gone downstairs and out into the street in his nightshirt. Sowerby claimed that Campbell, having taken down his number, then assaulted him, whereupon the officer 'merely put or pushed him into the house'. This set off further violence from the husband, wife and daughter, the last wielding a shovel. In overpowering all three, he tied the mother and daughter together with a 'home-made manacle – a kind of handcuff – consisting of a strong cord passed through two holes in a short stout piece of wood'. Sowerby's evidence does not altogether ring true. He did not clearly explain what exactly he was doing with the prostitutes, or why Mr Campbell saw fit to take his number and seemingly attack him without provocation. The policeman's case did not improve when the Athol Street bridewell keeper noted that Sowerby failed to mention anything about water being thrown over him. Mrs Campbell's evidence, on the other hand, answered quite a few questions regarding

Sowerby's behaviour that night. She recounted to the court how she, on looking out of the window, saw the policeman 'attempting to get a girl in the cellar'. She then remonstrated with him, telling him that this was not the way to do his duty, and he replied with 'disgusting language'.[29] Thus it would appear that Sowerby had picked off one girl for his own use and was trying to chase away the other women, who noisily objected to his behaviour. The case suggests that the officer thought that he could do what he liked, in this instance attempted rape, with a prostitute.

The respectability of the victim of a police assault, as in the case of one Annie Williams, often proved to be the crucial element in making a successful complaint against the officer. Although picked up and assaulted for being a prostitute out late at night, Annie was able to prove that she was a respectable waitress on her way home. The magistrate, in passing judgement against one of the three policemen implicated in the case, said he had made 'a very stupid mistake'. This seems to imply that, had she been a prostitute, the assault would have been forgivable. Where individuals were known to be 'bad characters', such as dock porter James Ware, constables could act with impunity. Ware's charge of assault against one of the dock police was dismissed when he was described as 'one of the worst characters on the pier-head'.[30]

The realities and practicalities of policing duty (especially the night shifts) and the fact that constables were working-class males, with working-class male attitudes to violence, are important themes which require further consideration. Issues of authority, reputation and male 'hardness' were all bound up in the question, who rules around here? If the police constable, through an unofficial show of force, beat up a local rough, then his reputation for hardness would have undoubtedly been enhanced and a grudging respect might well have been accorded him, thus making his job easier. However, if the reverse occurred, that is, the policeman lost a fight, then the rough's reputation increased accordingly. In a one-to-one fight, before a crowd of Liverpool cornermen, PC Stratton lost to a rough named Roberts. All we know of this challenge and encounter was that Roberts was prosecuted, but one wonders how Stratton coped thereafter on his beat.[31] In other cases men came out of the pubs and issued public challenges to constables, which inevitably led to scuffles. But such cases rarely led to charges of police violence.

Some policemen were inclined to use force when the legality of their acts was queried or challenged by members of the public. (Modern research has confirmed that public condemnation and criticism of policing can trigger police violence.) For example, two constables were seen beating up a man they were arresting; this brought forth a complaint from a publican's wife, who said to them, 'Don't murder the man'. PC John Kerr took umbrage at this remark and turned to the woman and kicked her to the ground. In one of those strange coincidences, Kerr, who was fined in the magistrates' court the following day, was immediately arrested on stepping down from the dock because a woman, claiming to be his first wife, stood up and shouted that he had committed bigamy.[32]

In a more complex case, PC Whelan was brought before the magistrates for assaulting Margaret Patterson. It transpired that he and another constable had arrested Patterson for failing to answer two summonses. Witnesses to the arrest told the police that they had the wrong woman – it was her sister they were after – but this information appeared only to enrage the arresting officers. Their defence in court was based on the claim that they were simply trying to do their duty under very difficult circumstances. This was accepted by the stipendiary magistrate, who said to Whelan that he should be more careful in future when executing warrants.[33]

In another complex case, teetotaller John Callinson witnessed an arrest in which he believed unnecessary violence was used. As a consequence he went to the police station, where he made a charge against one of the officers. In the ensuing mêlée, he was punched in the eye and thrown out of the station onto the street. When the whole matter came to court, it appeared that many constables were struck with amnesia or confusion, so much so that the bench agreed that the complainant had been punched 'but by whom was not known'. The defendant, PC McKinley, was allowed to go.[34]

Occasionally it appears that the fighting had arisen out of tensions which had little to do with the defendant being a policeman. This is especially true where a constable was in civilian clothes and made no reference to his being in the force. The fight in such an instance might be construed as private and personal, and as such had little to do with the misuse of authority and power. However, even in cases such as this, interpretative complications may still arise. Take the prosecution of Jonas Mitchell, a Liverpool policeman, for the assault of Matthew Murray, of Leeds, in January 1862. The incident took place on Christmas Eve in a hatter's shop in St John's Lane. According to Murray, the policeman, who was in plain clothes, gave him a black eye and also jumped on him after he had been knocked to the ground. Mitchell, on the other hand, claimed that Murray had pulled his whiskers and generally 'chaffed' him about his facial hair. It should be observed at this point that Mitchell sported 'an enormous beard, which makes him a conspicuous character in the Liverpool force'. Murray's claim that he was new to the town and hence did not know that Mitchell was a policeman was fairly crucial to his defence. Mitchell claimed that Murray knew very well who and what he was, as he had complained that 'he had to support them and that they [the officers] were fed on meat that was given to dogs to feast on'. He also, according to a police witness, called them pigs and donkeys. Provocation was acknowledged by the magistrates when they fined the officer a mere five shillings and costs.[35]

Community relations and assaults on the police

A NINETEENTH-CENTURY policeman's lot was far from easy, especially in a borough like Liverpool. Regarded to some extent as a class traitor, he was viewed with suspicion and contempt by his social equals and inferiors. For the middle classes and civic dignitaries he was regarded with a mixture of disdain and patronizing affection. He was, after all, a public servant. As the century progressed, outright hostility towards the police abated to a small extent, but it would be wrong to believe that the job was not, at times, a perilous one. In examining public hostility towards the police it would be as well to separate violence directed at them in the course of their job (making arrests, breaking fights up and so forth) from the violence they attracted because of their very existence as an institution. How much violence was directed towards them? It is difficult to arrive at any satisfactory answer. The statistics for assaults on police officers are fairly complete for the borough but they need to be handled and analysed with care. Figures 1 and 2 relate to summary prosecutions in the magistrates' courts.

When considering convictions for assaults on the police, historians need to be aware that they may include cases where defendants were 'stitched up', so to speak, by individual constables keen to hide their own aggressive behaviour.[36] It is not inconceivable that officers also provoked drunks into fights in order to arrest them on more serious charges. Equally, some assaults on officers never entered the statistical record, as some police, for whatever reason, chose not, or were not in a position, to make arrests. The published figures are thus a very incomplete record but they still contain

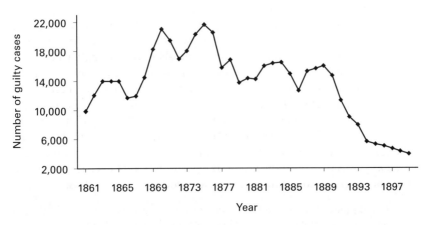

Figure 1 Annual totals of charges of drunkenness with 'guilty' findings in magistrates' courts, 1861–99. (Numbers taken from LvRO, 353 POL2, Head constable's reports to the Liverpool watch committee.)

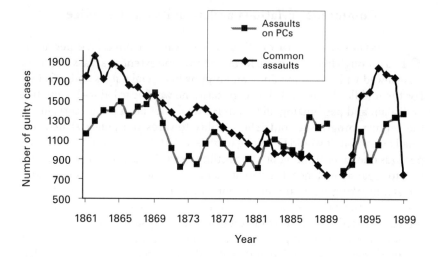

Figure 2 Annual totals of charges of assault on a police officer or common assault with 'guilty' findings in magistrates' courts, 1861–99. (Numbers taken from LvRO, 353 POL2, Head constable's reports to the Liverpool watch committee.)

some useful information. The rises and falls in assaults do follow patterns and are related to social and economic forces, not least the state of the local economy and the amount of alcohol consumed by the population of the town (the latter is plotted over the period in proxy fashion in figure 1, which gives the annual number of convictions for drunkenness).

It was generally argued by the police that whenever working people experienced full employment and high wages, it followed that convictions for drunkenness increased. As a consequence of increased drunkenness, convictions for assaults on policemen would also rise. This pattern is borne out in 1887, for example, when the head constable noted a 'revival' in trade. The number of assaults on the police rose by 363 when compared with 1882, and the number of convictions for drunkenness rose by nearly 2700. There are some divergences to this pattern towards the end of the century, when methods of recording and counting crime changed, in 1893. The other problem with the statistics, and it is one alluded to by Shimmin in the *Porcupine*, was that the police were in a position to influence the recording of offences, specifically drunkenness. He noted cynically in 1878:

> Drunkenness is a very difficult offence for the constable to deal with. On observing a drunken and disorderly person, the constable must first reflect whether it has been officially stated that drunkenness is on the increase or decrease. If drunkenness is said to be on the increase, he must arrest his man; if on the decrease, he must let him go. By a judicious arrangement of this kind,

this pernicious vice can be made to appear increasing or decreasing, according to the will of the operator – a sweet and subtle fact that portrays most beautifully the unspeakable value of official statistics.[37]

Whether this occurred or not is impossible to tell; however, it is hard to deny the dangers confronting the police in their day-to-day duties. Almost universally despised along streets like Scotland Road, individual officers, and even those working in pairs, had to face up to crude insults at best or violence at worst almost daily. This violence, while rarely lethal, accounted for about 50 officers on average being absent from daily duty because of injuries received during the course of their work. By far the most dangerous duty was that between 10 and 12 on Saturday night, 'the two blackest hours in the week for producing drunkenness' according to the head constable's report of 1868. A weekly return on drunkenness in 1872 shows that Saturday accounted for 30% of the weekly arrests, followed by Monday, with 19%. In terms of time of day, arrests for drunkenness between 9 p.m. and 1 a.m. accounted for 59.5% of Saturday apprehensions.

Not surprisingly, the vast majority of people arrested for assaulting the police were male, local and working class. In 1867, 80% of those guilty of being drunk and assaulting police constables were male, and exactly the same percentage was returned in 1880. In terms of male occupations, labourers, sailors and carters/carmen accounted for over 60% of the arrests. For women, the occupational descriptors were less varied: 'no trade', prostitution and hawking accounted for as much as 94%. The place of birth of those arrested for assaulting the police did alter over time; in 1868 Irish-born immigrants accounted for 40% of these assaults, Liverpool-born people for 36%, those from other areas of England for 14.5% and foreigners for just 2%. However, by 1898, Irish-born immigrants accounted for a total of only 8%, foreigners 2% and those from elsewhere in England 12%, while the proportion committed by people born in the city had risen to 71%. These sets of figures suggest that newly arrived immigrants from Ireland were charged most frequently with charges of drunken assault. Given that those aged 21–30 years were the most heavily represented for such crimes, it seems that the many people arriving in the borough during the 'Great Hunger' of the 1840s had had trouble assimilating into Liverpool society but that, by the end of the nineteenth century, this was no longer the case.

But drunkenness was no respecter of social class and social class did not necessarily guarantee the so-called respectable middle classes would escape the close attentions of the men in blue. In 1856, for example, a Mancunian solicitor, Thomas Blair, was seen knocking at the doors of houses in Catherine Street and then kicking an angry resident at 1.15 on a Monday morning. Although he denied striking PC 56, he was found guilty and fined the usual 40 shillings plus costs. Although no occupation is cited for Mr William Richardson Buckley, it is apparent that he was not a typical example of a police assailant. Before the details could be made public to the court, Buckley instructed his solicitor to pay not only for the cost of replacing superintendent Martin's hat, but of allowing himself to be bound over to keep the peace and never annoy Mr Martin or anyone connected with him. Unlike others charged with similar offences, Buckley was only bound over to his own recognizances to keep the peace for six months, along with paying for the costs of the case and the hat.[38] Such cases, however, were comparatively rare.

Some of the anger and violence directed at the police suggested there were some within the Liverpool community who had a deep and lasting hatred of them, bordering on the pathological. Some, like James Murphy, appear to have been waging a lone war. He was well known for his 'repeated and violent attacks' on the force. More commonly, assaults on a policeman would involve a group of people, often escalating from a small incident involving perhaps one or two individuals to a crowd. When Sergeant Carnes went into a Cheapside pub, described as 'a resort for thieves and characters of the lowest description', to arrest a pickpocket he had seen in the street the publican, Cropper, threw him out. The sergeant returned with two of his men and a mêlée kicked off in which Mrs Cropper was seen handing a life-protector (a kind of leaded truncheon) to one of the customers. Carnes was hit with this and another officer had a poker broken across his back, while the third policeman was disabled after being hit. No one was arrested.[39]

When major incidents occurred, one is unsure whether to marvel at the police's bravery or stupidity; perhaps foolhardiness best describes their behaviour. On one occasion in February 1851, a crowd of dock labourers and Irish navvies piled out of a pub in Snowden Street. It was estimated that they numbered between 100 and 150 and were mostly drunk and rowdy. Onto this scene arrived just two constables, PCs 100 and 598, who asked them to disperse quietly. This brought a show of defiance from the crowd, who told the two officers to leave, or else 'they would knock their brains out'. Upon receiving this advice, the two men went to the Athol police station and returned with three more colleagues – hardly enough to control a drunken and aggressive group. Nonetheless, their increased numbers initially appeared to do the trick and the street was cleared. This, though, proved to be only a tactical retreat, for the men returned armed with shovels, picks, bludgeons and stones. As soon as one man was arrested in the act of throwing a paving stone, his friends immediately started throwing stones and beating the police 'in a fearful manner'. Only later were the less seriously injured officers able to identify some of those who had taken part. In all, nine men were arrested.[40]

There were occupational hazards and tensions that brought the police into conflict with various communities. The police were most vulnerable in a number of situations: making an arrest, walking the arrested through the streets to the nearest bridewell, the policing of alcoholic consumption, dealing with sectarian conflicts and implementing the 'move on' order to prevent men and women from loitering on street corners. The last police duty was particularly irksome to the so-called 'cornermen' and prostitutes. While underemployed dockers frequently spent their days off congregated on street corners, the police appear to have had ambivalent attitudes towards this kind of behaviour.

In years of social unrest and moral panic over violent behaviour, as in 1874, constables were keen to move people on. In August 1876, just two years after the Tithebarn Street murder (already mentioned and discussed in chapter 7), PC 952 (Stratton) came across a large group of roughs assembled at the notorious corner of Sawney Pope Street and Scotland Road at 9 p.m. Ordering them to disperse, most obeyed but one refused and turned on the officer. During the struggle the policeman was knocked down and stabbed in the neck and head five times. Three hours later PC 974 ordered 20 roughs to move on in Tichfield Street. Again, just one, this time an Andrew Mularkey, refused to comply and swung a punch at the policeman. This was the sign for the others to wade in with their fists, boots and belt buckles. Mularkey was sentenced to two months' imprisonment with hard labour.[41]

However, in other years the act of standing on street corners did not unduly worry the police. It also depended on who was doing the loitering and whether it attracted other forms of anti-social or criminal behaviour. When PC 789 took exception to a group of prostitutes standing together on the corner of Hanover and Paradise Streets late one Friday night in 1862, he ordered them to move off. This upset two nearby sailors, Charles Martin and Samuel Jackson. The former shouted out, 'What do you want to move them for?', and he then picked up a large stone and flung it at the constable. It struck him just above the left ear. Unusually for this period, a passing pedestrian who witnessed the assault gave chase and caught Martin. His friend Jackson was prosecuted and found guilty of assaulting other officers in his attempt to rescue Martin.

Pitch-and-toss games played on pavements were viewed as both obstructions and a form of gambling; consequently, they were broken up and the participants moved on. This could be regarded as a provocation to the players and gave rise to fights. 'A tall, rough-looking fellow' named Patrick Murphy was fined 20 shillings or a month in gaol for having refused to budge when ordered to move on by PC 700. He hit the policeman on the head; while he was subsequently being taken to the bridewell, his friends returned and attacked the officer.[42]

Generally speaking, street activities were more heavily policed towards the end of the nineteenth century. Assaults on police officers arose out of their stopping football, illegal street trading and pitch and toss. One football case, which took place in Raleigh Street, Bootle, was sparked off when PC Adair began to take the names of some boys playing in the street. This action angered some men, described as 'rough-looking fellows', standing on the corner of the street. In all, five men were gaoled for two months with hard labour for their assaults on three constables.[43] This suggests that by the 1890s the Liverpool streets had become more orderly; it may also suggest that the police and the city council displayed greater intolerance towards behaviour that could be construed as disruptive or potentially disruptive.

The other great problem for the Liverpool police for most of the nineteenth century was the escorting of prisoners through the streets to the bridewell. One can easily imagine the name-calling, abuse and jostling aimed at the police from the watching crowd. The following news item from the *Liverpool Mercury* conveys the problem rather well:

THE DIFFICULTY OF TAKING PRISONERS TO BRIDEWELL

A young rough named Thomas Telford was brought up in custody charged with assaulting P-c 315 who stated that on Saturday about midnight there was a great deal of disturbance in Scotland-road in consequence of two men fighting. An officer interfered and took one of the men into custody, but as he was conveying him to the bridewell, he was attacked by several fellows who endeavoured to release the man. The prisoner came up to him, struck him on the side of the head and ran up St. Augustine-street. The witness whistled for assistance and succeeded in making No. 729 hear him. The latter officer took charge of one man and the witness pursued the prisoner whom he captured at the top of St. Augustine-street. He was taking him to bridewell when a man not presently in custody struck him on the head with a brick inflicting a very serious wound from which he was now suffering. After considerable trouble the prisoner was conveyed to the bridewell but even then the mob went to the doors and annoyed the police....[44]

The introduction of police wagons, an idea taken from Boston and New York in 1892, considerably eased the transport of arrestees to the police bridewells.[45]

The docks carried their own particular pressures for the police, who had, among other duties, to guard against theft on the quaysides, a duty made somewhat easier with the construction of the dock boundary wall. Like the move-on policy, the policing of quayside theft was probably not diligently and consistently enforced. Collusion between dockers and the police at the gates almost certainly went on, and any 'spoiled' cargo taken home by the dock force had probably attained the status of traditional work perks, to which some policemen would have turned a blind eye in receipt of a backhander. However, this did not mean that other workers, carters from outside the docks for example, could help themselves to the goods lying around on the waterfront. Making arrests in such circumstances could lead to violence. James Edwards, with 15 previous convictions and a sentence of four years' penal servitude to his name, was presumably well known to the police. He was spotted shortly after midnight, standing near a barrel of nails at No. 2 Canning Grave Dock. On being followed by PC 278 to the north end of Canning Dock, he was able to evade his pursuer and creep up on him and deliver a heavy blow to the officer's head with a ship carpenter's coppering hammer. Amazingly still conscious, the stunned officer was able to call out for the assistance of PC 41, who took Edwards into custody. Fifty pounds of copper nails were found in his possession.[46] This case highlights the very considerable violence that could be directed towards policemen during the course of their duties. The killing of police constables has been, historically, comparatively rare in Britain. That murders and manslaughters were so unusual is surprising, given the state of nineteenth-century medical science and the lack of treatment for infected wounds. The Liverpool police did, like most other city forces, have its roll call of officers killed while on duty. This included PC Sunderland, stabbed to death in November 1853 in an election fight in Scotland Road, Sergeant Tinker, killed in June 1855 by a hammer while intervening in an Irish fight, and Thomas Burns, killed in October 1866 at the Queen's Graving Dock.[47]

In the case of PC Sunderland, a man named Copeland, though charged with his murder, was found guilty of manslaughter and sentenced to trans-portation for life. That the trial and sentence left a bitter feeling among Copeland's supporters was evident in the magistrates' court case against Patrick Radigan, 'a blackguard looking fellow' and baker from Eccles. He was charged with using threatening language against shopkeeper Ann Houghton of Cavendish Street. She had, it transpired, acted as a witness for the prosecution of Copeland. Since the trial, Copeland's friends had set up a campaign of threats against Houghton. In this particular case, it was reported that Radigan had come to her house, kicked her and warned 'I'll have your life: you shall have no quarters. You got £50 to hang the man' and as he turned towards the door to leave he took out his knife and thrust it towards his dog, saying, 'You —, I'll serve you the same as the dog, and the dog as same as you [*sic*]: I'll have your life before I've done.' For these threats Radigan was given the comparatively mild sentence of finding bail with sureties to the sum of £40 to keep the peace towards Houghton for one month; failing that, he was to be gaoled for a month.[48]

While violence leading to police fatalities appears to have been rare, far more frequent were the murderous attacks and serious assaults to which they were subjected almost weekly. The details of some are surprising, given the urban nature of Liverpool policing. In February 1850, for example, at Kirkdale and Litherland seven officers of the county police were gathered to prevent potato stealing, a considerable problem at the time. About 30 men armed with pikes, brickbats and stones were spotted. To cries of 'Come on, ye pikeman', a pitched battle took place in which Sergeant Helsby was knocked down and stabbed in the back. Although forced to retreat, the police were able to arrest Patrick Brannan, with a load of potatoes, in Bootle.[49]

What made the police's job all the more hazardous were the frequent, though unpredictable, knife assaults they faced when attempting to act as peacemakers. For example, John Johnson, an officer stationed at West

Derby, was called to Petticoat Lane, where a domestic incident of wife beating was reportedly occurring. On persuading Hugh Walker, a 33-year-old butcher, to leave, PC Johnson walked with him up the lane, whereupon Walker turned round and stabbed him in the face. Another policeman nearby was cut in the hand when he went to the aid of his colleague. For these assaults Walker was sentenced to a mere 12 months' imprisonment. Officer John Quinn (PC 261), on duty in Bankfield Street, Bootle, came across a noisy group of drunken men standing on the street corner. At this point he asked them to go home and a local resident escorted 'a powerful-looking' coal-heaver named William Leonard home. The latter returned shortly afterwards carrying a massive piece of timber and 'let go' with it on Quinn's head, shouting out as he did so, 'Death to one of you, you —'. The policeman was left unconscious on the ground. A charge of attempted murder was brought against Leonard.[50]

Another butcher, Edward Tomkinson of Queen Street, called out to rooky PC 772, 'Come here, officer. You are a sensible man, and I can talk to you.' The policeman walked over to him, whereupon Tomkinson produced a cleaver from behind his back and hit the officer on the head. Fortunately, his helmet took the full force of the blow and the cleaver only just touched his head. A charge of murder could have easily resulted if it had not been for the helmet and Tomkinson was fortunate to receive just six months with hard labour.[51]

Policing the streets at night generally provided officers with the most problems of law enforcement. There was, however, one location that, in Victorian times, provided them with something of a conundrum – the home. This was, as will be shown (chapter 9), a significant location for violence. The problem for the police was whether or not to intervene, or interfere as the Victorians viewed it, and stop what could be often brutal violence from taking place. The police's jurisdiction was somewhat confused and this confusion was seen in their hesitant and uncertain inter-ventions. The residents of homes and rooms into which the police ventured were adamant that law officers had no right to be there. The home was, after all, the domain of the male head of the household and his word or fist was meant to go unchallenged. Time and time again, defendants in domestic disputes complained that the police had no right to intervene. This implacable attitude often led to assaults on the police, as in the case of James M'Carroll of Ford Street, off Vauxhall Road, who told officer Riley 'that he had no business interfering in family squabbles'. M'Carroll, whose hand had been amputated and replaced with an iron hook, struck Riley, seriously injuring his left eye. For this potentially lethal attack M'Carroll was fined only 10 shillings or 14 days' imprisonment in default. In Joseph Melling's case, he used the back of a hatchet to fell two constables who had run into a court off Stanhope Street, where he was chasing his wife in a drunken rage. 'Domestic' disputes did not always take place in the home but could occur in the street, where both husband and wife openly fought one another. In such cases the warring parties could still regard the argument or fight as a private matter, requiring no third-party interference, and either or both parties might take offence at a policeman's attempt to put a halt to the dispute. PC 307 came to Mary Huskisson's rescue when he saw her husband, John, beating her in Bevington Street, whereupon she turned on the constable. Having decided to lock her up for the assault, he was then assailed by husband John with a crutch. Both were found guilty and ordered to pay 40 shillings in fines, or spend two months apiece in gaol.[52]

One way of attempting to gauge the comparative popularity of the Liverpool police is to identify times when members of the public either came to their aid when they were physically being attacked, or supported them in making an arrest. Newspapers were generally keen to publicize such support, since it was considered both newsworthy and unusual. When PC 309 went to quell a disturbance in Vauxhall Road he was set upon, kicked, bitten and abused by a number of men. A cotton porter, named M'Quilliam, who was passing, asked some of the watching crowd to stop the officer from being killed. People replied that it was no business of theirs to intervene and some even suggested joining in to hurt him further. M'Quilliam bravely announced he 'would "wire in" to the first who tried it' and helped the policeman clear of the fight. A few months earlier two 'gentlemen' came to the assistance of an officer who was being attacked by two drunks in Westmorland Place, one of whom received a black eye from a spectator in the watching crowd.[53]

In other instances, major rows could blow up from nowhere, the details of which are almost impossible to discern. The evidence in the ensuing court proceedings appears almost as confused as the fighting on the actual night. Take, for example, what should have been a fairly straightforward case in which the police very properly came to the rescue of Thomas Stanley, a brass-founder of Kent Street, who was escorting two sisters, Mary Ann and Elizabeth Williams, home from work along Everton Road shortly after midnight in September 1871. The sober group met the frightening prospect of three drunken Dragoon Guard soldiers, linked arm in arm, coming the other way. Despite crossing into the road, the soldiers accosted them, and one grabbed Mary Ann around the waist. Her male companion hit him, which in turn set off a general fight and chase. Before long, police officers clashed with soldiers from the Rupert Lane barracks, led by a Captain John Bates, in a general set-to (illustration 2). The police on the one side claimed that the captain stood on some rails before the growing crowd and called out, 'People of Liverpool will you stand this; will you see one of our men taken by these — police? If they take him to the bridewell we will call out the guard, and sack the place.' The good captain, for his part, claimed that he was only enquiring of the police the nature of the disturbance, after which he was assaulted and manhandled by a drunken constable. Not surprisingly,

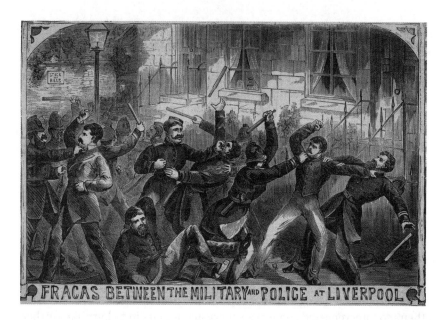

FRACAS BETWEEN THE MILITARY AND POLICE AT LIVERPOOL

Illustration 2 The events on Everton Road, as depicted in the *Illustrated Police News*, 23 September 1871. Reproduced with the permission of the British Library, Colindale Newspaper Library.

Mr Raffles, the magistrate, was unable to uncover much of the truth of the incident and left it to a higher court to adjudicate.

When the borough sessions met in the autumn, 'the fracas between the military and police' attracted considerable attention. The recorder, in his charge to the grand jury, suggested that little would be gained by pressing charges against Captain Bates and two soldiers of the Fourth Dragoons if either the police or the military expressed 'regret' for the incident. Sure enough, charges were dropped against the captain and all but one of the soldiers, although this appears to have been merely a diplomatic move in order to allow Thomas Clarke, the only soldier charged, to voice an apology through his counsel. The barrister was, he said, 'instructed to express his very great regret that he should, in a moment of thoughtlessness, have done anything to call for the interference of the police. This expression of regret having been made, he trusted it would not be necessary for the prosecution to proceed with the case.' The *Mercury* added, by way of comment, that the captain and his fellow officers offered a disclaimer 'as to any feeling by the military towards the police, and the somewhat Irish hope was expressed that, having had a good row with each other, the soldiers and the police will be better friends than ever'.[54] Such was the quality and generosity of English justice.

Conclusion

IT WOULD APPEAR that the Liverpool police, like so many other police forces around the country, were not popular during the first 60 years of their existence. In the 1850s the newly arrived Irish clashed frequently with a predominantly Protestant police force; in the 1860s and 1870s there was a more widespread hostility between the Liverpool working class and an increasingly disciplined and confident police force led by Major Greig. Much of the popular resentment against the force during the third quarter of the nineteenth century was rooted in the perception that the police were interfering in working-class activities such as drinking, standing on street corners or street betting. The Liverpool police, for their part, were slow to learn that in order to win the grudging support of the majority they had to discipline themselves and use as little force as possible.[55] Their use of the truncheon or night stick appears to have been, at times, counterproductive, but their reliance on such tactics may have been, in part, a reflection of the *esprit de corps* which Greig had instilled in the force after he arrived in 1852. This togetherness and discipline had its downside, though, insofar as some constables had an 'us versus them' attitude when dealing with the public, which emerged on occasion as police brutality or as acts of perjury.

By the 1890s the local press was reporting fewer instances of police violence; nor was overt hostility to the police, very evident earlier in the century, so apparent in the pages of the newspapers. Outright anti-police feeling had, perhaps, by the 1890s, narrowed to those engaged in what was perceived as anti-social behaviour such as street betting, and to the poorest elements of the community, particularly in the north end of the city and in Bootle. The unpopularity of the police had, by that decade, also waned with the middle classes, who had come to approve of their usefulness in so many areas of civic life. The head constable, Nott-Bower, also thought that the calibre of the officers had improved enormously by 1900, and such improvement must have contributed to a more widespread acceptance of the force. The police were now perceived as part of the street furniture, part of the city landscape. No amount of complaining, fighting or resisting them was going to remove the police from society; they were here to stay.

Part III
Violent crime in Liverpool

CHAPTER 5

The fighting Irish

... the Irish form but one-fourth of the population, and yet they give very nearly half the criminals.[1]

The influx of the Irish into Liverpool brought poverty, disease, dirt and misery, drunkenness and crime, in addition to a disturbance of the labour market, the cost to ratepayers of an enormous sum of money.[2]

T HERE HAS ALWAYS been a strong Irish presence in Liverpool, predating even the 'Great Hunger' or the 'Irish Famine' of the mid to late 1840s. However, the number who sailed in during those crisis years and then put down permanent roots in the borough was enormous. The Irish-born population of Liverpool rose from about 49,600 in 1841 to 83,800 in 1851, representing 17.3% and 22.3% respectively of Liverpool's population. No other city or town in Britain had such a large preponderance of Irish-born immigrants. This was hardly surprising, given the proximity of Dublin to the port of Liverpool. But what so upset contemporaries – churchmen, politicians, magistrates and the people of Liverpool – were the perceived social problems they brought with them. Disease, poverty and crime, to name but three, were singled out for special mention. These prejudices did not necessarily recede with the passing of time and the reduction of Irish immigration to the port. The generation born to the Irish immigrants who had settled in the borough, the Liverpool-born Irish, were culturally and politically Irish. This group, who largely settled in the north end, close to the docks, were also regarded with suspicion and antipathy. Anti-Irish and, by association, anti-Roman Catholic sentiments and prejudices put down deep roots in the town, notably in the form of Orangeism, and featured throughout the remainder of Queen Victoria's reign and beyond. Thus, sectarian tensions and conflicts made Liverpool different from other English towns and cities, and contributed greatly to the criminal profile of the town.[3]

The Irish and crime

THE IRISH were considered more criminally inclined than native-born English people. Whether they were actually so has been argued over by historians for the last 20 years.[4] However, all are agreed that the Irish appear to have been over-represented in the official records for crimes associated with violence and drunkenness. These included assaults, both common and assaulting police officers, as well as the more serious crimes of doing grievous bodily harm with weapons, which were tried at the sessions and assize courts. What do the stark statistics show? Should we trust them anyway, or is it a case of 'lies, damned lies and statistics'?

Even before the influx of Irish migrants in the 1840s, the English had already labelled the resident Irish criminal. They were, it was argued, 'almost three times as likely to face prosecution as their English' counterparts. In terms of their presence in the crime statistics, they were heavily over-represented relative to their presence in the community as a whole. By 1848, Liverpool's stipendiary magistrate Edward Rushton presented the nationalities of those appearing in the magistrates' courts. A total of 40% were Irish; when broken down by gender, 37% of male and 46% of female defendants were Irish. Undertaking a similar analysis in 1853, Rushton showed an even stronger Irish criminal presence in Liverpool's courts. Of the totals arrested and charged with felonies, 45% were identified as Irish. Neither the 1848 nor the 1853 censuses actually identified how many Liverpool-born Irish were counted under the 'English' heading. It would have emphasized the disproportionate presence of the Irish in the crime statistics still further. By looking at the numbers of committals to Liverpool borough gaol broken down by faith (i.e. into Catholic and non-Catholic), however, one can glean an approximate figure of how many Irish in total (Irish-born and Liverpool-born) were present in the criminal statistics. Catholic committals to the gaol between 1864 and 1876 never fell below 56.5% and were as high as 69.9% of the prison population.[5] What does this tell us? That Roman Catholics and the Irish, Irish women in particular, were true to the popular stereotype of being innately criminal and immoral?

The short answer is no. The Irish, and by implication Catholics, might initially appear to have been over-represented but when historians break down and analyse Liverpool's population by social group or class, it becomes clear that the Irish were not over-represented at all. They had entered the town with nothing but the rags on their backs, hungry and penniless, and as a result could be regarded as belonging to the unskilled working class, the very group regarded as most likely to commit crime; indeed, Irish people accounted for some 40% of the port's unskilled working-class population. The apparent over-representation of Irish women in the criminal statistics is, however, more striking and significant. One cannot be sure if one or two drunken Irish women kept reappearing in the annual criminal returns, thus inflating the statistics. Mary Doolan, for example, in 1898 made her seventy-third appearance in court for being drunk and disorderly and for assaulting a police officer. This was surpassed in 1890 by Bridget M'Mullen, described as elderly, who made her two hundred and forty-second appearance for drunkenness and other felonies.[6]

What kinds of offences were thought to be peculiarly Irish? Drunk and disorderly behaviour was, without doubt, perceived to be the minor offence for which the Irish were most frequently convicted, closely followed by other charges arising out of drunkenness, such as minor assaults and assaults on policemen. More serious crimes of violence, such as wounding, stabbing and grievous bodily harm, could also arise from drunken disputes and street 'rows', which were regarded as peculiarly Irish. In terms of crimes such as theft, robbery and prostitution, the Irish population had a mixed reputation. Michael Whitty, Liverpool's first head constable and a Roman Catholic, did not regard them as thieves, but the police later in the century had a low opinion of young Irish people in particular, who were, the authorities argued, sent out by their parents to steal. Prostitution was not perceived to be an Irish practice in other parts of the country, whereas in Liverpool it was.

To what extent was the stereotype true of the drunken Irish person resisting arrest, cursing and fighting their way to the bridewell? In the annual criminal returns for assaults – aggravated, common and of policemen – and drunken and disorderly behaviour in Liverpool's magistrates' courts for the second half of the nineteenth century, the numbers tried who were Irish-born represented around 40% in the early 1860s. By the 1890s, the Irish-born tried for assaults was as low as 11%, and for drunk and disorderliness 19%. This decline mirrored the decline in Irish immigration to the city. On the other hand, the figures for those tried in the courts who were Liverpool-born (whether English or Irish) displayed a reverse trend to the Irish-born figures. In the early 1860s Liverpool-born people constituted 28% of those charged with assault and 22% of those charged with drunk and disorderly behaviour. By the 1890s these figures had risen to 67% and 55% respectively.[7]

The newly arrived Irish lived in the poorest slum housing and had the most casual jobs on the dockside, if they had jobs at all, in the 1850s and 1860s. They were bottom of any social and economic barometer by which one would wish to measure society. By the 1890s, most Irish people would have been Liverpool-born and thus it is impossible to separate them out from Welsh, Scottish or English Liverpudlians. Irishness in itself did not suggest innate criminality and violence. Being very poor and being bottom of the social and economic ladder did, on the other hand, contribute to the high numbers in court for drink-related crimes and minor assaults.

The prejudice which associated Irish nationality with crime was evident within the criminal justice system. During the 1875 sessions, for example, the recorder sentenced William Hardy to 10 years' penal servitude for inflicting bodily harm to two Liverpool policemen. Hardy, though only

24, was described as a 'thoroughbred rough' and 'a genuine "old savage",
a terror to all who knew him, and at perpetual war with society and its
special guardians'. He had, during his brief life, 31 previous convictions
since starting his criminal career back in 1860, when he was sent to Soho
Street industrial school for stealing lead. Thereafter he was in and out
of industrial schools, reformatories and prison for drunken and riotous
behaviour, assaults, wilful damage, threatening behaviour and theft.
However, what surprised Shimmin was the manner in which the recorder,
in sentencing Hardy, decided to discuss what he took to be the prisoner's
nationality and religion. 'In justice to the Irish population', wrote Shimmin,
'there was no evidence as to the probable religious status of Hardy, who had
been an inmate of both Catholic and Protestant reformatories, and no body
is so foolish as to assert that all Liverpool criminals are Irish'. Hardy, who
hanged himself immediately on returning to Walton gaol, had previously
had a 'private interview' with the Protestant prison chaplain, David Morris,
who told the coroner's court that Hardy had said 'he should never be a
better man until he left Liverpool, for when he went out of gaol he had
nowhere to go to but his old haunts, and no society to go to but that of his
old companions'.[8] There was nothing in Hardy's name or history to suggest
that he was Irish but the recorder chose to air his own anti-Irish feelings.

Nationality and religious affiliation were not without consequence when
it came to crimes of interpersonal violence in the borough. Many of the
bar-room brawls, the street 'rows' and late-night drunken fights contained
within them implicit, and occasionally explicit, anti-Irish and anti-Catholic
sentiments. There was a kind of background rumble of sectarian hate that
was ever present but contained until the twice-yearly flash points of 17 March
(St Patrick's Day) and 12 July (the Orange celebration of the Battle of the
Boyne, when the new Protestant monarch William overthrew James II)
sparked greater trouble. The lesser Irish Catholic festival of St John's Eve
(23 June) could also occasionally provoke tension.

Sectarian tensions and Irish riots

SECTARIAN TENSIONS probably dated back to 1819, when Liverpool staged
its first 12 July procession. These annual affairs then continued until the
early 1850s, by when the enormous influx of Irish Catholic immigrants
meant that such processions had become increasingly offensive and objectionable to a growing section of the community. To make matters worse,
large numbers of the Liverpool police force were, by this time, members of
Orange lodges, and were consequently anything but impartial to the Irish
Catholic poor. The early 1850s were years of great sectarian tension and
violence and the authorities not unnaturally regarded the months of March
and July with some trepidation. Their fears proved entirely justified when, in

1850, after the Orange Day procession, which went off reasonably quietly, despite the firing of pistols, a crowd of angry Irish gathered outside a north end pub in Chadwick Street. Here, publican Henry Wright was entertaining fellow Orangemen who had gathered for drinks once the march was over. On the second day of disturbances, shots from an upstairs window of the pub were heard and three people lay wounded in the street. One, John Sangster, a 19-year-old youth, had suffered serious gunshot wounds, from which he later died. Wright, the publican, was arrested and charged with the killing. During his trial the role of the police was censured by the judge, who said Wright had not been given sufficient protection. Witnesses also claimed Wright shouted at the crowd, 'Come on, you bloody Papists, and we will blow your brains out', and then shot at them. He was found not guilty of manslaughter.[9]

The following year, despite advice from the Home Secretary and the mayor to stop any Orange marches, the head constable, Mathew Dowling, complacently allowed it to go ahead on 14 July. While the Orangemen gathered in London Road, a Catholic Irish crowd, who numbered up to 1000, moved up from Shaw's Brow to challenge them. At first, the Catholics drove the Orangemen back but when the latter received reinforcements, some armed with pistols and cutlasses, the Protestants were able to repulse the Irish. The absence of the police suggested Dowling had totally miscalculated the threat of disorder. He further miscalculated by allowing the parade to proceed. It was the largest the country had ever seen, numbering thousands rather than hundreds, and included bands and floats. The police, an estimated 150 of them, brought up the rear of the parade, ostensibly to prevent further riots, but to Catholic eyes their presence in the procession suggested a very different message – that of support and partiality for the Protestants. While the procession went off with only a few fights, it proved a spark for later, more serious trouble. Like the year before, another person, John Malley, was shot dead in the street and two others were wounded outside an Orange pub, the Wheatsheaf in Scotland Road. By the end of the evening the police had arrested 70 Irishmen and not one Orangeman. This brought further accusations of police bias.

One of the constables, PC Green, who was present when Malley was shot outside the Wheatsheaf, was later stabbed outside his own home in Penryhn Street, and a man called Jones who came to his aid with a swordstick was killed in the fight. At the subsequent inquests of Malley and Jones, witnesses claimed Green had not only beaten Malley before the shooting but had also witnessed it and then done nothing about it. Although a man named Weaver was identified as the killer, he provided an alibi and so the jury returned a verdict of manslaughter, not murder, even though Malley had been shot in the back while being chased. At a subsequent magistrates' court hearing it transpired that PC Green was an Orangeman, in spite of the 1842 ban preventing the police from being members. While the order prohibiting officers from joining parties or organizations was repeated in the early 1850s, there came another serious incident between the Liverpool police and the Catholic Irish which suggested that large numbers of the force had ignored the order.[10]

This was all too evident in the infamous Holy Cross Chapel case of 1852, when members of the Liverpool police force were accused of an unprovoked attack on members of the chapel, and also of falsifying police records afterwards. The incident largely hinged on the anti-Irish and anti-Catholic prejudice of the borough police, who mistook a crowd of worshippers fleeing the chapel for rioters (or used that misapprehension as an excuse for attacking the Irish Catholics): inside the chapel a beam had given way with a loud crash during the service, causing panic among the congregation, who fled out into Standish Street. Here they were met by the police, who, in the words of the press, 'beat and assaulted them without any distinction either as to age or sex, or without the slightest reason whatever for doing so'. One of the first officers on the scene, Sergeant Tomlinson, soon learnt of the real reason for 500–600 people rushing out into the street. He also witnessed the arrival of police using their sticks on the panicking crowd and wrote of this in his initial report of the incident. Unfortunately for Tomlinson, head constable Dowling and a superintendent ordered him to tear out the original report and write out a new report, which failed to mention the police violence. All this came to light during a hearing in the magistrates' court. The head constable rather bizarrely claimed to have been high on opium, a medication for his 'ill health', and could not recall the events. He was suspended and dismissed soon after, a disgraced and broken man.[11]

With Dowling's 'retirement' came a cleansing of the Augean stables that was the Liverpool police. Riddled with anti-Irish and anti-Catholic prejudice, the force had become a breeding ground for the Orange Order and had declined in a few years, according to the *Liverpool Mercury*, from having a reputation as 'a fine, orderly, well disciplined, well conducted body of men ... into a band of insubordinate, worthless, mendacious, and corrupt despera-does'. Over 300 policemen were either dismissed or resigned from the force between 1852 and 1853, which suggests that, despite the 1842 ban on Orange Order membership by officers, a large number must have been members of Orange groups. The new head constable, Major Greig, was determined to improve the force's discipline and the public's trust in it but he found the rising sectarian tensions of 1852 and the killing of Margaret Baines at the hands of the police (see chapter 4) difficult hurdles to surmount. However, one important step was taken by Greig and that was the ban on marches and processions within the borough boundary. This ban was primarily aimed at the Orange parades, which were then forced to meet on the outskirts of the borough for the remainder of the nineteenth century. This only exported the problem to Old Swan, Wavertree and West Derby Road, where, in the words of Shimmin, 'reeling wretches, yelling, swearing, fighting, and exchanging brickbats', met to celebrate the Orange anniversary.[12]

For the thousands of poor Irish who had come to Liverpool to escape the hunger of the late 1840s, the food shortages of 1855 must have induced dread and panic. The food scarcity and with it rising unemployment were begun by an easterly wind which blew during January and February 1855. Ships carrying food were unable to enter the port and many of the dockside unloading jobs, usually carried out by the Irish, were not required, adding further to the distress of the Liverpool poor. On 19 February 1855, a large crowd gathered in Vauxhall Road and Scotland Road, ostensibly to receive charitable relief. After a 'signal', attacks were made on bread shops and provision stores: doors and windows were broken and the stores were ransacked. Bread, flour and other food stuffs were thrown out into the street, where waiting women gathered up the booty in their aprons. The *Liverpool Mercury* was quick to identify these 'barbarian tribes of the north' of the borough as 'some of the lowest and vilest men and women' in the community. 'They consisted', the paper continued, 'for the most part, of females of the lowest class, youths familiarly known to the police, mixed up here and there with some more noted dock plunderers and "ruffs," who seemed to direct operations'. The working class of Liverpool were not, the paper emphasized, involved in the rioting, but the 'undeserving poor' were. Over the three days of disturbances, 106 were arrested, of whom 83 were Irish. This fact brought predictable outrage from the Liverpool Conservative press, which fuelled the sectarian divide by referring to the rioters as 'the scum of Irish popery'. 'This influx', the *Liverpool Courier* continued, 'of semi-savages brings all the turbulence and disorder of Popish Ireland with it'. With an improvement in the weather and the wind direction, the docks started operating again and with it came full employment and a measure of social order.[13]

Everyday sectarian violence

SECTARIAN DIFFERENCES AND HATREDS certainly continued to dominate Liverpool life throughout the second half of the century, but how seriously or how viciously it is impossible to determine. Historians can never be sure what issue kicked off a street fight or a bar-room brawl. Clues in the dates of the assaults or the names of the protagonists may suggest national or religious rivalries were to blame. Or reported racial insults might appear in the newspapers' accounts of hearings in the magistrates' court. While tensions undoubtedly remained, it is possible to argue that such tensions fluctuated, becoming quite extreme because of national politics such as Home Rule for example, or the activities of the Fenians and events in Ireland, or during local borough elections. These acted as sparks to the tinder of sectarian distrust, and could bring about sudden flare-ups of violence.

Seemingly small symbols and gestures took on significant meanings in Liverpool. Orange-coloured clothing and orange-coloured lilies could give, and were meant to give, offence, especially if worn around 12 July. In 1860, Margaret Mercer, for example, was fined £1 or one month's imprisonment for attacking a woman carrying an orange lily and a man, who came to her aid, in Lime Street. The colour of the flower appeared to anger her so much that Mercer then followed the two retreating victims into a nearby pub, where she continued her assault. Trouble flared up in Baptist Street, an almost totally Catholic street except for one Protestant resident, Thomas Douglass, who stabbed John O'Hare. When arrested, Douglass told the police that 'It's all through an orange lily which I had in my window'. The shamrock could cause equal offence to Protestants. Two men were hospital-ized on St Patrick's Day 1895 in the south end of the city for wearing (and refusing to remove) a shamrock on their hats.[14]

Most pub brawls and street fights were not reported as having been fuelled with sectarian hatred. It would be wrong to assume that sectarian-ism lay behind these everyday scenes of violence, since, increasingly as the century drew on, the Catholic and the Protestant poor tended to live in their own distinct neighbourhoods. The Liverpool Irish lived down close to the docks and the Protestants up on Everton Heights. At the south end, the religious divide was less clearly defined. Nevertheless, neighbourhood quarrels and fights did occasionally contain an explicitly religious element. Sometimes the clue lies in the date of the disturbance. In March 1850, two women of opposing religious persuasions were fortunate to be let off with nothing more than a caution by the magistrate, even though a bread knife had been wielded in a fight between them. In 1868 two drunken women, Kitty Muldoon and Margaret Thompson, had a furious bar-room fight in which the former called the latter 'a blood-red Orangewoman, "although I am only a Tory, and hoorayed for Church and State"'. '"Oh, but you cursed, Mr. Gladstone," complained Muldoon, "and swore he was an archbishop of the Jesuits, and you sent the Pope to a hotter place than a coal-mine..."'. Others provoked neighbours by hanging out orange flags on 12 July.[15] The magistrates, to their credit, condemned such displays of religious bigotry and vainly attempted to eradicate it.

The religious geography of the town probably had some bearing on the assault of Michael O'Toole, when he was returning from Old Swan to his home in Fontenoy Street in 1889. When he and his friends came to the corner of Heyworth Street and Beacon Lane they were accosted by a group of men who wanted to know to which religion they belonged. They were immediately set upon. Although mixed marriages became increasingly frequent, hidden resentments might surface in moments of drunken rage. Protestant Thomas Johnson cut the nose 'clean off' his Catholic father-in-law, who had allegedly called him an 'Orange dog'.[16]

In July 1864 a furious row broke out in Key Street between neighbours, in which the house of a man named Sharkey came under attack, with the throwing of bottles and bricks. This continued the following evening.

During the hearing, in which four defendants were tried, Mr Holme, the magistrate, remarked that 'one would be apt to fancy that he was living in some of the savage settlements of New Zealand instead of the civilised town of Liverpool. It would seem that in these Irish rows the laws of force was the only thing recognised, and therefore the law must step in and show its force to those who chose to disregard it'.[17] This incident sounds very much like what were called 'faction fights' – fights between Irishmen, which may or may not have been sectarian in origin.

Another such incident in 1870 concerned Thomas Finnegan and Martin Flagherty, who fought in the notorious Ben Johnson Street. The two belonged to opposing factions. Just days later, another Irishman was committed for the murder of a fellow countryman. The actual killing had taken place on Christmas Day 1869, when Joseph M'Grath's windows were broken by a group out in the street; 'Let the Leinster — come out', they shouted. An hour later, M'Grath was set upon by a man named M'Donough and a woman by the name of M'Hale, among others. Their Irishness was in many ways an irrelevance to the actual argument, which, by all accounts, concerned some bad mouthing, but the judge made a point of emphasizing the nationality of the combatants. In sentencing M'Donough for man-slaughter, Justice Wills said:

> it was a terrible thing to think of that people coming from the other side of the water, because they were better off here, and had more employment and higher wages, and could live better, and who must perfectly well know that so long as they conducted themselves well they would be treated with perfect fairness, and have an opportunity of bettering themselves – it was a terrible thing to think, that by reason of their folly and their tendency to drink that they should upon such an occasion as Christmas, break out into a proceeding more suitable to wild Indians than civilized people and fall foul and maltreat one another.... He could not think without a feeling of sadness and shame of the disgrace which was brought upon people coming from Ireland by such conduct as this....[18]

After this blanket condemnation of the supposedly inferior Irish people, who, in the judge's opinion, stubbornly ignored the superior English ways of life and equity, M'Donough might have expected to receive a heavy sentence. He was fortunate in receiving just 12 months' imprisonment with hard labour, while M'Hale remained at large.

Fenianism and Home Rule

ALTHOUGH THERE REMAINED an anti-Irish and anti-Catholic prejudice among English people which occasionally flared up, there occurred during the second half of the century occasional build-ups of tension that were related to Ireland and the politics of that country. First came the Fenian panics of the 1860s, which associated some Irish patriots with what were regarded as terrorist activities in the north-west of England. Looking back to 1866, when there had been rumours of a Fenian uprising in the north-west of England, the *Liverpool Mercury* claimed in 1882 that 'Fenianism was a real power in Liverpool far more so than was then realised or will probably be known'. Liverpool, being '"the halfway house" between Ireland and the United States', experienced latent Fenianism in many roundabout ways. 'I'll stand six months for the sake of my Fenian brotherhood', a drunken Patrick Byrne announced. Newly arrived off the Cork steamer in 1865, Byrne took a swing at PC 458 in Dublin Street. A contrite and sober Byrne told Mr Raffles, the magistrate, that he did not know what he was doing when in drink.[19]

Of much more concern to the authorities were apparent conspiracies involving weapons. Working closely with their Irish counterparts and tipped off by informers, the Liverpool police arrested four Irishmen, who were brought up on charges of possession of government firearms at the Liverpool assizes in December 1866. Although the *Liverpool Mercury* alluded to the judge's comments about a Fenian conspiracy in his opening charge to the grand jury, the paper failed to report the details of the actual trial. This may be because all four were found not guilty, even though it was proved that they had moved five crates of rifles, 38 bayonets and 200 sticks of phosphorus from a warehouse in College Street to the corner of Chaucer Street and Grosvenor Street. What the prosecution could not prove was that the accused knew what was in the crates; nor could the prosecution identify the mysterious man who hired the four to move the crates. This case coincided with a demonstration conducted by Major Greig of a chemical compound containing phosphorus found in Salisbury Street. He created in effect 'Molotov cocktails' and threw bottles of the chemical at the bridewell wall, where they exploded. He claimed that this cache of explosives was going to be used by the Fenians for a widespread arson attack on English towns and cities.[20]

The threat from Fenianism was taken so seriously that the Liverpool police requested and received arms from the government. Detectives were armed with revolvers in the autumn of 1867, 'a period of much anxiety', and muskets were sent to temporary depots. How this affected relations between Liverpool's Irish community and the local police is difficult to assess. However, accusations of racist taunts from local constables were made in a case concerning Peter and Alice Nugent and Michael M'Taggert, who were charged with assaulting a constable and attempted rescue. Witnesses claimed one policeman called Nugent a '— Fenian', but this was denied by the officer concerned. Raffles, who took the police's side in the affair in the magistrates' court, claimed he would have instantly dismissed any officer who was proved to have said the 'Fenian' word.[21]

Tensions peaked shortly after the trials of the three 'Manchester martyrs', who were convicted and sentenced to death for the murder Sergeant Brett of the Manchester police. After their execution on 23 November 1867, Liverpool supporters organized a 'funeral procession' in their honour. It was proposed by Liverpool Fenians to assemble supporters of 'the three men strangled in Manchester' at Stanley Road and then process to Scotland Road. Posters were put on walls around town and handbills were distributed outside Catholic chapels calling on Irishmen to demonstrate 'in their thousands'. The police and local priests did all in their power to prevent the circulation of such advertisements by tearing down the posters and denouncing the procession from the pulpit. What made the proposed demonstrations so dangerous for Liverpool was the large presence of Orange supporters, who warned the mayor that they would hold a counter-demonstration, which would have inevitably led to large-scale rioting, had not the funeral procession been called off on 13 December.[22]

The success of the police in cracking down on the Fenians in the north-west led to a 'general stampede' of its leaders across the Atlantic to America and to 'a gradual decay' and final extinction of the movement in the region. Notwithstanding the excitement of 1881, when two men were tried and found guilty for bombing Liverpool town hall and the police section house in Hatton Garden, and when dynamite and 'infernal machines' (bombs) were found on two boats from Boston, there was no popular response among the Liverpool Irish. The brief flurry of revolutionary activity brought in a secret force of 2000 troops, who were placed around the city in small detachments.[23] More typical were the 'Irish rows' concerned with Home Rule. These invariably involved street fights among the Liverpool Irish. The police attributed one particular faction fight to 'mid-day drinking amongst women'. Women were also heavily involved in the fights between 'Hibernians' and 'Home Rulers' in the Scotland Road neighbourhood in September 1878.[24] These faction fights had, according to the police, been a 'constant source of annoyance' for the past three years.

Conclusion

THE LARGE NUMBERS of poor Irish who came to Liverpool did contribute to the distinctive character of the town. They were often its poorest citizens and many took work at the expanding docks, consequently living in the poorest and densely populated courts and streets in the north end. They were regarded by their often conservative host Liverpudlians as not only poor and dirty but also, above all, criminal. They were perceived as thieves, drunkards and brutal savages. This perception was partly a self-fulfilling prophecy, insofar as the Liverpool police in the 1840s and early 1850s, at just the time of a large influx of Irish immigrants, were not only Protestant but Orange members too. The police were, therefore, not neutral when it came to controlling marches, processions and the food riot of 1855.

Their failure to respond sympathetically to the potential disaster unfolding in the Holy Cross Catholic chapel in 1852 led to the head constable's sacking and the reform of the force. Improvements in the way the police, now under the leadership of Major Greig, treated the Irish and the Liverpool Irish were evident, but it would be wrong to conclude that anti-Irish feeling was eradicated in the town at large. Sectarian tensions remained and occasionally flare-ups occurred, not least when the politics of Ireland and its troubled relationship with Britain intruded on domestic politics. During such times, Irish nationality was relevant to the question of criminality.

Were the Irish of Liverpool criminal and did they contribute to the town's violent reputation? The statistics do appear to suggest an over-preponderance of Irish criminality, but when it is considered that the Irish were a large and significant proportion of the town's poor, a group which disproportionately contributes to crime figures, it may be possible to conclude that the Irish added to the town's criminal profile because they were poor, not because they were Irish.

Chapter 6

The fist, the boot and the knife: male-on-male violence

The fatal prize-fight at Aintree

On Sunday, 1 August 1875, Sergeant Shaughnessy and PC Jackson stood on duty in Rice Lane when a crowd of up to 400 'town roughs' walked by on their way to Aintree. His suspicions aroused, Shaughnessy followed them to the racecourse, where some men held running races while others lolled on the grass. On learning that the real purpose for this gathering was a prize-fight, he requested the men to disperse, but 'they did not pay any heed to what I said'. Shortly afterwards the crowd quickly formed a ring 'without ropes or stakes. About a dozen men', Shaughnessy reported, 'were acting as ring keepers and were, with sticks and belts which had buckles at the end, keeping the crowd back'. Two men, bare-chested and stripped to their trousers, stepped into the ring, shook hands and commenced bare-knuckle boxing. The fight lasted, according to the on-looking yet powerless police, from 4.15 to 4.55 p.m. and covered between 16 and 20 rounds. Shortly before 5 p.m. the victor, John Mahoney of Gay Street, knocked his opponent, Simon Looney, to the ground. The fight ended suddenly, and quickly the crowd and all those involved in the fight rushed away from the waiting police, who had been reinforcing their numbers during the bout. The group carrying the unconscious Looney were stopped and arrested. The police, however, took the injured boxer to Bootle hospital, where he died early the following morning without regaining consciousness. In all, five men, dockers and carters, were immediately arrested for organizing the prize-fight. They were: Michael Farraher, Joseph M'Cann, Thomas Glennon, John Coyle and John Jones. All came from streets in the vicinity of Vauxhall and Scotland Roads, including the notorious Chisenhale Street.

As was usual where a fatality had occurred, an inquest was soon held, at the Dolphin Hotel, Bootle, where the main witness to the fight, Shaughnessy, told the coroner and the jury that 'It appeared to be a fair stand-up fight. Everything seemed to be conducted fairly. I saw no kicking. I did not see the man kicked while he was on the ground'. The coroner emphasized both the sergeant's testimony and that of Mahoney, who had given himself up to the police within 24 hours of the fight ending. The coroner reiterated that there was 'no evidence of anything unfair or foul having taken place in the fight.… The fight seemed to have been a stand-up fight from first to last, and there was nothing unfair or foul in the fighting'. Furthermore, he went on to say that Mahoney was 'little to blame' in comparison with 'those who were aiding and abetting, and who urged the men on to fight':

> These men liked to stand by and see others knock themselves to pieces, and took care not to fight themselves. He looked upon such persons as being far more reprehensible than the poor fellows who were fools enough to stand up and beat each other for the amusement of others.[1]

At the subsequent assizes at St George's Hall, at which six people were committed to trial for manslaughter, the presiding judge, Mr Justice Archibald, informed the grand jury:

> There is nothing which is more characteristic of the English people than their desire to encourage athletic sports and manly exercises, and, so far as they are kept within the bounds of law, they must have approval of every one. The exercises of cricket and rowing, and riding and fencing, and even boxing with gloves for the purpose of acquiring the art of self-defence, are not in any way objectionable; but a prize-fight, where two men meet to fight for money, and to maul and maltreat each other until one is subdued and has given in, is one of the most brutal and brutalising exhibitions that can well be, and is, moreover, a direct breach of the peace and a violation of the law; and is, in truth, a practice which it is impossible for the law to tolerate; and if death ensues, those who are engaged in it immediately, and those who are encouraging it by their presence and by those taking part in it in any way, are guilty of the crime of manslaughter.[2]

During the actual trial the only new material evidence that had not already been published in the press concerned details of Mahoney's reluctance to fight. In his statement to the court, he told how he was approached by Looney, who challenged him to a fight. 'Mahoney, I want to fight you badly', to which Mahoney relied, 'What for?' 'That's the for [*sic*]. If you don't fight me, I shall — —.' In reply, Mahoney said, 'I don't think I am man enough for you'. Looney then emphasized his desire for the fight by boasting that he could raise plenty of financial backing in the town. Even Looney's wish to have the fight on a Sunday was initially unacceptable to Mahoney, who did not want to break the Sabbath. However, the Sunday following the challenge was chosen, even though his family – wife, mother and brother – tried to talk him out of going. Reluctantly Mahoney finally arrived at the racecourse, where, according to his evidence, a policeman came up to him and said, '"We shall have a fight." I answered him back for to fight himself as he was so fond of it.' This short interchange suggests that some of the police were probably looking forward to the boxing match as much as the other spectators. Once the fight began, Mahoney realized that he was getting the best of it from round 5, and attempted shortly before the end, when Looney was tiring badly, to halt the match. The crowd, however, rushed forward and threatened to knock his head off if he did not finish it properly, which he did by laying Looney unconscious with a blow to his left ear.[3]

There were many mitigating circumstances in Mahoney's favour, not least his stated reluctance to fight, which the court accepted; also, he was 'a decent working man of good character' and had handed himself into the police once he had heard that Looney was 'in the deadhouse'. This evidently worked to his advantage, as the sentence was a mere four months' imprisonment with hard labour. Those who acted as seconds and bottle holders received six weeks.

This fight raises many significant and interesting issues. At its heart is the notion of a 'fair fight', a concept accepted by all the onlookers, including the police, and then later by the coroner. Only when the case got to trial did the judge put forward arguments concerning the brutality of the fight and the fact that it was not a display of the art of self-defence, the aim of the fight rather being to batter a man into submission for a monetary prize. The case brings out the tensions in mid-Victorian society between, on the one hand, manly sports and exercise and, on the other, the law; between fighting for money as against amateur displays of skill; between working-class notions of manliness and middle-class notions of respectable masculinity. At root, this fight represented a clash between popular customary attitudes and practices of how men fought and the state's insistence that such behaviour was both brutal and illegal; moreover, it was disruptive of the public order.[4]

Mahoney's behaviour in this case suggests that he was a man who held ambivalent attitudes to the ways and methods of settling a dispute. He reluctantly abided by the working-class notions of fighting and maintaining his reputation, while wishing, contrarily, to adopt the new Victorian and essentially middle-class virtues of respectability, Sabbath-keeping, self-discipline and non-violence. His evident desire to refrain from violence was emphasized yet further in March the following year, when he and his wife were confronted in Tenterden Street by a group of about 15 angry men. 'You killed a good man', William Jacobs said to Mahoney, and added, 'I shall be hung for you'. Mahoney kept his hands deep in his pockets and even allowed Jacobs to inflict the ultimate humiliation of knocking his cap off. When Mahoney bent down to retrieve it, Jacobs slammed a paving stone onto his head, at the same time remarking, 'Dead men tell no tales'. Later Mahoney told the police that he had not retaliated or risen to the bait of having his hat knocked to the ground, as he was afraid Jacobs would have drawn a knife.[5]

Manliness and violence

IN ATTEMPTING TO MAKE SENSE of some of the actions of those broadly involved in the prize-fight, the reasons for which are never stated, it is necessary to examine briefly how violence was dealt with by both the authorities and the people in general. Historically, interpersonal violence was regarded, with the exception of murder and manslaughter, as private and something to be settled by the combatants, usually out of court, through financial compensation. Very often fights led to festering private enmities or feuds that were not entirely settled over the course of decades. By the beginning of the nineteenth century, violent behaviour was increasingly deemed intolerable, especially according to middle-class sensibilities. Prosecution through the courts was expected and short prison sentences (of up to two months) became normal for those found guilty of common assault. Thus, criminal statistics for violent behaviour appeared to rise significantly in the nineteenth century, although there had not necessarily been any change in male behaviour. Men, who had from time immemorial fought to defend their honour, manhood and status, were now expected to defend their honour and reputation in ways other than through fighting. The middle classes had, for example, successfully banished and outlawed the duel, preferring civil actions and financial recompense for any perceived public loss of character.[6]

The working classes were perhaps slower in accepting these refinements in public behaviour and civility; moreover, they could not financially afford access to the courts to right wrongs. They therefore still felt the need to defend their reputations and emphasize their masculinity through the use and power of the fist. In many working-class streets of Liverpool, 'violence and brutality' were, reported the *Liverpool Review*, 'the accepted signs of manliness'. Although most acts of violence had been outlawed by the nine-teenth century, the deeply embedded associated attitudes and values were retained by the working classes, and continued to be expressed through the unwritten rules of the 'fair fight' or the 'up and down fight'. This partly explains the ambivalence of Victorians, who admired the masculine virtues of physical prowess as displayed in boxing and wrestling. 'There is', argued the *Porcupine*, 'some good, yes, much good in a man developing his muscular power, and being able skilfully to apply it in his own defence', but there had to be a dividing line between 'the manly art of "self-defence" and downright ruffianism'.[7] Where this dividing line fell was often determined by the courts. A man who defended his status or reputation through the use of the fist in front of witnesses, and who ensured fair play for both combatants, was deemed by many to be acting honourably. In these circumstances the law and those charged with its enforcement – the police, magistrates and judges – could, on occasion, show surprising leniency towards men who had behaved in traditional male ways, even though serious injury had occurred to the defeated victim in a fight. A man's respectability and character were not necessarily lost or damaged if he was charged or convicted of assault or some other act of interpersonal violence. It all depended on the context of the violence.

During the nineteenth century, important distinctions came to be drawn with regard to different types of male-on-male violence. Modes of fighting and the use of weapons were increasingly examined and attitudes hardened against the use of the boot, clog and knife. This in turn led the authorities to pass value judgements on those involved in the fighting. Distinctions were drawn between 'violence' and 'brutality', with the latter being the preserve of the underclass of roughs, bullies and ruffians.[8] This was the group with a no-holds-barred approach to fighting, who, in the eyes of the press, police and the courts, terrorized honest society and who needed to be treated harshly by the courts, with some of their own medicine. Flogging was seen to be the answer for the street bully and garrotter. Legal punishments and official attitudes hardened towards those convicted of violent and brutal behaviour and the general public increasingly viewed violence as unacceptable and intolerable.

The fair fight

WORKING-CLASS male honour and status were defended or enhanced largely through physical prowess and strength. Although strictly speaking illegal, the 'fair fight' possessed codes and rules of fighting that were respected by men of all classes and which allowed men a measure of self-respect whether they were the victors or the vanquished of a fight. So long as the rules were adhered to by both sides, the fight was seen as an honourable means of settling a dispute. The general rules stipulated that the specific arrangements for the fight had to be agreed upon by both parties, that no weapons were to be used and that just two people were to be involved. Handshakes were exchanged between the combatants, witnesses were on hand to ensure that fists rather than boots were used, that a man was not hit when down, and that neither party received any unfair advantage from the spectators, who formed the ring. A fight would end with a victor, but honour would have been satisfied by both sides. There was nothing dishonourable in defeat so long as the fight had been fair. Nor was the fight necessarily illegal, even if a fatality resulted.

In July 1896 James Duxbury agreed to meet Edward Wilson at a stable in Gill Street after they had exchanged words in a Dansie Street pub. It seems that the two men had taken up a quarrel begun by their respective wives, who had argued and fought on two separate occasions and had had to be separated by the police on each. The husbands, however, appeared to have continued the disagreement in a drunken yet amiable fashion. Both men went to John Eyres, a coachbuilder, who owned a stable in Gill Street. Duxbury sought Eyres' permission for 'a friendly set to' in the stable, which Eyres was reluctant to allow; the former replied, 'Mr Eyres, there will be no harm'. With witnesses present, the two men struggled rather than fought, in what was described as a 'hugging match'. At the end of the fourth round Wilson fell backwards over the shafts of a trap, taking Duxbury with him.

Both fell awkwardly, although Wilson appeared to have the worst of it, as his head fell against some iron. Despite that, a fifth round was fought, with Wilson getting 'the best of it' and, at its conclusion, Duxbury announced he had had enough and they left by separate exits.

On the way home, Wilson fell in the street and had to be carried back to his house, where he told his wife that 'Mr Duxbury had put his knee on his stomach'. He repeated this to the doctor at the Royal Infirmary the following day, adding, 'but, hush; I want to hear no more about it now that it is done'. The formality of his language and the manner in which the fight ended suggest very little animosity on the part of either combatant. Three days after his admission to hospital Wilson died; the post-mortem showed the cause was blood poisoning from 'the absorption of the bowel contents into the abdominal cavity'. The inquest was particularly concerned to discover whether an old rupture to the abdomen, four years previously, was, in part, the cause of death. Dr Stockdale, the infirmary's house surgeon, reported that 'there must have been a recent rupture of the bowels which might have been caused by a man falling on top of him'.[9] Consequently, the jury returned a verdict of manslaughter, a charge that was brought against Duxbury earlier on the same day as the inquest. He was eventually discharged at Liverpool assizes later that July, as no evidence was offered against him. The medical evidence was inconclusive as it turned out but it also came out in an earlier magistrates' hearing that Wilson had challenged Duxbury to a fight and the latter had refused. Wilson then called him a 'cur' and a 'coward', insults which most men of this period would not have been able to leave unanswered. Thus all the evidence suggested that the deceased had provoked a fight which was then witnessed and pronounced 'fair' by those present.

The Duxbury case was by no means unique. Magistrates commented on the methods of fighting on a number occasions and, by implication, supported the legality of 'fair' fighting. This was understood by a number of defendants facing charges of assault. Thomas M'Conville, who was 'one of a gang of fellows who were the terror of Windsor' – known as the Windsor lambs – claimed his assault on James Washington was a 'stand up' fight and hence fair. The notion of fairness was supported by magistrates if certain conditions were met during a fight. The fight, in their opinion, had to be mutually agreed upon and fought in a sober and disciplined fashion; weapons and feet were not to be used; combatants must not hit or kick each other if one of them was on the ground; and there had to be good reason for the fight in the first place. A personal insult to a man or his female companion was considered to be adequate reason for a set-to. When sailor William Salmon came before the stipendiary magistrate for knocking down and kicking John Roberts, who had 'blackguarded' the woman Salmon was accompanying, the magistrate announced, 'If the man insulted any respectable woman with whom you were walking, you did quite right to knock him down, but nothing can excuse your kicking him when he was down'. In another case the magistrate told Stephen M'Dermot, who had been charged with a stabbing, 'If you fellows would confine yourselves to the use of your fists I might have discharged you; but I wish all you fellows to understand that as soon as ever you use a knife you shall be dealt with according to the law'.[10]

The knife and racial stereotypes

THE NOTION OF THE 'FAIR FIGHT', that is, premeditated non-brutal interpersonal violence, continued to exist throughout the nineteenth century. In parallel, however, a great deal of fighting of other sorts went on as well. Racial stereotyping figured large in Liverpool when it came to fighting. The Irish, it was argued, had their free-for-all rows in which anything to hand was used during drunken brawls; foreign sailors invariably used the knife and the 'low-born' English, especially Lancastrians, favoured their heavy boots or clog-clad feet. All were considered uncivilized and, hence, un-English methods of fighting. As with all stereotypes, there were elements of truth, exaggeration and prejudice in all of the above portrayals. Interpersonal violence in all these cases was classed as unmanly and, above all, brutal.

Examining how each of the stereotypes was broadcast in the press offers some kind of insight into notions of supposed English superiority. In an 1866 article on the American Civil War, the *Manchester Courier* observed:

> When two Frenchmen or two Italians begin to talk loudly and throw their arms about we look on with more amusement than curiosity, for we know that with them neither strong language nor violent contortions will lead to blows. But when we witness the same demonstrations in this country we expect a more serious result, since neither the Anglo Saxon nor the Anglo-Celt is given to using threats which he does not mean to fulfil.[11]

Setting aside the condescension, the suggestion contained within this item was that foreigners made empty gestures and a lot of noise, whereas the British, and the Irish, once riled, followed up their words with force. The inclusion of the 'Anglo-Celts' is noteworthy insofar as the Irish were regarded as brutal fighters, easily inflamed when in drink. In one manslaughter case heard at the Liverpool assizes in March 1870, Justice Wills complained, when sentencing Irishman John M'Donough, that the Irish were more like 'wild Indians than civilized people', whereas England was a land of fair play and opportunity, which the Catholic, drunken, brutal and uncivilized Irish misused.[12]

Despite the *Manchester Courier*'s haughty dismissal of the French and Italians as all wind and no action, many Victorians believed Europeans, and foreigners in general, fought in an underhand and unfair manner. It was, the English believed, cowardly and unmanly to rely on the use of knives, rather than the fist, to settle arguments and disputes. How true were these prejudices against foreigners? Liverpool, as a port, constantly received sailors from all round the world and it was they, magistrates argued, who were responsible for the relatively high incidence of knife assaults and woundings. Stipendiary magistrate Mr Raffles on a number of occasions ordered notices to be printed in many languages 'cautioning sailors against the use of the knife'. In 1861 and 1862 he ordered bills to be posted around the docks in seven different languages warning against 'the dangerous practice of sailors carrying knives in the public streets'. In the poster he requested captains of ships coming into Liverpool and boarding-house keepers 'to dissuade' sailors from carrying sheath knives and other dangerous weapons when in Liverpool.[13] Sadly, he observed that the use of the knife had got 'naturalised' in England and that local people used them on the slightest pretext or provocation. The notices, though well circulated in 1862–63, did not have the desired effect, according to the head constable, who reported a continued rise in the number of woundings and stabbings. In a very typical case of wounding heard at the 1889 Liverpool assizes, sailor Henry Flynn was tried for wounding fellow shipmate Andrew Hayden with intent to do him grievous bodily harm. It transpired that they had had a quarrel after coming on shore but then had shaken hands 'as friends'. Immediately following the handshake Flynn lunged at Hayden and stabbed him in the neck. For this act he received the heavy sentence of five years' penal servitude.[14]

Foreigners, however, it was argued, did not value human life as highly as the English, for whom the fist merely hurt or bruised both the body and the ego of the combatant, whereas a knife could be lethal at worst and, at best, disfiguring. In defending an Argentinian sailor who had stabbed a German with 'a long Spanish knife', his counsel maintained that 'foreigners too frequently settled their quarrels with knives, and unfortunately did not look on life so seriously as Englishmen did'. The magistrates' courts frequently heard cases of foreigners using knives. Spaniards, Greeks, Norwegians and Danes were all prosecuted for knife fighting either in Liverpool or during voyages, in which case they were arrested and prosecuted when they reached port. Interestingly, Mediterranean men had their own rules and modes of fighting, which were regarded as legitimate, if not 'fair'. Such fighting involved knives but combatants did not intend to kill or seriously injure their opponents. Like fist fighting, the purpose was to injure or 'blood' one's opponent enough for him to surrender, thus allowing both sides to withdraw with honour intact. Where knives were involved, the combatants tended to slash out at each other's arms and legs, which might indicate that customary constraints were again brought into play.[15]

Not surprisingly in an environment and a society like nineteenth-century Liverpool, nearly all men carried knives, ranging from sheath-style ones used for work to small tobacco knives used for cleaning pipes and cutting tobacco. Whatever the style or type of knife, they could all be used in fights, by both foreigners and locals. The continental style of fighting in fact became the norm for sailors from all countries or nations. In an 1856 case involving two sailors on a British ship, it was reported that the accused made a cut with his knife 'in the usual mode adopted by Spaniards, who aim at the legs or thighs, and not with the intention of striking about the body'.[16] Good relations between the two men resumed shortly after the fight, which suggests there was no lingering ill-will between them. In fact, given the non-lethal form of fighting and the subsequent peace between the two men, the captain of the ship expressed his anger when the prosecutor took the case to court: he considered it 'malicious' to prosecute. Even knife fights between British people did not necessarily incur the wrath of the courts. When a sailor was brought up in 1854 on a charge of threatening to stab William Brand, a lodging-house keeper in Surrey Street, he was exonerated and discharged. The sailor had owed Brand between £3 and £4 for rent but had done a 'runner'; the lodging-house keeper had spotted him one month later down at Trafalgar Dock about to board a ship bound for Swansea. Not unnaturally, Brand collared the man and demanded payment, but the sailor denied owing the debt and drew a knife and tried to stab him. The magistrate, hearing the case, argued that Brand had no right to collar the sailor, even if he was owed money, and, further, that few men would have had the 'patience to submit to such a procedure' (i.e. to be detained by someone other than a policeman). Even though it was 'cowardly' and 'exceedingly improper' to draw out a knife, the magistrate felt he did not have the power to intervene in this particular case.[17]

The argument that the use of knives for fighting had somehow been imported into Liverpool late in the middle of the nineteenth century, as the magistrate implied, is not fully borne out by the facts. Instances of stabbings between men, and not necessarily sailors, can be found in earlier court reports. However, the fact that knives had been used was often flagged up by the newspapers in their reports, with headlines such as 'THE USE OF THE KNIFE' and 'SERIOUS STABBING CASE IN LIVERPOOL'. The *Manchester Courier* described the use of knives in Liverpool as 'common' in early 1864. Six years later, at Altrincham petty sessions south of Manchester, two men from Birkenhead were charged with a brutal assault. Having kicked and 'knocked him [their victim] senseless', one of the accused told his fellow accused to 'give him the Liverpool cut', whereby a knife was drawn and the victim was cut at the left corner of his mouth.[18] It is difficult to know what to infer from this phrase, 'Liverpool cut'. Was this slashing of the mouth a common trademark in fights on Merseyside, or was it a piece of bravado by the accused, who were attempting to appear as tough outsiders who knew how to handle themselves, unlike 'soft' Cheshire folk? The latter explanation may well be the more likely interpretation, as the newspapers in Liverpool failed to particularize cuts around the mouths of victims in their news reports of knifings.

While the knife was commonly regarded as an unfair weapon in fights between men, the boot, too, came in for much criticism, because it was associated with the notion of kicking people when they were already down. However, unlike the knife, with all its associations with foreignness, the boot and clog were not only English but, more specifically, northern and Lancastrian weapons. This became evident during the Tithebarn Street murder, when Richard Morgan was kicked to death (chapter 7). Within days of the murder the deputy judge at the Liverpool summer assizes announced that the courts were 'determined ... to stamp out a crime which is peculiar to Lancashire – that of kicking or "purring". In many parts of the county', Mr Higgins, QC, continued, 'and especially in colliery districts, men used their feet more freely than their fists, no matter whether the object of their wrath be a male or a female'. 'Purring' was a distinctively east Lancashire form of fighting with clogs, especially in and around Wigan. In the spring of 1874, Shimmin wrote that 'purring' 'is the art of fighting with the feet encased in boots specially formed for kicking, and the highest perfection in "purring" is to kick your antagonist to death'. Purring became known as an 'inhuman Lancashire practice'.[19] The proximity of Wigan and its environs to Liverpool and the fact that many cases of violent crime from that area were heard at the Liverpool assizes meant that Liverpool and the county tended to shade into one and the same place in the minds of southern readers, which did nothing to enhance Liverpool's already tarnished reputation.

Pub violence

STREET ASSAULTS were not the only types of violence which men had to live with on a daily basis. The pubs and beer houses found on virtually every street corner in the working-class parts of the town were potentially dangerous locations, particularly for men. There were so many possible flashpoints, ranging from a wrong look in the bar or the spilling of drinks to accusations of cheating that provoked initial angry words before escalating into a fight or even a brawl. Most male-on-male violence was alcohol fuelled and combatants could often become aggressive and threatening for the smallest of reasons. Most vulnerable to physical injury were the people behind the bar. In examining 85 assault cases, reported in the *Mercury*, arising out of fights between customers and bar staff, including publicans, barmen and barmaids, 64 (75%) were assaults on bar staff. More often than not the trigger to a dispute was a refusal to serve drink to a customer. In the 1870s, when John Fowler, a barman at a pub in Moorfields, refused more drink to James Long because he thought he had had 'enough', Long reached over the bar and seized the barman with one hand. With his other hand Long picked up a glass and smashed it on Fowler's temple. During the police court hearing the barman informed the court that his employer had given him orders 'not to serve any persons who were in a state approaching drunkenness'. The magistrate sent the case to a higher court, where compensation could be decided upon. In addition to refusing to serve customers, ejecting them from the premises could lead to violence. Barman Patrick Kitterick of the Naylor Street vaults, for example, was felled by a large cinder thrown by Daniel Costigan, who had been refused drink because it was after the midnight closing time.[20]

The most extreme violence towards bar staff occurred in February 1898, when in two separate incidents shots were fired at them. In the first, sailor Peter Olsen got into an argument with barmaid Matilda Swainson in a Frederick Street pub. When asked to pay for his glass of rum Olsen refused and drew a revolver, saying, 'I will pay for it with this'. Fortunately, the bullet missed Swainson and hit the counter. Olsen had recently been found guilty of drunkenness and discharging firearms in the street, for which he had been fined just 40 shillings. For this latest offence he was fined £5 or six weeks in prison. In the case of Francis Burge, who shot barman Thomas Naylor and PC William Flood after he was refused drink because he was deemed to be drunk or very nearly so, the court adjudged him to be insane and detained during her Majesty's pleasure. Fortunately again, his revolver was not very powerful and the wounds were of a superficial nature. This had not been the case in 1892, when a publican was stabbed in Houghton Street. The perpetrator, Woolf Bendoff, 'professor of boxing', originally charged with attempted murder, was, however, found guilty of wounding with intent to inflict grievous bodily harm, for which he was sentenced to six years' penal servitude.[21] The argument arose over the fact that the publican, William Atherton, had asked Bendoff to take his custom elsewhere when he entered the pub. Bendoff refused to move and was finally ejected by two policemen. Later that day he had returned from his lodgings with a carving knife and stabbed Atherton in the face and then, when on the ground, stabbed him in the throat.

While bar staff were particularly vulnerable to violence from drunken and irate customers, they themselves were not averse to being violent towards their customers. In 25% of cases, bar staff were charged with violent behaviour by their clients. How much of this violence was provoked or arose out of disputes about serving rude and abusive customers is hard to judge but we must assume that tensions arose which tipped bar staff and publicans over the boundaries of legality. In Edward Brien's case, both the police and the magistrates argued that he had the right to throw out a drunken marine fireman named Whitty from his pub in Great Homer Street. The court heard how Whitty had been ejected twice before receiving a third and final more violent eviction. Bar staff had an array of weapons and whistles under the counter which could be hurriedly brought into use as and when the circumstances demanded it. Thomas Hanlon, of Vauxhall Road, received only a five-shilling fine for 'bursting' John Lynch's right eye with a hammer. Another publican was found guilty of using a life-preserver against a customer whom he was ejecting. On the other hand, David Francis, landlord of the Australian Vaults in Hood Street, was found guilty of assaulting a Spanish seaman who had been causing trouble in the dancing saloon attached to the vaults. His mistake was to kick the man whom he had thrown into the street. James Houston, a publican in Deacon Street, made a similar mistake when ejecting a woman who had come fetch her husband. He was playing in the alley by the pub and refused to come home and so Houston threw her out and kicked her. He was fined 20 shillings.[22]

On occasion, the barman or manager was as drunk as the customer he was serving, if not more so. When in May 1892 carter Thomas Heyes went into a Sefton Street pub at 10.00 p.m. for a pint he received more than he bargained for. When he placed 6*d* on the counter for his drink the manager, Thomas Bell, put the coin in the drawer and said he would use the change to buy himself a whisky. Heyes, however, wanted his change before he left but Bell, somewhat the worse for drink, came round and tore his coat and hit him. After more arguments outside the pub Bell returned to the front door with a loaded revolver, which he aimed at Heyes. Fortunately, he missed and was immediately disarmed by two policemen. Amazingly, at the subsequent assizes Bell was acquitted of attempted murder and grievous bodily harm. He was discharged with a warning from the judge that there should have been some way of punishing him for having let off a revolver. Bell did, however, lose his licence to sell alcohol.[23]

The early 1870s, it would appear, were the years most fraught with tension and danger for bar staff and drinkers alike. There were public debates in the town regarding the licensing laws, the behaviour of customers in and around licensed premises, and opening and closing times which made publicans nervous about serving drinks to already inebriated customers. Publicans and bar staff were fined for allowing drunken behaviour and fights on their premises, but those who attempted to stop such brawls by going into the street and blowing their whistles to alert the police were accused of being police spies. Henry Lowther who acted in this way when there was a street row going on outside his premises on the corner of Collingwood Street and Scotland Road was fined 20 shillings, but he was seen to strike an innocent person twice on the mouth.[24]

Racist violence

IN ADDITION TO the sectarian rows that periodically broke out and the annual fights between Catholics and Protestants on St Patrick's Day, St John's Eve and 12 July, there were regular instances of racist violence. Liverpool, during the nineteenth century, was home to a sizeable black population, and received large numbers of visiting black seamen, particularly from America. There were a number of racist assaults, especially in the years between 1850 and 1880, on 'coloured' seamen. In the 1870s, John Williams, for example, was struck by 'a black bottle' for singing 'nigger songs' in a pub. The 'n' word was also used against chief steward James Bellamy when his steamer docked in New Orleans. The engineers called him 'vile names', as in 'kill the … Nigger'. The two men were charged and prosecuted when their ship, the *St Louis*, docked in Liverpool. They were fined 20 shillings and made to pay a guinea to Williams.[25]

When racism was mixed with sexual jealousy the outcome could be fatal, as in the case of William Morgan, who was tried for the murder of coloured seaman Alexander Montgomery, newly arrived on the *Aleppo* from New York on 29 October 1866. In a typical male confrontation over a woman, Morgan said to Catherine Patterson, who knew both the victim and the defendant, 'Will you talk to a — nigger?' Montgomery's companion, a white sailor named Hill, replied 'are you going to insult a man?' Catherine, too, made a point of taking Montgomery's side, by taking his arm and entering Ford's pub in Oldhall Street. Meanwhile, a slightly inebriated Morgan was seen pacing outside in the street promising to cut 'the guts out of the black tonight'. Later that evening, when Hill left a neighbouring singing room, he was accosted in the street by the still angry Morgan, who called out 'You are the man that took the — nigger's part', to which Hill replied that he had done so and would do so again. This was seen as a challenge by Morgan, who invited him around the corner into Rigby Street to 'fight it out'. During the fight Montgomery emerged from the pub and intervened because he had been called names by Morgan, who then stabbed him in the stomach. In what can be only be described as a surprising and unusual summing up of the case by Mr Justice Smith, Morgan was found guilty of manslaughter rather than murder and sentenced to 10 years' penal servitude. The judge told the jury:

> Drunkenness was no excuse whatever, and no justification in law but it was a circumstance the jury might consider in forming their opinion of the state of a man's mind when he committed a particular act, and it might affect their judgement, because a sober man, after being excited, sooner recovered the control of his passion, whereas a drunken man might remain longer under the influence of injury having been done, and of course to some extent had lost control of his reason. The question upon which the jury were to determine the character of the offence was as to the provocation the prisoner received from the deceased previous to inflicting the blow.

The jury, it was reported, 'almost immediately returned a verdict of man-slaughter'. It would not be anachronistic to state that this court decision reflected the racism of both the judge and the jury. In many other cases judges were careful to warn juries that the drunkenness of defendants was no defence. Furthermore, the arresting constable had booked Morgan for being drunk but 'not very much so' and another witness had said Morgan was neither drunk nor sober. What makes the proceedings all the more suspect is the judge's reference to the provocation of the defendant. When the narrative of the evening's events is gone over it is obvious that the provocation was all towards Montgomery. The racial insults were directed at both him and his shipmate, who was referred to as 'a — Dutchman' by Morgan. The only provocation, if that is what it can be termed, occurred when Montgomery was determined to seek redress from Morgan in the final and fatal fight, in which the former used only his fists. It was at that point that Morgan kept his earlier promise of cutting Montgomery's guts.[26]

It is clear from examining other cases involving black men that racist insults were used. In some cases the people doing the insulting were the complainants in court, who also claimed they were attacked without any provocation. One such case occurred in Tithebarn Street in February 1856. James Hammond, described as 'a powerful looking coloured seaman', was charged with assaulting Edward Gallagher late one Saturday night. However, when the magistrate, Mr Mansfield, heard that 'offensive language' had started the fight, he felt that the provocation of Hammond was serious enough for him to stop the case going to a higher court, even though Hammond had inflicted serious harm with his life-preserver. The defendant was fined £5 or two months in gaol in default of paying the fine.[27]

The 1850s appear to have been a troublesome decade in terms of racist assaults and this may reflect the possibility that black people were starting businesses for the large group of itinerant black seamen who passed through the port and who required friendly lodgings. When George de Morce, a black boarding-house keeper in Titchfield Street, went out for a walk with three of his lodgers, also 'coloured', they were met at the end of the street by a hostile group who hissed at and insulted them; the name calling included the word 'darkies'. De Morce advised his friends to do an about turn and not offer any cause for offence, but this failed to defuse the situation. Having refused to 'treat' one man with either tobacco or drink, the group were surrounded and attacked by a 'mob', who chased them back to the boarding-house, where windows and chairs were smashed. The police intervened and arrested four men, Samuel Fearend, William Lee, William Ivers and Christopher Winters. The former two were fined £5 and the latter remanded. On another occasion some men were insulted and then assaulted in the Vauxhall Road area 'because they were black'.[28]

Racist insults did not only involve local white people and visiting black sailors. Occasionally racial slurs were exchanged between blacks and other foreign sailors. One Brazilian 'coloured' seaman, Emmanuel Bravo, was reported to have said 'Look at the young Zulu coming' when Joseph Seabrook came into the shipping office at the Sailors' Home. The black sailor replied, 'If I'm a Zulu, you are a Diego'. This latter term was regarded 'amongst coloured sailors as a term of reproach to natives of South America'. Later in the day the same insults were again exchanged, sparking off a fight in which

Seabrook was stabbed in the neck and shoulder. Bravo received five years' penal servitude; had he been English, the judge said, he would have received a longer sentence.[29]

The casual racism of this era was apparent not just in the streets of the slum districts. The newspapers also reflected a white supremacist view of the world. The language of the press reports of incidents in which black people were involved shows this all too clearly. Under a headline 'SHOOTING AFFRAY – A ROW AMONG THE NIGGERS' a local paper reported the court hearing involving George Washington Dickson, who was charged with shooting 'a brother darkie, glorying in the name of Jeffrey Jackson' at a boarding-house in Banastre Street. From the evidence submitted to the court, it appeared that Dickson had had a fight with an unnamed black shipmate of Jackson's on the dance floor at the boarding-house. The paper primly noted that the female companions of the black sailors 'were of a fairer complexion'. The racist language apart, this report serves to show that men of whatever colour or race were prone to fight over female company, or the lack of it.[30]

Conclusion

THIS CHAPTER has moved a long way from the Aintree prize-fight of 1875 for which Mahoney received the comparatively light gaol sentence of four months. His crime differed from the later Duxbury case inasmuch as he fought for money (the purse was reportedly £10). Moreover, it was public and had attracted hundreds of 'roughs'. The police made value judgements about the event and those taking part. The authorities assumed that a group of working-class, largely Irish, men walking out of the courts and slums of Scotland Road and Vauxhall Road to the suburbs meant trouble and so they regarded the fight as a public order problem. It was found later that many of the accused were able to present good character references from employers, and Mahoney himself appears to have subscribed to many of the virtues so admired by middle-class Victorians. The context and the actual time of the event, occurring so close to the 'black assize' of late 1874, meant that the authorities not only labelled those taking part, they also had a lower threshold for crimes of violence. However, the leniency of the sentences would appear to bear out Wiener's point that by the 1870s judges were keen to convict participants and their seconds in prize-fights but not to punish them severely with heavy prison sentences.[31]

The Duxbury–Wilson fight, on the other hand, was a comparatively private dispute held in the privacy of a stable and clearly did not constitute a public order problem. What makes it so interesting is that it took place in 1896. Studies by other historians, particularly by John Carter Wood, have shown how, through the law and policing, there was a concerted attempt to alter working men's behaviour and their attitudes towards 'fair fighting'. This 'civilizing' process, although evident from the late 1860s and early 1870s, had not been successfully accomplished in Liverpool by the end of the century.

The use of the fist, however, was deemed less dangerous and less brutal than the use of either the boot or the knife. Liverpool was a melting pot of masculine fighting styles and traditions. The use of the knife was a particular problem, as there were so many sailors who brought not only their weapons but their own styles and customs of fighting. These did not conform to 'English' notions of the fair fight, in which manliness was achieved or enhanced through muscular strength. Locals, Irish-born Liverpudlians and foreign sailors all appear to have indulged in knife fighting, despite the fact that magistrates assumed it was foreign and un-English. The dockside posters in seven languages urging sailors to lay aside their knives on landing in Liverpool appear to have been ignored by all and sundry.

Taking all these issues into consideration, we can conclude that living, working or drinking down near the docks was fraught with danger. A wrong look, an accidental nudge on the pavement or a curse in the public bar of a corner beer house could lead to a sudden show of aggression. For the respectable working man, and for visiting and resident black sailors, the streets and bars of nineteenth-century Liverpool could be unpredictable, edgy and dangerous, as the following chapter will show.

CHAPTER 7

The Liverpool cornermen, gangs and garrotting

What have been mildly termed 'corner-men' now congregate in greater numbers than ever.... Many of them are well-known dock loafers; beings who will do anything and everything but be honest and work for a living.... They are beings who are really no earthly use to society.[1]

The Tithebarn Street murder of 1874

LIVERPOOL'S NATIONAL NOTORIETY as a place of violence and danger was firmly established with the news of the murder of Richard Morgan in Tithebarn Street on Monday 3 August 1874. That evening, it being the end of a public holiday, Morgan together with his wife and brother Samuel returned from a day out at New Ferry, and were walking up from the landing stage via Chapel Street. By all accounts sober, the group were just passing the corner of Lower Milk Street when John M'Crave (also known as Quinn) – one of three 'young rowdies', together with Michael Mullen and Peter Campbell, lounging at the corner – asked Richard Morgan for sixpence for drink. This request was refused, with Richard adding, 'Go and work for money as I do', whereupon one of the roughs, reportedly Mullen, replied, 'We work at knocking down such men as you and taking it off them if we can', and then hit Morgan suddenly and violently on the side of the head, sending him crashing to the ground. The papers reported that this was the 'signal for the commencement of a scene of brutality such as is rarely witnessed in the streets of Liverpool'. Despite brother Samuel's brave efforts and his wife's screams and attempts to shield her husband, between three and seven young men (witness reports differed as to the number) kicked Richard's head, face, neck, back and legs. Such were the force and violence of the kicks that witnesses claimed that Richard's body was moved across the street, 'like a football', a distance of some 30–40 feet. The noise and the spectacle attracted a large crowd of onlookers, some reportedly cheering on the fight and others calling for the police. After five minutes of fighting a cry of 'Heck, Heck' was heard – other witnesses said the shout was 'Nix, Nix' (but anyway cries of warning) – and the men broke off and ran away.[2]

What happened next is open to dispute. The *Liverpool Mercury* originally reported that Samuel Morgan, along with others, gave chase and cornered John Quinn, alias M'Crave, nicknamed 'Holly Fly', who drew a knife and threatened to stab Samuel. For his own safety, the newspaper reported, onlookers 'dragged' Samuel away from Quinn, who ran off and who was later pointed out to the police and arrested. At the first magistrate's hearing, the following day, Samuel Morgan told the hearing that when he had cornered John M'Crave or Quinn, the prisoner's friends helped him get away and 'a lot of women' stopped Morgan going into a yard in pursuit of the prisoner. However, 'some lads' told Morgan where M'Crave was and consequently he was able to have him arrested. Meanwhile, Hugh Shimmin, in the *Porcupine*, reported that 'a large crowd looked on calmly and did not interfere' while the three roughs kicked Morgan for about 15 minutes, and that no policeman arrived 'until the worst was over'.

This sad case, from the very beginning, began to take on a life of its own within the pages of the press and soon brought to the surface all kinds of social fears and debates about violence and personal security on the streets. The Tithebarn Street murder came to symbolize and represent so many different crime issues that its amplification makes it difficult to discern truth from mere press exaggeration. The victim, Richard Morgan, very soon attained the mantle of respectability and even martyrdom status. He was described as 'recently married, known as a steady and faithful servant' and as 'an industrious and respectable man' who, when challenged for money for beer, sarcastically and fearlessly told the scroungers to get work and earn money like the rest of decent society. His innocence, bravery and respectability were neatly juxtaposed against the characters of the three accused, two of whom already had criminal records and one of whom had only recently been released from gaol for an offence of robbery with violence. This immediately introduced into the debate the further question of the efficacy of punishments for violent crimes and whether they were harsh and effective enough to act as deterrents.

And what of the Liverpool community? Why did the crowd not rush to the aid of the victim? Were they, as some reports implied, on the side of the roughs, thus signifying a terrifying and depressing breakdown in the social fabric of Liverpool society, or were there other explanations for the crowd's behaviour? Where were the police? This was a further question posed by journalists, who appeared bemused that a busy thoroughfare on a holiday evening appeared to be totally unpoliced. How was it that a man was murdered over a matter of minutes (rather than seconds) without any kind of intervention from law officers? Finally, Mullen, M'Crave and Campbell came to personify a group within society who had proved troublesome and incorrigible for the last three decades of the nineteenth century and were to continue to prove problematic into the twentieth. They were perceived as a kind of criminal class who were identified under different names and titles, 'ruffians', 'rowdies' and 'roughs' being the most commonly used.

'The worst and most hopeless part of the story', reported the *Times'* editorial on 17 December 1874, was that Richard Morgan:

> was knocked down and kicked to death, and his wife was kicked off his prostrate body, in the presence of a considerable crowd of Liverpool men, no one of whom seems to have thought that it was any business of his to interfere. Nay, more, the sympathy of the spectators seems to have been on the side of the assailants. All through the horrible scene, while the one brother lay senseless in the road and the other was doing his utmost to defend him, and while the wife, casting off all the timidity of her sex at the sight of her husband's danger, was striving at the peril of her own life to shelter him, the crowd was literally enjoying the struggle, hounding on the murderers and encouraging them to greater violence.

Were the people of Liverpool on the side of 'brutal lawlessness' as the *Times* so publicly asserted? Or were there more complex responses and attitudes on the part of the spectators which prevented them from going to the aid of the Morgan family? Despite press assertions of a complete lack of assistance, 'loud calls for the police' were made by some of those present; nor should it be forgotten that M'Crave was followed, identified and captured very soon after the murder. Furthermore, many in the Tithebarn Street crowd would not have seen the initial assault and thus would not have been entirely sure who was the assailant and who was the innocent victim. A drunken brawl or 'an ordinary street brawl' was what one witnessed initially assumed was taking place.[3] This was a common enough sight on the streets of Liverpool and not something to become involved in, as one witness at the subsequent trial indicated when asked by one of the defence barristers why he did not intervene. 'What was the use of interfering with a lot of men like them? Why, I should get killed myself.' If one lived in a 'low neighbourhood' such as Vauxhall Road or Scotland Road, one did not 'interfere' in other people's fights. Shimmin, in his usual provocative manner, came up with another reason. Under the heading 'THE REIGN OF TERROR', he argued that the murder emphasized how ineffectual the law and the police were when confronted by such an act. Therefore why did the press attempt to hide the 'defects' of the law and the police 'by blaming the lookers-on'?[4] Their inactivity was due neither to cowardice nor to heartlessness but was, paradoxically, claimed Shimmin, due to 'fear of law and of the police'. A 'poor man' was, if he intervened in a street fight, in danger of losing his character and his liberty, of ruining himself and his family, because who were the police to arrest when they eventually turned up to stop the fight? And if arrested by mistake, how then could an honest poor man regain his liberty without finding witnesses? Shimmin's 'Reign of Terror' strikes a chord with the modern reader, although his assertions may well have been exaggerated. This terror of the legal system, policing in particular, was 'crushing' every feeling of liberty out of the people. 'Home, privacy, everything is being invaded, if not by, at least under the name of the law. The police may now go everywhere; into your house any time, night or day.' Other newspapers, however, argued that the law did not go far enough in protecting law-abiding members of the public. The *Pall Mall Gazette*, in what can only be described as a Victorian form of 'zero tolerance', argued for stringent police supervision in the north end of Liverpool:

> Let them feel that every exhibition of drunken violence, every street quarrel, every act which may conceivably lead to crime if left unchecked, will be visited with instant arrest. A body of police should patrol the district large enough to make the inhabitants aware that there is not an angry word or a loud cry, or a rough jostle which will not bring the eye of a constable upon them.... These are the methods by which disorder has been put down in Ireland and India, and there is no reason why the disease should be harder to control in Liverpool.[5]

In some areas of the country, particularly London, it would seem that the town of Liverpool was being viewed as a foreign land, and one that required subjugation through an occupying force. The Tithebarn Street murder had suggested to many middle-class readers that they were sitting on a rumbling volcano of criminality. What were the constituent parts of this Victorian criminality that occasionally spewed out a moral panic every 10 years or so, endangering in the process the all-to-vulnerable respectable classes? Most crimes of violence brought press and public attention to the triumvirate of masculinity, excessive drinking of alcohol and the idea of an underclass.

The identification and evolution of the Liverpool rough

MUCH OF THE EVERYDAY male-on-male violence was blamed on a specific but large group of young men who mainly lived in the narrow courts in the north end of town. Casual brutality was seen as a way of life for these men, so far as the newspapers were concerned. They were variously labelled during the course of the second half of the nineteenth century. Early headlines identified them as 'desperate characters' and 'incorrigibles', but greater value judgements by the press in the following decades led to them being labelled 'loafers', 'roughs', 'savages', 'brutes' and 'cornermen'; by the 1890s these same groups were 'cowards of the worst type', 'cowardly scoundrels' and 'cowardly cornermen'. The rough was identified and singled out as the main threat to an orderly Liverpool society. To what extent were these men a threat? Who were they? Were they, in part, a media exaggeration? Did they belong to what the Victorians called the criminal class?

First, some kind of definition is required in trying to identify who (or what) were cornermen and roughs. Some Victorians, like Charles Dickens, appear to have made very fine distinctions between roughs, rowdies and ruffians. In 1868, when roughs were first coming to public notice as an identifiable public concern, Dickens bemoaned the 'euphonious softening' of the term 'Ruffian' into 'Rough'. For him the ruffian was 'either a Thief, or the companion of Thieves'.[6] And the rough was quite distinct from a disorderly working man who, though occasionally troublesome, worked hard. Roughs were identifiable in the streets by their dress, furtive manner and the way they stood in groups at street corners. Their very name probably came from the way newspapers described them in their reports, namely 'rough looking'.

Six years later in an article comparing the American 'rowdy' with the English 'rough', Dickens attributed further characteristics to these 'savages', such as:

> their ignorance, their recklessness, their ferocity, their intemperance, their filthiness of speech, the cruelty of their amusements, and their utter disregard of all decency, propriety, and respect for the feelings, or even existence of other people. They form a class, or caste, by themselves, speak a jargon which respectable people do not always understand, and are the veritable pariahs of our civilization.[7]

This emotive definition was created in the immediate aftermath of the Tithebarn Street murder and encapsulates, clearly, general attitudes towards this dangerous 'sub-group'. The roughs or cornermen belonged to the 'other', a group whose very existence gave meaning to the police, for the police had to control the streets and make them safe for decent men and women. The roughs also gave meaning to what kinds of public behaviour were not to be tolerated. In short, the 'roughs' were a necessary evil. This does not make them a figment of the newspapers' imagination, for there were groups of rowdy young men congregating on the corners of the streets – in Liverpool, notably in and around Scotland Road and Vauxhall Road. It was, however, only in the 1860s, significantly, that they were first perceived to be threatening. Crime during that decade came to dominate the political and public agenda, at least as reflected the national news, with the reporting of the London garrotting panic of 1862, the first English rail murder in 1864 and the continuing worries about the 'ticket of leave' prisoners, who gained early release because of the ending of transportation abroad for serious crime. In short, there were public panics into which the roughs and cornermen neatly dovetailed. In one of the first instances in which the *Liverpool Mercury* used the word 'rough' (in 1865), it described how 'a gang of "roughs" ... were in the habit of congregating about the corner of Price-street and Duke-street'.[8] They, without provocation, abused, insulted and assaulted all who passed that way. In Athol Street, site of a police station, a correspondent to the *Mercury* in 1871 asked why 'street roughs and public house door loafers are permitted to hang about the street corners, greatly to the disgust and annoyance of the passersby?' 'Athol-street', continued the writer, 'from top to bottom, at the present time is inundated with idle roughs of a most dangerous class without any visible means of subsistence'. Not to be outdone, another correspondent wrote to the paper complaining of the 'gorillas' whose 'repulsive and shocking' language and laughter upset some of the residents of Prince's Terrace, Derby Road, Bootle. Again, the police were nowhere to be seen according to the correspondent.[9]

How dangerous were these cornermen and did they constitute a threat to the respectable members of society? Their crude and profane language, their high spirits and their numbers at street intersections made many people uncomfortable. Leaning against the walls of a public house, these 'man-hawks', as one journalist described them, seemed to stand watching, eyeing up possible victims, to cadge money off, or to insult, mock, challenge, assault and rob. Their 'crimes' were numerous and anti-social. For many of these young men, lacking status and self-esteem, and who relied on casual labour, intermittent wages and alcohol to see them through the week, fighting offered opportunities and diversions. Modern-day criminologists have shown how men typically take up a challenge or a fight if there is an audience of male friends present. A reputation for being a hard man, a tough, or the 'terror of Scotland-road' could give a man status and self-esteem. So when M'Crave asked Morgan for money that August evening in Tithebarn Street he was partly begging and partly issuing a challenge. A refusal, he knew, could quickly escalate to a fight.

Being 'king' of the street was important to a cornerman. The criminal courts had (and have) to deal with many cases where small, insignificant challenges and provocations have led to assaults and robberies. In 1878, young roughs James Gallagher, James Shearen and John Farrell were arrested in Byrom Street for pushing people off the footpath and assaulting the police officers who went to arrest them. Gallagher, who already had 16 previous convictions, was sentenced to six months' imprisonment. Two weeks later Stanley Ralph was charged with assaulting John Wilson in Lime Street. As in the previous case, the defendant was drunk and claimed that Wilson had 'shoved' against him and 'knocked me off the footwalk'.[10]

Sometimes a fight would be provoked as a means to robbery. A common provocation was to knock a man's hat off or to push it forward over his eyes. This was known as 'bonneting' and had the obvious advantage for the assailant of momentarily confusing the victim and leaving him vulnerable. A man's hat was, after all, a very personal and precious item, and he would go to considerable lengths to recover it. Hairdresser John Duckett was assaulted by a man who stepped forward from a group of friends on the corner of Wigan Street and shoved his hat over his eyes. The prisoner, who had already served five years on the reformatory ship the *Clarence*, put him in a head lock and rummaged through his pockets. He found nothing, and Duckett was beaten up.[11]

Frequently featured in accounts of cornermen was their love of drink. M'Crave had asked the unfortunate Morgan for sixpence with which to buy a quart of ale. This kind of cadging, or asking for 'a treat' as it was called in Liverpool, was common. The *Porcupine*, in the months following the Tithebarn Street murder, recounted stories of 'poor labouring men' being threatened by groups of roughs. One man was reportedly stopped on a corner in Scotland Road and asked for 'threepence "to make up a quart"'. 'The fearful lesson of Tithebarn-street', continued the journal, 'came before the man. He was not strong, and they were a desperate lot before him. He gave them the threepence, and they allowed him to pass on.' The same man had, it was claimed, refused to hand over money on another occasion and was seized and had his pockets turned out. Another, it reported, was lying in hospital, having been kicked by a gang in Blundell Street. Although he knew their names, the man was too frightened to identify them.[12]

On one occasion the roughs were mobilized for political purposes, probably by the local Tory brewing interests and publicans in the town, to demonstrate against changes in the licensing laws, particularly the early closing (at 9.00 p.m.) on Sundays. The mass meetings, according to the *Mercury*, were, 'simply displays of unmitigated rowdyism, where the Liverpool rough disported himself to his own amusement and satisfaction'. On Sunday, 3 November 1872, a motley crowd gathered in front of St George's Hall; as well as the roughs 'who came for a row', there were a few 'misguided men who went to "protest" against the action of the magistrates; a number of temperance advocates who went to "improve the occasion" by holding forth upon the evils of drunkenness; and a large body of spectators who assembled out of curiosity to see what some of them called "the sport".' They were not disappointed. The roughs, it was reported, enjoyed the sport 'like terriers in a rat ring. They pulled and tugged at each other, fought, drank, and blasphemed, and altogether conducted themselves more like savages than civilised beings.' By 3.30 p.m., a crowd of 25,000 had gathered on the steps of the hall; opposite stood magistrates calmly smoking their cigars by the windows of the North-Western Hotel. The latter appeared confident that the protest was not going to degenerate into working-class violence and vandalism, for they had 350 policemen ready and troops on standby. Amid this strange crowd moved a group of foreigners with their interpreter, evidently amazed at such a meeting but clearly not feeling threatened by the crowd. Humour and pantomime-style jeering and hooting up at the magistrates appeared to be the order of the day as it was almost impossible for any speaker to get more than a few sentences out. The main fun was to be seen on the steps of the hall, where an 'unruly mob composed of the most rowdy class of ruffians in the town' amused themselves and the spectators with their horseplay and mock speeches. After about an hour Major Greig moved the police into position and, in a pincer movement 'worthy of Wellington', the hall steps and Lime Street were cleared quickly and quietly.[13]

When the pubs closed that Sunday at 9 p.m., a crowd gathered once more. This time its composition was not as diverse as in the afternoon gathering, being made up of 'the lowest class' of 'the veriest roughs which Liverpool could produce'. Crude speeches were made by some roughs, 'red fire' was lit around the Wellington monument and hats 'blocked off' the view of those who stood by watching. Later, as the police swept the crowd back into their slum quarters, fireworks and red and blue fires were lit and set off, amid much hooting and yelling.

What strikes the modern reader about this episode is the relative absence of violence among the reportedly lowest, least civilized members of Liverpool society. Anger at the changes in the opening hours and class hatred are evident from their behaviour and language but the whole episode appears to have been overwhelmingly good-natured and not too threatening. The *sangfroid* of the magistrates, smoking their cigars on the balcony of the hotel, was in part born out of confidence that they had sufficient forces ready if the crowd became violent and in part probably a confidence in the Liverpool crowd, whom they knew to be rowdy but essentially deferential.

The roughs and the criminal class

THE LANGUAGE ADOPTED in the press to describe these roughs and cornermen – as well as their female equivalents (and female admirers) – suggested that many of the 'respectable' classes located such people within what Victorians termed the 'criminal classes'. Who or what constituted the criminal class? This is a difficult and complex question and depends, in part, on whom one reads. The definition below, developed by J. J. Tobias in the 1960s, serves as a useful introduction to the Victorian concept of a criminal class:

> When nineteenth-century commentators spoke of criminals they meant the class which lived a life of its own, separate from the rest of the community, members of which were usually easily distinguished by their clothing and habits and lived wholly or largely on the proceeds of crime.[14]

While not all Victorians necessarily subscribed to the above definition, most were agreed that the criminal class were incorrigible, habitual, irredeemable, professional law-breakers who were not only the antithesis of society, but were also a danger and a contagion to the working poor who lived among them. Henry Mayhew, in his massive study of the London poor, identified this group as those who 'won't work', a kind of non-working working class.[15] Victorians were keen to identify and label the world around them, the better to understand it. This specific application of scientific rationalism, which many of us are familiar with through the works of Karl Marx and his analysis of history as a war between classes, was particularly common on the part of social thinkers and even government officials when dealing with, for example, the 'undeserving' and 'deserving' poor. Once a social group had been identified as a problem and a label attached, a solution or a cure could be tried, be it a workhouse, prison or asylum.

By the 1860s fears that a criminal class was present and endangering society had become a common discourse in books, newspapers and journals. With crime rising up the political and social agenda there came an element of self-fulfilling prophecy about who constituted members of the criminal class. Did the cornermen and roughs belong to this species of inferior humanity? A closer reading of the commentaries of the day shows clearly how confused and contradictory the thinking was on such classifications. The notion of a criminal class became, for some, a useful label and stick with which to beat the poorest and underemployed members of society. Others came up with interesting sub-groups, one might almost say Darwinian sub-species. Take the *Times* on 31 December 1874, which, commenting on an article from the *Liverpool Albion* about crime statistics in the town, stated that:

> the authors of crimes of violence have more and more become a class by themselves. They are grouped and ticketed apart ... this criminal class has become more daring and more reckless of consequences to themselves and to others. This is a perfectly natural result. As criminals become more marked off from the rest of the population, they associate more with one another, and become more confirmed in evil courses.

Only three months previously the *Pall Mall Gazette*, in a piece headed 'THE ROUGH TERROR', had stated:

> the violent class was more separated from the ordinary population than it is now. It was associated more closely with the openly criminal class, and consequently could be more easily avoided. At present the rough forms an intermediate type. He belongs to the criminal class as regards his tastes and amusements, but not necessarily as regards his employment. The man who finds his evening's recreation in inflicting scientific kicks has probably spent the morning at honest work. It is not possible, therefore, for his victims to avoid him. He walks the same streets, and very possibly lives in the same house with them. They have to pass him lounging at the corner as they come home at night, they have to push by him before they can enter the publichouse where they go for beer.[16]

Shimmin, on the other hand, approvingly quoted the 'extreme views' of a gentlemanly correspondent who argued that these men and women 'never earned a shilling honestly in their lives' but gained their livelihoods through 'robbery, plunder and prostitution'.[17] Opinion on who these people actually were and what degree of threat and menace they represented to the rest of society was clearly divided. Had the bullies taken over certain working-class areas of the town to the extent that the honest respectable poor dared not complain or report these roughs to the authorities, or was the apparent lack of policing a genuine reflection of the comparative lack of a threat posed by such groups? Was the Tithebarn Street murder a one-off event which the press then magnified into a local panic?

The police did come in for heavy criticism, both specifically for not being close to the scene of the 1874 murder, which took place on a busy street, and also more generally for allowing the rise and perceived domination of the cornermen on public thoroughfares. Shimmin, a usually reliable observer of Liverpool life, wrote of the cornermen being 'permitted to infest the public-house corners of nearly all the streets' in certain neighbourhoods of town. This point was endorsed in one correspondent's letter to the editor of the *Liverpool Mercury*, who, when she ('a Gentlewoman') reported a kicking row to a policeman, was informed that 'he would not interfere in the Tithebarn rows'. The constable added that the police 'always left them to fight it out'.[18] While anonymous correspondents should be treated with a degree of caution and scepticism, the policeman's point– that it was better to leave the roughs to fight and kick among themselves – does have an air of credibility. The *Times* went much further, in claiming that the cornermen had

> taken such entire possession of their own districts that they can do literally as they please in them. All who presume to approach their territory must do so at their own peril. They will almost certainly be assailed, and will not impossibly be kicked to death as a consequence of their rash intrusion…. There seems, in fact, to have been a sort of unwritten compromise between the guardians of the public peace at Liverpool and the peace-breakers. As long as the 'Cornermen' are content to keep to their own regions, nothing more will be demanded of them, and they may act, therefore, without restraint within the quarters to which their sway is limited.[19]

Setting aside the hyperbole and exaggeration contained in the opening sentences of this editorial, the accusation that the police had adopted, in effect, a pragmatic approach to policing the back streets and courts of the north end of Liverpool does not seem unfounded.

In the aftermath of the Tithebarn Street murder, the whole question of policing in the town became highly politicized both by the recorder at the winter sessions and in town council meetings, where the chairman of the watch committee had to defend the police against accusations of inefficiency and failure to undertake their duties and responsibilities. The recorder, in his address to the grand jury, made a telling point:

> supposing the system of 'corner-men,' instead of existing in Tithebarn-street, Chisenhale-street, and the lower parts of town, existed at the corner of Falkner-square or Abercromby-square, and if, instead of a person like Richard Morgan being assaulted and murdered, persons in their [the grand jury's] class of society, or persons in the class of society like the magistrates, the Watch Committee, and those who regulated the police force, were molested, did they believe that Falkner-square or Abercromby-square would have been left with only a small number of police walking about as before? He did not think so, nor did he think anybody else would.[20]

In the police's defence, the head constable, Major Greig, had immediately initiated an enquiry into how many policemen were close to the scene of the murder on 3 August at about 9.30 p.m. If his inspector is to be believed – and there is no reason not to, as there was a shift change at Rosehill station at 9.00 p.m., which meant the police were following routine procedures at the time – the murder spot was visited by six constables, an inspector and an acting inspector between 9.15 and 9.45 p.m. One actually walked down Lower Milk Street at 9.25, a mere five minutes before the murder.[21] This kind of detail appeared to exonerate the police from accusations of being both absent from Tithebarn Street and slow to answer calls for help. The press, however, chose to ignore such facts, preferring instead to emphasize the more newsworthy fiction that the police were not only absent but that they allowed the cornermen to take over the streets of Liverpool. Referring to the press's accusations against the force, Major Greig used a parade at Rosehill police station in January 1875 to accuse the newspapers of having 'heated imaginations' in their exaggeration of the dangers of Liverpool's streets. In 20 years' experience, he claimed that he had never seen anything 'beyond a brawl' which could be witnessed in any town. The police never, he emphasized, 'shirked or feared danger'. The chairman of the watch committee spoke of the exceptional nature of the murder and said that such events were impossible to prevent unless police strength were increased from 1500 to 15,000. Just a week earlier Greig had reported to his watch committee that, compared with streets like Marybone, Tithebarn Street 'is an orderly place'.[22] Moreover, police numbers were increased whenever certain days came up on the calendar like 17 March (St Patrick's Day) or 12 July (the date for the Orange parades). This planning had ended not only the major processions but the fights that used to accompany them. Neither had there been any 'well grounded complaints' about ruffianism.

In reading his report, one is struck by the 'flannelling' of some his explanations and justifications for the absence of riots and sectarian disputes. Of most interest is his penultimate paragraph:

> Although the mere assembling at corners of streets has not hitherto been held as punishable, except on the ground of obstruction, the Police have full instructions to prevent any assemblage, even in small numbers; and in few cases have they been obliged to compulsion.

This suggests that the police, despite what some historians have claimed, did not always consistently and energetically enforce the much-derided 'move on' order whenever a constable found a group of 'loafers' standing at the street corners by the doors of a public house.[23] Evidence for this irregular enforcement of obstruction laws can be found in the press when there were periodic crackdowns against cornermen. For example, the magistrates' court dealt with 17 cornermen on 1 April 1884 for loitering, on 2 April the police requested summonses against 25 men for loitering on streets and outside railway stations, and on 8 April 18 were prosecuted. Interestingly, only three defendants attended court, while the remainder sent their mothers and sisters. Many refused to give an address. Yet more prosecutions took place on 15 and 22 April, when a further 60 were prosecuted or summoned. It would appear that most were young men, many with unstated previous convictions, who were fined between 1 and 20 shillings for obstruction and loitering, in Vauxhall Road, Wigan Street, Chisenhale Street, Oriel Street, Stanhope Street and Scotland Road. It would not be unreasonable to conclude that March and early April 1884, so soon after two killings, saw something of a crackdown by the police on the 'cornermen nuisance'.[24] By this time the police had at their disposal a new by-law, passed in 1877,[25] aimed at 'roughs of the "street corner" order', who could be charged with 'standing, loitering, or remaining on the footway without reasonable cause, so as to obstruct the free passage of the streets'. The very first men to be charged under this by-law had previous convictions for stabbing, drunkenness and robbery. A fine of 10 shillings would have seemed a relatively minor imposition.

The High Rip and other gangs

CORNERMEN WERE, on occasion, referred to as 'gangs'. Was this a simple descriptive noun being used to refer to loosely organized and constantly shifting groups of young men hanging around street corners? Or did the newspapers mean that these bands of men were tied together in a more organized and tight-knit fashion, through blood or neighbourhood links? We are familiar with the whole gamut of gang cultures, from the extremes of the Mafia through to the criminal networks of the Krays, for instance. More recently, the news media have worried about youth gangs and their territorial fights in London and Manchester, for example. This latter city had, in the nineteenth century, its very own gang culture, based on the Scuttlers, who formed numerous groupings in and around Manchester and Salford.[26] Were the Liverpool cornermen and roughs anything like them or were they simply a loose group of 'yobs', for want of a better description, bent on low-level anti-social crime and acts of violence and petty thieving?

Take the case of Richard O'Brien, aged 26, Joseph Smith, 20, John M'Nally, 23, and William Connolly, 24, all labourers, but described in the press as '"roughs" of the roughest type', who were charged in 1878 with two counts of stealing. It seemed from the statement of the principal witness and victim that these men waited close to the docks, where two of them simply helped themselves to goods off the backs of carts, in this case a tub of butter. The remaining two men stood in a threatening way at the corner, waiting either to help themselves to more goods if the carter gave chase or to beat him up. This latter experience had happened the previous day to the carter. On three of the defendants being found guilty, the recorder noted that 'the prisoners apparently formed one of the most dangerous gangs of thieves in Liverpool, and one of the most dangerous gangs which could possibly exist in a large town'. Its leading member, O'Brien, or 'Dick the Devil' as he was known to his friends, had in his short life been 40 times in gaol for acts of violence and other crimes. For this robbery, 'by means of terror', he received 10 years' penal servitude. Short of tracing O'Brien's criminal life and associates, it is difficult to arrive at any conclusion about whether he belonged to an organized gang or simply mixed with like-minded friends who committed opportunistic crimes. In an earlier case, 'Dick the Devil' and two women had kicked and assaulted a pregnant woman in Frederick Street, in what looked suspiciously like a premeditated ambush. When the magistrate, Mr Whittey, said to O'Brien, 'I know your face very well', he replied, 'Sure the world knows it (laughter in court)'.[27]

Evidence contained in the press and the head constable's regular reports to the Liverpool watch committee on the presence of gangs is contradictory. This makes any historical judgement tricky, to say the least. In the 1880s there arose in Liverpool a phenomenon called the High Rip Gang or High Rippers. In a memorandum for the Liverpool watch committee on 19 October 1886, Captain Nott-Bower, the head constable, wrote:

> During the last few weeks a Liverpool Paper has brought very prominently before the public the subject of an alleged dangerous organisation of Ruffianism at the North End of the City.
> It is suggested:–
> 1) that there is an extensive conspiracy for purposes of assault and plunder and that those concerned are banded together in a Secret Society known as 'The High Rip Gang.'
> 2) That by the operations of this society the safety of the inhabitants of the North End is in serious danger, as the assaults committed are increasing in severity and number and, (owing to Police incompetence and the state of terror which exists among the people) those made amenable for these assaults are very few and becoming fewer.[28]

Organized violence had, it was claimed by some newspapers like the *Liverpool Daily Post*, been allowed to flourish under the very nose of a police force which was both expensive and ineffective. The High Rip Gang was, therefore, to some extent a politically motivated scare which coincided with local elections in November 1886. This was not the first nor will it be the last time that crime is used as a political issue. Were the High Rip Gang, and the other Liverpool gangs – Logwood, Finnon Haddie and Dead Rabbits – brought to brief prominence by some elements of the local press which exaggerated both their importance and the dangers posed by them?[29]

Historians have claimed that the High Rippers dated back to the murder of a Spanish sailor in Blackstone Street by a so-called leader of the gang, M'Lean, in 1884, although contemporaries made no mention of the gang name at the time. A more definite reference appeared in 1885, at the winter assizes, when two 17-year-olds, Boylan and MacConnell, were tried for a malicious wounding. The *Liverpool Mercury* went on to report that the term 'High Rip Gang' was 'a familiar description applied by witnesses on both sides to a band of youthful residents of the notorious locality of Back Portland-street'. The police constable involved in the case spoke of being aware of 'a heavy gang' which was led by, he believed, MacConnell. When asked by the judge what the gang did, the constable replied, 'They carry old knives and swords, or any weapon they can lay hold of', and would go 'up and down the streets, and knocking any body down they can meet'. Both youths were found guilty and given the comparatively light sentence of six months with hard labour.[30]

Two months later the local press headlined reports of prosecutions in the magistrates' courts with 'THE "HIGH RIP" GANG AGAIN'; this case involved two young men who, after an argument in a public house, assaulted two men in Scotland Road with knives, belts and sticks. The 1885 spring assizes witnessed yet another case in which the High Rip Gang was implicated. It concerned the wounding of Hugh Cunningham by a 19-year-old carter, George Whitehead. This case arose out of the earlier court hearing, insofar as Cunningham, it was alleged, had acted as a prosecution witness against those two members of the gang. The defendant was found guilty and received just five months with hard labour. Further allegations were made against individuals at New Brighton, on the August bank holiday, when four young men from Liverpool fought among themselves and then stabbed a butcher from whom they were stealing pork pies.[31]

News stories relating to the gang appear to have tailed off for about 12 months after the assize trial of August 1885. However, in the late summer of 1886 the High Rippers made an unwelcome and notorious return to the pages of the Liverpool press, particularly the *Daily Post* and the *Echo*. The existence of the High Rip Gang was beginning to appear more tangible, credible and less elusive. First came news of an incident involving 32-year-old John M'Shane, who was arrested and charged with shooting 20-year-old Harold Buck in his foot. M'Shane had gone out of his house with a seven-chambered revolver and shot into a crowd; those in the crowd were, he claimed, members of the gang. A week later William Hignett was knocked to the ground in Scotland Road and brutally kicked by members of the High Rip Gang because he had had the temerity to refuse them money for 'spruce' beer.[32]

On 28 August 1886, there occurred 'the march on Walton gaol' by over 100 High Rippers hell-bent, it was claimed, on attacking and killing a witness to an earlier case whose testimony had landed some gang members in gaol. This same march was to be opposed by the Logwood Gang, a vigilante-style group of men armed with logs whose ambition was to put an end to the High Rippers. Fighting broke out both outside the gaol and in Marybone, where the gangs clashed with each other and the police, who had got wind of the Walton gaol march and the gang war. Three members of the Logwood Gang, John Jeffers, Edward Sebborn and Michael Davy, were later charged and found guilty of riotous assembly and disturbing the peace. Rather surprisingly, Mr Raffles, the magistrate, dismissed their behaviour as a 'great nuisance' and bound them over to keep the peace for three months. Such a low-key magisterial response, together with such a lenient sentence, suggests the authorities were not unduly concerned with the gang wars supposedly taking place on the streets of north Liverpool.[33]

This was not the initial reaction of Justice Day, who presided over Liverpool's November assizes that same year. The earlier M'Shane case, held over since August, came up for trial. Interestingly, the police acted as prosecution for Buck, who, M'Shane claimed, was in the crowd which was part of the High Rip Gang. They had, he said, been annoying him by coming to his house and damaging his windows and door panels and calling him a 'police spy'. Again, witnesses such as neighbours and the local beat constable confirmed the existence of the gang, which was said to have control of a neighbourhood known as Sebastopol. Significantly, PC 507 said in cross-examination that members of the gang were not present at the shooting and that the area was not only more peaceful than it used to be, but that the inhabitants did not live in fear.

Justice Day struggled with what he had heard during the trial and observed:

> He could hardly believe it is possible that in any part of Liverpool the streets were given up to the control of ruffians, that the authority of the law was unknown, and that it was necessary to seek police protection to pass along the streets, or to carry firearms for the purpose of self-defence.

The next day, Mr Justice Day presided over another case in which the defendant, 29-year-old Patrick Webb, claimed to have been acting in self-defence against the gang, who thought that he had acted as a witness against 'our two lads this morning'. These two cases suggest either that the High Rip Gang was becoming a major social order problem on the streets of Liverpool or that it was being cited as something of an excuse, a defence, to be used in cases where extreme violence had occurred. The gang's existence could indeed have been a convenient fiction for both defendants and newspapers wanting to believe that the police no longer had control of streets in the north end of the city. Towards the end of the same assizes, two more 19-year-olds, Peter Tedford and Edward Higham, were tried for stabbing John Jeffers, of the Logwood Gang, who himself had been up before the magistrates at the end of August. They received the severe sentence of 15 years' penal servitude.

At the conclusion of the assizes Justice Day, in order to clear up any 'erroneous impressions' which he might have given relating to the existence of the High Rip Gang, stressed that 'nothing that had come under his observation led him to believe that such a society did exist; and he paid a high tribute to the efficiency of the Liverpool police force'. This change of heart may have been due to a secret tour of the less salubrious northern streets of the Scotland Road police division, which he undertook with Nott-Bower, two detectives and Mr Justice Grantham. For three hours this unlikely group toured the district after the pubs had turned out their customers. The poverty and the squalor clearly shocked the judge and perhaps gave the learned gentlemen some insight into the lives of the inhabitants in that quarter of the city.[34]

On the other hand, the existence, indeed infamy, of the High Rippers was such was that they were written into the Christmas pantomime that year, *Robinson Crusoe*, at the Rotunda Theatre:

> Mrs Crusoe: Well, Liverpool has had its spell of crime.
>   'The High Rip Gang' has had a high old time.
> Will Atkins: (a pirate): Brave.
> Ally: Where were the police? I'm fairly puzzled.
> Mrs Crusoe: The police were catching dogs that went unmuzzled.[35]

The High Rip Gang, however, faded almost as quickly as it had appeared. One of the final stories relating to its activities concerned a robbery with violence and a malicious wounding on 4 February 1887 in Scotland Road. Four young men, John Baker (aged 20), George Baker (19), Francis M'Tavey (20) and Bernard M'Call (20), who all lived together in a lodging house in Sylvester Street, first attacked a young man who passed by them at the corner of Westmoreland Street, by knifing him in the head. Then they ran down Scotland Road, where they charged by a pawnbroker's shop. Here they attempted to steal some display goods; however, and rather tellingly, they were surrounded by a hostile crowd. M'Tavey having flailed at them with a knife, the group then went to another pawnbroker and stole some clothing, before moving on to a confectioner. The catalogue of assaults and thefts was then outlined to the court:

> The prisoners next made their way to the confectionery shop of Mrs Reid in Latimer-street. The daughter of Mrs Reid was standing at the door with a baby in her arms, and the prisoner George Baker struck the child in the face and M'Tavey, who had a knife in his hand, kicked Mrs Morris on the thigh. John and William Reid ran to the rescue, and a struggle took place, in which John Reid was severely cut on the head and William Reid wounded in the back. The shop of a butcher named Smith, in Latimer-street, was also attacked and Smith was stabbed in the back. The prisoners next assaulted a boy and an assistant at Newport's pawnshop in Scotland-road, and tried to steal a number of white frocks. When running down Dalrymple-street, they also knocked down two women and struck a child, and when they again turned into Scotland-road they attacked Agnes Howarth, an assistant in Mr Hunter's shop.[36]

This 'steaming', or rampage of mayhem, left eight people with wounds of one sort or another. In addition to gaol sentences ranging from 15 to 21 months' imprisonment with hard labour, Mr Justice Day ordered them to receive a total of 60 lashes in three separate floggings. The resort to the 'cat' was seen by many as an excellent deterrent and was largely given credit for the ending of the High Rip fears in the north end of town. This is not to say that peace reigned on the streets around Vauxhall and Scotland Roads, for Raffles, the stipendiary magistrate, complained in the spring of 1887 that 'he had never had such experience of the knife being resorted to by boys as had recently come before him. This new development was far worse than the assaults of the High Rip Gang.'[37] One cannot help but feel that the gang phenomenon and the youths with knives were one and the same thing, but given different labels.

When the events of 1885–87 are examined, there is little solid tangible evidence which gives credence to the High Rippers' existence as a dangerous gang. Reports speak of 'alleged' members and hint, by implication and association, at the gang's existence. The *Liverpool Review*, which was initially a firm believer in it, even claimed that the gang had settled in the Islington neighbourhood, because the area was 'a kind of neutral zone into which policemen seldom come', the area between Soho Street and Canterbury being identified as the worst. What exactly was the gang doing there? The roughs, the paper reported, congregated on and monopolized the pavements, where their 'favourite "game" appears to be solitary females who, without being subjected to further personal violence than a rough jostle, are insulted by the coarsest ribaldry'. Men, for their part, it was claimed, had their hats crushed and 'upon any retaliation' they were attacked. This was, by any standards, low-level, albeit very frightening, rowdyism that would hardly be worthy of the term 'gang behaviour'. The same journal, in an article on the North Dispensary, recounted that out of 176 cases treated in one week, 100 were wounds, 'such as fractures of the skull, stabs, cuts, scalp wounds, bruises and broken bones'. And yet there had been 'not one case of a prosecution'. Using rather uncertain maths, the *Review* then estimated that between 8000 and 9000 cases of violence a year went unreported and unpunished in the north end of Liverpool. The reason for this high figure of unprosecuted crime was, according to the paper, the lack of faith in the police. 'There is as much intimidation and terrorism in the portion of the city lying between Scotland-road and the river, as there is in the most disturbed district in Ireland that ever was filled with troops and constabulary'. In a sarcastic reference to the head constable's denial that the High Rip Gang existed, the *Review* went on:

All this is mere sensation no doubt, but pessimists may be permitted to doubt whether High Rip Gangs are not much more substantial entities than the Liverpool police force. The former, at any rate, give striking evidence of their existence while the latter appears to have become a purely ornamental body, or at any rate as far as the suppression of disorder is concerned.[38]

The police view of the so-called High Rip Gang was probably nearer the truth. There were groups of young men and lads who hung around on street corners insulting all who passed and who, on occasion, assaulted and robbed the innocent. But equally they appear to have fought among themselves. That they represented a major danger was perhaps an exaggeration. The crimes of violence and robbery attributed to them were little different from what had been occurring for decades; it was a case of new wine in old bottles. There was one significant difference from the earlier cornermen scares and that was the age of these youths, who appear to have been in their late teens or early 20s. Young men have always been considered an unruly and threatening cohort in society and the High Rippers were no different. They were not, however, in the same league as the Scuttlers in Manchester, who appeared to form more permanent neighbourhood gangs. Even the *Review*, in a remarkable *volte face*, wrote in March 1887: 'For ourselves, we may freely confess, since we have never made any secret of our conviction on this point, that we have always regarded the stories of the High Rip outrages as somewhat mythical, at any rate to the extent that we believed them to be worked up to a point of obvious exaggeration for sensational poster purposes'.[39]

Five years later, the *Liverpool Mercury* was reporting 'brutal stabbing outrages' very similar in character to the 'High-rip Gang' attacks. One instance concerned John Saunders, of Adelaide Street, Everton, who was stopped in Scotland Road by a group of roughs demanding money from him. When he said that he had none they knocked him to the ground and gave him a severe kicking, and finally stabbed him in the chest. Another concerned an Everton man who was likewise kicked and stabbed after refusing to hand over money. In a similar incident in late December 1893, two 'cowardly cornermen' were gaoled for six months each for three separate assaults in Boundary Street. As Mr Stewart, the magistrate, intimated, this kind of assault and robbery by groups of 'cornermen' was still a regular feature of the north end of Liverpool, especially during economic recessions or when the dock labourers were on strike. In the latter case, the men congregating on street corners were dockers in dispute and they saved their insults and shouts for the 'scabs' who had continued working.[40]

It may be possible to conclude that the High Rip Gang phenomenon was a heady brew of press exaggeration and sensationalism when the expense of the police was a local political issue. Underlying this froth was the persistent and endemic criminality among certain age groups in the north end, usually known by the label of cornermen. The High Rip Gang belonged on the spectrum of male-on-male violence. There was, for a short time, among some males in their late teens and early twenties, a fashion for gang warfare. How serious a problem they presented to the police is difficult to judge. The authorities, for their part, appeared remarkably sanguine about the so-called gangs, perhaps regarding the situation as no different from what they had been use to policing. On the other hand, it could be argued that the police were bound to play down the seriousness of the gang phenomenon. By admitting to their existence the police would have been highlighting their own ineffectiveness.

Street robbery and garrotting

WHAT WAS NOT TEMPORARY was the persistent problem of street robbery, usually accompanied by violence. In other cities, especially London and Manchester, such crimes, commonly labelled 'garrotting' from the 1860s, generated a moral panic. Garrotting became a media fear and received widespread coverage in 1862 when a Member of Parliament was assaulted and robbed within sight of the House of Commons. This particular incident set off a panic in the capital and the term was used to describe similar violent street robberies in other towns and cities.[41] That Liverpool did not join this media scare may have been significant, inasmuch as these crimes were neither particularly newsworthy nor especially threatening to the middle-class readership of local newspapers. Brutal street robberies in Liverpool tended to occur in the slum quarters, especially those close to the docks. Moreover, the victims of such attacks, if not poor themselves, were often sailors, newly paid off after lengthy voyages and carrying plenty of cash. Neither group of victims was considered important; nor were such attacks threatening to the middle classes, who seldom ventured into the slum neighbourhoods. On one rare occasion a couple were advised to leave St John's Market as they were 'too respectable for that neighbourhood'. Unfortunately, the warning came too late, as they were followed out of the market into Murray Street, where they were attacked and robbed by two men.[42]

Looking at garrotting in a bit more detail, there is little to distinguish this phenomenon from other crimes of violence. Indeed, garrotting as a crime was counted under the heading or highway robbery or robbery with violence for the purpose of police and judicial statistics. However, there was a qualitative difference between highway robbery and garrotting in the eyes of the press. The difference lay in method and style. Garrotting, which the *Cornhill Magazine* elevated to a 'science', usually involved between two and four assailants, one often being a woman who acted as a lure or distraction to a male victim. The strongest of the gang took the victim from behind, blocking his windpipe with his hands or elbow to almost strangulation point, while one or two others rifled through the victim's pockets. This latter role and that of the lure were the most vulnerable so far as the assailants were concerned, as they could later be identified by the victim and thus be arrested and prosecuted. The main distinguishing factor of this form of street robbery was the choking or garrotting of the victim. It was rare in such attacks for victims to be either permanently harmed or subjected to violence in which a weapon, a knife for example, was used. Strictly speaking, the newspapers did not consider street robberies where weapons were used (belts, knives, knuckle-dusters, skull-crackers or swords) to be garrotte robberies.[43]

In Liverpool it is possible to identify areas of the borough that were prone to garrotting and street robbery with violence. The main thoroughfare of Scotland Road and many of the smaller streets branching off it had many attractions for both locals and visiting seamen such as pubs, beer houses, markets and brothels. Not surprisingly, this area could prove dangerous for the unwary. Other 'hot spots' of garrotting lay between Lime Street, St John's Market and Williamson Square. The street that could claim to be the most dangerous in Liverpool during the nineteenth century was without doubt Chisenhale Street. Its notoriety attracted a *Mercury* reporter in 1873, shortly after a murder, and his report and description of the locale must have sent a vicarious thrill down the spines of the paper's readers:

> – a mother killed by her son, and in a locality in which crime is so common, as to be little heeded; a locality in which crime is so common that the inhabitants become callous, and the last spark of true sympathy seems crushed out. It is not the first time that the foulest crime – murder – has taken place in Chisenhale-street. Some years ago the 'long entry' became famous for a deed of blood, and three of the 'boys' were sent across the seas for their country's good.[44]

There followed lengthy descriptions of some of the courts, the crowded and unfurnished homes with their emaciated and semi-naked inhabitants. Although no reference is made to Ireland, the reader is left in little doubt as to where these people had originally come from, as the reporter makes a point of describing pictures of 'His Holiness Pius IX' and 'The Bleeding Heart' in a house close to the scene of the murder. Though the vicinity lacked both a church and a school, the street had three public houses and a beer house 'within something like 100 yards'. The reporter, however, failed to make reference to Chisenhale Street's most notorious spot, the bridge over the Leeds–Liverpool canal. Reports on a number of occasions alluded to the dangers in the vicinity of the canal bridge. In June 1853 a Portuguese sailor was thrown into the canal by 'ruffianly-looking fellows' – James Rosseter and his unidentified friends. The sailor told the policeman who fished him out of the water that he and shipmates had been stopped on the bridge by a group of men who demanded money. On refusing, he was picked up and thrown over the bridge. Only a fortnight earlier 'coloured' seaman Horace Jordan was robbed of 40 shillings and some dollars by John Monks. As in so many street robbery cases, the victim was asked to 'treat' the protagonist and, in this particular case, Jordan refused and ran into a pub for safety but on the way he had his cap snatched off his head. He came out only on the promise that he could have his cap back if he paid a small fee. This was an old trick, for when he got his purse out someone came up from behind and snatched it away.[45]

In both cases the assaults and robberies were examples of 'levying', the practice of demanding money with menaces. On the same night that the

Portuguese sailor was thrown over the bridge, another man escaped the clutches of William Smith, who, along with others, demanded a levy when crossing the bridge. Even as late as the 1890s, Chisenhale Street's notorious reputation remained, as pedestrians were still being asked to 'stand' drinks or face assault and robbery. In August 1892 police officers fished a woman from the canal and in March 1895 cattleman James Boylan of Newry was found unconscious on the bank of the canal close to the bridge. He was taken in the horse ambulance to the Northern Hospital, where he died four days later. The coroner's court decided he had, in an intoxicated state, fallen over the bridge, but given the history of this locality the death has to remain suspicious.[46] Sailors were frequent victims in this part of town partly because they were purposely directed from the docks up Chisenhale Street towards Vauxhall Road.

The frequency of assaults and robberies in Chisenhale Street raises that commonly asked question put by Victorians, where were the police? Interestingly, by 1870 the police had established a bridewell at the end of the street but this had done nothing to make the neighbourhood more law abiding. When one reads the court evidence relating to street robberies and garrottings it becomes evident that many victims were drunk when assaults occurred, and/or naive, and often these assaults took place within earshot of patrolling officers (which in itself suggests that the assailants were stupid, careless and/or desperate). One other possible explanation for the continued frequent violence on the streets of the north end of the town aired by newspapers and some members of the public was that the police allowed it to continue. Why should the police, so the argument ran, risk their lives ensuring the safety and security of people who cared little for them and the law, and who were little different from their assailants? This cynical logic was put forward by both the *Mercury* and the *Porcupine* in the immediate aftermath of the Tithebarn Street murder.

Victims were often selected because they were vulnerable in some obvious way. Drunken sailors staggering out of pubs and into the streets were a common target. Moreover, they often carried a pocket watch, the most frequently stolen object, and cash. Patrick Higgins received three months with hard labour for assaulting an intoxicated sailor and stealing £4 in Gerard Street. He also assaulted a witness to the assault, who had called for the police. Being new to Liverpool and asking for directions could place a person in danger. Old man Phillip Farley, fresh from New York, asked two men, one a returned convict, for directions to a hotel. Their friendliness and their keenness to help should have alerted him to the danger of assault; this duly occurred in Carlton Street. Farley had on him £25 in gold and silver, a cheque for £60, a gold case and toothpick and a copy of a will which left £10,000 to some people in Ireland. Drunken sailor John Fairhurst asked where he could find lodgings for the night. Michael Carroll, who had previously served nine months for 'killing a police officer', found only 1s 9d on him.[47]

Assailants seem to have displayed little fear of the consequences. Many were caught almost immediately by patrolling constables or they remained in the immediate neighbourhood, where they were later identified by the victims. This seemingly casual disregard for the law and the police may have been, in part, brought on by the fear (even 'terror') they were able to engender in the slum neighbourhoods. Take Thomas Parry and James Hession of Bootle, who were tried for assault with intent to rob in 1894. When the judge asked the arresting constable about the two defendants, he was told that they seldom worked and belonged to a gang 'who hold the shopkeepers of Derby-road in terror. Sailors are also afraid to go up Dundas-street ... unless they are in sufficient numbers to protect themselves'. It transpired that shopkeepers were afraid to give evidence against these youths and foreign sailors were reluctant to start prosecution proceedings.[48]

Conclusion

THROUGHOUT THE SECOND HALF of the nineteenth century there existed in Liverpool, particularly in the north end, bands of young men, poor, casually employed and apparently unafraid of the police. They did not hide their presence, for they congregated on street corners close to the beer houses and from these prominent locations watched, begged, threatened, abused and occasionally assaulted passers-by. During this period they went under various labels, not least roughs and cornermen, and their existence on occasion induced panic and fears. This was especially after a working man was murdered before a large crowd on Tithebarn Street in the summer of 1874. The crowd's reaction to this event was widely commented on in the national press and gave Liverpool a reputation for being a violent town, inhabited by people who, if not brutalized themselves, were fearful of bearing witness against these brutal men.

There was, throughout the 50 years, a spectrum of male violence that incorporated frequent street robberies, muggings and anti-social behaviour on the streets, which may have shaded into gang fighting. The latter induced a panic in the 1880s, when the so-called High Rip Gang was portrayed in some Liverpool newspapers as terrorizing streets in the north end of the town. The gang's existence was disputed by both the police and some local newspapers, which argued that the actual threat presented by these groups of young men was highly exaggerated. Whether the High Rippers constituted a proper gang is very difficult to judge. The most recent and detailed study, that by Macilwee, suggests that they were, to all intents and purposes, a gang. On the other hand, the High Rip Gang does not appear to have possessed longevity, a clear identity or purpose, in contrast to what Davies identified in the Scuttling gangs of Manchester and Salford. Whether the High Rippers constituted a gang is, in many ways, beside the point, for they belonged to that underclass of men who had always been perceived as a threat to the rest of Liverpool society. The police, for their part, always appeared confident in their dealings with this criminal group. However, the police were repeatedly criticized for their perceived inactivity and even invisibility whenever fears of these men were amplified. Whatever action the police took, the threat of the cornermen never went away, for they were still on the streets of Liverpool in 1900.

CHAPTER 8

Female savages and tippling viragoes: violent women

Criminal Women, as a class, are found to be more uncivilized than the savage, more degraded than the slave, less true to all natural and womanly instincts than the untutored squaw of a North American tribe.... As a class they are guilty of lying, theft, unchastity, drunkenness, slovenliness.[1]

WOMEN WHO COMMITTED CRIME were, in the eyes of respectable Victorians, traitors to their sex and far worse than criminal men. They were doubly bad for being both criminal and female. Why were they subjected to such vilification? Victorians had constructed an ideal model of the woman with all her 'natural' qualities and virtues. Within this construct, women were thought to be gentle, caring, unselfish, pure, patient and submissive. Moreover, they were able to achieve fulfilment of these qualities within the confines of the home and child rearing. In short, the Victorian middle classes created an ideal of the domestic goddess. In the reality of a Victorian Liverpool slum the construct was a nonsense but this did not prevent the newspapers from castigating women who fell short of this ideal. Headlines such as 'FEMALE SAVAGES IN CIRCUS-STREET' or 'ONE OF THE FURIES', the latter for an article which reported how a 'masculine-looking' Catherine Flynn with 70 previous convictions was sentenced to two months for assaulting a policeman, indicated to readers the type of women who turned to violence.[2]

If a woman failed to attain this ideal, with all its attendant virtues, she was regarded as deviant and possibly criminal. The stigma of the 'fallen' woman haunted Victorian do-gooders. Prostitutes who sold their bodies, and who tempted and enticed men in Eve-like ways, were thought to be contaminating society, both morally and physically. 'A bad woman', one commentator argued, 'is the worst of all creations'. Lacking the supposed feminine virtues and qualities such as compassion, kindness and selflessness, criminal women typically indulged in such crimes as petty theft, pickpocketing and shoplifting. Women represented, nationally, only about 15–20% of those tried in the higher courts. The present-day figure is of the same order. Liverpool women sent to trial for serious offences against the person were in the order of 20–27% in the Victorian period. In the lower courts women were frequently summarily charged with common assault and drunk and disorderly behaviour. The figures for the second half of the nineteenth century suggest the borough had an unusually high percentage of violent women, varying between 24% and 34% of all cases tried summarily in the magistrates' courts. In Liverpool the same faces and names came up before the courts with depressing regularity. Towards the end of the century, however, new ways of analysing female crime were emerging: instead of female criminals being 'bad', deviant women, some at least were now objects of pity and medical scrutiny and labelled 'sad' and 'mad'.[3]

Violent women were unusual and murderous women rarer still. For that very reason they became the focus of newspaper hyperbole. They were the very antithesis of all that was regarded as feminine. Journalists painted word pictures of these hard and uncaring 'monsters' who had defiled the home. *Famous Crimes*, the 'penny dreadful', described Catherine Flanagan, the infamous Liverpool poisoner of the 1880s, thus:

> Her fat sides shook with laughter at the lewd banter which passed for wit in the circle in which she shone. Her snub nose, typical of her race [Irish], her gross, fresh-complexioned, freckled face, her scarred eyebrow, her pendulous ears, whose deformity was emphasised by the heavy gold rings which depended on them, her abundant crop of wavy, greying black hair, and her strong Milesian [i.e. Irish] accent....

It left the readers in no doubt that here was an evil and ugly woman.[4] During the nineteenth century women who killed represented just 15% of all those committed for acts of homicide, if the figures for infant killing are removed from the statistics.

Infanticide

WOMEN, as we have seen, were far less violent than men. However, there was one crime peculiar to them and that was the killing of newborn children, legally termed infanticide. Theoretically, mothers who killed their illegitimate children were liable, under an act of 1624, to execution, but this was rarely enforced. From 1803 the law recognized a new crime – concealment of birth – which covered most cases of infanticide and which carried a maximum sentence of two years' imprisonment.[5] Children under one year of age were by far the largest group of homicide victims in Victorian England, and Liverpool was no exception. The coroner's court register for the borough between 1852 and 1865 records a total of 182 murders, of which 114, or 63%, related to children under one year of age.[6] In London in the 1860s, 80% of all coroners' courts verdicts of murder were applied to infant victims. One reason for the higher murder figure in the capital was probably related to the fact that coroners in London in the 1860s had been medically trained, whereas in Liverpool the coroner was legally trained. Legally trained coroners were less inclined to advise juries to reach murder verdicts if there was insufficient or imprecise evidence, whereas medically trained coroners, such as Middlesex's Edwin Lankester, were not averse to advising juries to find murder verdicts based on probability.

These very high percentages probably do not begin to explain the full scale of the deliberate killing of infants in Liverpool. The coroner's court registers for the 1850s and 1860s identify a further 160 suspicious infant deaths, for which juries reached the following verdicts: manslaughter, chance medley, found suffocated, exposure to cold, want of attention at birth, whether stillborn or born alive no evidence, stillborn, accidentally smothered and cause of death unknown. Some of the cases were probably hidden murders and may well have been interpreted differently in Middlesex. Of the different verdicts, 'chance medley' is the most intriguing. It was applied to infants who had suddenly died in their first year. This legal term covered apparently accidental deaths which had occurred in suspicious circumstances; it was not unlike the manslaughter verdict. In reality, coroners' juries might reach a verdict of chance medley where the infant had died of an overdose of the drug laudanum, as in the case of 17-day-old Ann Arron of Sparling Street in 1852. Whether the overdose was deliberately given to the baby was impossible to prove.

The sudden deaths of infants worried newspaper journalists and coroners alike. Hugh Shimmin wrote an impassioned article on the large number of inquests on smothered infants in Liverpool. There were, he wrote, 'for the year ending June 30th, 1862, inquests held on eighty-one smothered children! A very large proportion of these were slain on Saturday evenings or Sunday mornings'. Why this was the case was not, according to Shimmin, difficult to fathom. The cause of infant suffocation among Liverpool's working poor was, in his opinion, 'set down to the frightful prevalence of the vice of DRUNKENNESS'. Mothers, out on a spree on a Saturday night, would come home and drunkenly fall into bed where, during the night, they would roll on their infant and smother it. Although such instances were treated as accidental deaths and not 'deliberate murder', he felt that parents of 'intemperate, vicious, or degrading habits' should be held criminally responsible for their overlain children.[7]

When Liverpool's coroner, Frederick Lowndes, analysed the borough's inquests on newborn infants between 1869 and 1871, he discovered the following numbers of verdicts: murder, 28; want of attention at, during, or after birth, 19; found dead, 24; still-born, 34; other verdicts, 22. He clearly thought the murder figure was an underestimate and approvingly quoted a Mrs Meredith, who in conversation with female inmates of Brixton Prison, London, was told that older prisoners taught the younger ones how to kill newborn infants without being found out.[8] Obviously such claims cannot be proved, although there were occasional news items which suggested the possibility of illegality. In 1873, for example, the mother of a newborn infant, her mother and a neighbour were all cleared of the infant's death. The earlier inquest on the child's body had concluded that suffocation was the cause of death but had been unable to provide evidence of how this was achieved.[9]

Five years earlier, the *Liverpool Mercury* cast light on the role of midwives and the suspicious economics of burial. This arose from a case in which a woman in labour claimed she had attempted to attract a neighbour by banging on the thin dividing wall between their houses. However, she had, she claimed, fainted just before her child was born. On the arrival of a midwife, the mother told her that she had not heard the baby cry and, as a consequence, 'did not want a coroner's inquest over it'. The midwife duly obliged by certifying the child as stillborn, for whom the cost of burial would amount to a mere 2s 6d. On presentation of the certificate to the coroner's office, the beadle suspected there was something wrong and he stopped the burial. A post-mortem examination was then undertaken on the child's body and this revealed, according to the examining doctor, that the child had been born alive 'but had died from exposure and want of attention after birth'. No further action was taken, however, other than the censuring of the midwife for handing out a false certificate. This example hints at the important role a midwife might play in misleading the authorities as to the true scale of infanticide. One wonders how many of the 644 stillbirths buried in four Liverpool cemeteries in 1868 were what they were claimed to be.[10]

Infanticide, although not consistently viewed or counted as murder, did have an adverse impact on Liverpool's homicide statistics. Chapter 1 related how the port appeared to be in the grip of a murder epidemic in the second half of the 1860s. A closer reading of the head constable's annual reports shows that for a brief period infanticides were being counted as full-blown murders. In 1867–68, for example, 23 of the 27 murders listed in the report were in fact 'verdicts against persons unknown for the murder of infants found exposed'. This sudden interest in infanticide as murder reflected the official and popular concern for this crime at the time. The borough coroner, Mr Clarke Aspinall, wrote to the Home Secretary on the subject and was authorized by the government to offer rewards of £100 for information leading to the arrest and prosecution of persons guilty of killing infants. No rewards appear to have been claimed.[11]

Where doubts or suspicions occurred over the sudden deaths of newborn babies, smothering or suffocation were the most frequent causes of death. Foul play may have taken place, as in the case of a woman called McCann, who made no preparations for the arrival of her child. Historically, if a woman, on trial for infanticide, could prove that she had bought either clothes or bedding prior to the arrival of her baby, this was normally sufficient evidence for a jury to acquit her. The preparations, it was argued, were proof that the baby's arrival was welcomed. In McCann's case the baby's arrival was anything but welcomed. In response to her midwife's admonitions for her lack of preparations, she replied, 'It did not matter, the child would not live'. A day later, when the child was hungry and McCann was warned it might die for lack of food she exclaimed, 'And a good job too'. Within 48 hours the child was dead and yet the coroner's court and jury, while finding the circumstances surrounding the baby's death highly suspicious, returned an open verdict, which effectively ended any further investigations.[12]

When Louisa Brough admitted suffocating her newborn child, the jury decided she had been temporarily of unsound mind at the time of her confession. As a result, they found her not guilty of murder, manslaughter or concealment of birth. Suffocation as a means of killing was very hard to prove with or without an admission of guilt on the part of the mother. However, in an unusual case in 1893, widow and charwoman Mary Quinn was actually caught by the police in the act of smothering her newborn. Neighbours obviously had their suspicions about Quinn, as did the police, who were within yards of her door when she gave birth. One can only surmise they suspected her of killing an earlier child, in 1891. Unable to prove that killing, neighbours informed the police that Quinn was close to confinement and that she should be closely watched. When the police broke into her home it was initially reported that they found Quinn in the act of placing 14 bed irons on her mattress. On removing the weights and the mattress they found a newborn baby, seemingly dead, but a doctor was able to bring the child back to life. During a thorough search of her room the police found a box in which were the remains of a long-dead infant, presumably dating back to 1891. She was charged with attempted murder and concealment of birth. To the latter charge she pleaded guilty but she was found guilty of the former. For the two crimes she was sentenced to 15 years' penal servitude.[13]

The interest in the 'overlaying' of infants had coincided with the counting and inclusion of coroners' court murder verdicts on the newly born in the annual police statistics during the late 1860s. It would appear that infanticide was the predominant worry of this decade. Letters began to appear in the *Liverpool Mercury* in October 1865 highlighting the number of inquests on infants who had met their deaths 'through (as the verdicts say) being accidentally overlaid by their mothers'. Like Shimmin, the correspondent felt that drink was the primary cause and that the mothers were culpable of, at the very least, negligence. Twelve days later the same correspondent hinted that burial society membership may have been behind some of these mysterious deaths. By paying 1*d* a week, members, it was claimed, could collect £3 10*s* on the death of their children.[14]

The coroner, Mr Curry, at the conclusion of his court on 20 October 1865, informed the jury 'that they had had on some occasions lately as many as ten or twelve [overlayings] a week. How to put a stop to it he did not know. If there was evidence in the case of the parties being intoxicated he recommended their being sent for trial.' Just occasionally charges were indeed brought against women for overlaying. Sarah Ruddy, 'a wretched looking woman', was tried at the 1868 winter assizes for feloniously killing her two-month-old daughter Margaret. On coming home drunk, Ruddy asked her landlady to bring her child up to her bed so that she could breast-feed her. This was done, but when the landlady returned to Ruddy's room she found her asleep on top of her daughter. The court heard that she had been a good mother and that she had displayed sorrow for the death of her daughter and, as a consequence, the jury returned a verdict of not guilty.[15]

Even when the mother was wracked by guilt, as Margaret Shaw was, the courts had great difficulty in returning a guilty verdict. In Shaw's case, early in 1870, she, along with her husband, went to a policeman in Tithebarn Street, where she drunkenly told him, 'I have come to give myself up. I have lain upon my child and smothered it.' This was the second of Shaw's children to have died from smothering; the previous case had been investigated by the coroners in 1868. She was nonetheless acquitted at the following assizes.[16]

Such 'not guilty' verdicts highlight a problem peculiar to cases of alleged infanticide, namely the difficulty of interpreting the evidence. There were, by the mid-nineteenth century, a number of approved tests which most doctors believed provided evidence of foul play in the sudden death of infants. The most important was the lung test, in which the child's lungs were removed in order to see if they floated in water. If they floated, it suggested to doctors that the child had been born alive. Beyond that, however, there was little agreement between the experts on whether other post-mortem procedures pointed to the murder of newborn children.

Diverging medical opinion as to the cause of death remained a problem right through the nineteenth century. When widow Mary Jane Lunt of Bickerton Street, Lark Lane, was arrested on suspicion of having killed her child, the evidence against her appeared very damaging. In a desperate attempt to hide her shame, Lunt told her doctor that she was married to a man 'in a high position' and that her confinement had to be kept secret. On examining the body of the infant, which Lunt had claimed was stillborn, Dr Campbell refused to write out a death certificate. He told the police that death was the result of strangulation and neglect at birth. Dr Bennett, who carried out the post-mortem examination, thought death was caused by neglect and that whatever had been tied around the neck had not resulted in the baby's death. This difference of opinion led to a third doctor, no less than Dr Paull, professor of medical jurisprudence at the University of Liverpool, to adjudicate. He concluded that the baby had been born alive but had been strangled. Mary Lunt's response was to claim that she had felt ill and retired to bed, where she fainted or fell asleep. On awakening she found that she had given birth to the baby, which died in the following two or three hours. This highly unlikely story was not believed by the coroner's court jury, who concluded that death had been due to both neglect and strangulation. Initially, the police were, regardless, not going to offer any evidence against her when she was brought up before the magistrates the following week. However, news of 'some sensational evidence' ensured that the police had a change of heart and kept Lunt on remand. The sensational new evidence concerned the possible identity of the father, the lodger in Lunt's house, named Thomas Must, a constable with the county police force. He was, it was claimed, in the room at the time of the birth and removed all traces of the birth and the child. Such was the thoroughness of the job that Lunt's neighbour who slept with her that night told the court that she had had no idea that there had been a confinement. The assize trial in which both Lunt and Must were tried for murder hinged on the medical evidence. Disagreement existed between three doctors as to the cause of death, asphyxia, strangulation or death by neglect. In such circumstances a jury could hardly be expected to find the defendants guilty. The widow and her lodging constable could count themselves very fortunate in being acquitted.[17]

The example of Mary Lunt, though typical in that she was not found guilty of any crime, was unusual in one respect when it came to the sudden death of infants and the newly born. It was common to read in the pages of the local press of infants having been found wrapped in old clothing, newspaper or parcelled up in brown paper and abandoned on waste ground, in ash-pits, or even on doorsteps. A more symbolic and disturbing form of 'child dropping' was the not uncommon disposal of newly born infants in privies and cisterns. Some were, in all probability, stillbirths, while others displayed obvious signs of violence, such as blows to the head. Another method of disposing of unwanted babies was to throw them into the canal. Most disturbing of all was the discovery of live children partially buried under soil.[18]

A key aspect of infanticide cases concerned the identity of the mother: usually young, single, alone and in domestic service. These girls, in their desperation to remain 'respectable' and apparently chaste, killed their newborn infants. This, then, was the paradox: in order to prevent shame, they had to commit crimes that, if detected, would bring even greater shame upon them. This could lead, as in the case of Hannah Poole, to sad and poignant events. On being asked by her employer, Mr Roberts, hairdresser and owner of pastry shops in Castle Street and Church Street, if she was in the family way, Hannah 'distinctly' denied this was the case. However, shortly afterwards evidence was found in the kitchen where she lived of someone having delivered a baby in the night. When news of this was passed to the police, detective Carlisle arrested her and also discovered the body of a child in Hannah's box of clothing. A post-mortem examination suggested that the baby had been born alive but it was impossible to prove that Hannah had killed it. She was sentenced to 12 months with hard labour for the concealment of the birth.[19]

In what was headlined as a 'Shocking Case Of Child Murder In Liverpool', 22-year-old domestic servant Elizabeth Plent (or Plant) was arrested when it was discovered that she had cut the throat of her newly born child with a pair of scissors. A murder charge was inevitable, as she admitted to having killed the baby. Her case was an interesting one when it came up for trial at the March assizes. Her defence barrister put forward a number of arguments, not least that there was insufficient evidence to show that there had been a live birth. Moreover, even if the child had been born alive, he continued, then death had either been accidentally caused by the mother during self-delivery or while she was 'suffering under temporary mental derangement'. All these points were enough to convince the jury that she was guilty only of manslaughter, with the usual recommendation for mercy, rather than murder.

The judge, before sentencing Plent, gave a remarkably candid and unusual speech in which he and the jury 'had been ingenious' in finding a way of reducing her crime from murder to manslaughter and, having done so, it was his duty to sentence her on the basis of what he 'believed to be practically the truth'. On this he was most explicit, for he was convinced that the child had been born alive and that she had killed it in order to conceal her shame. 'He feared much', he continued, 'that it was more than mere manslaughter; he feared much that if they had acted according to the truth of the case the prisoner would have been found guilty of murder, and nothing else'. It was murder in all but name and this is why, in part, he rejected the jury's recommendation of mercy. He continued:

> The jury had recommended the prisoner to mercy. It was obvious why; for, after all, the prisoner was a woman – a young woman – and nobody could look upon her, fallen as she was, ruined as she was, without the pity which must fill the heart of every man who saw a woman, even if brought there by her own crime, in such a state. But he (the learned judge) must think of what happened throughout the country; he must think of the common occurrence of this crime; he must think of the horrible iniquity which prevailed in this country, where new-born child after new-born child was killed for the sake of hiding the shame of the mother, and where women who did this horrible thing became degraded, and degraded each other, unless the crime can be put an end to.

During this speech, the reporter noted the prisoner's 'most eccentric manner in the dock, interrupting the proceedings with angry remarks, and at times crying bitterly'. Given the content of the judge's speech, her behaviour would seem, to modern eyes, rational and understandable. The judge's words indicated he was going to be severe towards her and he sentenced Plent to 10 years' penal servitude.[20]

As the judge had indicated before passing the harsh sentence, the law, juries and judges generally found ways to mitigate the punishments for women who killed their newborn infants. All sorts of explanations were put forward to lessen the woman's guilt or punishment. As shown above, the most influential so far as the courts were concerned was the medical evidence, or the lack of it. Proof of independent life for the child was notoriously hard to establish and this left the way open for women to claim that they had experienced stillbirths. Women in such circumstances remained liable to punishment for having concealed the birth, for which the maximum penalty was two years' imprisonment. Other medical arguments in defence of women who killed their children ranged from ignorance concerning what to do once the birth had taken place (for example, how to deal with the umbilical cord) through to the mental health of the mother. Puerperal fever, causing temporary mania, was a well known illness afflicting women after childbirth. It was widely accepted that they could harm or kill their infants when suffering from the effects of the fever, but they were not considered responsible for their actions and would be acquitted of any crime.

More difficult to assess was society's attitude towards single women who killed their illegitimate offspring. As the judge in the Plent case above indicated, a measure of sympathy was patronizingly offered to women who found themselves pregnant. An understanding of the shame they may have felt or been made to feel by society at large is evident in juries' frequent recommendations to mercy. Moreover, there was an often unspoken recognition that women, in their ignorance or naivety, could have been seduced and thus found themselves almost innocently caught up in an unwanted pregnancy and birth, abandoned by their male lover or partner. For all these reasons, juries and judges, usually, found ways to acquit women accused of killing their children, or at least to punish them leniently. This partly explains the very low statistics for infanticide and concealment.

When it came to married women, even if widowed, who concealed the birth of children whom they had had out of wedlock, society and the law displayed little sympathy. In the case of Elizabeth Kirkbride, a seemingly respectable widow who had taken apartments in Sutton Street, Tuebrook, the public learnt with mounting incredulity of the serial discovery of tin boxes containing the bones of babies. In all, six skeletons were found in Tuebrook and Penrith, where she had previously resided. Given that three of the bodies had been found further north and that all six infants would have been born in either Westmorland or Cumberland, where Kirkbride had lived for a number of years after the death of her husband, she was delivered into the custody of the Cumberland police. Followed by a large and noisy crowd, composed mainly of women hooting and booing her, Kirkbride was put on a train at Lime Street. Her behaviour was closely scrutinized by reporters, who picked up on and described any of her mannerisms deemed to be unfeminine or indicative of her guilt. She was described as 'sullen and downcast, and indifferent to the curiosity' of onlookers. She had shed not a single tear since her arrest. Eventually tried at Appleby, Kirkbride pleaded guilty to concealing the birth of three children at Helton, Westmorland, which meant that she was able to evade any difficult questions relating to the six bodies, one of which was found with a ligature around its neck. This suggested strangulation but the doctors who undertook the inquests were never able to prove whether the babies had been born alive. In sentencing her, Justice Manisty said:

> Neither he nor Baron Huddleston [the other presiding judge] had the slightest moral doubt that the prisoner had been guilty of violence to those children when they were alive. In three cases out of five it was perfectly clear that violence was resorted to, and in two cases there were clear marks of violence which would have caused death. She must answer to her conscience whether she did tie those cords and did cause the death of those children.

After these stern words he indicated that she deserved more than the maximum two years' imprisonment for each concealment. Rather surprisingly, he sentenced her to a mere nine months with hard labour for each of the three children, making a total two years and three months. One wonders if her attempt at exposing and shaming the father of these children had won her some sympathy. She alleged he was Thomas Moss, a tea and ham and bacon dealer of Askham, near Penrith, who had, she alleged, repeatedly promised to marry her but then married another.[21]

The killing of young children

THE LAW and those whose duty it was to implement it displayed far less understanding and flexibility when it came to adjudicating on the killing of older infants and children. Nonetheless, in many respects the circumstances surrounding the killing of the very young were similar to those of the infanticide cases. Instances of suspicious deaths can be found in the local newspapers, such as the body of a four-week-old baby girl floating in the canal near Vauxhall Road, that of a two-month-old boy found in the canal near Burlington Bridge, or the mysterious death of 22-month-old Catherine Devitt, whose body was examined as a result of her sudden demise. The surgeon reported finding a ruptured liver, 'arising from violence', and several other marks of violence on her head and body. Her mother, who had only recently come out of prison, was not charged. Another mother to fall under suspicion for the double murder of her children, Bridget Cochrane, a hawker of St Martin Street, was found not guilty of poisoning them at the summer assizes of 1857.[22]

The fate of Joseph Edwards, 21-month-old son of 'unfortunate' Mary Ellen Edwards of Blake Street, brought to light how easy it was to kill a young child. A neighbour reported seeing a wet counterpane, later described as a toilet cover, on the child's face. Joseph was found dead with the wet cloth still on his face. Other evidence indicated little in the way of maternal feelings on Mary Ellen's part. She had frequently ill treated her son, starved him and had said, 'I will not rear him for the father, I will kill him', and 'he is my child, and if I kill him I shall have to suffer for it'. It transpired during the trial that he had only recently been returned to his mother because she could no longer afford to pay someone else to bring him up. Clearly the child was unloved and unwanted. Edwards was fortunate in being tried for and found guilty of manslaughter, for which she received 10 years' penal servitude.[23]

One of the notorious scandals of the Victorian era, and one which writers and journalists highlighted, concerned 'baby farming' – the commercial killing of babies under the guise of child rearing or fostering. Some women would offer to bring up babies for about six shillings a week and the mothers, who were either desperate to keep their reputations intact or needed to work without the encumbrance of child rearing, would pay them a lump sum of £1 for example, with a promise of more payments later. Needless to say, the women often gave a false name and address, which meant that once the money had been spent by the foster mother there was no more forthcoming. At this point the women had to get rid of the child or attempt to place it in the workhouse.[24]

In Liverpool only one such major criminal concern came to light during this period, although others undoubtedly existed but presumably escaped detection. Although headlined as 'THE TRANMERE BABY FARMING CASE', on account of where the two defendants were arrested, it soon transpired that they had, in 1874, operated out of Liverpool. Husband and wife John and Catherine Barnes (alias Hamilton, Hall and other names) were arrested in September 1879 and charged at Birkenhead magistrates' court with the murder of two infants through gradual starvation. During the course of police enquiries into the couple's movements, it was found that they had lived at seven or eight different addresses in Liverpool and its neighbourhood. In that time it was thought between 30 and 40 children had passed through their hands and that 'their lives have been sacrificed by starvation or some other method'. The police were able to identify and trace at least 18 children who had been with the prisoners during the previous 10 years. However, only three infants were cited as victims at the murder trial at the end of October at Chester.

The Barneses would place and answer advertisements for children to adopt, in one particular case going as far as Hereford to collect Alice (one of the deceased infants) and £30 from the single mother. That agreement read: 'I agree to take your little girl for ever, and bring it up as my own, for £30, and not to trouble any one belonging to her again from this date.' In addition to receiving the infant and the money, the Barneses took ownership of a considerable amount of baby clothing and blankets, which fetched a good sum at the pawn shops. The next child, Mabel, was collected from Leeds, but this time a Mr Blythe of Scholes, near Wigan, who had answered an adoption advertisement in the *Manchester Courier* and was father of the child, negotiated to pay only £15. During his summing up the judge strongly condemned such fathers who appeared anxious to be rid of their children at any cost. The mothers, however, were in his opinion more worthy of pity, as they often appeared reluctant to give up their children. Lord Justice Brett told the defendants after they were found guilty of manslaughter:

> you have been found guilty of a series of premeditated crimes. You have for years carried on the vilest trade that human malignity ever invented, and you have carried it on with a brutality and cruelty that cannot be exaggerated. The woman had been unsexed, the man has been unhumanised, and a more dangerous and a more fatal course of conduct with regard to these children I cannot imagine. I have not a doubt that during the past ten years you have decoyed into your possession as many as 18 children. (sensation in court)
>
> And I cannot doubt but almost all those children have died in consequence of your conduct. The jury, guided by me, have taken that merciful view which the law of England requires. It may be that in your brutal minds you had not the definite intention that these children should die, but you were utterly reckless and careless whether they died or not, and your minds were made up to treat them with the greatest cruelty and neglect. The jury have rightly abstained from finding a verdict of murder ... but they have found you guilty of as bad a case of manslaughter as was ever brought to the attention of a court. You have been guilty of crimes, of successive crimes, carried on for years from the vilest and the most mercenary motives, each of which crimes was only by a hair's breadth short of murder. Manslaughter is a crime which may be slight, but it may be, and sometimes is, a hair's breadth from murder. Your crime is but by a hair's breadth from murder.[25]

He then sentenced both to penal servitude for life, which brought forth 'slight applause'. The case, which had attracted enormous interest and crowds in and around court, had not only exposed the limitations of the Infant Life Protection Act of 1872, it had also set off a scare in the Merseyside area. 'A number of women in Toxteth-park', the *Times* reported three weeks after the trial, 'have applied to the parish authorities to relieve them of the nameless children they had undertaken to bring up, the parents being young women of respectable appearance who had failed to continue contributions for the maintenance of their offspring'.[26] The Poor Law guardians refused to take on these extra burdens, arguing that the women should have made more careful enquiries into the parents of the farmed out children.

Murder of their offspring by mothers was considered altogether unnatural and women who committed such crimes could be labelled 'mad', 'sad' or 'bad' depending on the circumstances of the child's demise. These three labels were by no means exclusive: a woman could be both mad and sad, although when deemed 'bad' she would receive neither the sympathy of society and the court nor the explanations of the burgeoning science of psychiatry. The case of Charlotte Elliot is an interesting one, in that it appears from the court proceedings to have encompassed all three headings at some point. Her story reads like a Victorian tragedy. She had been seduced, made pregnant and abandoned. Overcome with shame at the birth of her illegitimate child and weighed down with depression, Elliot cut the baby's throat. It was quite clear that she had won over the sympathy of the jury and local press but this did not prevent the judge going through the theatre of donning his black cap and sentencing her to death. Her reprieve came two weeks later, the *Mercury* noting that 'it would have been an undue stretch of the law to have exacted the extreme penalty in such a case as this'.[27]

Women who killed adults

RARELY DID WOMEN kill adults, and even more rarely did they suffer the most extreme punishment of execution. When 30-year-old Mary Williams, of Raleigh Street, Bootle, was executed on 30 August 1874, the local newspaper noted that she was the first woman to be hanged at Kirkdale gaol for over 30 years. Betty Eccles in 1843 and Betty Rowland in 1836 had been the two previous unfortunate victims of the noose. And even in Williams' case it was assumed that she would receive a last-minute reprieve because she was a woman and, more importantly, because she had 'received great provocation from the man she killed'.[28]

From a sample of 29 women who were tried for killing other adults in Liverpool between 1850 and 1900 some surprising patterns emerge.[29] It was thought by Victorians and by historians that women, because of their physique and lack of physical strength, tended to use their guile in killing their victims, who were usually close relatives. This was often thought to mean that poison was their method of choice, for women through their domestic duties had access to arsenic (used as rat poison), which they could disguise in the cooking of rice pudding, for example. In the study sample, however, poison was used on only four victims. Obviously, there may well have been many more cases of poisonings which were successful and undetected: that was, after all, the whole point of deploying such a method of killing. However, in the known cases it was well down the list of methods of killing. The most frequent means, with nine cases, was the use of a poker or other household implements such as irons and fenders. Broken glasses and bottles as weapons were used in four cases, and stabbings and general fighting each similarly led to four deaths. Shooting and the throwing of oil lamps accounted for two deaths apiece.

The other surprising result concerned the victims of these killings. Most, 14, were neighbours or fellow house lodgers, followed by friends – six victims. Only three relatives were found among the 28 victims. Sixteen of the victims were female and 12 male. Of the 29 defendants, five were found guilty of murder, 13 of manslaughter and two of unlawful killing, while six were discharged or acquitted. There were two main reasons for the high manslaughter count: first, both the victims and defendants were often drunk during a fight and as such it was difficult to prove intent to kill; second, in five cases death resulted some time after a fight, when infection, erysipelas, was found to have been the cause of death. In only eight cases did the defendants act in the company of others, and in all but two cases this was with other women.

The profile of homicidal women is really not very different from that of male killers. They fought, used weapons, lost their tempers and got into drunken fatal brawls in the same manner as men. One significant difference does present itself, however. Their victims were nearly always known to them. Only one victim appears to have been a total stranger and that was when drunken Susan Campbell stabbed a sailor who had refused to buy her a drink.[30] Most killings were the result of drunken rows with fellow house lodgers and immediate neighbours over mundane, but important, matters such as money, debt, petty jealousies and even noise. Headlined 'TRAGEDY IN LIVERPOOL. LIFE IN THE SLUMS. SHOCKING DEATH OF A WOMAN', one report painted a detailed picture of Lower Blenheim Street, a slum street which in 1899 had yet to be cleared away by the council. Here a domestic row upstairs between Catherine Levens and her husband at 2 a.m. brought shouts from John Tracy in the room below for quiet so that he and his wife could have some sleep. After an argument with the Tracys in their rooms, Mrs Levens went back upstairs but returned with a lighted paraffin lamp, which she hurled at the couple, who were in bed. Immediately the couple and their bedclothes burst into flames and, despite the efforts of neighbours, both died from the burns and shock. Later that year at the assizes Levens was found guilty of murder and sentenced to death, although this was later reprieved.[31]

Neighbourhood rows in the poorer districts of the city, where overcrowding would have stoked festering hatreds, occasionally blew up into fatal tragedies. In such places silence on the part of possible witnesses was not unusual. In 1895 the coroner's court met to investigate the death of Mary Digman, of Kempston Street, but had to adjourn because the police had trouble obtaining evidence. When the trial resumed witnesses seemed to give confusing or contradictory statements, so much so that the jury returned an open verdict, which seemed to clear Jessie Burgess, the chief suspect.[32]

Not all unlawful killings occurred in such mysterious circumstances. When Patrick McDermott took his drunken and disorderly neighbour Bridget Daley by the arm and led her back to her cellar in a court off Grosvenor Street, he was hoping to prevent her from doing greater mischief than throwing dirt at her neighbours. When cries of 'murder' from the cellar were answered, two men found McDermott lying on his back and Daley kneeling beside him, repeatedly striking his head with a cleaver. When the trial came up at the following assize she was found guilty of manslaughter. Before the judge could sentence her she fell on her knees in the dock and swore that 'when she got out she would have it out' of a woman who had given evidence against her. She added that the people of her street were 'all strangers to her, and were a false bad lot'. It was highly unlikely she would have ever had it out against the witness, as the judge sentenced the

62-year-old to 20 years' penal servitude – a heavy sentence, influenced, no doubt, by her 10 previous convictions for assaults and drunk and disorderly behaviour. She was, the judge said, not only a woman of a 'treacherously cruel disposition', but she had attacked her victim like 'a tigress more than a human being'.[33]

Another defendant who was unpopular with some of her neighbours was Mary Williams. Abandoned by her father (her mother being dead) at the age of 12, married unhappily for 10 years, mother of seven and still breastfeeding an eight-month-old child, she had many mitigating factors in her favour. However, her adult life was remarkable for its brutality, poverty and ignorance. In her favour were the events which were said to have led her to shoot dead her neighbour, Nicholas Manning. It was reported that she had been held against her will by Manning and some of his relatives a few weeks prior to the shooting. On the day of the murder, she once again had been beaten by two sisters and a brother-in-law of Manning, the scars of which were evident when the police came to arrest her.

Against these factors was her reputation as a 'virago' with a quarrelsome disposition. Furthermore, there were the damning eyewitness accounts of her shooting Manning from close range and her unrepentant confession of 'Yes and I'll do it again; and there's two or three more before the night's over as I will do it to'. Later, when the prospect of a reprieve began to retreat, she repeatedly proclaimed her innocence, citing her husband to be the guilty party who pulled the trigger. However, her status as a mother and the support from the Bootle community where it was said she had been 'subject to great brutality at the hands of …, it now transpires, … a savage brutal fellow and the terror of the neighbourhood', were not sufficient to save her.[34]

The *Liverpool Mercury*, in its treatment of Williams, was in part sympathetic to her plight, dwelling on her final farewells to her children, who 'clung about their unfortunate mother' in the condemned cell in Kirkdale prison. They were, however, also mindful of her crime and her reputation prior to the murder. She did not quite fit the stereotype of the murdering woman in the same way that two sisters, Flanagan and Higgins, did in 1883–84. These two women poisoned at least four people in order to claim the insurance money which they had previously taken out on their victims' lives. This was Liverpool's most notorious crime of the nineteenth century and one which attracted the attention of the nation's newspapers.

Flanagan and Higgins: 'the Liverpool poisoners'

THE STORY OF Catherine Flanagan (variously spelt Flannagan, Flannigan) and Margaret Higgins (illustration 3) has been frequently and ably told by historians, especially by Angela Brabin.[35] Their known murders – four victims in all but there were almost certainly six more – eventually came to light in late 1883, when the brother of the fourth victim went to the coroner's office after neighbours had told him of their suspicions. After stopping the burial in dramatic fashion – the wake was halted just when the body was about to be placed in the coffin – doctors conducted a post-mortem examination on the spot. Some organs were removed which later revealed traces of arsenic in the body of Thomas Higgins, husband of Margaret. Further enquires and exhumations revealed the deaths of: 18-year-old Margaret Jennings, long time lodger of Flanagan in January 1883; John Flanagan, son of Catherine, in 1880; and Mary Higgins, 10-year-old step-daughter of Margaret, in 1882.

It is worth dwelling on why Victorians found this case, headlined 'THE WHOLESALE POISONINGS', so shocking and notorious. First, the victims were either related, through marriage or blood, or were otherwise close to the murderesses. By killing such victims, the women were portrayed as under-mining not only the core social relationships of Victorian Britain, family and marriage, but also epitomized the very reverse of nineteenth-century female domesticity. Second, by poisoning their victims, these women were actually using the very domestic skills considered so essential to home-making to achieve their nefarious ends. If the family were not safe in the bosom of the mother and the home, then they were not safe anywhere. Much emphasis was placed on the way Catherine Flanagan 'nursed' the dying Thomas in his Ascot Street cellar. The final point of interest for Victorians concerned the motive for these murders, namely pecuniary gain. One often repeated turn of phrase from their trial was emphasized by the press. It was reported how

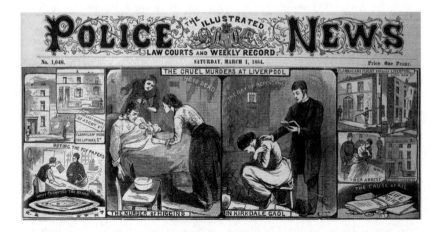

Illustration 3 'The cruel murders at Liverpool' (Flanagan and Higgins), *Illustrated Police News*, 1 March 1884. Reproduced with the permission of the British Library, Colindale Newspaper Library.

the judge characterized the crime 'as one so horrible, carried out so cruelly and relentlessly, and for motives so sordid, that it made one shudder to think of the depths to which our common humanity was capable of sinking'. Although neither woman was able to read or write, Flanagan was cunning enough to spot a (literally fatal) weakness in the way life insurance business was carried on. She was able to insure her victims' lives without their knowledge. In the case of their last victim, Thomas Higgins, he was insured with five different companies for over £100. Her ingenuity also extended to extracting arsenic from 'Infallible fly papers' and putting it into liquid form for her victims to drink. Whether the two women had themselves thought up this system of obtaining poison and insuring the unsuspecting victims is hard to determine, as it was reported that they had told the police of three other women who had practised similar methods. Arrests were widely anticipated but none appears to have been made.

Although the other victims were insured for considerably less, it would seem that murdering a victim on a regular basis would have provided a tidy annual income for these poor women, who, it was alleged, were fond of drinking. Their trial was a sensation, with vast and angry crowds congregating daily for three days outside St George's Hall. It would seem their fury had much to do with the callousness and scheming of the two women, who had slowly and deliberately poisoned people close to them. It was the ultimate betrayal of trust. From the moment of Flanagan's capture at 39 Ono Street, Wellington Road, Wavertree, she received very little sympathy from the people of Liverpool. Followed by a 'jeering crowd of villagers', the county police had some difficulty in preventing onlookers from assaulting her during the handover to the city police. When the two sisters were finally executed, over 1000 people braved bitter weather and falling snow outside the gates of Kirkdale gaol. In fact, the only time Flanagan experienced support was when she went on the run for 11 days after the wake for Thomas Higgins had been halted and before her arrest in Wavertree. During that time she moved lodgings on a number of occasions and in at least one case her identity was known but no one reported her to the police.

Fighting women in the neighbourhood

THE CRIMES OF Flanagan and Higgins were not typical of the violent female actions brought to the notice of the police and magistrates on a weekly or even daily basis. This raises a number of important questions. Who fought and whom did women fight? Why and where did they fight? And how did women fight? In posing such questions, there is an underlying assumption that women fought differently from men. Apart from being unladylike, feminine virtues did not include challenges to strip off and fight fairly; women were thought to engage in particularly vicious and 'unfair' methods of fighting. Hair pulling, scratching and biting, to name but three, were commonly regarded as female. One stipendiary magistrate, in a throw-away remark when dealing with a case of a man found guilty of biting, complained that biting 'used to be confined to women, but now men were doing it'.[36] The supposedly feminine tactics involved close engagement between the combatants, clinging on with their hands or teeth, and drawing blood through gouging the nails into flesh, as opposed to the brief, but no less vicious, punch of the fist. Basically, hair pulling, scratching and biting were considered 'below the belt' tactics if used by men. But how true is the stereotype of 'wild' women using their bodies as weapons?

The mechanics of fighting have first to be considered. Women wore cumbersome skirts which reached down almost to the floor. Taking that into consideration, along with their relatively smaller and lighter physiques, in comparison with men, kicking was not necessarily a practical mode of fighting for women. Although there are occasional references to women kicking their opponents, it would be fair to conclude that this method was not favoured by women wanting to do serious damage to their victims. Biting, on the other hand, was reported in the press, and was usually headlined 'CANNIBALISM'; in one particular case, 'BITING AN EAR OFF AND EATING IT' was used. This latter headline referred to the case of Caroline Rogers, who was accused of biting 'a large portion' of Lucy Saunder's ear off. She was then seen to '"crunch" something in her mouth, and the inference was that she ate the portion bitten off'. Witnesses alleged she then threatened 'to eat' anybody who came near. When Isabella M'Cann tried to break up an argument between a sailor and Mary Ann Douglas in Crosshall Street, the latter bit a four-inch chunk out of her arm and spat it out on to the street. The surgeon noted that the tendons and muscles of the victim's arm had been left exposed. Such a method of fighting was, in the eyes of the press and magistrates, the work of 'savages'.[37]

In examining a sample of over 500 cases in which women were the primary aggressors, the feature which strikes the modern reader is the sheer variety of weapons used by them. Women appear to have grabbed whatever was close at hand when stepping up a quarrel to a fight. Table 4 illustrates this. The weapons specified in table 4 were not always used to the exclusion of others. For example, when women fought in street rows, bricks, pokers, fists and crockery were probably deployed by the warring factions but the press tended to describe the chaos in general terms. The weapons listed are the ones cited in the press reports as being the primary cause of an injury to the victim.

While the list is remarkably diverse in terms of both modes of fighting and the weapons used, some of the objects echo the domestic circumstances of the confrontations. Knives were not of the same type as used by men, for example, but were what was lying on the kitchen table at the time (carving or bread knives, for instance). Other domestic implements,

Table 4 Modes of fighting and weapons used by women, 1850–1900

	Number of cases
Assault (unspecified), including kicking, scratching, punching	147
Stabbing, slashing: with knives, oyster shells, scissors, cans, forks, fire-scraper, etc.	119
Domestic implements: pokers, jugs, crockery, rolling pins, chamber pots, candlesticks, fenders	114
Glass: tumblers, bottles, glasses	36
Biting	24
Hitting with bricks, life-preservers, hammers	38
Boiling liquids, acid, lamps, etc.	13
Shooting: firearms, slingshot	5
Throwing out of window, downstairs	5
Poison	3
Total	504

Figures calculated from cases reported in the *Liverpool Mercury* between 1850 and 1900.

not least pokers, crockery and jugs, again suggest the fighting started in or near the home. When women 'glassed' others, it could just as well have occurred in the pub as in the home. General assaults tended to occur in the street, when women were drunkenly wandering home, and often involved policemen struggling to arrest them.

Was fighting gendered? That is, did women fight in different ways from men? They did not conform to the simple stereotypes and clichés of scratching and hair pulling, which were commonly thought to be the female practice. Rarely, though, did they emulate men in their ritual of calling their opponents out to 'fight fair' in the street. Stripping off the top most garments down to the bare chest was not something women would have resorted to. Jane M'Nee, however, behaved very like a man when she followed Margaret Thorpe out of the magistrates' court and challenged her to fight. She 'partially stripped' off before striking her opponent. Stand-up fights between women did take place, or so it was claimed on occasion by witnesses at trials, but one does wonder if they made such statements only to try to get their female acquaintances out of trouble. When Bella Murphy clashed with neighbour and beer house keeper Ellen Bowen in Jamaica Street pokers had first been used. However, a witness claimed it was a 'fair stand-up fight', during which they fought for some minutes in front of a crowd who were there 'to see fair play'. One male onlooker told the court that the two had fought '"manfully and womanfully", and neither of them had much to complain of, but the prisoner was the "best woman"'.[38]

Women commonly moved with little warning from verbal argument or abuse to fighting. The typical male signals of the challenge, the threatening pose or stance, were not in women's body language vocabulary. Ellen Barton, for example, argued with Annie Curran about drinking with her husband. Suddenly the latter struck Ellen in the face with a pair of scissors, disfiguring her in the process. Aiming at the face and head was, in fact, a feature of female fighting. Victims of both sexes were frequently slashed or cut by women. Jane Higgins of Gerrard Street was arrested after stabbing Patrick Lavelle seven times 'about the face, neck and ears'. After expressing regret for what she had done Higgins added, 'but I will kill him when I get out'.[39]

Almost invariably women knew their opponents. The violence does not appear to have been random, opportunist or casual in the way that men's acts of violence often were. Therefore the 'who', 'why' and 'where' of female violence are often interlinked. Neighbours and fellow lodgers figure heavily as victims. Such assaults and fights highlight the petty jealousies, poverty and overcrowding of the slums and court life in Liverpool. Not surprisingly, money, or more accurately debt, was often cited as a reason for fights. When Mary Burns, occupier of a cellar in Sherwood Street, told Theresa Cochrane, the landlady, that she could not pay the rent, the latter called in Rose Maria Boyle to take 'the rent out of her in blows'. The two women struck Mary with a jug, a pair of bellows and a poker. Cochrane, who was smiling throughout the court case, was reprimanded by the magistrate, who remarked that she 'seemed lost to all sense of propriety and decency, and were fit only to live in a country of savages'. Mary Scohill was charged with wounding her lodger, Richard Cannell, whom she caught doing a moonlight flit with his furniture from her Shaftsbury Street home. By striking him on the head with a cup, Scohill had set off a street-wide 'row'.[40]

Frequently resort was made to moneylenders, usually when it was no longer possible to pawn items of clothing. Non-payment of debts with interest was then a cause of woman-on-woman violence. Most moneylenders were women and many of their customers were also female. Husbands very often did not know their wives were borrowing. It was considered shameful not to pay back money owed and this fact was exploited to the full by the moneylender. The latter knew that if she made a row on the doorstep of the debtor, this would disgrace and shame her in the eyes of her neighbours. Other female moneylenders used 'personal terrorism to enforce repayment', by breaking into the house, armed with pokers, and threatening debtors with personal injury. The case between moneylender Annie Welsh and her customer Ann Connor brought to light the enormously high interest rates charged by the former. In lending Connor four shillings, Welsh charged 800% interest but became unconvinced that she would ever be repaid. This led to a drunken fight between the two, of which Welsh was accused of being the instigator.[41] By the turn of the century, the usual rate of interest was approximately 17% (specified as two pence in the shilling) for the first week, rising to 25% in the second week.

Simmering resentments, gossip and 'tittle tattle' appear to have presaged more physical confrontations. Caroline Charnley, fined only 20 shillings, complained in court that her neighbour, Ellen Woodruff, had been name calling her husband, but that hot bacon fat, which was in her frying pan, accidentally slipped from her pan onto Woodruff's face, burning it severely. Jealousy, sexual or otherwise, lay behind a number of cases where wives claimed their husbands were drinking or socializing with other women.[42]

The notorious murder in 1873 of Mary Corrigan by her son Thomas forced neighbours in Chisenhale Street to take sides. Julia Maddocks of the same street upset neighbour Mary Eccleston when she said that it 'serve him right, and anybody else who would do such a thing to their parents', when he was sentenced to death for the offence. This appears to have enraged Eccleston, who struck her on the head with a piece of iron and then called to her son, 'Kick the head off her, and give her the same as Mrs Corrigan got'. She received a fine of 20 shillings. This was not the first time the Corrigan murder had created tensions in the neighbourhood. Chief prosecution witness Mrs Joanna Harris was visited by nine women, some of whom were drunk, and threatened with death by ringleader Ellen Peacock for perjury against Thomas Corrigan. In her defence, Peacock claimed that she was upset that Mrs Harris had done nothing to stop Corrigan killing her mother. This was not believed.[43]

Interfering with or threatening witnesses in court cases was a particularly common and peculiarly female crime throughout the Victorian era. The preponderance of females found guilty of assaulting and threatening witnesses may suggest that men interfered with male witnesses in similar ways but the latter were expected to deal with the threats by themselves, without recourse to the criminal justice system. However, groups of women lay in wait outside the magistrates' court for prosecutors who had either reported their friends or themselves. 'Two women of disreputable character', it was reported, waylaid an elderly female witness who had given evidence against two male pickpockets a few days earlier. In order to protect witnesses, Mr Mansfield, the magistrate, sentenced one to either pay a £5 fine or in default to serve three months with hard labour. Other relatives or partners of the recently prosecuted waited until witnesses arrived back at home, as in the case against Catherine Scavey of Great Crosshall Street. Scavey knocked out witness Mary Ann Houghton, who was responsible for six people being placed in gaol. Houghton had also to put up with being followed by the friends of one of the suspects. In this case the magistrate, Mr Raffles, threatened to lock up the entire street if need be to stamp out witness intimidation. Such 'snitching' could lead to long-term animosity. Ann Binds of Stockdale Street, for example, was stabbed on her left eyelid by Margaret Muldoon because she had acted as a witness two years previously, against Muldoon's husband, who had been sentenced to five years.[44]

This allusion to intimidation being a neighbourhood problem was not altogether far-fetched. In the Toxteth Park area of town, a complicated row escalated from an argument between two women to a serious assault of a mother and her daughter. In the subsequent magistrates' court hearing there were charges and counter-charges brought by the two sides. One of the defendants claimed she had given evidence in an earlier case and had received no peace since. The impossibility of determining where the truth lay meant that the magistrate had to discharge the defendants. However, that same day, after the court proceedings, one witness for the defence returned home and waved her shawl in victory, which antagonized supporters for the original prosecution, who then attacked the original defendants with pokers. This time the magistrate felt able to believe the complainant's side and her witness, and so 15-year-old Ellen Green was sent to gaol for six weeks with hard labour.[45]

As some of the cases above imply, women-on-women violence could escalate into street-wide rows, some of which were, in all probability, sectarian in origin. Under the headline 'FEMALE ROWDYISM IN LYON-STREET', the *Mercury* of 15 July 1896 reported how up to 20 women had been swearing and fighting for a number of nights over the previous week, in disturbances which the police had had trouble quelling. The women, it transpired, ran indoors at the first sight of a uniform and thus evaded identification and prosecution. A week later Christian Street was reported to be in uproar, with men and women throwing slates and bricks from roof tops into the street below. It was estimated that 2000 people had congregated in the street either to participate or to view the goings-on. Not all street disturbances were sectarian or political in origin. In a court off Henderson Street, police found a cartload of bricks after a fight 'worse than the battle of Waterloo'. It was, the police told the magistrate during the committal of Alice Smith, 'the usual custom ... to fling bricks from the housetops, which practice had led to the almost total demolition of the chimneys about'. This row appears to have been concerned with the illegal distilling or brewing and the sale of drinks. Competitors of such trades did their utmost to prevent or discourage others from trading.[46]

In what must have been one of the last bread riots which any major British town experienced, Liverpool women were identified as playing a leading role in attacking bread and provision shops in 1855 (see chapter 5). The participants were deemed to be different from the honest working class. 'They consisted, for the most part, of females of the lowest class, youths familiarly known to the police, mixed up here and there with some of the more noted dock plunderers and "ruffs," who seemed to direct operations.' They were the 'vicious and dissolute' of Scotland Road and Vauxhall Road, who broke down the doors and windows in order to take away flour and loaves. Many of those arrested bore Irish names and women figured as frequently as men in the magistrates' courts and police cells in the subsequent round-ups.[47]

The implication in some of these reports of female intimidation is that the women bullies belonged to the same class as the cornermen. This was not altogether surprising, since there were the female equivalents who garnered notorious reputations as terrors of the neighbourhood. One mother and her daughter were, reportedly, the 'Terrors of Midghall'.[48] In fact, in the sample of over 500 cases of female violence described above (table 4), all but one of the women were working class, as were their victims. Even this observation requires further refinement, as the press reports explicitly and implicitly associated violent female behaviour with an underclass of prostitutes, basket women and drunkards.

'Drink', wrote Father Nugent, the Catholic prison chaplain, 'is making terrible havoc upon the female population of this town ... changing wives and mothers into brutal savages'. This became increasingly evident as the century moved to its close. Much female violence occurred in pubs and beer houses, where refusal to be served drink or eviction from the premises could trigger violent assaults from inebriated women. Glasses, bottles and tumblers were thrown or pushed into the faces of bar staff. In this respect these women were no different from men guilty of similar offences.[49] Alcohol features prominently in cases where women were prosecuted for inter-personal violence. Not all of it occurred in the street, as there was a growing tendency during the nineteenth century for women to drink at home. Very often sending their children out with jugs, or going themselves, to the local pub, women could drink and, on occasion, argue and fight with their female drinking partners behind closed doors. Such was the case in Nash Street, where four basket women, a notoriously poor group, were drinking. In what was claimed to be an accident, Mary Langham told the police that 'Lizzie Gaffney threw two cups at my head and also struck me with a bottle. I threw a glass at her in return, which struck her on the arm'. The glass cut Lizzie's main artery in her wrist and she, as a consequence, bled to death. However, even drinking at home could still present problems for some women when they went to the pub to get refills. When Sabina Cannon was refused entry to a pub on Sawney Pope Street by Bridget Moylan, she smashed her jug on the publican's wife's forehead.[50]

Conclusion

LIVERPOOL HAD, according to successive head constables, a higher than normal crime rate when compared with other ports and cities in Britain. One factor which made the city distinctive was its high rate of female criminality and this was, in part, caused by heavy alcohol consumption by women. Women and drinking were, according to Liverpool's head constable in the early twentieth century, Leonard Dunning, associated with prostitution, assaults (especially on the police) and cruelty to children. Violent women, the very antithesis of nineteenth-century femininity, were one of the city's defining features in terms of its criminality. Living in appallingly overcrowded slums, having limited work opportunities, raising families on very little money and being victims of patriarchic disciplining from frequently drunken husbands, some women found Victorian values irrelevant to their situation. Preferring alcohol to see them through, these women fought and argued with neighbours, borrowed from female money-lenders or stole to pay for their addiction and behaved in ways normally associated with men.

CHAPTER 9

Women as victims of domestic and sexual violence

Nowhere is the ill-usage of woman so systematic as in Liverpool, and so little hindered by the strong arm of the law; making the lot of a married woman, whose locality is the 'kicking district' of Liverpool, simply a duration of suffering and subjection to injury and savage treatment, far worse than that to which the wives of mere savages are used....[1]

These, then, are the localities wherein Wife-torture flourishes in England; where a dense population is crowded into a hideous manufacturing or mining or mercantile district. Wages are usually high though fluctuating. Facilities for drink and vice abound, but those for cleanliness and decency are scarcely attainable. The men are rude, coarse, and brutal in their manners and habits, and the women devoid, in an extraordinary degree, of all the higher natural attractions and influences of their sex. Poor drudges ... of the crowded and sordid lodging-house, they lose, before youth is past, the freshness, neatness, and gentleness, perhaps even the modesty of a woman, and present, when their miserable cases come up before the magistrate, an aspect so sordid and forbidding that it is no doubt with difficulty he affords his sympathy to them rather than to the husband chained to so wretched a consort.[2]

The killing of Dinah Quigley

ON WEDNESDAY EVENING, 18 December 1867, in No. 5 Court, Vernon Street, labourer Thomas Quigley came into his house. Seeing his wife Dinah was not at home he sent his nine-year-old daughter, Mary, to the house of neighbour and widower Andrew Matthews, to see if she was there. The daughter, in fact, spied her mother through the keyhole but went home and lied to her father, saying that she was not there. Her lie did not convince Quigley, who went himself to the neighbour's house, where he saw Dinah running towards the coal cellar. From there she was dragged out by her hair and back across the court into her own house, where her husband repeatedly beat her with a poker as she lay on the floor. He later hit her with a stick, a 'big table' and kicked her in the throat.

Mary, the main witness to this savage assault, told the coroner's court how her father jumped on her mother 'three or four times' and then 'rested himself between the times and sweated'. He then picked up her younger sister and threw her against Mary and 'dashed' them down the yard. The beating had attracted a lot of attention in the court, where neighbours not only heard the cries of the woman but could also see through the window some of the brutal events, before Quigley closed the window shutters and put out the light. Neighbour Ann Keegan, who had seen him beating his wife with a piece of wood, asked him 'to have patience with his wife'. In reply he said it was 'hard for me to have patience. She was drinking yesterday with Peter Lawler, and to-day with Andrew Matthews, and was worse than a prostitute'. One neighbour, Julia Sackey, asked two constables, who came to the court entrance, to enter Quigley's house but this they refused to do as Dinah was, in their opinion, drunk. They did, however, look in and saw the woman lying on the floor. Later three more constables entered the court and helped lift Dinah onto an armchair and carry her by stretcher to the Northern Hospital, where she died on 23 December. Being informed of the impossibility of her recovery, she provided a deposition statement to the borough magistrate, Mr Caine. The post-mortem examination showed that she had three contused scalp wounds and another on her cheek; bruises on both ears and under the jaw and on the neck; seven fractured ribs; fractures and bruises on both arms; bruises on the lower half of her body; and a fractured leg.[3]

The *Porcupine*, under the headline 'A Shocking Story', chose to highlight the apparent police inactivity by posing the following question: 'Do you know where Vernon-street is?' Contempt and outrage in equal measure rose from the page when Shimmin answered his own question: 'It is close to the Police Court and Offices; close, also, to the Bridewell. It is, one might say, perpetually under the bull's-eye of police officialism. If any part of Liverpool ought to be free from and safe against acts of violence, Vernon-street and all its tributary courts ought to be.' In a more florid description of Dinah's assault than that of the daily local press, the *Porcupine* noted that the first set of police officers to attend the incident spoke both to a neighbour, who had told them of the wife beating, and then to the husband.

> They [the police officers] did not seem to think there was any occasion to make much fuss about that. The woman urged them to go into the house where Quigley's wife was, and they did, in fact, look in; but bless you, they saw nothing there worth noticing, there was only a woman lying in a heap on the floor. Drunk, of course? Well, the person who had just appealed to them thought not; but the police understand these things better. Oh yes, Mrs Quigley was drunk, no doubt, nothing more. So the officers chatted a little with Mr. Quigley: perhaps expressed a hope that he had not beaten his wife more than a Briton has a right to do, and then they went away. Quigley followed their example: he went away too.

The woman on the floor, whom the two constables had quickly glanced at, was, in Shimmin's words: 'A hideous, battered, mashed, bleeding heap of broken bones'. This case is unusual in one respect: Dinah Quigley was killed as a result of the violent beating she received from her husband. In many other respects this case highlights significant features and issues common to domestic violence during this period. First, the event took place in full view and earshot of the neighbours, some of whom appear to have tried, initially, to halt the violence by verbally remonstrating with the husband. All these neighbours were women. Second, the only male witness, widower Andrew Matthews, did nothing when Quigley came for his wife. His main concern appears to have been that the husband should beat his wife in their own home. Third, when the police first entered the court, they spoke to Thomas Quigley and saw his wife lying on the floor but thought nothing of it and dismissed the incident as a 'drunken row'. After they had left the court, Thomas Quigley likewise made a hasty retreat and disappeared on a steamer to Rotterdam, where he surrendered to the Dutch authorities on 2 January 1868. The case therefore raises issues concerning public attitudes to domestic violence. Did the husband have, according to popular and traditional sanctions, the right to beat his wife? If so, where was the line drawn between excessive and 'legitimate' violence? What was the attitude of those whose job it was to ensure the law was being upheld? Did the Liverpool police, in what Shimmin suggested was a 'disgusting and shameful truth', think 'a husband has a prescriptive right to beat his wife as often as he likes…?'[4]

The home, the law and 'the wife'

DOMESTIC VIOLENCE APPEARS to have occupied some kind of grey, indeterminate moral area between legality and illegality, both in the popular mind and within the legal establishment. To what extent was this ambivalence continued during and immediately after the trial, in which Quigley was found guilty of murder but recommended to mercy by the jury? Although a sentence of death was passed on him, a memorial from 'a number of influential persons' in Liverpool persuaded the Home Secretary to issue a reprieve and altered the punishment to one of penal servitude for life.[5] On what grounds were the feelings of sympathy based?

The home, contrary to popular misconceptions then and now, was the most dangerous place for a woman. Why was this? There were many forces pushing in the same direction. First, there was the ever-growing Victorian idealization of both the home as a place of domesticity and the 'angel' who presided over this domestic sanctuary, namely the wife, mother and homemaker. The home was increasingly portrayed as refuge from a world of business and work, where the man could seek the love, care and joys of family life. His job was to provide, protect and care for his wife and family; in return, his wife was to obey and provide domestically for him. These were, then, the badges of Victorian respectability. How these attitudes could contribute to domestic violence is not difficult to understand. The home was seen as a private space, away from the prying eyes of officialdom, exemplified by the saying 'an Englishman's home is his castle', in which the master of the house could do much as he pleased.

This new idealization of the domestic home was grafted on to a centuries-old popular belief that the husband had the right to chastise his wife (that is, hit her) if she disobeyed him. How hard and with what were matters open to debate, but there was the popular 'rule of thumb' that a man could hit a woman with a stick no broader than his thumb. This principle had never been enshrined in law but it did not prevent people, both men and women, believing in it. This meant that if a man beat his wife or partner in the privacy of their home it was no one's business to intervene.

The final force which contributed to the notion of the dangerous home was, paradoxically, the introduction (nationally) of the 'new police' from the late 1820s. Their role was one of surveillance but this was initially restricted to the streets and thoroughfares of the towns and cities. As the public spaces became more orderly through close inspection and patrolling, so it could be argued that interpersonal violence was pushed indoors and out of sight of the police. It should be emphasized that the average beat constable in Liverpool, or anywhere else for that matter, was a working man who generally subscribed to the same beliefs held by the people he was policing. Thus he too may have believed in the husband's right to hit or beat his wife and he too would have felt unwilling to forcibly enter someone's home uninvited. This would have been regarded by all and sundry as an invasion of privacy.[6]

The law, however, increasingly criminalized violent behaviour, especially male violence. Domestic violence was singled out in 1853, when the Aggravated Assaults on Women and Children Act was passed. This new act allowed magistrates to pass more stringent sentences, up to six months with hard labour, on men found guilty of aggravated assaults. Newspaper reports commented on the heavier punishments given to wife beaters, such as James Houghton of Nash Grove and Emanuel Hellyer, who held the distinction of being the first in Liverpool to receive maximum sentences under the new act.[7] In the latter case, Hellyer had been 'upwards of a dozen times for assaults upon his wife, and the various terms of imprisonment he had undergone amounted, in aggregate, to four years and ten months. Though the parties had been married 17 years, they had only lived three years together.' In the former case, Houghton went home at 2 a.m. and ordered his wife out of bed to pull off his boots. When she refused, he seized a piece of iron and repeatedly struck her as she lay in bed. These were defined as assaults involving the use of a deadly or dangerous weapon. The more frequently used charge of common assault was typically used against husbands who gave their wives and partners black eyes and bruises. The maximum sentence for causing such injuries was three months. Further laws passed in 1878 and 1895 not only increased magistrates' sentencing powers (to one year in these cases) but, more importantly for women, also allowed wives to separate from their husbands and receive maintenance of up to £2 a week.

While the law and legal attitudes appear to be relatively clear cut and unambiguous on the question of violence to wives and children after 1853, in reality they were a little more complex. Take the headline from the police intelligence news column in the *Mercury* on 2 February 1855: 'WIVES, OBEY YOUR HUSBANDS'. In the case described in the column, the stipendiary magistrate, in presiding over a complicated family dispute in which the wife had left her mother-in-law's home and returned to her own mother's, declared:

> It is the first duty of a wife to obey her husband, and when you marry you give up entirely your own family. I must say that, so far as this case is concerned, he did quite right in refusing to allow you to go to your mother's, though I am very sorry that a blow should have been inflicted, because from the man's general demeanour in court he does not seem to be a violent man. You had better return to your home and your duty, and then you will probably live more happily together.

This case shows the tensions which existed between, on the one hand, Victorian attitudes towards women and their inferiority to men and, on the other, the law making violence to wives illegal.

Increasingly through the nineteenth century, domestic violence attracted growing condemnation from both the law and respectable opinion, as expressed in Cobbe's 1878 essay on 'wife torture' quoted at the start of the chapter, but this is not necessarily reflected in the crime statistics of the period. Domestic violence was, and is, the classic example of a hidden crime, one which went largely unreported and unprosecuted. There is no way of knowing how big the dark figure of unreported wife beatings was; one can only assume it was huge. Under the 1853 law on aggravated assaults of women and children, between 1863 and 1893 Liverpool returned the figures set out in table 5. These figures should be treated with extreme caution because they do not all relate to prosecutions for wife beating. The number of women prosecuted for aggravated assault was quite substantial, accounting for a quarter to a third of all those charged. Most of them would have been charged with violence against other women or children. Very rarely were they brought to court on serious assault charges against their husbands.

When one considers that the population of Liverpool rose from 376,000 in 1851 to over half a million in 1891, it is obvious how low was the reported number of serious wife beatings. Peaking in 1867 with a mere 210 individuals prosecuted, domestic violence was clearly a generally hidden

Table 5 Number of prosecutions for aggravated assaults on women and children in Liverpool, 1863–93, and the total numbers convicted for common assault

Year	Total prosecuted	Number found guilty	Convictions for common assault
1863	170	170	1707
1864	198	198	1865
1865	200	200	1819
1866	204	204	1649
1867	210	210	1626
1868	168	159	1537
1869	163	139	1302
1870	177	148	1461
1871	126	101	1372
1872	90	71	1302
1873	88	78	1343
1874	82	70	1427
1875	110	96	1413
1876	109	85	1325
1877	73	63	1227
1878	64	57	1176
1879	55	48	1145
1880	60	52	1062
1881	64	56	1013
1882	59	47	1191
1883	45	34	962
1884	50	38	977
1885	32	26	967
1886	50	44	925
1887	24	22	941
1888	10	10	843
1889	10	10	749
1890	unavailable		
1891	8	7	755
1892	9	9	957
1893	31	27	915

Figures taken from LvRO, H352 cou, Head constable's annual reports to the Liverpool watch committee for the respective years.

crime. Why was this the case? Wives and common-law partners were often loathe to prosecute their male partners, even after they had initially brought charges against them. The reasons were many and either revolved around economic considerations or personal safety for themselves and their children. Fear played an important role in women refusing to press charges. Unlike other crimes of violence, such as male-on-male street violence, the victim and the assailant in domestic cases were intimately related to one another, to such an extent that the emotions which lay behind a punch or a kick were deep seated and of long standing; nor were they likely to lessen or disappear once the violent attack was over. In short, the violence was often irresolvable; the best that wives, in such relationships, could hope for was a reduction in the possible trigger-points for their husbands' brutal assaults. Prosecuting them for domestic beatings did not often solve problems but often made matters worse.

In 1855, Mrs Roche, who gave evidence against her 'wastrel' husband who had left her for 10 weeks with only 4s 9d to live on, was met outside the court by a gang of '"ruffs" who were companions of the prisoner … waiting to assault the complainant'. Others would shout from the dock to their wives, threatening them with worse when they were freed from gaol. Such threats were not idle, as Patrick Doran's wife found to her cost when she met her husband on his discharge from prison for an earlier assault on her. He took nearly all her money, bought drink with it, knocked their child out of her arms and beat her to the ground. This assault was witnessed by a policeman, which meant she did not need to give evidence against her husband. Ellen Lewis, who had been repeatedly beaten by her husband, refused to come to court to give evidence against him as he had threatened to kill her if she did so. Failure to appear in court after having initially brought charges against their husbands for assaults was a common tactic and this would lead magistrates to discharge the prisoner. One stipendiary magistrate, Mr Raffles, frequently found it frustrating that 'cowardly fellows' took advantage of the fact that their injured wives had no enthusiasm to press charges and were thus able to continue to assault them with impunity.[8] By the mid-1860s the stipendiary magistrate, if the evidence of an assault was compelling, would ignore the wife's silence or the lack of witness evidence and find wife beaters guilty.

Many women, however, did attend the magistrates' court and reluctantly give evidence against their husbands but would plead for a sentence other than imprisonment. Mary Martin, wife of Edward, successfully asked that the charges be dropped against him because she had borne 17 children with the defendant. Fear of the workhouse may well have been the prevailing motive behind her plea, as this could be the outcome if a breadwinner was gaoled for two or three months.[9] Others asked magistrates to downgrade the punishment to separation orders and maintenance payments, which both parties were happy to comply with. In other cases magistrates ordered men to find sureties to keep the peace. These solutions, if that is what they can be termed, were increasingly resorted to in the later decades of the nineteenth century. This may partly explain the decline in the prosecutions for aggravated and common assaults.

Some wives would change their evidence and claim their injuries were the result of accidents, their own clumsiness, or their own provocative behaviour. Such instances often led to some unlikely stories in court. When PC 249 was called to Paul Street, off Vauxhall Road, he found Margaret

Markey lying unconscious on the floor in a pool of blood. On coming round she told him that her husband had hit her on the head with a frying pan and then kicked her in the abdomen. So bad was the assault that her life was feared for, so much so that George Melly, the magistrate, and his clerk, were sent to take her deposition. In it she stated:

> I called him names and provoked him. He said, 'If you don't hush I'll have to beat you.' And I dared him to do it. He gave me a slap about the stomach. I don't remember that he kicked me. He only gave me a slap in this room, and then went away. I ran after him into the street, and called him names. He told me if I followed him he would beat me. I still kept following and then fell. It was in this street that I fell. He then went away into the street he lives in. He was a good husband to me, and I don't wish to say anything against him: I don't know that I have said that he struck me with a frying pan or that he kicked me. I was raving mad all night, and do not know what I may have said.[10]

Her deposition was, in effect, a retraction of everything she had said the previous day, and she achieved this effectively by saying that there was no one present when they had had their argument; further, he had used an open hand – a slap – as opposed to a fist when he had hit her. She not only taunted him with her name calling but had followed him out of the house into the street, where she had, so she claimed, fallen. Anything she had said the previous day was, in effect, the ravings of a sick and feverish woman who was totally unaware of what she had said. Despite her attempts to get the charges dropped, her husband was sent to trial for attempted murder. In another case James Corrigan's wife claimed in her deposition that she had 'rushed against the knife' in her husband's hand during an argument. He had, she claimed, been cutting tobacco, when she 'fell'.[11]

Characteristics of wife beating

THE VIOLENCE INFLICTED in the home by men on their wives and partners was often extreme, lethal in some cases. It was often far worse, more serious and more frequent than anything which women might experience out on the streets late at night. This was in part due to the lack of intervention by neighbours and partly due to the manner in which the violence was meted out. Most commonly men used their fists on women. Such assaults, if ever prosecuted, were punished with a one- or two-month sentence. However, many of the cases that came before the courts were more serious in that weapons had been used, sometimes in a life-threatening manner. A commonly used implement of domestic violence (as well as street violence, as seen in chapter 6) was the working man's boot. Even *Punch* magazine in its 30 January 1875 edition, shortly after the Tithebarn Street trial, ran a cartoon, headed 'A Mere Trifle', in which one 'Liverpool rough' asks another rough who has just beaten his wife 'within an inch of her life': 'I soy, beel, what'll thee git for this 'ere?' To which the 'second Liverpool rough' replies 'Foin o' ten bob maybe, same as 'ad for walloping thay jackass, though ah've gived it to 'er smarter-like!' Over the page of the magazine there is a poem headed 'The British Boot: A New National Song'. The third verse runs:

> Are our spouses remiss? We'll their memory jog
> With a brisk application of Lancashire clog;
> That is better than manual punches or 'fibs'
> To smash in and settle importunate 'ribs'!
> Effective enforcer of marital rights,
> Companion and backer in 'five to one' fights![12]

While the boot was the weapon most talked about in the mid-1870s, men in their drunken or jealous rages frequently grabbed anything close to hand. Not surprisingly, iron pokers figure large in descriptions of wife beatings. However, many other implements were used, ranging from bits of wood, razors and frying pans, to knives, axes, cotton hooks used by dockers, boiling water and guns. It is a fearsome list and not surprisingly such items caused dreadful injuries to the victims. Perhaps most disturbing of all were the attacks which aimed to disfigure the woman. Under the newspaper headline of 'CANNIBALISM', it was reported how Charles Heath of Birchfield Street had tripped his wife up and then fallen on top of her. When he got to his feet it was seen that he had bitten the side of her nose away. In a similar kind of assault Francis Farrell told his wife he would disfigure her, whereupon he knocked her to the ground and bent over and bit part of her nose off. She was, according to the doctor at the East Dispensary, permanently disfigured. Drunken cotton porter Thomas Ireland shouted out 'I will spoil you now' as he stabbed his wife on the cheek and head when she refused to fetch him more drink.[13]

Ellen Conner's case was not untypical of domestic violence charges brought before the town magistrates. Still suffering from her injuries, Ellen, according to a local newspaper, 'bore a most wretched and helpless appearance'. The report continued:

> A white bandage encircled her head covering three large wounds, her eyes were blackened and the whole of her face was much swollen. Her left arm was splintered, her ring finger having been broken in two places, her right arm was so bruised and swollen that she could not use it and her legs were so badly injured that she could scarcely move them. Pc 163 said he apprehended the prisoner in his house in Bent-street, Scotland Road, about half past two o'clock yesterday morning and the woman was in such an exhausted state that he was compelled to take her in a car to the hospital. The unfortunate woman stated that the prisoner went out about seven o'clock yesterday morning making her give him a shilling to get drink with. During the morning she hunted all over the town for him but could not find him. He came in shortly before two o'clock much under the influence of liquor and immediately began to ill use her, calling

her very improper names. Seeing that he kept a knife continually in his hand she thought it would be best for her to get out of the house for which purpose she was going toward the door when he asked her for his breakfast. She told him it was on the table ready for him and went out through the door but he went through the back door and came suddenly round to her. He then dragged her into the house and locked the doors. He then deliberately commenced to ill treat her in the most savage manner battering her head with a three leg stool until the weapon broke in his hands, beating her about the head with a jug or anything else that came within his reach, next kicking her until he was himself actually exhausted, when he would coolly sit down to rest and afterwards renew his cowardly and brutal attack upon the poor helpless woman. The unfortunate creature went upon her knees and implored for mercy but that only seemed to exasperate the brute for he ran at her with a knife in his hand and swore he would be her butcher. He struck at her throat with the weapon and in order to save her life she raised her hand and the blade of the knife cut through the bone of one of her fingers. After renewing the attack at short intervals five or six times he sat down and fell asleep. She then managed to get out and crawl to the house of a neighbour but the good woman there kindly told her to go away or she would bleed to death in the house. After this she got into the court and was lying bleeding there when the officer found her and took her in a car to the hospital. Notwithstanding all the injuries she had received at the hands of her brutal partner, the woman begged that the bench would release him on his promising that he would not assault her again for 'he was the father of her three little children and was not a bad husband when all was said and done'. As the surgeon said the woman's life was still in danger the prisoner was remanded for seven days. Mr Mansfield said the woman must go back to the hospital and he requested Mr Clough to attend the children in the meantime.[14]

A week later Michael Conner was found guilty and sentenced to six months with hard labour. Unusually, Ellen's pleas regarding her children were addressed by the stipendiary magistrate, who awarded her a weekly allowance for the duration of the prison sentence. This case highlights the role of alcohol – Conner was drunk – and the most frequently cited trigger for an assault – the demand for food whatever the hour.

Husbands and male partners also took great exception to being humiliated by 'their' women in front of other men. Peter Harrison, for example, was committed to trial for stabbing his wife in a Scotland Road beer house. She had, he complained, been '"bothering" him to go home'. Labourer Henry McCarthy was sentenced to two months with hard labour for kicking and beating his wife who had gone into a Vauxhall Road pub to fetch him home.[15] Other typical characteristics of wife beating included the lengthy and often drawn-out nature of the assault and the different weapons used by the man. The silence, too, on the part of neighbours was deafening. In the Conner case above, the neighbour was unusually unsympathetic, but this nonetheless indicates how domestic violence was viewed as a private matter between husband and wife.

Popular attitudes and community responses

PRIVACY WAS OFTEN difficult to achieve for assailants in the narrow and crowded courts, where there would be at least a handful of neighbours on their steps at almost any time of day or night. In 1868, Robert Rimmer, who occupied a cellar dwelling in Halgrave Street, mindful of the attention his argument with his drunken wife was attracting, came out of his house and drove away a group of children who were standing by the railings looking down on the scene. He returned and locked the door and silently slit his wife's throat. Twenty minutes later he emerged, having cleaned up the blood, and went to a female neighbour, whom he asked to visit his wife. The inquest concluded that she died from natural causes and that the throat wound was a mere 'scratch under her chin'.[16]

There almost appears, at times, to be an element of theatre or spectacle to some of the quarrels. A domestic dispute could provide an entertaining distraction to neighbours, whose days were otherwise uniformly drab. When Peter Gregory quarrelled with his wife at their open door a crowd of onlookers gathered to watch the spectacle. In his anger Gregory grabbed a bottle of aqua fortis (nitric acid, used domestically for killing house-bugs) and threw it at the watching crowd. The faces of two men were covered; fortunately, no lasting damage was done to their eyesight.[17] How people reacted to their neighbours' domestic quarrels and fights defies any kind of generalization. Many different and complex responses were noted in the press. Fights took place in which no kind of help was offered to the woman being battered. We have already seen in the case of Ellen Conner, who crawled to a female neighbour's house, how she was asked to leave. This apparently heartless response was by no means unique. When Louisa Skelland went to neighbour Charles Graham seeking sanctuary – 'let me hide here; my husband is going to kill me' – he told her, 'Your place is with your husband' and shut the door on Louisa, leaving her standing in the court. Two other neighbours informed the coroner's court how they had seen her husband punch her to the ground and kick her. After she was dragged back into their house by her husband, one neighbour saw him punch her on the jaw and knock her into the cellar, where she was found dead the next day. No one, it would seem, had fetched a policeman or taken the unconscious woman to the dispensary.[18]

Domestic fights could be easily overheard, as the partition walls between houses were often no more than a brick's width. One neighbour to Elizabeth and Emmanuel Mavromatis, of Louis Street, heard three cries of 'murder' and then silence. Although he knew the couple frequently quarrelled, he was sufficiently worried to tell a neighbour, who went to the house and shop and found the husband coming from the back room. He immediately admitted to having killed his wife by slashing at her throat and face.[19]

Neighbours could be forgiven for being confused as to their rights to interfere in neighbours' matrimonial altercations. In a case involving the

Sinclairs, who ran a grocer's shop in Kent Street, a crowd had gathered outside the store to watch the row between the couple, in which the husband had vowed to kill his wife 'and would be hung for her'. One neighbour who went to Mrs Sinclair's aid claimed she was assaulted by the poker-wielding husband but the stipendiary magistrate concluded that 'Certain friends had interfered who had no right to interfere'. The charges against the husband on violence to both his wife and the neighbour were dismissed.[20] Neighbours had to weigh up a number of difficult factors in deciding when the moment had come to intervene or 'interfere' in a neighbour's domestic row. First, they would have to decide whether the noises coming through the wall from the neighbouring property were different and more worrying than usual. A heavy crash or screams of 'murder' followed by silence could often be a cause for their inquisitiveness. Second, and more important, were they, as interfering neighbours, placing their own lives in danger by stepping into what were often drunken, brutal fights? The evidence suggests that this was no idle fear.

When neighbour Mrs Kenny went to the aid of Mrs Tulley, who was being beaten by her husband, she was knocked to the ground with a brick and then kicked by him. Drinking 'out of sorrow' for the death of his son was how Metcalfe, of Fontenoy Street, defended his actions. During the wake, an elderly neighbour told Metcalfe to stop beating his wife, which enraged the husband so much that he bit the man's thumb almost off and then, while grappling on the floor, 'dragged' two of his teeth out. Just occasionally, intervening between a husband and a wife attracted the anger of both warring parties. When a postman came across the Hickeys arguing in Hanover Street, he stopped to watch. 'Both turned on him', the court was told, 'and the husband asked him what he was looking at, and told him to mind his own business'. Charles Morrison, the postman, replied that he would 'make it his business to send a policeman', whereupon the husband struck the postman and the wife hit his face with a tin can. Only Sarah Hickey was charged.[21]

The police, as has been seen in the Quigley case, did not always intervene on behalf of the battered wife. Was this typical? An element of confusion and uncertainty was written into the instruction manuals distributed to new police recruits. They were warned, where possible, not to become involved in purely domestic disputes; this was regarded by all concerned as interfering rather than intervening. When PC 668 (Cutler) answered the cries of 'murder' and 'police', coming from a house in Birkett Street, he told James Clark to stop hitting his wife. For his troubles he received a kick in the ribs from the husband and when his colleague went to arrest Clark, the wife began hitting PC 575 (Kerr) with a poker. If, however, the battered wife implored them to help, the police's first responsibility was to stop the violence and then, wherever possible, to persuade the woman to remain at home. This was Sergeant Johnson's initial reaction when he entered the home of Michael Fitzpatrick of Old Swan. On hearing screams around midnight he put his head round the door, to see Fitzpatrick laying into his wife, whom he was holding down. He was not, he told the court, 'inclined at first to take the prisoner into custody'. However, only when wife Ellen persuaded him that her life was in peril and that 'she would be murdered before the morning' if her husband was allowed to remain at home did he make an arrest.[22]

Dinah Quigley was not the only woman to die as a result of police reluctance to interfere. In the same month that the Tithebarn Street murder occurred, 33-year-old William Worthington, boatman, killed his wife, Ann. The circumstances surrounding her death 'seem to verge on the incredible'.[23] It transpired during the trial that the first witness heard continuous screams for 15 minutes before she looked out of a window on her way to bed. She saw Ann crouching down on ground close to Vauxhall Road and her husband standing over her and kicking. The witness shouted out of the window and another man, a Mr Kerr, asked Worthington what he was doing to his wife, to which the latter told him to mind his own business. Kerr fetched a whistle and blew for a policeman; PC Flint came up and saw Ann 'in so wretched a state, her face covered with blood and with dirt and mud'. Flint, though, refused to interfere or take the husband into custody, even when Ann said she would press charges. Unfortunately, the constable did not appear to understand her reply of 'Ay, taen him' (take him), most likely delivered in a broad Wigan accent, for that was where her family came from. He told them to 'go and settle it at the boat' for they lived on a canal barge with their daughter, who then witnessed the brutal kicking later that night and a final fatal one first thing in the morning.

When cross-examined during the trial, PC Flint was asked why he refused to arrest Worthington: 'I thought it was merely between man and wife', he replied. 'And is it', asked the judge, 'your opinion as a police-officer that whatever may be the injury a wife receives it is not a case for police interference?' 'I did not think it was so bad as it was', the hapless constable answered. Justice Mellor followed up by telling him that:

> when people said to him 'Look at the state of that poor creature', and pointed to a woman who had been ill used, it was his duty to interfere. A man was not to beat a woman because she was his wife; she had as much right to be protected as any one else. He must recollect for the future that he was not bound to wait until he had a charge made to him. If he saw the signs of recent injury, he, as a policeman, ought to interfere. Although slight matters between man and wife were better not to be meddled with, yet if the officer saw a wife injured in future he must interfere, without caring whether she gave her husband in charge or not.

Although the jury found Worthington guilty of murder, they recommended him to mercy but this was ignored. He was executed along with two of the guilty Tithebarn Street murderers at Kirkdale gaol on 4 January 1875.[24]

The fact that the policeman needed to be reminded of his duties and responsibilities towards victims of domestic violence was an indictment not only of police training in Liverpool but also of their apparent passivity when confronted with brutal and violent behaviour. In this particular case the violence was public and witnessed rather than restricted to the privacy of the home. This may have represented some kind of turning point for the police, since many newspaper reports of domestic violence after this date noted that individual constables would break into a house on hearing a woman's screams. This is not to deny that the police did intervene prior to 1874/75. Shortly after the notorious Quigley case there were reports of the police, on hearing screams of murder, entering homes and arresting husbands. By 1870, however, the police were again showing a marked reluctance to arrest wife beaters. The officer who patrolled the Gilbert Street area told the court that Hamilton Poole was 'in the almost nightly habit of abusing his wife.... The prisoner would come home at all hours of the night, and abuse her as if she was a man that could stand up to him, and would also turn her out of doors.' Arresting a wife beater would appear to have been a last resort. This kind of approach was confirmed in the case of wife beater James Edwards, whom two local beat constables had 'considerable difficulty in restraining', for a number of days.[25]

Wife killings

DOMESTIC MURDERS attracted considerable newspaper and popular interest. It was mentioned above that Thomas Quigley, though found guilty of the murder of his wife, never actually hanged. While this was not unusual, it would be fair to say that wife murderers generally experienced the full rigours of the law and were often executed, increasingly so, as the nineteenth century moved towards the turn of the twentieth. However, this does overlook one interesting characteristic of wife killing, namely the possibility that 'a suspicious and mysterious death' escaped prosecution altogether or that the murder charge was downgraded to one of manslaughter.

Infanticide was notorious for being under-reported and unprosecuted. Wife killing, too, may have been disguised on occasion. Reports from the coroners' courts and the assizes highlight how husbands and partners, as well as professionals, could introduce testimony which suggested other reasons for a woman's sudden demise. This clearly occurred in Robert Rimmer's case (discussed above) in 1868. In Mary Swift's case, doctors who visited her after she had been beaten by her husband argued whether she was suffering from delirium tremens or the infection erysipelas. It also transpired that she had fallen while being assisted out of a window by a police officer. With such conflicting evidence the jury found her husband, William, not guilty of manslaughter.[26]

Deaths that resulted from a push and a fall could very easily be termed accidental, or lead to a prosecution for manslaughter rather than murder. Rose Ann Quinn of Star Street, Toxteth, had been abused and beaten for two hours by her drunken husband. During the rest of the day, a Sunday, Mr Quinn came and went from home to pub, becoming more intoxicated as the day wore on. On each visit home he renewed his attacks on his wife. At 10.30 p.m. he opened the front door and took Rose Ann by the shoulders and threw her down three steps into the street. It appears that she did not break her fall with an outstretched hand; rather, she fell head first. For this unlawful killing he was sentenced to a mere eight months.[27] In the case of Ann Dabbs, the coroner's court arrived at a verdict of 'Died from the effects of violence, but how that violence was received there is no evidence to show'. This decision came even though she had moved lodgings in order to escape her husband's beatings. She had arrived at her new lodgings in Norfolk Street with two black eyes and bruises about her face and arm. However, there were no witnesses to the violence and only her word as to the identity of the perpetrator.

Where husbands were suspected of having thrown their wives out of upstairs windows, they were able to defend themselves by arguing that their partners had jumped or slipped during domestic rows. Two witnesses claimed to have seen Lydia Harrison being thrown out of a first-floor window in Division Street. Although Lydia claimed that 'Billy', William Fairclough, had pushed her, she later denied having made the accusation. Defenestration, throwing people out of windows, was not that rare in Liverpool. At the previous assizes in the town, John Lopez was sentenced to penal servitude for life for throwing his wife from a window in Upper Frederick Street with intent to murder her. Unusually, the judge indulged in what would now be called amateur psychology when he remarked that the wife's heavy drinking was probably a result of her trying to forget the awful treatment she knew was awaiting her every time her husband returned home. Her drinking was, in his opinion, the consequence of the brutality meted out to her.[28]

The lack of witnesses was a problem peculiar to domestic assaults and killings, since such attacks usually took place behind closed doors. Children were often the only witnesses but their evidence was not always considered credible and certainly not as reliable as that of an adult. In the case of Hannah Allen of Celt Street, Tuebrook, who had cohabited with Alfred Robertson for 17 years, an 11-year-old errand boy claimed to have seen her being assaulted by her long-term partner. He informed an inquest that, on knocking at the door and getting no reply, he had looked through the keyhole. Robertson was, he claimed, knocking Allen's head against a wall and slapping her face. Later, after she had picked up a knife, he set two dogs on her. When the door was finally opened, she sported two black eyes. Robertson, who was known to the police as a 'sober and steady man', claimed she was drunk and had fallen in the backyard. He admitted only to slapping her once 'with an open hand'. When the inquest jury reached a verdict of 'Death from violence, but not sufficient evidence to show how caused', Robertson was arrested. Days later he was discharged as the only witness was 11 years old and the police believed he could not have seen through the keyhole everything he said he saw. Children's reliability as witnesses was deemed to be especially question-able if they had spent some time alone in the company of the prime suspect before the police became involved.[29]

The 'good wife' and the 'drunken slovenly woman'

INQUEST REPORTS covering some of the above cases and newspaper coverage of court proceedings relating to domestic violence invariably wove into the facts of the cases moral narratives on the lifestyles of victims and their assailants. In some reports the women were portrayed as decent, god-fearing and temperate mothers married to drunken and worthless husbands. In other cases, as we have seen, the wives were portrayed as the drunks and the men as hard-working and responsible husbands. In some cases the news reports portrayed the homes and the relationships within them as chaotic, dysfunctional and uncivilized. Wife beating came to be symbolized as the brutal behaviour of an underclass who were marginal-ized from normal society. For such people the civilizing influences of the domestic ideals of homemaker and mother, on the one hand, and, on the other, the protector and breadwinner, who gathered the family round the hearth to listen as he read the Bible, was a laughable fiction. Many families, particularly in the north end, lived in cramp and dirty courts, often in just one room. Houses were shared and communal insofar as staircases ran from one floor to another within the living spaces of the residents. Cellars offered the greatest privacy but these had their downsides in terms of dampness, lack of natural light and poor ventilation. Poverty and overcrowding tended to nullify any Victorian notions of self-improvement.[30]

The press tended to pass moral and value judgements in their reports on domestic violence. Headlines offered the reader instant indications and signifiers of who had been to blame for the violence. Most emphasized the deviancy of the wayward husband: 'A BRUTAL WIFE BEATER', 'A COWARDLY WIFE BEATER', or 'A CRUEL, COWARDLY, WORTHLESS HUSBAND'. In the case of 'A COWARDLY WIFE BEATER', it was reported how Patrick Doran, who had been freed from prison 'only yesterday' for an earlier assault on his wife, was met by her carrying their baby in her arms. She gave him nearly all the money she had for drink, but refused to give him more when he returned shortly afterwards. The 'few coppers' she still had were needed, she said, to buy food for the child. Doran thereupon grabbed her hair and beat her, knocking the baby out of her arms and onto the street. At the subsequent court hearing the magistrate belittled Doran's masculinity by saying that 'those fellows who struck women were those who dared not exercise their fists upon men'. 'It made his blood boil', the report continued, 'to hear these cases day after day of such brutes as the prisoner who had women in their power'.[31] This short report had managed to convey very effectively the image of the 'good wife', by portraying her as a loyal and generous mother, whereas her husband was a gaol-bird and a drunkard cowardly brute.

This juxtaposition of the good woman and bad husband is a theme that runs through many of the cases. Alfred Dunn, a decorator living at Waterloo, was told by the committing magistrate that 'he had never met with a more unmanly and cowardly outrage committed upon a respectable, decent woman, within a short time of her confinement [she was eight months pregnant]. None but a brute would have been guilty of such an outrage...'. John Nolan was described as 'a worthless, idle fellow' who had lived off the earnings of his 'hard working' wife for nearly a year. He was in bed when his wife returned from her stall in the fish market. Having complained bitterly that she had not given him 'sufficient dinner and breakfast', he then slashed her face with a cotton hook.[32]

All these reports highlighted and emphasized the violent husband as a monster, a brute, a coward and unmanly. Wife beating was, in the opinion of the courts and the newspapers, a practice increasingly restricted to an underclass of alcoholics and slum dwellers. Such men were labelled barely human, as the following headline indicates: 'ROASTING A WIFE LIKE A HERRING – HORRIBLE CASE IN LIVERPOOL – A MONSTER IN HUMAN SHAPE'. Just occasionally, as the 1856 headline 'TABLES TURNED' suggests, there was a reversal of the narrative in the story of domestic violence. In place of the respectable good woman, there was the 'bad wife' juxtaposed against a patient, hard-working and responsible husband whose patience suddenly snapped. The 1856 headline alluded to Joseph Turner, who had been gaoled for violent and abusive conduct and threatening his wife. It was later discovered by the stipendiary magistrate that she was 'a perfectly worthless woman' and he was immediately discharged.[33]

What kind of behaviour was attributed to a 'bad wife'? Most commonly it was excessive drinking. Blacksmith Thomas Quayle of Toxteth Park was brought up on remand for assaulting his wife with a glass, the evidence of which was plain to see in the bandaged head of his wife. However, he countered this powerful evidence by telling Mr Raffles, the magistrate, how his wife came to bed 'beastly drunk'. Waiting until she was sober the following day, Quayle 'spoke to her about her behaviour', upon which she flew into a rage. Any injuries to his wife were, he claimed, done in self-defence. The arresting policeman added that their neighbours said she was a drunken woman and that he was 'a very quiet man'. His foreman at the shipyard likewise gave him a good character reference. All these factors weighed in his favour, to the extent that he did not receive a custodial sentence.[34]

In what became known as 'the Saltney Street tragedy', Peter Flynn was brought to trial for the murder of his wife of 25 years, named Margaret. Although no one witnessed the actual killing, neighbours heard the raised voices of arguing, followed by screams and cries of 'murder'. Only when the husband left the house and found a policeman to report his wife's death, accidental he claimed, did the truth start to emerge. In addition to the five wounds on her head, the post-mortem examination brought to light 13 broken ribs. It was obvious that Margaret had been subjected to a prolonged and brutal assault from her husband. During the trial he was portrayed as a 'quiet hard-working man' whose life had been ruined by a quarrelsome and drunken wife. For these reasons he was found guilty only of manslaughter, for which he received six years' penal servitude. The newspaper comment following the trial makes instructive reading. A household containing a 'tippling virago', the *Mercury* wrote, 'could not be otherwise than disorderly and miserable'. If full control was not exercised by the husband, tragedy inevitably followed. The husband's mistake so far as the paper and the judge were concerned was not that he killed her in a fit of 'ungovernable passion' but that he 'continued his violence with a kind of savage ferocity which had not previously manifested itself in his disposition'. Had he simply delivered one fatal punch he might well have received a year or two in prison but he had lost his temper. Even so, six years hardly appears a sufficient punishment for a brutal killing.[35]

Where wives were killed in matrimonial fights, husbands could use the inquests to portray their spouses in a poor light. Edward Cannell, of Wilton Grove, Old Swan, went unchallenged in suggesting his wife had 'intemperate habits' and so, by implication, had spent the insurance money, set aside for the agent, on beer. There was, on the newspaper's part, no possibility of labelling Cannell a brute or a monster. He was a sober workman, whose push to his drunken wife on a slippery floor had resulted in her death. The charge was limited to manslaughter, for which he was acquitted.[36]

A similar outcome occurred after the inquest upon Ellen Sherry in 1893. Her body, the doctor explained, was covered in bruises, the liver lacerated and a pint and half of blood found in the abdominal cavity. She had, he opined, been the victim of a series of kicks rather than falling down two or three steps as had been suggested. When the relieving officer came to fetch her to the workhouse hospital, her husband, dock labourer James Sherry, told him she had 'pawned his clothes, drunk the money' and had 'no food in the house for him'. She had, in short, failed him in most wifely duties. The coroner's jury found a verdict of manslaughter with the qualification that Sherry 'had had great provocation'. At the following assizes the prosecution offered no evidence.[37]

Drunkenness was not the only charge levelled against female victims of wife beatings who had transgressed the ideals of Victorian femininity. Recently married Daniel Smith complained to the court that his wife, Ann, 'had been guilty of the grossest neglect, which was enough to drive any man from his home'. She even spat in his food as she cooked it, he alleged, saying 'anything was good enough for him. If he asked her for 1½d to get a glass of beer, she would refuse, and say anything was good enough for a dog like him.'[38] Rather than gaol him the magistrate awarded the wife four shillings a week in maintenance. There was a fine distinction between being seen as a down-trodden husband and an upstanding but injured party. Smith in this case was very close to being regarded as the former.

The sexual purity of women, or as the Victorians termed it 'chastity', was a virtue prized by all classes of men. What was meant by this? Women were expected to be not only sexually faithful to their partners but also modest in their dealings and behaviour with other men. Not surprisingly, sexual jealousy figured among the stated motives of wife beaters. Dinah Quigley was, claimed her husband, 'nothing better than a prostitute' because she had drunk with two different men on consecutive evenings. There had been no suggestion of a sexual relationship between her and either of the two men but her being out of the house and enjoying the company of other men was enough to enrage her husband.

Patrick McLean, however, caught his common-law wife on the knee of another man, who was also kissing her. Although drunk, he waited until they had returned to their room in Beatrice Street to give her what he called 'a warming'. He punched her head so badly that she was unconscious for three days before her death. While McLean admitted giving her the beating, he claimed that he did not fully realize how bad a beating it was, because of his drunkenness. He was charged with manslaughter rather than murder. In a more extreme case, in which a tailor, James Davies of Bostock Street, jumped on the face of Robert Renses and stabbed him twice with a pair of scissors, when he found him in the marital bed, the judge said: 'It was also a principle recognised by law, and by every man of common sense that where a man found another in the act of adultery with his wife, if he killed either the adulterer or his wife he was not guilty of murder, but of manslaughter, and that of the lowest degree, inasmuch as the greatest aggravation one man could receive from another was to see him in the act of adultery with his wife.'[39] Davies was given a four-day prison sentence and was immediately released, as he had been on remand for the four days of the assizes.

Knowledge of a wife's adultery was normally sufficient for a husband to receive lenient treatment at the hands of the court for any charges related to domestic violence. Robert Bradshaw, a shoemaker living in Howe Street, certainly found this to be the case. Continually taunted by his wife, who boasted of her unfaithful behaviour to him, Bradshaw was charged with attempting to murder her. He was seen kneeling over his wife, while cutting at her hands and throat. He was found guilty, though, of the reduced charge of unlawful wounding and imprisoned for just three months, 'in considera-tion of the provocation he had received'. His wife, who had refused to give evidence, was brought before the judge and given a 'severe reprimand' for her conduct towards her husband.[40] Bradshaw was fortunate in the manner in which his case had been tried and dealt with because, in the eyes of the law, a husband normally had to prove that he had attacked his wife in the heat of the moment, when his judgement was clouded by passion and rage. If there was a time lapse between the discovery of the adultery and the violence, then a beating could appear premeditated. In Bradshaw's case he had long known of his wife's adulterous behaviour but her taunts and jibes appear to have tipped him over the edge on this particular occasion.

Sex crimes: from rape to indecent exposure

L IVERPOOL WAS PROBABLY second only to London for the scale of its sex industry. Brothels, often advertised as boarding houses, were to be found in abundance close to the docks. Here the paid-off sailors could indulge in their two principal pastimes, namely drink and women. Given the large numbers of prostitutes and the prevailing attitudes towards women in general, one would expect to find many instances of sex crimes. However, the Victorian idealization of women meant that those who failed to come close to achieving these feminine virtues were cast down into the mire of sexual degeneracy. Women were either Madonnas or Magdalens, sainted mothers or whores. If the latter, then men had licence to do with them much as they pleased. This would have impacted on the reportage of sexual assaults and made the crime, to all intents and purposes, invisible.[41]

When one considers that Liverpool had a population close on half a million by 1871, it is somewhat surprising to discover that only three rapes were reported to the police over 1871–72. 'Assaults with intent to abuse and ravish' totalled a mere 12 cases. Clearly, annual police statistics are of little value in trying to assess the prevalence of sex crimes. This remains the case today. However, statistics do provide an insight into conviction rates for sex crimes. In 2007–08, 6.5% of reported rapes led to a conviction. How does this appalling statistic measure up to the second half of the nineteenth century? Between 1862 and 1892, there were a reported 99 rapes in Liverpool, which led to the arrest of 94 people. Of that total, 27 (29%) were found guilty and 55 (59%) were acquitted or discharged without reaching trial. Although we are dealing with small numbers, this conviction rate appears quite reasonable by today's standards. In examining the assaults with intent, there were 431 reported crimes and 231 arrests. Of those arrested, 114 (49%) were convicted and 97 (42%) acquitted or discharged.[42]

Rape was a hidden crime and it presented many problems for both the victim and the police. First, the shame of going before a court and making an accusation against the assailant was sometimes too much for the victim to bear. When one hard-working widow was making her way home to Kirkdale she was attacked by labourer Thomas Carnes, who dragged her towards a 'lonely place'. Her screams, however, attracted the attention of a policeman, who gave chase and eventually, after a struggle, arrested him. 'Feelings of delicacy' prevented the widow from bringing a prosecution, so Carnes was fortunate to be prosecuted only for assaulting the constable. The production of evidence in the days before DNA was an obvious difficulty for the victim. The case might end up as one person's word against another. This could prove disastrous if the accuser came from a lower class or was of lower status than the assailant. In a story headed 'THE ALLEGED INDECENT ASSAULT BY A YOUNG GENTLEMAN', William Henry Powell of Breck Road was accused by one of the family's domestic servants of indecent assault. In support of her case two witnesses spoke of her being distressed when she told them of being chased from one room to another by 'young Mr. Powell'. Another servant complained that she too had been chased by the defendant. The servant's allegation was effectively undermined by the mistress of the house, who was also mother of the defendant. She was able to introduce doubt and conflicting evidence from an obviously distressed servant, who had initially complained of her son taking liberties. On the evidence presented in court the magistrates dismissed the case but the way the case was reported in the paper hints that something had taken place.[43]

Young domestic servants were clearly very vulnerable to the unwanted advances of their employers. In such cases the dividing line between civil and criminal law could be very fine and difficult to determine for examining magistrates. When 18-year-old Mary X complained to her aunt of being raped by her elderly master, bread and flour dealer Charles Robertson, the court heard conflicting evidence. For her part Mary spoke of having resisted the attack by screaming, but to no avail. She also informed her aunt that very evening of what had occurred. Robertson's defence argued that he had 'taken liberties' with her on previous occasions and consequently she was a 'consenting party'. The medical evidence proved insufficiently conclusive for the magistrate to send the case to a higher court, but he felt Robertson had behaved disgracefully, so much so that he felt Mary and her family could bring a civil case for seduction.[44]

Another important piece of evidence which could favour the victim's case was whether she resisted the sexual assault. If she screamed or struggled with the rapist and managed to attract the attention of passers-by, then her case against the defendant was strengthened. Newly arrived servant Flora, in search of work in Liverpool, naively allowed Corporal James Kelly to 'show her the way' back to her lodgings. When the pair got to St Martin's Field, he grossly assaulted her. Here her cries of 'murder' were heard by a patrolling constable, who rushed to the spot and arrested Kelly. In a most unusual case, 18-year-old Ann of Circus Street told the court how she met James Riley, a sweep, and Catherine Burkey, who invited her for a drink at 4 a.m. to a house in Baptist Street. While Riley tried to rape Ann, Burkey allegedly held down her arms and head. Neighbours who heard her screams immediately sent for a constable, who overheard conversation which indicated that an attempted rape had taken place. They were both later found guilty at the borough sessions and sentenced to six months with hard labour.[45]

Women who persisted in pressing charges could lay themselves open to possible character assassination from the defendants' legal representatives. Defamation of a woman's character by referring to previous extra-marital relationships was an effective way of undermining a prosecution. The fact that Ann X of Everton admitted in court that she had previously been seduced by a man who had since emigrated to Australia was used by the magistrates to summarily convict John Benson, 'of respectable appearance', for gross outrage on her. They argued that they were protecting her character when in fact it was an excuse to give the exceedingly small punishment of a £5 fine to Benson. A similar fine was levied on John Gibson, an ex-policeman, who committed an indecent assault on a policeman's wife. His defence was that she had 'encouraged' him with loose conversation and improper behaviour.[46]

In such circumstances, therefore, it is a surprise to find that one Liverpool woman whose reputation had been undermined was able to gain a conviction in a case of attempted rape. In the initial magistrates' hearing, the case appeared relatively clear cut. Mary Y, a married woman between 40 and 50 years old, was going home late after work. In Upper Frederick Street she had been assaulted by a young man, Edward Boulton, a complete stranger to her, who knocked her on the head and then sexually assaulted her in the street. The next day the case came up again. However, this time the court heard that Mary Y had lied the previous day. She had not been working and she was in drink at the time of the alleged assault. She had, she claimed, been watching the SS *Great Eastern*, the massive steam sailing ship, then in Liverpool. It was further claimed by the defence solicitor that she had made 'improper advances' towards Boulton and was 'little better than a common prostitute'. The magistrate replied that 'even if she were a prostitute that would not justify such an assault … and she was as much entitled to protection as any other woman'. This response was most unusual but it does chime with a remark, made later by a justice of the peace, who argued that it was disgraceful that women could not walk the streets without being assaulted.[47]

Neither the criminal charge nor the severity of the punishment for those found guilty of sex crimes necessarily reflected what kind of assault had taken place. Rape, for example, often led only to a charge of attempted rape, indecent assault or even common assault. This was done in order to increase the chance of a successful prosecution, as the level of proof required was not as great for the lesser crimes. When James Woods, a 21-year-old seaman, met Jane, a married woman, in Carnaevon Street, sitting on her doorstep, he invited himself into her home. Once in, he locked the door, took the baby she was holding from her arms and dragged her into the bedroom. Jane, desperate by now, began screaming and struggling, which brought neighbours to her door whereupon Woods punched her in the face and ran away. The punch was all that was witnessed by other people, even though his stated intention had been to rape Jane, hence his relatively mild punishment of two months with hard labour.[48]

Sentences could range from two months' imprisonment in the local gaol to 20 years' penal servitude in convict prisons. Where penal servitude was ordered, it reflected the severity of the attack. In 1867, following an Irish wake, basket girl Ann agreed to go to a pub with 21-year-old Hugh Tully M'Keown, where he was alleged to have put something, tobacco it was thought, in her drink. On leaving the pub he assaulted her on some wasteland and pushed the screaming and struggling Ann into a 10-foot deep hole. Here he raped the already injured girl and then continued to abuse and kick her for the next three hours. Her groans were heard by a policeman, who discovered M'Keown kicking the young woman. This was, said the judge, the sort of case which would have attracted a death sentence when rape was a hanging offence (it was so up to 1841). He ordered him to be kept in penal servitude for 20 years.[49] Penal servitude was also often reserved for men who raped their own or other children.

Lesser crimes of a sexual nature, such as indecent exposure, could incur two-week prison sentences or fines of up to 40 shillings. When self-styled 'professor of music' Carl Henrich raised a married woman's clothes up to her face with his walking stick he was charged only with being drunk and common assault. His defence was that he had been surrounded by prosti-tutes in London Road and, being afraid that they would steal his watch and chain, he had swung his stick around in self-defence. The fact that he was drunk and that there were no other people present other than the woman and her husband meant that he was found guilty and fined 20 shillings.[50]

Conclusion

Wives and female partners, while protected by specific laws, had to combat prevailing Victorian attitudes. Many people believed it was right and proper to hit women. More importantly, a battered woman had to be able prove her character was good and her behaviour temperate, obedient and modest. She was, in effect, locked into a role of subjugation. The husband, on the other hand, could drink, for that is what men did, demand total obedience and order his wife to cook at whatever times of the day to suit his whim. If she disobeyed she was a 'bad wife', who could then be slapped. The neighbours often subscribed to these domestic arrangements and would turn a blind eye and a deaf ear to any assaults in their court. Over time, the slapping could escalate to become a punching, a beating with the poker or a kicking. While the legislature and the courts attempted to outlaw such behaviour, and the press stigmatized those men who practised and continued such customs, and branded them as brutes, wife beatings continued. Popular sentiment, both male and female, proved very hard to change and wife beating continued to be an essentially accepted practice into the twentieth century. The location and the stigmatization of this crime as being more typical of the slum-living poor than of the other classes enabled the crime to be conveniently downplayed and hidden. It would appear from the available evidence that the police intervened more actively in domestic disputes in the last quarter of the nineteenth century than in the years around the middle of that century. Liverpool was in no way exceptional in terms of attitudes towards domestic violence. The frequency of such attacks on wives and partners was, in many respects, a reflection of the large amounts of alcohol consumed, the poverty and the cramped living conditions of the town. Such conditions could be found in most large cities and industrial towns. What marked Liverpool out was the cluster of violent crimes in the 1870s which gave the town a bad name.

Crimes of sexual violence, while apparently less frequent and certainly less recorded than domestic violence, displayed many similarities to these latter assaults. They all belonged on the same spectrum of violence towards women. The acts of violence, whether sexual or not, reflected male attitudes towards women and their domination and power over them. Women, in effect, had to know their place; even as victims of assault, they came under scrutiny for any moral failings which might invite chastisement. The law struggled over the years to alter prevailing male attitudes and men's acts of brutality towards women, but magistrates and judges did occasionally surprise society with their harsh sentences and their belief that women should be allowed to walk unchaperoned and unmolested along the streets of town.

CHAPTER 10

'A constant state of strife': family violence

D OMESTIC VIOLENCE, in which men hit their female partners, was and still is one of the most under-reported crimes. Even more hidden, though, was the casual brutality and verbal and physical bullying that commonly occurred in the courts and terraces between members of the wider family. While this kind of intra-family violence shared many of the characteristics of domestic violence, not least women being the main victims of male anger, this form of domestic brutality was regarded with particular horror by the press and the judiciary. Whereas conventions associated with male dominance and the notion of the right to strike one's wife were still popular within the community, no such conventions or traditions allowed for the striking of, for example, one's mother. Adult sons who struck either or both of their parents were viewed as 'unnatural' and 'unfilial' brutes.

A mother killed by her son

O N SATURDAY 1 NOVEMBER 1873, in Liverpool's most notorious street, Chisenhale Street, a murder was committed that was described by the *Liverpool Mercury* as 'the most horrible in its character which perhaps has ever occurred in Liverpool'. This was the killing of Mary Corrigan. What made the murder so shocking to contemporaries was that it was Mary's son, Thomas, who killed her. In what was described as a respectable boarding house, untypical of the area, there lived the Corrigan family, comprising father, mother and 25-year-old son, the latter's partner, Martha Knight, the Harris family of five and James Canavan. All were at home that Saturday evening. Mary was in the parlour, crying about the unwelcome presence of her son's partner, who was now co-habiting in the house, when a drunk Thomas Corrigan angrily descended the stairs to the kitchen, where he asked his mother for some tea. She replied that it was cooking in the oven, whereupon he checked by opening the oven door to find nothing there. In order to placate her son, she claimed that she had sent out for some, but by now it was too late to appease him.

Illustration 4 Thomas Corrigan as pictured in the *Illustrated Police News*, 8 November 1873. Reproduced with the permission of the British Library, Colindale Newspaper Library.

The manner in which he beat her was graphically described in the paper and in the subsequent coroner and court proceedings. First, he seized her by the shoulder and punched her in the face; he then grabbed her hair and dashed her head on the ground a couple of times. All this was done in front of three other men: his father, Harris and Canavan. Turning on them all, he shouted that he was going 'to clear the house', and threw punches at them until two of the three ran out. For some reason Harris and his wife were allowed to remain in the kitchen when he bolted the door. Turning his attention back to his prostrate mother, Corrigan grabbed the corner of the kitchen table for support and balance, then proceeded to jump on his mother (it was described as 'dancing') until she lost consciousness. At this point he called down his partner, who helped Mrs Harris undress and carry Mary Corrigan to a downstairs bed. On being revived by a glass of water thrown over her, the mother somehow found the strength to pull herself up the stairs, where she hid naked behind a lodger's door. On seeing the bed empty Corrigan rushed to the floor above and threw her back downstairs, where he recommenced his brutal assault. This time he used the buckle end of a leather belt wrapped around his knuckle. After repeated blows to her face, he 'danced' on her once more, again using the table as a support, until she was lifeless. The fatal assault had lasted just over two hours and had left Mary Corrigan with a ruptured eyeball, wounds to her head which went down to the skull bone and fractures to all her ribs on the left side of her body. Blood was seen to issue from her eyes, ears and mouth and her face was 'a mass of pulp' when the local Catholic priest, Father Ross, arrived on the scene. Neither he nor the local constable whom he had sent for believed Corrigan's claim that his drunken mother had fallen while in a street brawl. For good measure Corrigan had poured two glasses of spirits down her throat while she lay on the floor. He did this not to revive her but to enhance his story of her drunkenness.[1]

This atrocity shocked the town to its very core. Thousands visited the street and stood and gawped outside the house, and the *Mercury* sent its own reporter to describe this notorious neighbourhood so its readership could relish the horrors of Chisenhale in the comfort of their own home. This murder was, in short, a sensation. The actual manner of the killing apart – the 'dancing' on the stomach and head attracted most attention – the killing raised important questions as to the behaviour of witnesses and neighbours, who must have heard the woman's shrieks during the two-hour ordeal. Neighbourly non-intervention was explained by the frequency of domestic arguments and fights in that particular area. People were used to hearing cries of 'murder' and 'help' which never actually ended in anybody's death. In addition, as the *Porcupine* noted, 'neighbours are chary of interfering in these domestic dramas ... lest they might be set upon by both parties, and perhaps implicated in the broil'.[2] More difficult to explain, and for the magistrate, Mr Raffles, to forgive, was the apparent inaction of Mary Corrigan's husband and the spectators to the actual murder.

Described as a 'small man', the father and husband, Patrick, had been able to escape after the initial assault but he failed to alert the police. He had, he told the inquest, gone to the barber's and therefore did not witness the murder. 'It made one's blood boil', said the magistrate, 'to imagine such things could happen in a house among a number of people'. Those who were left locked in the house with Corrigan were, claimed the *Mercury*, 'paralysed with fear' and genuinely frightened for their own safety. Tommy Corrigan, one of the 'Red' Corrigans (the 'Black' Corrigans of the same street were their sworn enemies) on account of his sandy-coloured hair, had a notorious reputation for violence, having been up before the magistrate on five previous occasions. He was by all accounts a powerfully built young man, who occasionally worked at the docks and was regarded with 'terror' by all who knew him. He was found guilty and executed at Kirkdale gaol on the morning of 5 January 1874.[3]

The matricide of Mary Corrigan was an extreme case but contained within its narrative many aspects common to family-on-family assaults. First, the victims were commonly mothers, who suffered at the hands of their sons, who terrorized their families, fathers included. Second, the initial spark which set Tom Corrigan off on his drink-fuelled violent rage included, among other things, his mother's disapproval at his bringing a woman home to live in the house, and his demand for a meal which was not yet cooked. Both these reasons were cited in other cases where sons beat mothers. The other main cause cited in cases where sons assaulted their mothers involved disputes over money. In most cases, the sons were invariably portrayed as worthless, idle loafers, while the mothers were usually seen in positive terms, as homemakers, trying under very difficult circumstances to make the best of the situation. So when sons refused to contribute to the family budget, or raided their mothers' purses for drink money, they were viewed as contemptible. Often, evidence cited in court suggested that such sons repeatedly behaved badly at home. Robert Lovett, for example, son of oyster seller Mrs Lovett of Williamson Square, was brought before magistrate Mr Mansfield for the third time for assaulting his mother. Typical punishments for such assaults on one's mother ranged between three and six months' imprisonment with hard labour. James Shields of Upper Frederick Street must have counted himself fortunate when he received a sentence of a mere one month of hard labour when he came home in a drunken rage and broke up the furniture and hit his mother.[4]

Occasionally mothers were portrayed in critical terms. This was certainly true of Ellen Jenkins of Gascoyne Street, who was killed by her son Joseph. Tried for manslaughter, he was described as a 'very good son', who always took his weekly wage home to his mother. However, on the night of the killing both he and his mother were the worse for drink and instead of taking Joseph's trousers out of pawn as requested, Ellen spent the money on more drink. This started an argument in which the mother struck out at her son with a poker and he kicked her. Other witnesses spoke of Ellen in disparaging terms as a drunken and violent woman who regularly pawned her son's clothes for drink money. On being found guilty of manslaughter Joseph was sentenced to just one month with hard labour.[5]

When Robert Foster, aged 23, was charged in 1896 with killing his mother, Annie, in Upper Mann Street, witnesses, including his sister, described the mother as a habitual drunk who ate very little. Although he was seen to drag her by the hair out of a neighbour's house and into the street, where he hit her 'with an open hand' and then kicked her three times, the post-mortem examination showed that Annie suffered from a diseased liver and kidneys as well as fatty degeneration of the heart. All these factors, the physical assault apart, weighed heavily in the son's favour. He was charged only with manslaughter and he was allowed out on bail until the assizes. Unsurprisingly, his mother's intemperate habits and the poor state of her internal organs were emphasized during the trial and Foster was acquitted.[6]

'Home Rulers': adult sons

OTHER MEMBERS OF THE FAMILY, fathers and sisters particularly, were sometimes beaten by these brutal and often drunken young men. In a play on words the *Mercury* ran a headline 'A HOME RULER' for an article that recounted the behaviour of 20-year-old Charles Squire, whose father, unusually, was described as a 'private gentleman'. In what must be regarded as a typical encounter, his mother began cooking him a meal on his return home from having been out all night. During the course of this domestic scene Mrs Squire told him not to bring his friend to the house, which infuriated Charles. He leapt up, smashed the frying pan into the fire, lashed out at his sister with a knife and 'conducted himself in a most overbearing and tyrannical manner to the family'. The father complained to the court that his son expected to be maintained until he was 21 years old and that he was unable to control the stronger younger man. The son received one month with hard labour.[7]

While women members of the family were the most vulnerable, brawls between male in-laws were not unusual. Again, drink lubricated and heightened emotions which may have been, in more calm moments, suppressed. Sectarian differences between man and wife could provide ready triggers for some quite serious disagreements. When Thomas Johnson got into a fight with his father-in-law in Kew Street, just off Scotland Road, he picked up a bacon knife from the counter in a shop where he had been hiding and cut the father-in-law's nose 'clean off'. When asked why he had done it he said that his father-in-law had called him a '— Orange dog'. In other cases mothers-in-law were victims of their son-in-law's anger. When ruling on a case in which John Shepherd tore off Ann Finnegan's bonnet, punched her in the face and then cut her ear while holding her down on the ground, the magistrate agreed that he had been provoked by the fact that she had spat in his face first. George Knowlson, on the other hand, received penal servitude for life for killing his mother-in-law on a reduced charge of manslaughter, in what can only be described as a vicious and prolonged attack. In a brutal assault which attracted many witnesses, all intent on watching the action, Knowlson spent up to 15 minutes beating and kicking Mary Garvey, who was looking after her daughter, who had left home about two weeks earlier. Although neighbours repeatedly separated the assailant and his victim in a fight that moved from an upstairs room down to the court outside, no one thought to call the police until it was over. During that time Knowlson had gone back to his house, fetched a bricklayer's hammer and, with a large crowd at his heel, returned and struck Mary Garvey on her head. What had provoked so extreme a reaction? Knowlson told witnesses at the time of the killing that his mother-in-law had cut him when she attacked him. 'She had', he angrily proclaimed, 'spilt my Protestant blood, and I will have her Papist blood'. An unhappy mixed marriage, therefore, lay at the heart of this domestic tragedy.[8]

To modern eyes, the Knowlson case looks like a *prima facie* case of murder rather than manslaughter. He had, after all, attacked his mother-in-law over the space of about 20 minutes, taking time off to go home and return with a bricklayer's hammer. This suggests a certain amount of premeditation on his part. Witnesses spoke of Knowlson kneeling on the pavement in a public and ritualized manner, and striking the ground and demanding that he would have 'blood for blood'. More damningly, it was alleged that, as he went back into the house clutching his hammer the second time, he had said 'Now for it'. Although the prosecution put it to the jury that Knowlson had committed murder, the defence argued that he had been attacked by his mother-in-law, which brought about his drunken rage. His murderous attack was, thus, not premeditated and, as he acted in a passion, the killing was manslaughter. The jury, perhaps reluctant to place a man on the scaffold – capital punishment was becoming less popular by this time – found the prisoner guilty of 'aggravated manslaughter'. This was a new and remarkable finding, which suggested the dividing line between murder and manslaughter was now very fine indeed.

However, violence was sometimes used to stop domestic violence. Patrick Scholls, for example, hit his son-in-law for ill using his daughter, while Charles McKay stabbed his brother-in-law, who had interfered in a domestic dispute between his sister and her husband McKay.[9] In both cases the assailants were acting in a traditional male role, as protectors of their female relatives. Such incidents could end in tragedy. When a drunken James Hanney, the elder, demanded from his wife more money for drink, he threw a chimney ornament at her and shouted offensive language. This enraged their son, James Hanney, the younger, who had a tussle with his father and cut him in his chest, which led to his death. In attempting to lessen the charge and punishment, the son's defence team called James the elder a drunkard, who routinely acted in a brutal way towards his family. The son was, the defence claimed, only coming to his mother's aid. Found guilty of manslaughter, the judge conceded that the son had been provoked but the fact that he had used a weapon meant that he was sentenced to five years' penal servitude.[10]

Wives, mothers and daughters

NOT ALL FAMILY VIOLENCE was initiated by men; women, as shown in chapter 8, did not always conform to the stereotype of the passive and modest female figure to which Victorian respectability expected them to adhere. In particular, the mother–daughter relationship could, at times, be stormy. When Catherine Kearns, mother of seven children, was brought before the magistrate for stabbing her daughter Mary Anne, arguments as to who was the more disreputable were put to Mr Mansfield. The mother, in her favour, claimed she had been abandoned by 'her man' in St Helens and left so destitute as to force her into putting her children into workhouses in Liverpool and St Helens. In addition, her daughter was, she alleged, visiting a Scotland Road herbalist with a view to buying items to bring about an abortion. The daughter, described as a 'decent-looking young female' and respectably employed in domestic service, was able to tell the court that her mother had abandoned her children when she went off with 'her man'. This appears to have led to the argument and the mother's assault on her daughter's face with a knife. She was gaoled for three months with hard labour.[11]

More typical were assaults by daughters on their mothers over issues which resonate with the present day. When Eleanor Valaley's mother told her off for stopping out all night with her 'fancy man' while her husband was away in Australia, the daughter 'leathered' her with a poker and a toasting fork before pushing her downstairs. Mary Ann Keating, on the other hand, attacked her mother in the street when the latter refused to give her money. She knocked her down and kicked her in the body and face, blinding her in the right eye in the process.[12]

Wives were exhorted to obey their husbands, to be passive and submissive in their relationships with their partners, but was this always the case? How did the male partner or husband appear to the outside world if he prosecuted his female partner for assault? What took place in the home usually stayed in the home, be it a case of domestic violence by the man on his wife or, more importantly and humiliatingly for any Victorian man, the wife's attack on her husband. When such domestic tiffs did find their way into the court room, the press and even the court officials adopted a comical tone. The man, instead of being portrayed as master in his own home, was regarded as weak and emasculated. In what turned out to be the equivalent of a divorce proceeding, George Urquhart summoned his wife, Elizabeth, for assaulting him with a brass candlestick. She had, one newspaper noted, 'attained a mature age, as indicated by the whiteness of her locks, but she retained all the vigour of youth, if the violence used to her spouse and her conduct in court might be taken as a criterion'. Although the magistrate initially told her 'to go home; to coax, caress and endeavour to make the complainant comfortable', he was happy to accept the husband's offer of five shillings a week as a separation allowance. Judging by the woman's reaction, all smiles as she left the court room after the judgement, the violence she had employed may well have been a tactic to gain the separation.[13]

In an article ironically headlined 'MATRIMONIAL BLISS', the *Liverpool Mercury* reported the case laid before the magistrates' bench concerning the unhappy marriage of Patrick Hagan, 'a thin, dark-looking Irishman' who looked 'well henpecked'. He complained of having been beaten by his wife, Bridget, with a poker without any provocation. However, the more the magistrates enquired into the case, the less sympathetic they were towards Patrick, who, it transpired, was a returned convict. The magistrates negotiated a weekly allowance of 15 shillings for his wife and two of their children, a feather bed and some furniture, on the understanding that she was not to annoy Patrick in the future.[14]

Although the courts sometimes made light of these incidents and held the husbands up to ridicule, these domestic quarrels often signified deep-seated hatreds and had serious outcomes. In five cases which had fatal outcomes for the male partner, none of the women was found guilty of murder, although some were tried under that charge. Sarah Brady was found kneeling over the prostrate body of her husband by a neighbour, who reported that Brady's fingers were so tightly wrapped around the muffler which she had used to strangle him that she could not release her fingers. Only when a policeman came and cut the neckerchief could the drunken Brady release her hand. During the trial it was said that the couple did not have a happy marriage but there was evidence only of them quarrelling, rather than fighting. However, on the day of James Brady's death, neighbours swore to having heard Sarah say that she was going to kill him. Found guilty of manslaughter rather than murder, she was sentenced to 10 years' penal servitude.[15]

As one would expect in cases like these, trial evidence often suggested that the female defendants had themselves been subjected to physical violence for many years. The killing of their male partners thus represented the women's solution to past experiences of domestic violence. Whether these acts could be construed as premeditated or, conversely, done in a passion proved to be a difficult and controversial legal problem. When 'respectable' Sarah Corduroy (alias Lyon) of Upper Frederick Street stabbed her 'husband' Edward to death it caused a 'considerable sensation' in the neighbourhood. What started out as an argument over a lack of gravy for his steak for lunch turned into domestic violence when Edward struck Sarah. They tussled on the ground until a neighbour separated them. On getting to her feet Sarah Corduroy grabbed a table knife, which she plunged into Edward's chest. In addressing the jury on her behalf, Mr Sidgreaves argued that, at the time of the fatal knife attack, Sarah was acting in fear of her life and grabbed the nearest thing to hand with which to defend herself. This argument proved successful insofar as the jury found her guilty of manslaughter, with a strong recommendation to mercy on the grounds of provocation. It was a recommendation to which the judge concurred, as he sentenced her to only four months' imprisonment.[16]

When 44-year-old Mary McAleavey went to her neighbour's house in Tamworth Street she told her, 'The brute is rowing me again. Look at my fingers. He has crushed them in the door.' She was, it was said in court, 'very much frightened of him', especially when he was in drink, which was most of the time. Her character was further enhanced when she was described as a 'very hard working woman'. Her husband, the inquest was informed, died from a fracture of the skull, produced by either a fall or a blow from a poker. Although Mary admitted to hitting him on the head with a key during a fight in which he was beating her, the coroner's jury came to a verdict which appears to have favoured her. The jury accepted that death was caused by the wound to the head but 'that there was insufficient evidence to show how the wound was caused'.[17] This finding may well have led to Mary's discharge from police custody, as the case never appeared again in the press.

Where the wife had a less than favourable character and fell short of the domestic ideals set by society for married women, the courts showed little sympathy. Catherine M'Donald, tried at the winter assizes for attempted murder of her husband, John, was painted as a drunken, violent and neglectful wife. Although described by John as a wife 'as good as any in Liverpool' when off the bottle, his pleas for her not to be gaoled went unheeded. She received the comparatively severe sentence of seven years' penal servitude and he was admonished by the judge for being weak and requiring protection from 'the virago'. Her defence suggested that married life within the privacy of the home was rather different from that portrayed to the court by the 'steady, hard-working' John. She complained of being all alone and having to put up with her husband and his mother. The former had, she alleged, been standing over her during the fight, with a poker in his hand, which he had used to beat her to the floor. She had stabbed him with a bread knife, fork and chisel.[18]

Conclusion

DOMESTIC VIOLENCE or, more accurately, violence in the working-class home ranged far beyond the archetypical drunken and violent husband who thrashed his miserable, careworn and submissive wife to the ground in front of a family of small terrified children. All members of the nuclear family and both sexes indulged in brutality with other family members. 'Surly' wives and adult sons particularly were the main protagonists other than the husband/father, although it was the mother who was often the main target. Not surprisingly, neighbours were loathe to intervene or interfere in these family rows, even though they were often the first port of possible refuge for victims.

CHAPTER 11

'Boy brigands' and 'young savages': juvenile criminals and their young victims

> Even crime has its regular habits and respectabilities, so to speak, its laws and etiquette, its proper times and seasons, which it must keep to on peril of being deprived of its official and statistical reputation. There is a proper and expected age for different kinds of misbehaviour; lying has its age, unhappily often a very early one; theft begins later, and brutality later still.[1]

THE ASSOCIATION BETWEEN children and violence is perceived in a curious and at times contradictory manner. Children are, on the one hand, defenceless innocents killed, as in the recent cases of young Rhys Jones (caught in the crossfire of a Liverpool gang vendetta in 2007) and of Sarah Payne (murdered in 2000 for the pleasure of a predatory and dangerous adult); on the other, they are themselves 'little monsters', like Jon Venables and Robert Thompson, who murdered James Bulger in Liverpool in 1993. In this latter role children have been branded as 'evil' and as capable of any terrible act as the most degenerate and violent adult. It is almost as if they were born bad rather than being themselves victims, on the receiving end of a constant barrage of violent forces in which moral boundaries are wholly absent and which, by degrees, turn them bad. In much the same way that 'video nasties' were invoked as causal agents in the late twentieth and early twenty-first centuries, plays about highwaymen heroes in the nineteenth were thought to act as catalysts which unleashed the evil lying dormant within children's small frames.

This chapter is concerned with children who turn to violence, children who kill even. Their presence and their actions can haunt a generation of adults; they can trigger doubts and anxieties within society and raise fears for the future which go far beyond the individual acts of aggression. In that sense, violent children can frighten us more than violent adults. We can, as a consequence, learn a great deal about a society through the manner in which it views, reacts to and treats or punishes children who are violent. In this respect, Victorian Liverpool offers considerable evidence on both violent children and their victims (invariably other children) and, as such, was probably typical of many large towns and cities during the nineteenth century.

Children and the age of criminal responsibility

FOR MANY CENTURIES the law, and hence the courts, have had difficulty in setting the age of criminal responsibility for children. This need to establish an age point when a child could differentiate right from wrong, good from evil, was important inasmuch as punishments, and in the case of murder capital punishment, had to be determined and meted out by the judicial authorities. Since the medieval period it has been accepted practice to set age boundaries that divide infancy from childhood and childhood from adulthood. For example, children below the age of seven years have never been held responsible for any felony they may have committed because the courts believed they were unable to discern right from wrong. However, children aged between seven and 14 years have offered the courts, and in particular judges and juries, a particular set of problems. It became the responsibility of the judge to determine at the outset of the trial whether a child defendant aged between seven and 14 knew right from wrong, what is known as *doli capax*. The test to determine this took on a number of different forms, not least a simple question–answer session in which the child was asked if he or she had heard of God, the Bible and the Devil. The test might then have moved on to more specific but simple ethical issues to do with theft. On the basis of the answers received the judge decided whether the child was old enough to stand trial. The jury, too, at the completion of the trial evidence, would make a judgement on the age issue when reaching their verdict. If, in their opinion, the child was too young to have understood the full import of the actions, they would acquit the defendant. In other cases they might find the defendant guilty, but either on a lesser charge (manslaughter rather than murder, for example) or with a recommendation of mercy for the defendant on account of age. The law then, as now, allowed for discretion and recognized that children matured intellectually, physically and emotionally at different rates. But the law's very imprecision might also mean that there was a lack of uniformity of practice. By the nineteenth century, the law with regard to children and adolescents had, though, become fixed: children aged seven and under could not be held criminally responsible, while those between eight and 14 could be deemed to be responsible and liable for their actions.[2]

'The ghastliest murder on record': child killers and their young victims

FIRST AND FOREMOST, the killing of children by other children has often been viewed as extremely unusual. This raises the question, how unusual? A number of authors have identified child killers from the past, going back to the eighteenth century. Infamous and notorious children appear at fairly long but regular intervals during the nineteenth and twentieth centuries.[3] It has been possible to select a sample drawn from north-west England between 1853 and 1899, comprising 21 killings committed by children aged 16 years and under. In terms of suspects, there were 30 boys and just one girl. When this group is broken down by age (where known), 11 were aged between 13 and 16 years, 2 between 10 and 12 years, and a surprisingly high figure of eight were under 10 years.

When we examine the cases relating specifically to Liverpool, there were 12 killings, involving 16 individuals, all boys. Only five of them were charged with murder and eight with the less serious manslaughter charge. In the remaining cases the charges were either dropped or not brought against anyone, as the case never proceeded beyond the coroner's court. Only one, 16-year-old Michael Lavelle, was found guilty and sentenced to death but he was reprieved, on account of his youth, in 1886. His trial and sentence gave rise to public anxiety and concern in Liverpool about the death penalty for young people more than any other case during the nineteenth century. In light not only Lavelle's youth but also the circumstances surrounding his murder of Maxwell Kirkpatrick, who had constantly bullied and insulted him at Tickle's Timber Yard, Blackstock Street, the death sentence outraged many in the town. A subscription and petition were set up on Lavelle's behalf, and any outstanding money was sent to Kirkpatrick's widow.[4]

Where the boys were under the age of 10, four in total (two murders each involving two accused), they were closely assessed for their criminal responsibility by the juries, both before standing trial and at the trial's completion. In both cases where the boys were under 10 years old, they drowned their victims, who were younger than themselves. The first of the two cases concerned John Breen and Alfred Fitzpatrick, both aged nine years. One summer's Sunday evening in July 1855 seven-year-old James Fleeson failed to return to his home in Saltney Street. By the following Wednesday Fleeson's father, also called James, went in search of work at the Stanley Dock, where, by some strange coincidence, he saw a body floating in the dock pool. On removing it from the water he identified his son, whose head showed signs of having been hit before the body was placed in the water. At this point in the narrative, it is worth noting that the Fleeson family, who lived in a poor neighbourhood, had made 'every enquiry' into their son's whereabouts, but nowhere is it reported that they had informed and involved the police in any search. The other detail which one can only speculate on concerns the coincidence of the father finding his son in the water two and half days after the killing. Had someone in the neighbourhood told him to look there? This thought does not seem altogether unfeasible when the details of the subsequent police investigation became known at the coroner's inquest and later at the assize court. The main witness, nine-year-old James Hawkins, described as 'a sharp little fellow' from the same street as the victim, told the police how he, Fleeson,

Breen and Fitz (as Alfred Fitzpatrick became abbreviated) had gone to play in the neighbouring brickfields along with some other boys. Here, while playing 'leap on back' (leapfrog), Fitz accused Fleeson of not having taken a fair jump. According to Hawkins, the argument lasted about half an hour before Fitz took up half a brick and struck Fleeson on the temple, and struck him again while he was on the ground and experiencing convulsions. Fitz, along with Breen, then dragged Fleeson by his arms and legs about 40 yards to the Leeds–Liverpool canal and threw him in. That Fleeson was still alive at this stage was never doubted, for, as Hawkins later recalled, he 'struggled for a minute or two on top of the water and then sank'.

All this had occurred in front of a group of boys and one woman who claimed to have seen the fight but not the drowning, yet no one had attempted to intervene or rescue Fleeson. Hawkins did go home and tell his parents, although he failed to follow up his threat to Fitz and Breen that he would tell Fleeson's father. Thus, between Sunday and the following Thursday morning, when the police were notified, 'the matter was kept secret ... though the fate of little Fleeson was generally known in the street', where all the families concerned lived as neighbours. 'A kind of agreement', reported the *Liverpool Mercury*, 'was entered into to keep it from the ears of the police'. When Fitz was finally arrested his father tried to stab the police inspector, while his mother was in Brownlow Hill night asylum awaiting an order of passage to Ireland for herself and her three children, Alfred included.

When, at the subsequent inquest, the coroner's jury was asked to reach their decision, the coroner reminded them of the law and the culpability of children between seven and 14 years of age. The jury, rather unusually, stated that in their opinion the boys had committed murder but were reluctant to express this finding. Once the coroner had eased their concerns regarding the death penalty and the fact that the children would almost certainly not hang if found guilty of the capital offence, the boys were committed to trial on the charge of murder. It was apparent that while the court and the press viewed this murder as extraordinary, they placed it in the context of the children's poverty and poor upbringing. Both defendants appeared to be in a state of neglect, being 'bareheaded and barefooted', thus punishment would place them in better care than they had been used to. In short, the boys were thought to be reformable. On being found guilty of the lesser charge of manslaughter, they were sentenced to Walton gaol, an adult prison, for 12 months, where they were taught, in separate cells, the craft of shoemaking and to read and write.[5]

The second case occurred in 1891 and involved the drowning of eight-year-old David Eccles by nine-year-old Samuel Crawford and eight-year-old Robert Shearon or Sheeran, in a pit on a building site at the corner of Victoria Street and Stanley Street. This case was significantly different from the other case, in that the stated motive was to steal Eccles' clothes, although a reading of the evidence emphasizes the callous, cool indifference of the children. From the account of witnesses who saw the incident developing, two lads, one of whom was dressed only in a sackcloth (later identified as Shearon), were seen to 'entice a well-dressed' little boy behind some hoarding where there was a plank, known as 'the rafts', laid across a pit full of water within an unfinished building. The evidence suggests that Crawford and Shearon ordered him to walk onto the plank, where he was pushed off into the water. He was then dragged out and stripped naked and pushed in twice more. It soon became evident that this was no 'ordinary clothes stripping' (quite a common crime in Liverpool), for, during the third ducking, Crawford knelt on Eccles' head, which was face down in the water, for five minutes. After waiting to see if he moved the boys left the building site at 9.00 p.m., having divided up the clothes. Shearon took Eccles' coat, trousers and shirt, and Crawford his vest. The boots, socks and cap were thrown back into the pit.

As in the 1855 case, witnesses entered into conversation with the children. In this instance some apprentice printers sensed something was amiss when they saw a lad with 'nothing but a sack and the remnant of a coat about him' and some other boys trying to get a boy with a 'corduroy suit and stockings on' over some hoardings. The boy with the sack told one of the witnesses that his clothes had been stolen, when, in fact, according to his mother, she had sent him to bed naked and had hidden his clothes. This punishment came about as the result of Shearon having stayed out for two consecutive nights. Another significant difference from the 1855 killing was the apparent desire of the witnesses and the mother of one of the accused to involve the police. The printers claimed they had sent one of their number to find a policeman before the killing had taken place but he had failed to locate one. We may have to treat this evidence with a little caution, insofar as the apprentices wanted, no doubt, to cast their actions in the best possible light, hence their unsubstantiated claim to have looked for a policeman. If, on the other hand, they had done nothing and subsequently learnt that they had been passive witnesses to the killing of a young boy, they may have felt an element of guilt and shame. Whatever the truth of the matter, the fact that they felt a policeman should have been involved suggests that a sea-change in attitudes had occurred during the second half of the nineteenth century. The police had, by the 1890s, become very much an integral part of city street life. This was emphasized still more by the fact that Shearon's mother came to the detective office because her son had come home in strange clothing and she had read of the drowning in the papers. Clearly she had had her suspicions about her own son and thought the police should be involved.[6]

The general reaction to the news of the killing within the city appears to have been more one of sadness than of outrage, and a concern for Liverpool's reputation throughout the rest of the country. In London the *Pall Mall Gazette* headlined the story 'THE GHASTLIEST MURDER ON RECORD'. Warming to the theme, the then Liberal paper continued:

We doubt if the rest of the civilized world ... has ever been confronted with a passage quite so hideously black. What is it in the dreary annals of murder – in the study of that half-explored region of human nature ... what is it that makes one crime stand out among its fellows? Is it inadequacy of motive? Pitiful inadequacy of motive is here. Cold, savage deliberation in compassing [sic] the crime – horror and cruelty in the circumstances of its accomplishment? Such deliberation, such cruelty, were never more revoltingly displayed than here. But over and above all this, as the last bid for ghastly pre-eminence, which seems to put this Liverpool murder in a class by itself, there is one circumstance which may be told in a sentence. Murdered and murderers all three were infants.[7]

In the annual sermon on behalf of the city's ragged and industrial schools, the Reverend Stubbs warned that the killing 'must give to our city for all time the most revolting prominence in the national annals of crime'. He went on to argue that social problems and the 'evil conditions of city life' were the root cause, rather than the children themselves.[8]

When the case came up for trial at the winter assizes in December 1891, the boys' defence was concerned with the key question of their level of understanding. That is, it was argued that as children aged seven and under were incapable of committing criminal acts, the court had to be totally satisfied that the defendants, as eight- and nine-year-olds, were 'conscious of the nature and quality of their acts and of their moral gravity'. The jury found the boys guilty 'of having committed the act, but not responsible on the ground of their youth'. Consequently, the judge entered a 'not guilty' verdict and had them sent, with their mothers' permission, to training homes; one went to Father Nugent's Home, a residential school for poor children. The jury's decision provoked outrage in some quarters. In an article headed 'WHAT SHALL WE DO WITH THEM?', the *Pall Mall Gazette* complained that the trial of the 'Boy Murderers' at Liverpool raised 'some of the deepest problems which confront a civilized society'. The paper argued that 'the young savages' should not have been set free. But what were the alternatives? The paper was unable to put any before its readers other than to agree that the eventual compromise of sending them to homes was a solution, albeit an unsatisfactory one for a 'deliberate act of killing'.[9]

In some of the other cases of children who killed children, homicides arose out of playing, like the Fleeson case, but did not result in murder charges, for a variety of reasons. Herbert Corrie in 1853 was felled by a stone while playing cricket with his pals, but his killer was never identified. This incident bore the hallmarks of class resentments if the local newspaper is to be believed. Herbert, the son of an Everton broker, was attacked by some 'rough lads' in the fields close to York Terrace and twice hit by stones thrown by them. The same report mentions that stone throwing was a serious problem for the police in 1853. Over 100 cases of stone throwing in the streets were heard by the magistrates in that year alone. Two boys, 16-year-old John Dixon in 1874 and 12-year-old John Cunningham in 1896, were found guilty of manslaughter as a result of throwing stones in the street. In the latter case, Cunningham and his 16-year-old victim had fallen out after a game of baseball in Stanley Park. One other boy, six-year-old Stephen Heney, died while out playing. An unidentified boy placed a red-hot rivet down his back, when they were larking about down near Brunswick Dock. Suffering violent convulsions, he died two days after incident. No witnesses came forward and so the inquest returned an open verdict. General larking about and the teasing of a drunk resulted in two 13-year-old boys, James Woolley and William Duffy, being charged with manslaughter. Their cases never got further than the magistrates' court, as Mr Raffles threw the case out when he heard that the drunk, William Connor, fell into the path of an omnibus when retrieving his hat which the boys had knocked off his head.[10]

In another mysterious death, that of shoeblack John Stokes, aged 15, the coroner's court returned an open verdict after he had died from erysipelas. He claimed, shortly before his death, that another boy had hit him between the eyes and that this had led to the infection which killed him. One wonders if his death had similar origins to that of an older youth, named Gibbons, who was beaten to death by two other shoeblacks, Philip Mack, aged 18, and James Halloran, aged 17: trade rivalry. 'Let him stop in his own street', Mack had said of Gibbons, and this had led to the fatal fight.[11]

In the one remaining case where some kind of explanation for the killing is apparent, however insignificant, the children's behaviour appears little different from that of adults. At the inquest into the death of Sarah Sigley, aged 10, of Gay Street, her mother told the court how her daughter had returned home complaining that a boy, a complete stranger, had been hitting her head against a wall. She stated that her attacker had asked her if she was a Protestant and that she had replied that she did not know. This seemingly neutral response brought on the boy's vicious assault. His identity remained a mystery.[12]

Juvenile non-fatal violence

NON-FATAL VIOLENCE by children displays a number of distinctive features. The use of knives figures prominently in reported cases. If the non-specific 'assaults' are put to one side, stabbings account for 50% of the reported cases. This surprisingly high figure is probably inflated because many incidents of child violence were simply under-reported and not deemed worthy of prosecution, namely fist fights and scraps in the street. So infrequently were prosecutions for child fights reported, it has to be assumed that they were generally either condoned or informally dealt with by parents, other children and the police. Where they did come to the notice of the courts, something unusually serious had occurred. Take the case of 16-year-old Donald Macdonald of Bala Street, Bootle, who was remanded for assaulting another youth, Francis Owen. If the evidence presented in the summary hearing in the magistrates' court is to be believed, little aggression and hatred were apparent. It was more a contest of strength and reputation. Macdonald, on being arrested, had said to the police:

> Some girls told me Owen said he would fight me, so I met him and asked him if he had said he would fight me. He said he would fight me any time. I said 'to-morrow will do me.' He replied, 'I will fight you now.' I said, 'all right, let us go into the little square between Matthew-street and William Henry-street.' We went there, and both of us struck each other. I fell one way and he fell another, and he must have struck his head against a stone when I saw him lying on the ground. I carried him and put him on a doorstep, and got him a drink of water.[13]

Obviously Macdonald was trying to put himself in the best possible light but his evidence does have the ring of authenticity. Although further details were not forthcoming, as Owen was too ill to attend the first hearing, the court was left with the impression that an accident had occurred between two lads who had been egged on by girlfriends.

In other cases of fighting, the police were often the primary victims of teenage anger, especially if officers were trying to put a stop to anti-social behaviour like drunken fights in the street. In one case a constable was assaulted when he attempted to halt a group of young boys who were noisily smashing cups and throwing crockery about in a St Anne Street cocoa room.[14] But most often, in cases which ended up in the courts, boys fought boys with knives. Fourteen-year-old John Travis was arrested for drunkenly wielding a knife and threatening to stab another lad. Injuries, unlike in adult knife fights, appear not to have been too serious and court sentences tended to reflect this. This could range from the surprisingly generous discharge in return for a promise not to offend again, to 10 months with hard labour, as was received by John Murphy for stabbing Georgina Plummer in her back during an argument. His victim, unusually and significantly given the length of sentence, was a girl. Boys appear never to have stabbed adults, and nearly always fought with lads of roughly their own age. Fourteen-year-old Thomas Reeves, for example, flung an open knife at Edward M'Culloch during a quarrel on Queen's Dock quay.[15]

More worrying for the police were fights involving groups of boys, usually against other boys. These were not often, in Liverpool, organized, reckless violent gang confrontations of the kind seen in nearby Salford and Manchester, where 'Scuttling' (a gang culture based on the Scuttlers) became a notorious law-and-order problem during the last three decades of the nineteenth century. No doubt issues of territory, and perhaps religion, featured in some of these street battles, but for the police they were about maintaining order on the streets and public safety. One of the occasional crackdowns by them led to large numbers of boys being arrested in March

1874. Of the 22 boys picked up by the police, 14 were found guilty of throwing stones. A similar police operation against young people breaking the new earthenware insulators on the telegraph lines also took place in 1874. Stone throwing and general juvenile delinquent high spirits remained problems throughout the remainder of the nineteenth century. 'Aggrieved residents' from West Derby and Old Swan wrote letters complaining of the 'young ruffians' throwing brickbats at street doors, 'mud at the windows, explosives thrust under doors and into letter boxes, knocking and ringing and running away.... The laws against stone-throwing and other like nuisances are violated hourly, constantly'.[16] Vandalism, especially during the new industrial age, clearly held novel attractions for these young layabouts. The practice of putting rubbish, wood and other detritus on railway lines became a particular problem in the north-west, although Liverpool did not figure particularly prominently in this respect.

Children with guns and revolvers, often regarded as a twenty-first-century fear, were an issue nationally but, again, Liverpool did not stand out as being exceptional or notorious. Occasional news stories of boys with guns or boys firing indiscriminately in the street pepper the pages of the press. Initially, such cases were fairly low key. William Ebans, for example, was fined only one shilling for shooting Michael Cregan in Kitchen Street, and William Morris was given a discharge for accidentally shooting a girl, Sarah M'Dowell, when he was playing with a gun. Nor were people unduly alarmed when two 16-year-olds, dressed like 'Jack Shepherds', were arrested following a couple of break-ins at Roby.[17] However, by the 1890s the idea of armed teenagers had been elevated to something closely approximating a national moral panic. The *Mercury* headlined one story 'BOY PISTOL GANGS – THE CLERKENWELL TRAGEDY', thus alerting its readers to the dangers of armed teenage gangs, especially the risk that innocent passers-by could become victims in the crossfire. In London, one 12-year-old girl was gunned down during a feud between the Chapel Street and Lion gangs. Only months earlier, four youths were found guilty of discharging firearms in Hackney Road. Again, one innocent passer-by was 'accidentally' shot in the leg. These London-based stories, undoubtedly, explain the slightly alarmist *Mercury* headline at the end of June 1897, 'EXTRAORDINARY SHOOTING AFFAIR – JUVENILES ARMED TO THE TEETH', which headed a report on James Caligari (aged 14) and John O'Brien (aged 15), who were arrested armed with three revolvers and a dagger. According to evidence presented to Mr Stewart, the stipendiary magistrate, the boys had been firing in a brickfield off Lower Breck Road, where they were disarmed by Christian Johnson, a stonemason's improver, who had been startled by something whizzing past his ear. A week later the 'Two Would-Be Dick Turpins' were sentenced to the reformatory ships the *Akbar* and the *Clarence*.[18] The spectre of armed juveniles combined with what the general public were reading, namely 'penny dreadfuls', which glorified the gun

culture of the American 'Wild West', produced a state of nervous excitement in the 1890s.

The identity of the victims of child aggression can provide clues as to
why an incident had taken place but, more often than not, motivation and
rational explanations for these assaults are difficult to formulate. Only one
or two appear to have been related to juvenile issues such as quarrels or
fights arising out of play. Two apprentices quarrelled after a game of cricket,
and an 11-year-old playing 'peggy' in Gerard Street stabbed a 13-year-old.
His defence was that he was only playing. Lads were occasionally charged
with pushing other boys into a canal. Thirteen-year-old Thomas Gill asked
his victim, John Moon, if he could swim as they walked by the canal near
Chisenhale Street before pushing him in.[19] Practical jokes and high jinx
could sometimes go badly wrong; two boys, for example, blew up a hut by
pouring oil down a stove pipe chimney at Garston, severely burning two
men inside. In many of the cases where some kind of motive is stated in
the press report, children appear little different from adults. Trade wars,
albeit low-level ones, connected with shoe blacking or the empty-bottle
trade for instance, could spark off fights and work arguments, and where
the police intervened matters could be made worse by resisting arrest. Not
surprisingly, protecting family members could lead to courtroom appearances, as in the case of messenger lad William Tear, who was charged with
beating up George Clarke, who had previously beaten Tear's young brother.
He was discharged.[20]

Dangerous mental instability can afflict the young as well as the old,
although it is very unusual to find cases in which children are deemed
to be of 'unsound mind'. Such a case occurred in 1891, when 13-year-old
Francis Dowling was charged with attempting to murder five-year-old
John Ambrose Evans. Taking the little child to a house in Empire Street,
Dowling blindfolded Evans and then tied his hands behind his back and
struck him three times with a poker. Evans' cries and screams of 'Oh
Joey [Dowling], take me to mammy and daddy; don't kill me' alerted a
neighbour, who went round to the backdoor, where she found Evans with
terrible head wounds. After his arrest and while on the way to the detective
office, Dowling admitted, 'A mad fit came over me, and I struck him twice
on the head with a poker. He fell down, and I ran away out of the house.
I could not help it. I was not right in my head at the time.' At the time
of the preliminary hearing, doctors appear to have given contradictory
advice. Dr Beamish of Walton gaol opined that 'he could find no trace of
intellectual disorder ... but he had a badly-balanced nervous system'. The
'transitory' insanity was, he thought, caused by 'a morbid desire to kill'. At
the trial it became evident that Dowling had been under medical care for
some time and was not considered to be of sound mind. Despite this, the
jury found him guilty and he was sentenced to three years' penal servitude
if he was found to be sane.[21]

Teenage kicks: on the cusp of manhood

A GROWING PROBLEM towards the end of the nineteenth century, not just in Liverpool but in all British major cities, concerned teenagers. They became the 'folk devils' who were perceived to be threatening decent and orderly society. At that time, many young people left school at 12 or thereabouts, and this poorly educated group went straight into unskilled, boring and repetitive work. Apprenticeships were few and far between in a port like Liverpool and many lads had to make do with labouring jobs like scaling boilers.[22] Others became shoeblacks, messengers and 'nippers' – lads who rode on carts as drivers' mates and errand boys. At the age of 14 or 15 many of these lads were made redundant because a new cohort of school leavers could be taken on at lower wages.

These youths, termed 'half-men half-boys', stood on the cusp of manhood and it was a culture of manhood which identified status with a particular form of manliness, one which admired brutality and violence, male 'hardness' in other words. Unchecked by social conventions and sobriety, these young men, like their elders, hung around on street corners, swearing and cursing, shouting lewd remarks at passing women and being generally anti-social. Concerns are evident among this age group with not losing face or being treated with 'disrespect' in some of the street violence. After the Grand National at Aintree in 1875, as the crowds made their way through Walton, two apprentices, M'Lean and Orme, held a running race. During the race Orme stumbled and fell, provoking much amusement among a watching group of inebriated race-goers. One of this crowd of spectators, Moses M'Grath, was later set upon and punched and kicked to the ground by M'Lean, who thought it was going to be 'another hanging match' when told of M'Grath's death. He was fortunate to be found guilty of manslaughter but the sentence of 20 years' penal servitude was at the extreme end of the sentencing spectrum.[23]

While fears of what the future held for society when these youths grew to adulthood lay behind the moral panic, there occasionally occurred terrible events which amplified these fears. On Christmas Eve 1883, 13-year-old Michael Burns met his friend George Fox at 9.00 p.m. and walked down Reading Street, where they both lived, to Commercial Road. Here they saw a group of lads circled round two other youths fighting on a vacant piece of land close to the Leeds–Liverpool canal. Intrigued, Burns and Fox crossed the road and watched the fight until it ended in a draw after a further five minutes. The two protagonists, George Campbell of Lemon Street and Thomas Nolan of Regent Road, shook hands and agreed to meet at 8 a.m. on Christmas morning. At this point, one of the other lads, Charles Vaughan, who had been acting as Nolan's second during the fight, whipped off his coat and angrily challenged to fight any boy present. 'What is the matter with ye, Charley?', asked one of his companions, 'who's been getting at you?' To which Vaughan replied, 'I will soon show you who has been getting at me. Here's one of them', and he went over and head-butted a lad named John Murray.

Not liking the way the fight was degenerating into a free-for-all, Burns and Fox crossed the road to be clear of the crowd and harm's way. Their movement was, unfortunately, spotted by the irate Vaughan, who crossed over the road, grabbed Burns by his coat and head-butted him. Burns fell to his knees and Vaughan dramatically pushed him to the ground. At this point, three other lads, known as the 'pad lot' because of where they used to hang out on a piece of land near Westminster Road and Stanley Street, William Price, 18 years old, Isaac Hadfield, also 18, and John M'Comb, 15, joined their mate Vaughan. All four then laid into Burns, kicking and beating him. Fox, his friend, managed to break free and was chased away. Eventually, when two adults came up the street and chased the youths away, Burns was able to crawl up Reading Street, where he was found by his mother on the doorstep. He had been away from home for just 10 minutes.

As there was no blood and in spite of telling his parents that he was 'killed and murdered', they put him to bed and checked him in the night. The following morning, Christmas Day, Bridget Burns found him dead in bed. The post-mortem examination found bruising and contusions to Burns' head and knees and bleeding in the space between the brain and skull. The police, very speedily, rounded up the suspects, many of whom were found on a nearby flat – a barge-like transport boat – drinking. The court case which followed is interesting for a number of reasons. First and foremost, the case has a resonance with the recent murder of Rhys Jones, who, as an innocent bystander, was killed by members of a gang engaged in a vicious dispute with a neighbouring gang. The second point of interest to the modern reader concerns the criminal charges brought against the four defendants.

It transpired during the various court hearings that the lads had been fighting as representatives of three local gangs: the Lemon Street Gang, the Regent Road Gang and the 'pad lot'. To what extent the word 'gang' can be used as a sociological defining tool for these groups of boys is a moot point. The local detective did not appear unduly concerned by the presence of these 'gangs', for, he told the court, 'the lads in each street combined together in lots, or gangs, for the purpose of play; and should there be any fall-out between lads in two different lots, they had a general scrimmage'.[24] His evidence suggests the police knew about them; his use of the word 'play' immediately cast the phenomenon in a non-threatening light. Did these points have any bearing on the criminal charge?

To modern eyes, when reading the reports of the killing of Michael Burns, the immediate presumption is that it is a crime of murder. Back in 1884, at every court hearing of the case, both coroner's and criminal, the question of whether the charge should be one of murder or manslaughter was raised. Although the coroner, in the initial hearing, left it to the jury to decide, he did imply that it would be very difficult to discriminate between the four prisoners and that they should be all charged with the same offence. The finding of manslaughter was accepted by the stipendiary magistrate at the first police court hearing. Mr Marks, the prosecutor on behalf of the police, thought the charge against the four should have been murder but Mr Raffles replied that no jury would ever convict on that charge. Why the reluctance to proceed with the more serious charge? It would seem there were a number of reasons. First, in order to bring a charge of murder, the prosecution had to prove 'an unlawful act that would deprive a person of life'. The four defendants would have been able to argue that it was an everyday street fight, which ended in tragedy. In addition, three of the four youths would have been able to argue that they had come to Vaughan's defence, because they had come late to the scene, when the fighting had already begun.

The judge, Justice Butt, having expressed surprise that they had not been indicted for murder, added that 'manslaughter and murder were crimes which approached so near to each other that it was sometimes difficult to distinguish one from the other'. His sentence, 12 years' penal servitude for Vaughan and 10 years each for the other three, reflected the seriousness of the manslaughter.

What made this case particularly disturbing for contemporaries was the fact that just half a mile down the road, in Blackstone Street, and 12 days after Michael Burns' death, another killing took place. Beneath the railway arches of Blackstone Street a gang of youths kicked and belted two Spanish sailors to the ground. While one managed to escape, the other, Exequiel Rodriquez Nuniez, was chased and 'hunted like a dog' and eventually stabbed three times in the back and neck. While the five youths arrested for the murder were slightly older than those tried for the killing of Michael Burns, three were teenagers and worked as scalers in the same workshop as some of the witnesses to the Burns killing. This suggests a culture of violence among the young men in the north end of Liverpool. Of the two defendants found guilty and sentenced to death for the murder of Nuniez, Michael M'Lean, aged 17, had a history of violence, with charges of stabbing a policeman and robbery with violence to a lady. His sentence was not commuted, although he had entertained hopes that it would be. Before his execution, M'Lean addressed the reporters present in the following terms: 'Gentlemen, I consider it is a disgrace to the police force of Liverpool and the laws of the country that I am going to suffer death, and another boy [Patrick Duggan, 18] is going to suffer imprisonment for life, for a crime of which we are both innocent, as God is my judge.' While not denying being present at the assault of Nuniez, M'Lean claimed (as did Duggan) that William Dempsey was the guilty party. He had been acquitted at the trial and immediately set sail for San Francisco. This crime was later regarded as the first of the 'High Rip' outrages (on which, see chapter 7).

The *Liverpool Echo*, after the two killings, complained of 'bands of lads who prowled the streets ... and who were a terror to the neighbourhoods they infested'. To the newspaper, three points arose: that it was not apparent what the police were doing to break up these gangs of 'boy brigands'; that the parents of the boys were mainly to blame; and that 'boys of quiet habits should be taught not to loiter on the streets'.[25]

Measures to reduce criminality among young men were taken up enthusiastically. Boys' brigades were established with the avowed intention of occupying 'the attention of lads during the long winter evenings'. By 1887 their membership in the city numbered about 160 and the Liverpool brigade presumably attracted law-abiding youths, as a condition of membership was church attendance. Doses of military drill and scripture, even in the Empire and missionary years of the late 1880s, probably lacked what would now be termed street credibility with the young men of the north end. Potentially more promising and enticing was the formation of the Gordon Working-Lads Institute, which moved into purpose-built premises in Stanley Road, Kirkdale. Named after the hero General Gordon of Khartoum, who was killed in January 1885, the Institute was less overtly religious than the boys' brigade. Its stated aims were to 'provide instruction and recreation for destitute lads from 14 to 21 who have poor homes, and whose only rendezvous is the street'. By trying to attract lads at a young age – the critical years were deemed to be between 12 and 15 – the Institute believed it would be able to mould their futures and prevent them being 'initiated into the arts of vice and crime'. By 1887, it claimed an average of 200 lads attending evening meetings, and that 1500 had passed through its doors by May of that year. A drill shed was built in Upper Warwick Street, and clubs encompassing most sports, a band and a choir were also provided. In addition, technical classes on metal and woodwork proved to be popular.[26] Whether all these facilities contributed to a diminution of the 'youth problem' is very difficult to determine.

Conclusion

LIVERPOOL DOES NOT APPEAR to have had an unusually poor reputation when it came to child violence. When children killed other children, in Liverpool and other places in Britain, the events invariably attracted national prominence through the pages of the press. Child killers then, as now, presented society with a number of challenges, not least how they should be prosecuted and punished. These young killers also forced society to confront its own broader responsibilities to such children. Had the community at large failed them? Such questions continue to be posed. Concerns over juvenile crime appear to have been and continue to be a problem which periodically energizes the local press and politicians. The head constable's annual report complained in 1867/68 of an 'increase in juvenile offenders'. At the height of the debacle over the 1874 Tithebarn Street murder, head constable Major Greig received a letter complaining of shoeblacks and 'disorderly boys congregating under the arch way and opening into Sweetney-street', where they indulged in swearing and 'unseemly noises'.[27] In the north end of the city complaints about the rude conduct and dancing on street corners by the young men were evident towards the end of the century. Even as late as 1906, Leonard Dunning, the then head constable, was writing of the 'decay of parental control, the decay of which is producing the enormous amount of juvenile delinquency in the country'.[28] It would appear certain traits never change a great deal.

CHAPTER 12

'A most unmerciful beating':
adult violence to children

... this city presents a spectacle in the way of juvenile vagabondism unparalleled in any city in the world. News-boys, shoe-blacks, match-sellers, chip-vendors, and a whole army of unattached skirmishers are to be encountered at all hours of the morning, afternoon, and night, in the squares, streets, crossings, bye-ways, courts and alleys of our streets, unwashed, tattered and uncared for, almost naked in summer and half frozen in winter; their little faces pinched with want and prematurely aged with starvation, abandoned by everybody and sternly ignored by the School Board.[1]

The law and violence to children

THE NATION, as a whole, can take little credit in the fact that there was a 60-year gap between the foundation of a society for protecting animals and one for the protection of children. In 1883, Liverpool was able to lay claim to being the first city in Britain to establish a charitable group for the protection of children, with the foundation of the Liverpool Society for the Prevention of Cruelty to Children (LSPCC). Six years, later the National Society for the Prevention of Cruelty to Children (NSPCC) was formed (from the London Society, itself established in 1884). Liverpool, it would seem, could take pride in being the first city in the country to protect its children, a truly historic achievement (on the other hand, it could be argued that this merely reflected the fact that so many of the city's poor children were so badly treated that they required some kind of protection).[2]

This 60-year delay between the formation of societies for the protection of animals and children can be explained partly by the argument that the law already provided some protection, albeit limited, for children from assault, as with any individual. However, the Victorians, like their pre-decessors, regarded children as possessing a limited range of legal rights by virtue of their being children. In an 1883 report in the Liverpool press of one (admittedly unusual) case headlined 'SPARE THE ROD AND SPOIL THE CHILD', Mr Raffles, the stipendiary magistrate, decided to let 10-year-old

William Brown free in a case where the lad had been charged with the theft of his sister's dress. The discharge was conditional on Brown's father giving him a whipping. In reply to this request, the father replied, 'Your worship, I dare not do it; she won't let me' (pointing to his wife, who was standing near him). To which the magistrate, clearly exasperated, spoke to Brown's wife: 'You are a silly woman; "you spare the rod and spoil the child." You promise me that you will not hinder his father whipping him, and I will discharge the boy.' After the mother had reluctantly agreed to this order, Mr Raffles finally turned to Brown the elder and said that 'he ought to be master in his own house'.[3] This case encapsulates another important set of Victorian attitudes – those regarding the sanctity and the privacy of the home, where the head of the household was to all intents and purposes a despot. It would appear that the law, even in the same year as the formation of the LSPCC, encouraged corporal punishment of a kind and degree which to modern eyes would be considered cruel and abusive.

In cases where children were deserted and abandoned, the law was, as John Smith Mansfield, stipendiary magistrate, explained to the chairman of the Soho Street industrial school, less clear. The latter had brought to court the case of a six-year-old boy thrown out onto the street when his parents separated and his house closed up. After living rough and off scraps of food given him by neighbours in the court where he used to live, he was finally taken in by them and then passed onto the Poor Law guardians, who were keen to make the parents responsible for their child. Mansfield, in a telling statement, said that such cruelty cases were 'so uncommon because so unnatural that the law had not made that provision'. Most parents, in other words, did not abandon their children, because it was against their instinct to do so. Headlines to reports of cases before the magistrates of parental violence reinforce the perception of the unnaturalness of such cruelty; Eliza Whitson was termed an 'INHUMAN MOTHER' for deserting two of her children and attempting to kill a third. And the case of Ann Chatfield was simply headlined 'A BAD MOTHER'; she had assaulted her five-year-old daughter while drunk in Houghton Street.[4]

Children, because of their age, inexperience and, most important of all, their dependency on adults, were placed in positions subordinate to adults, be it in the home, where their parents ruled, in the school, where the teacher's will was supreme, or in the workplace, where the master or employer was the boss. In all these places and in their subordinate positions, children had to suffer a range of physical assaults if the adults in authority over them chose to inflict some form of corporal punishment upon them. There was little they could do to resist. They could, on occasion, attempt to win the support of one group of adults who might challenge another group of adults on their behalf. This kind of advocacy is seen in tensions between home and school, where angry parents sometimes confronted teachers.

In many of the situations in which children were assaulted, whether or not any sort of proceedings would be begun depended on considerations concerning the level of violence employed against the child, the context in which the violence was used and whether the law or other interested parties thought the violence inappropriate or excessive. The central problem when dealing with violence directed against children lay in the questions of interpretation and proportionality. The difficulty lay in judging when the hitting or beating became illegal or unacceptable. It was, in the nineteenth century, legal to hit children. Confusingly and equally important to understand is the fact that it could also be illegal to hit children even before the passing of the Prevention of Cruelty to, and Protection of, Children Act 1889. They were afforded the same protection under the law as any other individual in cases of assault.

Violence to children occupied a wide spectrum, ranging from legitimate corporal punishment, discipline and chastisement through to cruelty and torture. Knowing where to draw the line and identify when a flogging became unacceptable was mainly subjective, although the law was sometimes brought in to offer an objective test. The dividing line between legitimate disciplining and brutality also altered over the latter half of the nineteenth century, just as did the notion and concept of childhood. What might have been considered acceptable in the 1850s had, by the 1890s, become unacceptable, partly because the early years of life had increasingly come to be seen as a period of innocence, during which children required protection and the freedom to be children, rather than, say, 'small adults' earning a living. Childhood was becoming increasingly idealized, especially by the middle classes. This, more than anything, probably explains the arrival of the LSPCC towards the end of the nineteenth century.

However, middle-class notions of what constituted childhood and the experiences of childhood were rarely those of the working classes, especially the urban poor of Liverpool. Here, the reality of poverty, overcrowding and economic necessity meant that childhood was an altogether different experience. The brutality and neglect described in the pages of the local newspapers and reported from the magistrates' courts were very much located in the slum neighbourhoods of the city. Local readers understood the script, namely, poverty, overcrowding, alcohol and slum living gave rise to parental brutality. Such interpretations, while containing much truth, overlooked the fact that the majority of slum-dwelling parents loved and cherished their children as much as more affluent, middle-class parents did. Moreover, they raised their large families without resorting to the use of the buckle end of belts as weapons of discipline. Most families of both the middle and working classes slapped, smacked and disciplined their children within the terms of the law, as such behaviour was considered normal, useful and instructive to children in the laying out of moral boundaries for them. It was, in other words, part of the culture to hit children.[5]

Violence in the home

AMILY STRUCTURES in the twenty-first century are considered by many
people to be complex and frequently subject to alterations in parental
relationships. This could be due to divorce or simply partners moving on.
The assumption lying behind this kind of thinking is that family relationships were, in former times, simpler and long lasting, divorce being out
of the question for working-class couples for financial reasons. Closely
allied to this assumption is the belief that unstable families often lead to
violence and the abuse of children. Some of the more recent infamous cases
involved partners who had not been in the familial relationship very long
and were not the biological parents of the injured or murdered children.
How justified are we in believing that nineteenth-century families were
simpler affairs and that any violence to the children was perpetrated by one
or both of the biological parents?

When looking at the cases which came before the magistrates, it immediately becomes obvious that family structures could be as complex
as modern-day ones. Defendants in child abuse cases included biological
parents, separated ones, unmarried partners, step-parents and adults identified as 'aunts'. However, most defendants appear to have been the natural
parents of the child victims. It is not possible to state that the law treated
the mother and father differently. Widower and dock labourer John M'Fee
appears to have found the job of lone parenting of at least three children too
much, as he lost his temper with his daughter, aged three and a half years,
when she soiled the bed. He strapped her 'unmercifully' and threw her up to
the ceiling but caught her before she hit the floor. The child was presented
to the court with a swollen face, black eye and marks of violence on the rest
of her body. The father was gaoled with the comparatively heavy sentence
of six months, as was Ellen Reed of Wolfe Street, Toxteth Park, for her cruel
treatment of tying her children up when she went out for a drink. Ellen
Burns was classed as 'An unnatural mother' for assaulting her five-year-old
son. In what proved to be a comprehensive character assassination by her
separated husband, she was accused of being 'a woman of intemperate
habits', which had led him to leave her. Moreover, she had forbidden 'the
little fellow' from visiting his father and whenever she discovered that he
had 'stolen' a visit to him she would beat him 'most unmercifully'. It was
in such circumstances that Mrs Burns had seized the boy by his hair and
beaten him about the face so severely that his nose bled. As a result of this
brutality she was found guilty and imprisoned to three months with hard
labour, a heavy sentence even by the standards of 1855.[6]

Where stepmothers and stepfathers were defendants in cases of violence
to children the court frequently heard evidence of neglect and total want of
affection. When Mrs Hanwell was sentenced to six months for hitting her
stepdaughter on the back of the legs we can only speculate on the severity

of the injuries. Some cases give an insight into both the marital relationship and the neighbours' responses (or lack of them) to the violence. When Jane Tranter of Redmond Place, Circus Street, was charged with neglect and ill treatment of her seven-year-old stepson John, it appeared that she was taking the entire blame. Her husband, witnesses claimed, worked nights, was absent from home during the day and gave her his wages weekly. While this put him in a relatively good light, it became evident that he was aware of the state of his son, who weighed just 23 lb 13 oz, and had even complained and beaten his wife because of the neglect. John's terrible condition begs the question of whether the neighbours were aware of his appalling state and if so whether they did anything about it. Witnesses admitted to knowing of the 'almost daily' assaults for the previous 16 months. They had seen the stepmother using a rope, a stick and a strap to beat the child and had failed to alert the authorities.[7]

Parents charged with assaulting their children usually cited in their defence the fact that the child had been disobedient or had refused to complete a task requested of them by the adult. Obedience and servility were expected of children at this time and parents were within their rights to chastise their children who disobeyed. 'I thrashed her with a belt because she would not go to school', John Clarke told the arresting officer. The little girl was not his biological daughter, nor was he married to her mother, but Clarke clearly thought he had parental rights over seven-year-old Mary Ann, who was, said the superintendent, covered in bruises 'from head to foot'. In the case of orphan Margaret Fairclough, who had been ill treated by her adult cousin John Fairclough, a herbalist in the High Street, Wavertree, she had been hit with a strap on the eye and cheek and kicked. His defence solicitor claimed she was 'A bad girl' who stole money from him, lied and emptied ash rubbish into the wrong ash pit, thus causing problems with angry neighbours. He admitted to taking a strap to her and had, he claimed, accidentally caught her eye. In support of his defence Fairclough called upon his wife and Margaret's brother, who both claimed she had never had 'more than ordinary chastisement'. He was found guilty and Margaret was placed into the hands of the LSPCC, which had originally brought the case.[8]

In most cases which came before the magistrates, the violence and ill treatment had been occurring for a long time before they had come to official notice. Neighbours appear to have heard or known of the violence for many months before they reported it to the police or the LSPCC, but even then successful prosecutions could be difficult to achieve. The reason for this was that either the violence had to be witnessed by police officers or the complainant, that is, either the injured child or another parent, had to be willing to make a stand against the ill treatment the child was receiving. Either way, there were problems in getting enough evidence to secure a conviction. Nine-year-old James Doran, despite being blinded in one eye, refused to implicate his stepfather, who was, as a consequence, discharged. Moreover, it was usual for such abuse to take place behind closed doors, and if the victim had been badly beaten the parent could keep the child hidden away until fit enough to be seen in public. Alternatively, both assailant and the victim could swear that the child had met the injuries through an accident in the home. Medical evidence of black eyes and bruising on the body was not sufficient proof of ill treatment. Take the case of 13-year-old Susannah Bolton, stepdaughter to Thomas Bolton – 'a rather decent-looking man' – of Eaton Street, Windsor, who had kept house and cooked for her stepfather for the three months since her mother's death. On the Wednesday before Monday's court hearing, one of her father's chickens (which he kept in the cellar) strayed and he warned her not to return home without first finding the bird. Such was her fear of a beating when she could not find the chicken that she stayed away from home until the Friday, when he spotted her in a nearby court. Taking her home and locking her in the garret, he ordered Susannah to strip 'almost to a state of nudity'. He then beat her with a cane on her shoulders, back and legs. In the narrow confines of the court her screams were heard by the neighbours, one of whom immediately informed the police. Female witnesses described the dreadful condition, blood flowing from the cuts over her body, in which Susannah was brought from the house. As in other cases, the defendant attempted to justify his behaviour by describing his stepdaughter as 'a very bad child' who had been expelled from school for stealing. And in a throw-back to the old 'rule of thumb' belief, he argued that the cane he used on her was 'only two feet in length and a quarter of an inch thick'. In answer to his pleas for forgiveness and the promise of never doing such harm again, Mr Raffles, the presiding magistrate, replied: 'You seem to think you were justified in using a cane to a child in that way. Whatever the conduct of the child might have been nothing could justify such brutality.' Bolton was gaoled with hard labour for three months without the option of paying a fine.[9]

A complex, indeed mysterious family relationship between the victim and the assailant, and the involvement of neighbours, lay at the heart of a case involving the ill treatment of Robina Crawford by Agnes Macmillan of Rockingham Street, off Commercial Road. Robina, who did not know whether Macmillan was her aunt or her mother, complained of being over-worked and repeatedly beaten with anything that came to Macmillan's hand. On being thrown out of the house, partly clothed and with 'bleeding fresh' wounds, she went next door to a Mrs Davies, where she spent the night. Witnesses were able to testify that Robina had suffered 'shame-fully' and had been beaten 'until she was stupid'. The neighbour's lodger testified to being woken by the sound of Robina's head being knocked against the wall separating the two houses. Another admitted to knowing of the beatings for three years. In a 'long, rambling, incoherent statement' Macmillan admitted and then denied beating the girl with a poker. Robina, she said, was an orphan and a troublesome, dirty girl. Reading between the lines, it is possible to surmise that Robina had been taken on as an unpaid servant and nursemaid to Macmillan's six children. It was claimed that she, Macmillan, had even tied a line around her like a lead and told her husband to throw her into the canal. What is interesting about this case was the fact that Macmillan, the defendant, involved the police, whom she brought in to take back her 'daughter' from the neighbours. Even though she admitted to beating the girl, the constable did not see fit to arrest or charge her. Only when a neighbour came to the police court the following morning to report the assault was the 'mother' charged and later tried and found guilty. She was sentenced to two months with hard labour.[10]

The police's reluctance to become involved in child brutality issues during the mid-Victorian years was a reflection of popular and official attitudes towards the sacrosanctity of the home as a private sphere. It was a private space in which the father was, to all intents and purposes, a tyrant. Clearly, tyranny had its boundaries but judging when that boundary had been crossed was a difficult call for a police constable, especially if he, too, was lord and master in his own home. Even when all the evidence pointed to terrible abuse of a child, the policeman could still display a reluctance to arrest the guilty party. When PC 224 came across four hungry and distressed children in Latimer Street, just off Athol Street, late one evening, he returned them to their home. There he met a drunken Catherine Sherridan, the children's stepmother, who was clearly unrepentant in her behaviour and who further threatened to 'beat them to pieces'. Having returned them to their home the same constable met them in the street an hour later. This time the eldest boy complained of being beaten with a 'loaded life preserver'. Returning once more to Sherridan's house, he witnessed the abusive and drunken woman assault one of her stepdaughters and this led to her arrest. It transpired that other lodgers in the same house were aware and concerned about the woman's treatment of the children and had even informed the children's natural father, a fireman on a steamer between Dublin and Liverpool, of what was happening. This appears to have been met with threats to mind their own business. However, in the case of Catherine M'Donald, who was baby-sitting her five-year-old goddaughter, the local policeman had no hesitation in intervening to stop her dashing the child against the wall and floor 'till the blood gushed from its eyes and ears'. He had been called in by horrified neighbours who been too frightened to intervene. M'Donald was given 10 years' penal servitude for attempted murder.[11]

This and other cases highlight the vulnerability of children to violence from their parents or adults acting as their guardians in the mid-Victorian period. Even where the evidence of bruised, emaciated and partly clothed children confronted officialdom, the first instinct was to return them to the very source and cause of their misery. Only when the violence was witnessed first hand by a constable or only when the violence overstepped some unspoken line with the neighbours, presumably life threatening in their opinion, did a court case ensue. Even then, a prosecution could be a long time in coming, as the story of Edward William Jordan bears out. His case stands out for the simple fact that neighbours and the authorities knew of the ill treatment meted out to Edward for over 18 months by his single-parent father, an ironmonger and owner of two shops. At the first of four hearings Edward was presented in court with his ankles shackled by a padlock and chained together. The rest of his body gave evidence of frequent beatings. When asked by Mr Mansfield, the magistrate, how he came to receive such marks, the boy replied that his father hit him with a blackthorn stick. Why, asked the magistrate, did his father do this to him?

> My brother hit me on the fingers on Saturday, and I shouted and wakened my father. He came down to me, pulled me by the hair, and beat me. I have had this chain on since Saturday, and was chained to the bedpost. I was not in bed at all on Tuesday night (it was now Wednesday). – Mr Mansfield: You don't mean to say you have been walking about the street with this on? The boy: Yes sir. – Mrs. Duckworth (a neighbour): He got out of the house yesterday about one o'clock, and he was tied up from Saturday till then.

The boy added that the servant had begged his father to take off the heavy weight (56 lb) attached to the chain.

At the second court hearing, a week later, a very different picture was painted by the boy's father. Instead of being the blameless young innocent which he and the neighbours portrayed him to be, Edward was described by his father as a liar, thief, a truant and an 'incorrigible little rascal'. The servant, Jessie Taylor, told the court that he had often been 'saucy' to her and that 'beefsteaks were not good enough for his dinner'. In short, he was portrayed to be a juvenile delinquent who spent most of his time away from home – nearly half of the time in the last two years – and when at home brought back groups of boys against his father's wishes. Two very different Edwards were presented to the court. To a historian trying to weigh up the evidence, Edward's explanation for his long absences seems entirely credible, namely that he was afraid of his father, and the three women neighbours' evidence that he was 'exceedingly well-behaved' likewise told in his favour. The fact that he knew his mother, from whom he was taken at birth, but was not allowed to see her without receiving a beating, again suggests he had an entirely loveless home life. This is not to exonerate him from his delinquent behaviour, more an attempt to explain it. The court decided, ultimately, that the boy be found an apprenticeship by the defendant's solicitor, who had the difficult task of trying to placate the boy's father, who wanted to keep him for his business, and the boy's uncle, presumably his mother's brother, who wanted to find a trade for him to follow.[12] The point of this lengthy tale was that the lad had clearly been badly treated but the court did not find it appropriate to punish the father, partly because the boy was shown to be disobedient.

Adults were, to some extent, more liable to prosecution if they assaulted children in the street who were not relatives. In nearly all the news reports of such instances published by the *Liverpool Mercury*, defendants claimed that the children had been annoying them. The law did not always offer protection, especially to street urchins and other young beggars. When 'gentleman' John Slater was seen to strike 'a little, dirty, ragged, shoeless urchin', so small that a policeman had to hold him up in court as he could not see over the witness box, the defendant was able to win a discharge from the magistrates. It was never disputed by Slater that he had struck 'the brat' but he and his solicitor did dispute the policeman's right to take him into custody, as the constable had not witnessed the alleged assault. The fact that Slater was also drunk was likewise vehemently denied. His erratic behaviour was, he claimed, due to 'rheumatism' and 'paralysis', which 'might be mistaken for intoxication'. The bridewell keeper, in answer to the magistrates' enquiry on this detail, answered that Slater was 'positively drunk'. Despite this confirmation, the magistrates discharged him on the legal technicality that he had not hurt the child and that the constable should not have taken the charge of assault. They added that it would be better if troublesome 'urchins in the streets' were dealt with more often in Slater's fashion than for the magistrates to hear such 'paltry charges'.[13]

This was, admittedly, an exceptional case, since in most other incidents adults were invariably punished for assaulting children in the streets. The young, it would appear, took great delight in mocking, name calling, leg pulling and generally annoying people, especially drunken men and women. The fact that they were often the instigators of the fracas or, at the very least, baited the adults into reacting was rarely taken into consideration by the courts. Punishments for the adult assailants varied considerably and partly reflected the severity of the assault. In some cases adults were made to pay financial compensation, as in the case of Alexander Hunter, injured by a stone thrown by a boatman, Richard Gore. Groups of lads on the canal bank, he claimed, had been annoying the flatmen by Athol Street bridge. In other cases adults were made to pay small fines, sometimes as low as 2s 6d; this was the sum levied against a woman who had suffered 'rough music' in the form of the beating of tin cans as a celebration for her leaving the neighbourhood of Old Swan. Although she was found guilty of hitting a boy with a bottle, he, too, was told off for his provocative behaviour. After a similar episode in which neighbours were gathered outside Sarah Roughsedge's house in Fulford Street, she incurred a 12-month prison sentence, as she had rushed out of her house with a poker, struck out at an assembled group and hit 10-year-old Ann Adams on the head.[14]

Generally the attacks on children were violent and short-lived. Drunks kicking or punching could expect to receive sentences from as little as seven days, as in the case of drunken Thomas Lawson, of Robeart Street, for striking Thomas Ellis on the head with a poker, to as much as six months.

Many were given the option of paying fines, which, given most defendants' own parsimonious circumstances, they would have been unlikely to be able to pay. More serious assaults included lime being thrown into a six-year-old boy's eyes by a plasterer who was being annoyed by a group of children who climbed one of his ladders in Clayton Street. In two other instances boys were pushed into the water by assailants who did not know if they could swim or not.[15]

School teachers were, even in the nineteenth century, on uncertain legal ground when it came to disciplining their pupils. It is popularly assumed that school masters and mistresses could, until the 1950s and 1960s, freely inflict corporal punishment on their charges. This is a misconception. As early as 1879 the *Mercury*, in an editorial headed 'THE SCHOOL "CAT"', was already arguing that 'there is now no excuse for the brutalising application of physical force to the gentle operation of teaching an infant the mysteries of the three Rs'. The incident which inspired this editorial concerned the actions of a Dickensian-sounding teacher named Mr Twemlow, belonging to one of Liverpool's evening voluntary schools for very poor children. According to Twemlow himself, 'he lost his temper when he saw the boy "lift a slate as if in the act of going to strike him"'. This was, in the opinion of the *Mercury*, 'a leaky story, considering that Mr. Twemlow is a big strong man, and his victim a rather diminutive child'. The teacher then proceeded to 'pummel' the unfortunate child with his pointer, the consequence of which was a disciplinary hearing for Twemlow before the school board.[16]

What the law was concerned with whenever parents brought a case against a teacher for hitting their child was whether the punishment or beating was excessive. When James Jacques of Parr Street School was charged with inflicting excessive punishment to William Daly, he claimed the weals left on the boy's shoulders with his cane were not severe. The magistrate appears to have agreed but, on dismissing the case, he warned the teacher to be 'more cautious in future', which implied an element of guilt in this case. Schoolmaster Thomas Hall, of St Albans Roman Catholic school on Boundary Street, claimed that 'none but a savage would intentionally strike a boy across the face' when nine-year-old Thomas Gibbons accused him of striking him with a buckled belt across the arms, eyes and face. The bench was prepared to believe that it was an accident when a blow landed on young Thomas's face but the magistrates still found Hall guilty of assault (and fined him five shillings) because it was, in their opinion, the wrong way to strike a pupil. The magistrates clearly took the side of eight-year-old John Blackwell in his summons against head teacher Thomas Knight of St Simon's, Russell Street. Armed with doctors' certificates and the black and blue marks on his back, John and his father explained to the court how the headmaster had beaten him for truancy. It transpired that two other boys were used to hold John down during the caning. Presiding magistrate Mr Lawrence remarked, 'Any man who can treat a child as this child has been treated is utterly unfit for his post'. He continued, 'I am quite conscious that there are in some of our schools a great many punishments which are a perfect disgrace ... I would sanction no such cruelty as this'. The headmaster was found guilty and fined 40 shillings. The *Liverpool Mercury* also highlighted a case at nearby St Helens which involved a mother who was being prosecuted for the irregular attendance of her son. In her defence, she complained that her son was beaten twice a day, a complaint supported by the presiding magistrate, who said that 'he thought there was too much beating in schools, especially by the female teachers'.[17]

The LSPCC and violence in the home

INCREASINGLY TOWARDS the end of the nineteenth century the hitting of children came to be viewed as unacceptable. While corporal punishment from teachers and parental discipline were, with qualifications, still acceptable, many began to view other forms of chastisement as both unacceptable and illegal. Children required greater protection than formerly, partly because they were children and not young adults and, as such, had the right to enjoy and experience childhood as a period of comparative innocence. While, as we have seen, adults had been punished for beating and assaulting children up to the 1880s, it was thereafter increasingly felt necessary to create refuges and shelters for those at risk from parental ill treatment and neglect. Two men, Thomas Agnew, a Liverpool merchant who, on a visit to New York, came across a Society for the Prevention of Cruelty to Children, and MP Samuel Smith – active in the Young Men's Christian Association and child emigration schemes – combined their energies to promote further action against parental cruelty. With this in mind the LSPCC was formed on 19 April 1883 and shelters were established first in Nile Street and then Islington Square.[18]

It would, however, be erroneous to believe that the primary function of the LSPCC was to protect children by prosecuting violent parents and stepparents. The LSPCC case-load for the first 17 years shows how parental abuse could come in many guises and that violence was only a minor issue for the Society. Violence to children represented just 6.3% of the cases up to 1898. In its founding year, 1883, violence to children represented 13%, which suggests that early ambitions for the Society might well have centred on parental violence. However, it soon became obvious that cruel neglect, day and night begging, exposure and vagrancy, as well as immorality, were more important dangers to be confronted in the opinion of the Society. Children's status as victims who required protection and sanctuary had, in effect, risen in the final years of the nineteenth century.[19]

The minutes of the LSPCC indicate a sea-change in public attitudes towards violence and cruelty to children. By far the most important sources of information concerning ill treatment came from the general public; these sources included anonymous letters, neighbours and even the relatives of abused children (together representing 46% of informants by 1885). The Society did not, as a matter of course, initiate prosecutions against parents guilty of violence towards their children; rather it attempted to educate, persuade, warn and advise them. Prosecutions would inevitably, given the poverty of many of the accused, have led to gaol sentences. Prison was, as far as the Society was concerned, a last resort, for when the child's life was in danger or if parents had previously been warned about their behaviour. An examination of a sample of cases from the LSPCC's annual reports gives an insight into the ways in which the Society operated.[20]

> Case 153. – A girl of ten was bitten on both arms by her mother, her back scored with the buckle end of a strap, and her head laid open with a poker. The case was reported by neighbours, the [LSPCC] Superintendent brought her to the Shelter, and was followed by a large crowd, many of them from the street in which the mother resided; all appeared to rejoice in the girl's deliverance from a persistent course of cruelty which had extended over many years. The mother was taken before the Stipendiary, who sentenced her to three months' imprisonment with hard labour. The girl remains at the Shelter, while arrangements are being made for her committal to an Industrial School. The character of the home is too bad to admit of the return of this girl to her parents.

> Case 292. – A lad of eleven was savagely attacked by his father, for going out without leave. The father beat him on the head with his fists, kicked him on the leg, then thrust him, head downwards, through the broken seat of a chair, and bumped his head on the floor. A warrant was issued, but as the man had gone away to Rhyl, there was some delay, as well as a dispute respecting its execution; but he was eventually fetched by the police. When brought before the Stipendiary, a difficulty was experienced, as to the disposal of the children if the father was sent to prison. He was bound over in £20....

> Case 761. – A man in the Army Reserve was sent to gaol for two months with hard labour for stringing up his son by the wrists to a nail in the wall till the poor boy's toes barely touched the ground, and keeping him in this position at intervals during several days till the cords had penetrated the skin of both wrists. The boy was only eight years old. The man had previously been convicted of cruelly maltreating this child both with strap and fist.

> Case 1,675. – A boy of thirteen years of age was kicked in the face. The boy's mother had died four months before the occurrence, and in the interval the father had taken to drinking and immoral habits. The father had been in a respectable situation for fifteen years, and the bare suggestion that his conduct might be brought to the knowledge of his employers was sufficient to evoke strong expressions of regret and promises of amendment. In such cases, and the Society has many of them, remonstrance is more effective than prosecution, and subsequent visits by the Society's Inspector not infrequently show that the 'lesson' has not been forgotten. This case was first mentioned by the police.

These four cases highlight the difficulties which the Society had to consider. Should it prosecute or would a threat to inform an assailant's employer suffice? Or would it be too costly, as in case 292, for the Poor Law authorities if the breadwinner was gaoled and the children placed in the workhouse? Clearly, where the abuse amounted to torture and extreme violence, as in case 761, the Society had little difficulty in prosecuting, especially as the father had previous convictions for similar offences. Case 153 indicates among other things how the Society was willing to separate the child from a family for protection. It also hints at community anger at child abuse, although the case summary implies that the neighbours took up the girl's cause only after a long period of persistent and repeated cruelty, which they had presumably known about.

By 1900, Liverpool's children were better protected than they had been 50 years before; however, it is impossible to show that were they were less often hit, ill treated or abused. British society had, by the turn of the century, dramatically altered in its attitudes towards its own children. No longer were they deemed vital contributors to the family economy; rather, they were valued as young family members whose economic contribution to the family unit lay in the future. In the meantime, children, up to their early teens, were meant to enjoy a period of play, schooling and domestic familial security. This highly idealized picture of childhood bore little resemblance to the realities of overcrowding and poverty in Liverpool's courts and slums. However, even in these back alleys children were sentimentally valued and loved more than previously. Their status as victims of violence at the hands of adults – parents or strangers – had risen in the eyes of both the law and society and, as a consequence, there were more people (notably teachers and charity workers) looking out for their social and physical well-being.

A 'morbid curiosity': the murder of Nicholas Martin

UNDER THE HEADLINE 'SHOCKING DISCOVERY', the *Times* reported, on 20 May 1891, the discovery in Liverpool of a sailor's bag floating into Sandon Dock from the river. On retrieving it from the water, the bag was found to contain 'The mutilated remains of a boy about 15 years of age. The lad's throat was cut from ear to ear, and both legs were sawn off at the knees. The bag also contained a butcher's knife and a new tenon-saw, adhering to which were pieces of flesh and skin.' This was one of the city's most notorious child murders of the nineteenth century. It caught the media's attention for a number of reasons, not least the gruesomeness of the discovery, which called to mind Fanny Adams' mutilated corpse in Hampshire in 1867 – her severed head had been found resting in the corner of a hop field while the remainder of her dismembered body was found scattered over a number adjoining fields. Fanny, who had been playing with other children, had accepted money from a stranger, who walked her by the hand up a lane towards the hop 'garden', and the Liverpool murder similarly hinted of paedophilia, in that the murderer had perpetrated grotesque outrages upon his victim. What made the Liverpool murder notorious was that the victim was a boy. The killing also occurred during a period of heightened popular and media interest in murders. Jack the Ripper's Whitechapel murders had only just ceased and, moreover, the early months of 1891 proved to be period of other terrible crimes. Whitechapel yet again provided another body and in June 1891 the mutilated body of a little girl was discovered in Leeds. The shocking coincidence of two child killings in Liverpool and Leeds brought forth an editorial in the *Birmingham Daily Post* warning that 'the lives of children, however young, are not safe from murderous wiles, even within sight of their parents' home'.[21] The final element which added to the Liverpool murder's newsworthiness was the suspect himself.

Arrested within hours of the discovery of the body, thanks to good detective work, John Conway (aged 60), alias Conally, alias Brown, alias O'Donnell, was not only a fireman who sailed out of Liverpool but was also a paid delegate of the Southend branch of the National Amalgamated Sailors' and Firemen's Union (NASFU) and appears to have been the Liverpool secretary of the union. It had recently been involved in highly controversial industrial action against shipping magnates during a wave of industrial protest in support of 'new unionism', which saw the emergence of the new militant general unions for semi-skilled workers. In consequence, the Liverpool branch of the union was, initially, keen to place as much distance between itself and the suspect, even going so far as to issue the following resolution:

> the National Amalgamated Sailors and Firemen's Union do offer our most sincere sympathy and condolence to Mr. and Mrs. Martin in the bereavement which they have sustained through the horrible murder of their son Nicholas Martin. The circumstances connected with the crime make it particularly painful to us as members of the Union, but we trust that the loving memories which they retain of the deceased will be such as to buoy their spirits up in the most trying ordeal which they are called upon to pass through.[22]

Later the union offered Conway a solicitor but his services were soon withdrawn.

The walls and floor of the room above the union's office at 19 Stanhope Street were smeared with blood, despite the fact that someone had tried to wash it away. The victim, identified as 10-year-old Nicholas Martin, was last seen playing football near his home in Bridgewater Street on the previous Saturday evening. A witness came forward who saw the boy being addressed by a man: 'Oh, come, if you are coming'. The boy replied, 'Hold on, till I get my ball'. The man reportedly called out, 'Come on; never mind your ball, you won't want that any more'. The boy ran towards the man, who said, 'Here's sixpence'. The boy then put something into his right-hand trouser pocket. Looking at the ball in the boy's hand, the man said, 'You won't want that ball any more'.

At the ensuing inquest, details of the post-mortem examination carried out by Frank Paul (Professor of Clinical Surgery at the University College of Liverpool) and Dr F. W. Lowndes revealed that the boy's clothing was consistent with him having dressed himself and that 'there were no signs of the body having been outraged' other than the bruising on the face and the cut throat. Conway, it was proved by numerous witnesses, had recently purchased a sailor's bag, various saws and knives, a bucket and scrubbing brush. Moreover, a cabman came forward with evidence that he had given Conway a lift to George's Pier and that two dock gatemen at Sandon Dock heard a splash two hours before they fished the bag out of the dock. One further surprising detail emerged during the inquest: Conway had lodged amicably with the deceased's family 14–15 years previously, under the name of John Hooper.

Conway's defence hinged on the fact that he claimed that he had bought the bag in which the child's body was found for an unnamed foreigner whom no witnesses had heard of or seen. At the remand hearing on 5 June, he caused confusion when asked by the magistrate if he had anything further to say after the witness depositions had been read over and signed. 'I have nothing to say', Conway replied, then added, 'but that I am regular guilty of the charge preferred to me, Sir (sensation in court); but I wish to have that evidence produced in the public Press. It was a hidden thing until yesterday.' The court clerk read back the words which the prisoner had just uttered in court and asked if they were correct. 'No, Sir, I say distinctly they are not. I most emphatically declare my innocence in this court of the charge preferred against me.' Continuing to deny his initial admission of guilt, Conway was committed to the assizes, where, on 1 August, he was found guilty after half an hour's deliberation by the jury. He was sentenced to death and on 20 August was rather messily executed. A drunken hangman miscalculated the length of rope for the drop and virtually decapitated Conway.[23]

This murder and the public reaction to it are, to modern eyes, all too familiar. The funeral at Ford was attended by thousands and the route along which the hearse was drawn was likewise thronged with many mourners. There was outrage, shock, popular fear of paedophiles – although no evidence of sexual interference was found – and detailed media coverage on a national scale. But did it amount to a media-induced panic? On the face of it, the answer is no. The murder had caught the public's interest partly because it was so gruesomely unusual and partly because of its timing, coinciding with the murders mentioned above. The murderer, in this case, was associated with 'new unionism' and this lent the case an almost sub-liminal script in which general unionism was equated somehow with social pollution. Without being explicit, the papers held out the possibility that low-skilled and newly unionized strikers could also be vicious child killers. The fact that the murderer was caught so quickly and convicted on the basis of solid evidence meant that any underlying generalized fears evaporated and restored the crime to the realms of the unusual. Finally, immediately after Conway's execution, the prison chaplain read to the assembled press Conway's final confession of guilt, in which he emphasized 'my motive was not outrage. Such a thought I never in all my life entertained. Drink has been my ruin, not lust. I was impelled to the crime while under the influence of drink by a fit of murderous mania, and a morbid curiosity to observe the process of dying'.[24] Thus, the murder failed to generate panic among parents. Even within a day of Nicholas's body being discovered and the reports in the press, the *Mercury* described how children were playing out in streets very close to where the boy had lived.

A similar murder, the Blackburn murder of 1876, had likewise failed to generate any wider fears of paedophiles, although it did, briefly, capture the public's imagination, both in Blackburn and in Liverpool, where the trial took place, and in fact throughout the north-west. Again, it was not the possible paedophilia of the crime that attracted the main notoriety: it was more the circumstances of how the body of the little girl was discovered and who the murderer was. After much searching and arrests of tramps and vagrants (suspicion had immediately fallen on strangers and outsiders), a dog named Morgan, later to become a hero and the subject of a music hall song, picked up the scent of the little girl in a neighbour's chimney. The neighbour, a barber named Fish, fulfilled the press's and the public's expectation of what a child-killing monster would have looked like. With a misshapen head and of tiny stature, Fish was anything but normal to most people. Phrenologists had a field day analysing what the shape of his skull signified in criminal terms. All this was laid out in the press nationally, while in Liverpool the waxworks displayed a life-size model of Fish, which confirmed to many viewers the freakishness of the crime and the monstrosity of its perpetrator. It was not, therefore, assumed that child killers and sexual predators were hiding in the shadows waiting only for an opportunity to steal away and kill or ravish children.[25]

Sexual violence and child victims

WHILE THE SUBJECT of paedophilia was never very from the surface in the case of Nicholas Martin's brutal murder, it does not appear to have been overly threatening to many Victorian parents. This becomes evident when sex crimes against the young are examined. Few details remain of what actually took place, as newspapers were loathe to publish anything but the basic details of a case and few nineteenth-century witness depositions of sex crimes have been kept. Nonetheless, it is possible to draw a number of conclusions from the rather skimpy evidence which remains.

First, very few people were ever prosecuted for, let alone found guilty of, crimes perpetrated against children ranging from rape to indecent or criminal assault, and indecent behaviour. It becomes evident when examining the evidence that the charge levelled against a defendant did not always equate to the actual violence which had taken place. In other words, a girl might well have been raped but the charge was downgraded to one of attempted rape because the evidence was not conclusive with regard to actual penetration. Such a downgrading inevitably led to lighter sentencing if the defendant was found guilty. In one case, reported under the headline 'SUPPOSED HORRIBLE ATROCITY UPON A CHILD', master bootmaker William Roberts of Duke Street was charged with the criminal assault of a seven-year-old neighbour. The little girl, who ran errands for the defendant, fetching ale for him while he worked in his cellar, had had, according to a medical certificate, 'a horrible outrage' perpetrated upon her. Interestingly, the girl's mother had initially confronted the prisoner, demanding to know what he had been doing to her daughter. In the first magistrates' court hearing, the victim stated that the prisoner 'gave her a glass and two half glasses of ale (the glass being a small one), and then, placing his arm around her, said, "This is my little servant."' He then, it was alleged, choked her and she lost consciousness. During the second magistrates' hearing another doctor was called and although he opined that 'great violence had been used' he said there was no conclusive evidence that a felony (i.e. rape) had been committed. This meant the stipendiary magistrate, Mr Raffles, could find Roberts guilty only of a common assault, which carried a maximum sentence of two months' imprisonment with hard labour.[26]

This case highlights a number of difficulties facing the courts when trying such sensitive and distressing cases. Evidence, either medical or provided by eyewitnesses, was very hard to come by. In the above case there was another shoemaker present but he claimed both he and the defendant were drunk to the point of stupefaction; consequently, he was unable to remember a thing or provide evidence one way or another. The surgeon, too, appears to have back-tracked and was less confident in providing evidence of a damning nature. This meant a lesser charge was brought against the defendant, even though the magistrate believed the little girl's account of events. In other cases, any significant delay between the alleged indecent assault and it being reported usually led to the discharge of the accused, because any marks of violence would be no longer evident on the victim's body. This occurred in another case, coincidentally involving another Liverpool shoemaker. Not only did the domestic servant and alleged victim fail to seek a medical examination until a week after the event, but she had made no 'alarm' at the time of the alleged offence. Her silence during the violation could have been construed, rightly or wrongly, as consent. Where the victim cried out there was a stronger chance of witnesses being able to give evidence. Off-duty constable Joseph Taggert was fortunate to receive a mere two-month prison sentence and dismissal from the force for a common assault on an 11-year-old girl and daughter of a widow who lived on his beat. Her daughter's cries from the back parlour brought the mother running into the room, where the policeman was found lying on the sofa, inebriated and 'with his clothes disarranged'. However, a charge of sexual assault was not possible as there was so little evidence.

Even medical evidence was not always enough to secure a conviction. In 1853 a 10-year-old girl abandoned by both her parents, who had emigrated to America, was found on the streets in a 'destitute condition'. She was found to be suffering from venereal disease and was able to name the culprit, a 17-year-old lad, but as she had said and done nothing for four months the charges against the young man were dropped.[27]

When examining crimes of sexual violence against children in the Victorian era, it is impossible to come to any conclusions about the scale of the problem. Statistics on sexual assault of adults, let alone children, are, and have always been, notoriously unreliable, for a variety of reasons. First, there was the silence which hangs over the crime, especially if the assailant was the child's father. Incest was not a crime until 1908; however, fathers could be and were prosecuted, as will be seen below, for crimes of sexual violence against their daughters. Under-reporting of sex crimes has, therefore, always been a major problem. Second, the age of consent during the second half of the nineteenth century changed a number of times. In 1875 the age of consent was raised from 12 to 13 years and to 16 years in 1885, after the scandal and sensational news reports surrounding the child sex market, known as 'the Maiden Tribute of Modern Babylon', uncovered by the journalist W. T. Stead in his *Pall Mall Gazette*. This change in the age of consent signified the Victorians' confusion and doubts about children's sexual awareness and innocence. The raising of the age of consent also had the effect of changing popular attitudes towards sexual acts with children. Theoretically, this should have increased the number of press reports on the crime, but this cannot be verified. Louise Jackson, working on court records for Middlesex (i.e. London) and Yorkshire for the period 1830–1910, found that over 60% of all sexual assault cases involved child victims in London and over 40% in Yorkshire. Moreover, she noted in the court cases that there was a shift from adult to child victims in the last quarter of the nineteenth century, which may have been partly due to the growth of child rescue societies such as the National Society for the Prevention of Cruelty to Children in the 1880s.[28]

In the nineteenth century, the victim's identity was not kept secret when it came to news reportage of court cases and this may have prevented many families from reporting crimes perpetrated on their children. At the Liverpool assizes of November 1896 the judge, in his opening address, noted the large number of cases relating to the sexual assault of children and added 'that the details of assaults upon young children should be given in open court was a matter that he could not help regretting'. He felt it wrong that the 'minds of the idle' should be given all 'the revolting details' of the 'most degrading and beastly incidents'. He argued that the courtroom should be cleared of these idle men 'who thronged the courts', and to counter the charge of secrecy he argued that journalists could remain, along with friends of the defendant and the prosecutor, and members of the legal and medical profession.[29] While it was true that publicity led to the under-reporting of crimes, the judge's call for closed sessions never came to pass. However, the newspapers began to give fewer and fewer details of sex crimes on children to their readers towards the end of the century.

One argument for open, unrestricted and public court proceedings of criminal cases involving child victims was that it would prevent malicious accusations. Male legislators appeared to have laboured under the fear that victim anonymity would lead women and girls to make false accusations of sexual violence against men. In the 50 years covered for this research, only one case was found in which the charge against the defendant was dismissed because the accusation appeared to be false. It concerned Joseph Thompson, of Athol Street, described as 'a decent-looking middle-aged man', who was accused of indecently assaulting a nine-year-old girl. In dismissing the case the stipendiary magistrate, Mr Mansfield, said that there was no evidence against Thompson and that he was not guilty of any 'imprudent or unguarded conduct'. At the time of the alleged offence he had been in the company of a warehouseman, who acted as a witness for him. The report of the case then went on to add, rather mysteriously, 'He was only performing an act of duty and charity for which he had been very ill-requited by the conduct of a thoroughly corrupt and depraved child, who made a charge which, in the absence of such testimony as he was fortunately able to bring, might have ruined his character and prospects for life'. Verdicts of not guilty did not mean, however, that the defendants were necessarily wholly innocent of sex crimes. In a case involving 51-year-old Peter Tearney, the nine-year-old prosecutor described circumstances of 'the most disgusting and revolting nature'. Some of the girl's evidence, according to the judge, might have been true, but 'it was almost without the bounds of reason to believe it all'. Consequently, Tearney was acquitted, even though the judge's parting comment was that 'it was a case of great suspicion'.[30]

In all but a single instance of cases examined between 1850 and 1900 the victims were female. This suggests that sexual abuse of boys was even more hidden. The exception involved William Calton of New Quay, who was fined £5 for an indecent assault on a 15-year-old shoeblack.[31] In the other (female) cases, the assailant and victim were usually known to each other. Assailants were often cited as being a father or partner of the mother, a relative, neighbour or employer. Less frequently did a stranger attack and sexually assault a young girl, even though the myth of 'stranger danger' was evidently very apparent in Victorian thinking, if not in name, in the 1876 Blackburn murder case, when the police immediately assumed the murderer was a vagrant or tramp.

In 1866 a girl 'not yet nine years of age' was snatched up by a man while she was playing on the turnpike road in Knotty Ash and taken to a field near 'Old Joe's Stile', where the crime was committed. Although the court report does not relate how the prisoner came to be arrested so soon after the event, one is left with the thought that the man was both local and known to the girl. When a stranger attacked a young woman, 15-year-old Mary Bennett, the newspapers were as much concerned with the facts that she was stabbed and had received unwanted kisses from a young man close to Exchange Street station. Every detail reported in the press suggests that Mary was worthy of the readers' sympathy. First, she struggled and screamed when James Tearnon 'threw his arms round her neck, kissed her and made an insulting proposal to her'. This attracted a crowd, forcing Tearnon to run off. Apparently undeterred by this attack, Mary carried on with her errand of fetching a minister of religion to the bedside of a dying man. This small detail made Mary even more worthy of the readers' sympathy. Within minutes, Tearnon was following her, but this time 'pushed against' her and in doing so stabbed her in the ribs. He was arrested and brought before the magistrates on a separate charge of stabbing a man in Pall Mall on the same evening but was discharged as the victim was unable to make a positive identification. However, a woman in court who had witnessed the attack on Mary pointed him out to the detective sergeant, who arrested him on the spot.[32]

Other reported assaults by strangers lacked both the gravity of the one outlined above and the overt sexual violence of other cases, especially those in the home. Local parks appear to have been locations of potential danger. Stanley Park attracted its share of 'dirty old men'. One, George Thom, was gaoled for two months for indecent behaviour towards 'two little girls'. One park-keeper complained to the bench that there were not sufficient staff to prevent such incidents. Two witnesses to another indecent assault saw 'respectably-dressed middle-aged' Charles Cannell put his hand under an 11-year-old's clothes. A drunk was convicted for indecently assaulting children in Newsham Park, and at Mount Gardens, Windsor, and an old man was convicted of acting in a grossly indecent manner towards three girls. In the case of elderly Henry Atkinson, who had picked up a girl in Prince's Park two years before his court case, it was admitted by the girl that she had repeatedly gone to his house for money, even though he had, on two occasions, asked her to stop visiting.[33]

Paedophilia comes in many guises; one which tends to be overlooked is child prostitution. Most seaports, Liverpool included, had a large sex industry, and its workers required constant replenishment. Many young women, often newly arrived immigrants from Ireland, were tricked into prostitution on the promise of work, wages and shelter. Not all were girls in their late teens and early twenties: some could be as young as 13, as is made clear by a report headlined 'ENTICING YOUNG GIRLS'. A mother and daughter, Catherine and Selina Smith, were charged with keeping brothels. The case is interesting for a number of reasons, not least for highlighting the police's attitude towards prostitution in Liverpool. 'It was not intended', detective superintendent Kehoe informed Mr Mansfield, the stipendiary magistrate, 'to prosecute the keepers of all the houses of ill fame in the town, and it was necessary that in some places they should be tolerated'. But in this particular case Kehoe felt the innocence and the age of the four girls, three of them 13 years old and the other just turned 14, warranted their intervention. Newly arrived from Dublin and intent on seeing Hengler's circus, the four were described as children of 'decent, well-to-do persons'. They asked two girls where they might find lodgings for the night and were directed to 'a coffee and private boarding house' in Dawson Street. It was in fact a brothel owned by Smith the elder, who told them to wash and 'make themselves nice'. She fed them and told them to go out into the streets and 'look for men', and if winked at by one of these men they were to wink back and bring the man back to the house. Sensing that they had fallen into bad company the four girls ran off and were found crying in the street and taken to the police station. The elder Smith was committed to trial while her daughter was freed on the understanding that she gave up her 'house' in School Lane.[34]

The home and its immediate neighbourhood were the locations where the dangers of sexual abuse and assault chiefly lay. Invariably, prosecutions were concerned with working-class families; there is no evidence of middle-class victims of sexual assault, which is not to say that it did not exist, simply that sex attacks by middle-class fathers on their children have escaped the historical record. For contemporaries, the dangers of entire families living and sleeping in one or two rooms meant that child sexual abuse was regarded as a class-based crime and one rooted in poverty. One father, described as a porter but in fact the owner of two brothels, one in Hotham Street and the other in Springfield Street, was charged with attempted rape of his 13-year-old daughter. She described how, when sleeping in a bed with her brother in the kitchen, she was awoken by her father committing an indecent assault upon her. Because the charge was attempted rape, he was sentenced only to two years with hard labour.[35]

Not surprisingly, fathers could normally expect heavier sentences than neighbours and acquaintances if found guilty of violence to their daughters. Children were, after all, under their protection and such crimes consti-tuted the worst possible betrayal of trust. They were frequently branded as 'inhuman' and the crime as a 'horrible depravity'. One father was given 10 years' penal servitude for an unspecified crime upon his nine-year-old daughter in 1876 and what compounded the crime was the fact that her mother was on her death-bed. Although not related by blood, stepfathers or partners of the victims' mothers could likewise expect heavy sentences, of up to seven years' penal servitude.[36] In one case in which the accused was the victim's brother, the family sided with the latter against the girl. Consequently, the case was dismissed, although it is telling that the magistrate was sympathetic to the girl's plea to emigrate when the case closed. His reply, 'I will see what I can do', suggested that he more than half believed her story. There are also examples of uncles being prosecuted for sex crimes against their nieces.[37]

If we regard the extended nineteenth-century family as including, where income allowed, domestic servants, we immediately come upon a particularly vulnerable group of young women. If employed by a tradesman, or even a manual worker, such girls were both young and very poorly paid. One unusual case involved retired pork butcher Thomas Beeson, of Seymour Street. He accused his young servant of eating some preserves. On being met with her denials he hit her on the face and then 'lifted her clothes in the presence of two young men and inflicted shameful chastisement'. Beeson's behaviour not only demonstrates the power of the master over his servant but also encapsulates the reality of male domination over women in general in Victorian Britain. In the court case which followed, Beeson admitted assaulting the servant but not in the sexual manner implied by the victim. Despite dressing smartly, in the hope of influencing the court as to his personal respectability, Beeson was sent to gaol for a month's hard labour.[38]

In the case of Holland George Hesketh of Netherfield Road, who was charged with indecently assaulting his 15-year-old servant, it was the girl's actions and behaviour both during and after the alleged assault that appear to have vindicated the defendant. When it was alleged that Hesketh had entered the parlour where she was sweeping and forcibly laid her on the sofa to commit the offence, she did not cry out, strike or bite him. Furthermore, it was claimed that the defendant's mother and his wife were in the house, albeit 'two lots of stairs off'. After the alleged assault, the servant told no one until she left the job a few days later. Even then, the defending solicitor appeared to cast aspersions on her character by discussing, in court, her behaviour and appearance at the Zoological Gardens, where she danced until late and came home with her hair hanging down. The defence solicitor was, in other words, questioning her character and successfully portrayed her as possessing immoral, even sluttish habits. The poor girl was not believed and the case was dismissed.[39]

The vulnerability of domestic service is surely encapsulated in the sad story of the 16-year-old domestic servant attached to the shelter belonging to the LSPCC in Islington Square. In her desperation to escape the inspector's attempts to indecently assault her, the servant jumped from the window of her bedroom and fell 38 feet to the pavement below. She broke an arm and both her legs (one of the bones was reported to be protruding through the flesh). Although the case was unable to proceed because of the seriousness of her injuries, evidence was supplied that the inspector's coat was found lying on her bed. In the subsequent assize trial it transpired that the inspector, Michael Egan, had been in drink on the night of the attempted assault. He was found guilty and sentenced to four months with hard labour.[40]

The sexual assault of children, then as now, was regarded as outrageous and shameful. In relation to neighbours displaying improper behaviour towards children, women sometimes took matters into their own hands, especially if they felt the police or judiciary were letting them down. Women might collect at a neighbour's door and mob and hoot the man they felt responsible. This occurred to Patrick Hanly, of Standish Street, who had the previous day been acquitted of indecent exposure to some girls. The evidence had been found inconclusive. However, the mothers and their women friends gathered outside his door in a shaming protest against him. They at least succeeded in getting him gaoled because he came out of his house and struck one of the women with a poker. He was imprisoned for three months for the assault. Many taboos have surrounded sex crimes and consequently victims and their families were often reluctant to report these kinds of assault to the authorities. There were in fact other possibilities open to both them and the assailant. One such, which had been used for centuries, was for the assailant to pay compensation to the victim on the understanding that no criminal charges were brought against him. Cab driver David Cassidy attempted unsuccessfully to do this with the father of a seven-year-old whom he had raped.[41]

Young victims would tell their mothers of the abuses they had suffered, although a considerable lapse of time might have occurred between the assault and the discovery of the fact. Male abusers would tell the girls that it was a secret between themselves, provide sweets or money in return for silence or simply threaten them. Once informed of the abuse, the mother had to decide how to proceed. Should she confront the man, collect more evidence or even try to catch the abuser committing further acts of indecency against her daughter? Or should she do nothing? Popular attitudes towards child sex abuse become evident in the court detail of people's reactions and actions on learning of the crime. They are often complex and defy generalization, since victims' families often had a number of issues to consider before taking further steps. In one 1855 case, the identity of the abuser was considered crucial in determining how the assault should be handled. It transpired in court that the aunt of the victim chose to act on her eight-year-old niece's behalf because the mother, although 'perfectly aware' of what was happening, had chosen not to prosecute. The reason for her inaction was that her husband, and stepfather to the child, was the abuser. She and some other members of the family had decided to stay silent because her husband was the sole breadwinner and thus they could not afford to have him held in custody and gaoled. In her attempt to protect her daughter, however, she sent her to Manchester, to be out of the way for two weeks. After the child returned to Liverpool, her aunt was determined to bring the case to court but she needed proof. On two occasions she sent the little girl to her stepfather's office with his lunch. On each occasion she had hidden and witnessed the assaults. On confronting the man she was coaxed and then threatened to stay silent, which she rejected by going to the police. During his trial the stepfather admitted to 'meddling with the child' but pleaded with the magistrates not to be sent to prison, as he was the family's sole support. He was fortunate to receive only six months' hard labour. The matter did not end there, since the prisoner's sister-in-law assaulted the aunt and chief witness as they both left court. She was fortunate to be given only a caution.[42]

It is clear from the evidence that Victorians did regard sex attacks on children seriously, since some of the cases attracted very heavy punishments, such as the 12 years' penal servitude handed out to Michael Martin for his criminal assault on a 13-year-old at Huyton Quarry.[43] Moreover, the legislature raised the age of consent to the present age of 16 during this period. There were other continuities with the present day: relatives and neighbours rather than strangers were often the guilty parties; certain spaces like the newly created public parks were potentially dangerous; and conviction rates for crimes against children appear to have been low.

Conclusion

ALTHOUGH CHILD SEX ABUSE CASES appear to have occurred with depressing regularity throughout the period, they did not set off moral panics. National cases such as those of 'sweet Fanny Adams' in 1867 or Emily Holland of Blackburn in 1876 attained their notoriety for the ways in which the little girls met their ends and were disposed of. In the Blackburn case the manner in which the dog Morgan discovered the body and the subsequent dispute surrounding the dog's ownership and its commercial value (an offer of £500 was made by a music hall owner) lent the story added interest.[44] In addition, heavy prison sentences were not the norm for paedophiles: they were commonly given between one and two years' imprisonment with hard labour. This apparent leniency was due to a number of factors, not least the age of the victim, the difficulties of providing evidential proof, and the downgrading of charges from rape to attempted rape or indecent assault.

For non-sexual crimes of violence, children were, by the turn of the century, better protected than they had been in 1850. However, it is impossible to gauge how successful the laws for their protection and the establishment of the LSPCC were in prosecuting child abusers. Children were generally, by 1900, more valued by society than they had been in previous centuries and this may have led to a diminution in acts of violence on children.

CHAPTER 13

A conclusion. 'Giving a dog a bad name': Liverpool and its criminal reputation in the nineteenth century

O N THE JANUARY MORNING of the execution of two of the Tithebarn
Street murderers in 1875 (chapter 7), the *Liverpool Mercury* ran a piece
headed 'CRIME AND CRITICISM'. It began:

> The proverb which shows the consequence of giving a dog a bad name has
> lately received a forcible illustration in the case of Liverpool. Just at present
> we bear the ill repute of being the most brutal and lawless community in the
> kingdom. Two or three of our London contemporaries have fallen foul of
> us with unsparing criticism, and a crowd of lesser lights have taken up the
> censorious cry.[1]

The *Mercury*, in stoically defending the town against the calumnies put
forward by the *Times* and other newspapers, argued that Liverpudlians
would not have been able to recognize the lurid descriptions of the port
being published in other newspapers. The Tithebarn Street murder was,
the *Mercury* argued,

> commented upon just as though it was typical of every-day life in Liverpool,
> instead of being, as was really the case, almost unparalleled in local annals. The
> corner men are spoken of as prowling about every great thoroughfare, and the
> police as powerless to keep them in subjection.[2]

Herein lay one of the problems confronting Liverpool. Crimes like the
Tithebarn Street murder, the 'wholesale poisonings' by Flanagan and Higgins
in 1883 (chapter 8), or the killing of David Eccles in 1891 by two boys under
the age of 10 (chapter 11) were newsworthy to both the local and the national
press, but for different reasons. For the *Liverpool Mercury*, such events were
unusual and out of character. The paper's experience of covering the city's
news, and more particularly everyday crime, meant it had a different perspective. The three cases above were viewed as shocking, out of the ordinary and
untypical. In contrast, the reporting of Liverpool crime by national papers
and journals from other regions of the country was spasmodic and tended
to focus on the same killings from a totally different perspective. These
newspapers portrayed the killings as abnormally brutal but typical events in

the annals of the city's crime. Their treatment and memory of Liverpool were based on the previous stories they had occasionally published about the city in their pages. The national papers set the context of a particular Liverpool crime news story within the last news story their papers had published on Liverpool. This process of accretion, of journalistic hyperbole and exaggeration, branded an already tarnished town.[3]

News about Liverpool may also have served journalists in other ways. 'In the old days of journalism', reported the *Maidstone and Kentish Journal*, 'it was said to be the custom "to kill a child in Liverpool" or invent some other mild and vague catastrophe of the kind, whenever a corner paragraph was required to fill the newspaper'.[4] This single sentence, written over 135 years ago, manages to convey the relationship between Liverpool and the press. First, newspaper reporters, it would appear, customarily associated the town with violent crime and, in particular, the killing of children. Second, the newspaper displayed contempt and thoughtlessness in regarding the killing of a child as a 'mild and vague catastrophe' worthy of being only a newspaper filler. This journalistic proverb emphasizes yet further the weight of notoriety under which the port suffered. Liverpool crime became a source of fillers for many newspapers around the country. The head constable's annual reports were abridged and published in many provincial papers, acting almost like a barometer for the state of the nation's moral well-being.

This is not to say that Liverpool's reputation for being criminal and violent was entirely undeserved. There is considerable contemporary evidence, albeit of varying quality and reliability, which suggests that Liverpool was more criminal and more violent than many other towns and cities in Britain. Writing at the beginning of this period, the Reverend John Clay, Preston's pioneering prison chaplain and crime statistician, recorded the following in his 1849 report:

> It is obviously a great mistake to impute Lancashire crime to Lancashire manufactures. It is the *great seaport* of the southern division which throws its own dark aspect over the moral reputation of the entire county ... the combined criminality of Manchester, Salford, Bolton, and Preston – the great 'manufacturing centres' – falls below that of Liverpool....

For the Reverend Clay as for many other commentators, the port of Liverpool laboured under a further burden, namely the influx of poor Irish immigrants, in addition to an already existing 'dissolute class'; 'whatever may have been their habits at home, no sooner [do they] reach Liverpool, than such of them as are in a destitute state, either give way to the temptation to plunder round the docks, or become an oppressive and demoralizing burden to the town'.[5] This stigma attaching to the Irish was itself grafted on to the town, making Liverpool even more notorious throughout the country.

Throughout the second half of the nineteenth century, Liverpool added to its notoriety with national reports of the town's infanticide figures,

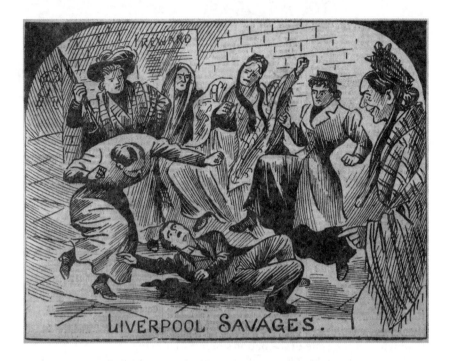

LIVERPOOL SAVAGES.

Illustration 5 The attack on William Nutting, as portrayed in the *Illustrated Police News*, 23 March 1895. Reproduced with the permission of the British Library, Colindale Newspaper Library.

its female crime (particularly prostitution), its drunk and disorderly, its vicious cornermen and its unruly juveniles. This substantial list stained the town's reputation. These deviant groups were still present on the streets of Liverpool in the 1890s. As late as 1895 the Lord Chief Justice, Baron Russell, complained of the use of knives bringing disgrace to the city. 'Men were charged', he said, 'with, on the slightest provocation, or on no provocation at all, taking out their knives – the husband against his wife, the neighbour against his neighbour, and the workman against his fellow workman'.[6] Witnesses, too, were still being assaulted after giving evidence in court cases. One young boy, William Nutting, was set on by a group of women in Smithdown Road for giving evidence at the trial of Edward Wedgewood, who had been found guilty of stabbing a woman. Eight women were charged with kicking him and breaking three of his ribs (illustration 5). On being arrested, one of the leading assailants, Annie Wedgewood, produced a copy of the *Police News* and told the constable, 'You need not have put it in the *Police News*. None of us had hats on. (laughter)'.[7]

There were also notable changes in the 1890s from the earlier decades. Foremost among them was the LSPCC, whose shelter in Islington Square provided a place of safety for young victims of neglect, abuse and violence at the hands of their parents. For older boys, clubs for lads and young men had grown in popularity since their formative years in the mid-1880s but rowdyism was still a persistent problem for the city. It was fortunate that it never reached the proportions it did in Manchester, with the Scuttlers.

One other feature noticeable in the crime and court reports was the increasing willingness of neighbours to fetch the police for certain kinds of violence, or when they merely suspected some foul deed had been perpetrated. In one sensational case from 1895, detailed under the headline 'ROASTING A NEWLY BORN CHILD', Ann Burke was confronted by neighbour Bridget Rooney, who wanted to know why Ann was no longer pregnant. When told the baby had been stillborn and that a nurse and a doctor had been in attendance, Bridget went and asked both the alleged medical helpers if this was true. They denied all knowledge of the affair and so she informed the police. Their arrival coincided with the burning of the baby. Having to force their way into the house in Leyden Street, one of the policemen noticed a bright fire and on closer inspection he was able to pick off from the top of the coals a baby's head.[8]

Fetching a constable, however, was not always the first response for some in the community, as there were many instances of fights occurring in which the help of the police was neither sought nor welcomed. Detective Lawson found this to be the case in 1895 when arresting a woman, named Morris, whom he suspected of stealing an expensive coat she was carrying. When they got to Mann Street, where she claimed the coat was given to her to sell, Morris threw herself onto the pavement and fought and bit the detective. A crowd gathered and tried to rescue the woman by throwing bricks and other missiles at Lawson but he was able to force a retreat into nearby shop, which the angry crowd proceeded to attack until police reinforcements arrived.[9] Thus, within the space of 10 days in 1895, two very contrasting narratives of Liverpool attitudes towards the police could be found. This ambivalence towards authority remained an issue well into the following century.

Taking media distortion and stigmatization into account, is it possible, then, to evaluate how violent Liverpool was during Victoria's reign and draw conclusions about its poor reputation? Providing answers to these two questions has proved remarkably difficult. First, the statistical data used by Victorians to damn the town were flawed and misinterpreted. Second, it is not possible to make objective comparisons between Liverpool and other British towns and cities. Liverpool had the largest police force outside metropolitan London; this in itself would inflate the crime figures, as there were more officers to make arrests. Likewise, the emergence in Liverpool of the purity and temperance campaigns and the vigilance committee meant the local police may have been less tolerant of drunkenness than were forces in other cities, such as Portsmouth.[10] Also, the police in Liverpool may have contributed to the seemingly high figures for assaults on officers by using the charge of drunk and disorderly as a catch-all for people they wanted to arrest but, more importantly, they were resisted more enthusiastically and energetically in Liverpool than in other towns.

For many of the town's inhabitants living through Victoria's reign, violent crime rarely, if at all, intruded on their lives. It was something they read about in the local papers; something which happened in other, poorer parts of the town. Violent crime was concentrated in particular neighbourhoods close to the docks, especially in the north end. The *Mercury* and other papers, as we have seen, identified and branded certain streets as being notorious. This notion of moral law-abiding streets and disorderly ones had been identified in the 1850s by the Reverend Hume. He drew up a map of Liverpool in 1858 on which he used shading to designate 'pauper' and 'semi-pauper' streets and some 'streets of crime and immorality'.[11] While we may object to his overly moral language and terminology in labelling particular streets close to Vauxhall Road and Scotland Road, many in Liverpool during the late nineteenth century would have held in their heads a mental street map representing a geography of dangerous and safe neighbourhoods. It was not a case of 'there be dragons' but of 'there be ruffians'. By the end of the century, the more dangerous areas of town appeared now to be in the north end, towards Bootle, although Chisenhale Street never shook off its notoriety before 1900.

For reporters and editors looking in from outside the region, the people of Liverpool were generally tarred with the brush of brutality. When the watching crowd failed to intervene during the killing of Richard Morgan on Titheban Street and when St George's Hall was besieged by masses of locals 'loud in their sympathies for the accused' in 1874, the entire community was, in effect, on trial. The death of Morgan was 'a stain on the good name of Liverpool which it is incumbent on her inhabitants to wipe away'. For the *Telegraph*, 'Fear is the only scourge with which these ignorant savages can be governed'.[12] It would be wrong, however, to condemn the majority of the onlookers for their apparent inactivity during the fight which killed Morgan. As Shimmin noted, all kinds of issues would have been playing out in the minds of the watching crowd. First, there was the spectacle of the street fight, which many did enjoy watching. Second, to get involved would have invited danger of injury from the assailants or arrest by the police when they eventually arrived on the scene. Finally, many would not have seen the beginning of the fight and would therefore not have known who was the aggressor and who was the innocent victim. Street fights and domestic arguments in Liverpool, as in many other towns and cities throughout the country, were regarded as private matters, not to be interfered with.

There was, nonetheless, a small minority within the town who supported Morgan's murderers and who were able to exercise a fear over the majority of law-abiding citizens. To 'snitch' was to invite trouble, as the many witnesses who were beaten up after providing evidence could testify. These roughs, ruffians and cornermen existed throughout the period, often under different labels but forming, nonetheless, a continuous threat to working people. Moreover, their habits of standing around at corners, close to the pubs, meant that more law-abiding, but temporarily unemployed, dockers and labourers were mistakenly identified as belonging to this criminal group. An impression could be formed, therefore, of a town over-run with idle vagabonds or 'man vultures' waiting their chance for some easy plunder off some unsuspecting passer-by.

It would have been unusual had Liverpool *not* been a violent place. The city was a major port with an economy that depended on a large pool of casually employed labour. The poverty and poor cramped housing conditions surpassed those of most other nineteenth-century cities. In such an environment, heavy drinking, thieving and fighting among the poor, of whatever nationality and of both sexes, were to be expected. Children, too, were scarred by their life experiences in the slums. The conditions that pertained in 1850 were still largely present in 1900. When, at the spring assizes of 1895, Peter Flynn was found guilty of killing his wife (chapter 9), details of the couple's squalid life in a narrow court off Saltney Street were presented by the defence. The evidence, all too familiar to readers of reports of Liverpool's criminal trials, highlighted the husband's steady reputation as an honest and industrious man who had patiently borne his partner's 'drunken habits' and 'quarrelsome disposition'. What elicited comment from contemporaries was the fact that, in the slums, 'drunken wives and mothers' were still a numerous class, and that Flynn after his initial assault upon his wife 'continued his violence with a kind of savage ferocity which had not previously manifested itself in his disposition'.[13] Men were, by the late 1890s, expected to exercise more restraint.

It was, thus, hardly surprising that Justice Lawrence, at Liverpool's 1891 winter assize, complained that it was the 'heaviest' calendar of prisoners since 1863. 'It was', he continued, 'disappointing to find in this city of Liverpool such a state of affairs, when there was such a sensible diminution of crime in other parts of the country'. Out of the 117 prisoners on trial, the calendar of violent crimes included three murders, five attempted murders, five manslaughters, 12 rapes or other sex crimes, and four woundings.[14] The *Birmingham Daily Post*, two months earlier, in an article comparing crime in 10 major British cities, reported that Liverpool maintained its 'unenviable pre-eminence in crime'. Woundings and shootings numbered 251 in Liverpool but in Birmingham and Manchester the figures were 28 and 10 respectively. In an apparent gesture towards balance and fair reporting, the paper acknowledged Liverpool's peculiarity as a seaport, where crime was to be expected, but it noted that the combined total for woundings and shootings in the five ports of Cardiff, Hull, Southampton,

Bristol and Grimsby was only 47.[15] The paper concluded that Liverpool's reputation was 'abundantly justified'.

Crime known to the police can and did fluctuate greatly; consequently, the authorities preferred to study how the volume of crime altered over a number of years. Such longitudinal studies ironed out any quirks in the year-on-year figures. When the head constable came to review the Liverpool police in his end-of-century report, he noted with pride how the numbers of indictable crimes, measured over five-year periods, had fallen in the city, from 30,889 in the 1885–89 period to 19,863 in 1895–99. Furthermore, this decrease was especially notable in crimes of violence, down from 1515 in the former to 790 in the latter period. He attributed this apparently enormous decrease, in part, to the equally dramatic decrease in drunkenness. This had been attained through close police supervision of the public houses, which ensured badly run premises were refused drinks licences at the annual brewster sessions. There was also, according to the police, a significant change in drinking habits, with an increasing switch to drinking at home. How significant these crime figures were is very hard to evaluate but the head constable and the criminal registrar who collected and collated the nation's crime statistics believed there to have been a marked improvement.

Given such a diminution in the city's reported crime figures it would appear that Liverpool was following the national trend known as the 'English miracle'. This referred to the decline in trials for thefts and violence between 1850 and 1914, just when the nation was becoming more urban and industrialized, conditions which were thought to contribute to increased criminality. The criminal registrar, in 1901, described it thus:

> We have witnessed a great change in manners: the substitution of words without blows for blows with or without words; an approximation in the manners of different classes; a decline in the spirit of lawlessness.[16]

Liverpool between 1850 and 1900 exhibited some surprising differences from, and similarities to, the Liverpool of today. Looking at the differences first, paedophilia in the nineteenth century does not appear to have provoked major social concern and outrage. Punishments, too, for those found guilty of such crimes seem to modern eyes remarkably lenient. The reasons for the muted concern and the comparatively short prison sentences are not altogether clear. Many of the cases examined for the writing of this book involved not strangers but men known to the children. This fact alone takes away one of the most important characteristics of the present-day fear, that of the predatory male stranger who can strike, without warning, and abduct and murder a child taken at random from the street. In the nineteenth century, newspapers were often reluctant to highlight or discuss paedophilia but they did indirectly acknowledge the crime's more typical domestic characteristics by citing the relationship of the accused to the victim in the brief reports of proceedings at the assize court. This recognition that the crime was usually perpetrated from within the family allowed relatives to confront the paedophile and bring pressure to bear either through the legal process or through extra-legal methods such as shaming.[17]

Another notable difference concerns the decline in female violence. The level and frequency of female violence, particularly in Liverpool in the second half of the nineteenth century, appear to have been particularly high. Many of the incidents of female violence arose out of the dire social and economic conditions in which they lived and, like men, women could be brutalized. As these conditions, housing, education and welfare provision improved, so instances of female brutality began to decline. However, this is not to deny the continued existence of domestic violence between men and women.

One final difference between now and then, and one particularly pertinent to Liverpool, is how society and the state view and treat children who kill other children. While both the most notorious cases, the 1855 and 1891 killings (chapter 11), were considered newsworthy and unusual, the child killers were deemed to be reformable. By today's standards the punishments received by the nineteenth-century child killers appear unimaginably lenient and even generous. In 1855, for example, Breen and Fitzpatrick were taught to read and write, skills that in all probability would have been denied to them had they led law-abiding existences. However, by 1891 a concern was being expressed that has remained with us. The *Pall Mall Gazette*'s question, 'what shall we do with them?', is still pertinent today. The question of the age of criminal responsibility, presently set at 10 years in England, the manner in which children should be tried in court, whether the trial should be open (with reporters and public present) and how young offenders should be punished were being raised then and are still being posed now.[18]

When examining violence nowadays, certain themes appear, not least the youth problem and gang violence, the drink question, and the masculine need for status and reputation. So how successful was the 'civilizing process'? That process can be understood as one in which the middle- and upper-class culture of restraint and propriety prevailed over the older working-class culture which legitimated physical confrontation.[19] Certainly in Liverpool, the roughs and cornermen, who were so closely associated with fighting, were increasingly identified and labelled as brutes and un-English from the 1860s. The ritual of the fair fight to settle personal scores was likewise increasingly condemned by magistrates. Nonetheless, it is difficult to draw firm conclusions on how successful the process was in an international port such as Liverpool. First, other fighting styles and customs, the use of the knife for example, had had a long established presence in the town. Second, in chapter 6 it was seen that as late as 1896 Duxbury was having a 'fair fight' with Wilson (see p. 81). What makes the Duxbury case different from earlier male confrontations was the fact it was held in private, indoors and away from the eyes of a crowd and the police. The issuing of a challenge and then a public fight between two combatants in the street was becoming unusual by 1900. Nonetheless, ritualized forms of fighting occurred contemporaneously with free-for-all and knife fights throughout the second half of the nineteenth century.[20]

Those who engaged in physical confrontations, especially those who used weapons or lost control of their emotions, were, by the final years of the nineteenth century, singled out, as Wiener has argued, for particularly harsh treatment by the courts. Take the case of John Donnolly, who was tried for the murder of Robert Devine in June 1896. The court heard how the men had 'sparred together' in Athol Street but had been separated by a policeman. They met again in nearby Sumner Street, where Devine issued a challenge: 'If you want to fight me, come now and fight fair'. Devine then produced a 'short stick' from his pocket, whereupon Donnolly reached into his trousers and produced a knife, which he used to stab Devine in the ensuing fight. Interestingly, Donnolly gave himself up to the police and the jury never left their box in reaching their guilty verdict on a reduced charge of manslaughter. In an earlier decade the facts of the case would have stood in Donnolly's favour, as they appear to have done so here. What was different from an earlier decade of the nineteenth century was the judge's sentence in 1896, of 16 years' penal servitude.[21]

Yet surprising leniency was still being extended to some men guilty of seemingly quite brutal attacks on their partners in the final years of the nineteenth century. Daniel Boyle, of Wigan Street, was gaoled for only three months after he punched his wife to the floor and then hit her head with a chair. Later he threw her downstairs and finally kicked her prostrate body. The court in addition to the gaol sentence granted his wife a separation order, custody of the three children and 12 shillings a week in maintenance. Carter James Gilboy evaded a charge of manslaughter after his common-law partner Elizabeth Connor died immediately after his violent assault on her in Downe Street. The cause of death, a brain haemorrhage, was not linked to the kicking he had inflicted on her and so he was gaoled for only three months with hard labour. John Regan was imprisoned for three months for blinding his wife. She was already blind in one eye before the assault, and the damage to her other eye appears to have been intentional, as Regan had told her prior to the assault that he would 'completely blind her, and then get a dog to lead her about'.[22] Many more cases can be found in the 1890s which suggest attitudes to violence, especially domestic violence, had not hardened during the second half of the century, although courts appear to have become more generous towards women in the granting of maintenance and separation orders. Whether Liverpool was typical in its leniency (Mr Hopwood, the recorder, had a reputation for inflicting short sentences, for instance), only further research on other towns and cities will confirm. Nationally, Wiener has identified a 'diminished tolerance' towards men who assaulted women.[23]

However, we have seen that Liverpool continued to stage very heavy assizes calendars up to the mid-1890s, which may suggest that the so-called

'English miracle' of declining crime had by-passed the city. On the other hand, the statistics show a marked decline in reported violent crime right at the end of the century, which may suggest that Liverpool was finally moving into line with the rest of the country. Perhaps it is possible to conclude only that violent crime in the city, as a whole, did decline, but, and it is an important qualifier, certain neighbourhoods and quarters of the city remained as lawless and violent as they had been in the 1860s. Many people living in these streets had benefited little from the improvements in living standards then evident in much of the country. They continued to live in overcrowded and poorly constructed slums and they continued to struggle to earn a living wage. Their lives and how they resolved their grievances with neighbours and other family members continued in the age-old manner of interpersonal violence. Early in the twentieth century the head constable reported, however, that the demolition of the 'old back-to-back courts' had led to a significant decline in fighting, particularly knife fights. 'The enclosed courts', he said, 'gave two quarrelsome people no chance of getting away from each other, but only gave them a fighting ground'.[24] The housing developments which replaced the old courts were now more spacious and easier to police.

The criminal registrar, mindful of Liverpool's distinctive criminality, noted the unusually high proportion of female criminals, the large number of juvenile offenders and the large proportion arrested who were not born in Liverpool, at 37%. His optimistic words, however, tended to echo those of Liverpool's head constable, who in his annual report for 1899 wrote:

> It must never be forgotten, too, in considering crime in Liverpool, that Liverpool is a Seaport, with an immense migratory population of all nationalities. When this is borne in mind, and the record of crime in Liverpool is compared with that of other great towns, it will be seen that pride, not shame, should be felt in the condition of the City. Comparing the crime of Liverpool (for 1898, the last year for which returns are yet available) with that of Glasgow, we find that Indictable Offences in Liverpool only number 6.66 per thousand of the population, whilst in Glasgow they number 12.62 per thousand of the population. Even in Manchester, an *inland* town, Indictable Offences number 6.88 per thousand of the population. To have a record better than that of an inland town like Manchester, and nearly twice as good as that of a seaport town like Glasgow, should certainly be a matter for congratulation.[25]

Statistics, which had been used to damn Liverpool for much of the nineteenth century as drunken and dangerous, appear, ironically, to have bolstered the city's reputation at the very end of the Victorian period.

Saturday night and Sunday morning: Hugh Shimmin's account of the Rosehill night shift

In the summer of 1857, Hugh Shimmin's 'fly on the wall' articles, under the title 'Liverpool Life: Police, Prisoners and Prisons', appeared in the *Liverpool Mercury*. He had, before the appearance of these lengthy articles on the Liverpool police, written for the same newspaper on a diverse range of topics, from music halls to taverns, and from dog fighting to gambling. The common theme running through these pieces was his concern to portray, to a largely middle-class readership, the underbelly of Liverpool working-class life.

Born of working-class parents who had initially moved from the Isle of Man to Whitehaven in Cumberland and later on to Liverpool, when Hugh Shimmin was still a teenager, his early life, as an apprenticed bookbinder, offered few clues as to his later success as a journalist. However, with energy and a strong belief in self-improvement through education, Shimmin initially succeeded in small business, before becoming a reporter and writer in the 1850s. With the success of his *Mercury* pieces, Shimmin became editor and joint proprietor of the radical and satirical paper the *Porcupine*, in 1860. This publication proceeded to provide its readers with acerbic, knowledgeable and witty opinions on a wide range of local topics, from the theatre to slum housing, from sanitary reform to local politics. At times, Shimmin was irascible and, as the title of the paper implied, prickly, so much so that he was gaoled briefly for libel in 1870. Generally well informed, and holding strong views, chiefly against alcohol, Shimmin's closely observed articles on Liverpool's courts and slums are notable for their detail and sensitivity. His subjective viewpoint does not, for historians, invalidate him as an accurate historical source. So long as present-day readers understand his likes and dislikes – especially his dislike of statistics – and remain patient with his occasionally flowery prose and frequent classical and literary illusions, which are surely present to validate him as well educated, literate and cultured, they will come to recognize that Shimmin was a gifted writer. In fact, it would not be overstating the case to say that he belonged to a group of talented chroniclers of English urban working-class life in the 1850s. This group included the famous novelist Charles Dickens and Henry Mayhew of *London Labour and the London Poor* fame, and the less well known but equally talented Angus Reach, who, along with Mayhew, wrote for the *Morning Chronicle*. He belonged, therefore, to a fine journalistic tradition of social commentators and chroniclers but, unlike his contemporaries, his critical gaze fell on a fairly narrow range of themes. Housing, poverty and alcohol figure greatly in his articles, yet he has little to say on the Irish. When he does comment on them it is usually, and this is very much to his credit, to chastise others for blaming the Irish for all Liverpool's ills. He was, in other words, no sectarian bigot.[1]

What we have in the extracts reproduced below are genuine, first-hand observations by Shimmin, who was taken round on night patrol by one of Liverpool's senior police officers. In them we read, no doubt embellished for literary effect, of the problems and issues confronting a constable on his beat. The lengthy series of articles quoted below (which appeared between 27 July and 24 August 1857) was followed later in the year by a similar set of articles on the punishment of criminals in Liverpool, focusing especially on the newly built Walton gaol. The police articles were written and published shortly after the Liverpool force had had its first national inspection and for which it was acclaimed as 'THE MODEL FORCE OF THE KINGDOM'.[2]

The whole series, which had started in late June 1857, is clearly very supportive of the police, who had, earlier in the decade, lost much of their moral authority as a neutral, disinterested and incorruptible force. With the arrival of a new head constable, Major Greig, the Liverpool police's reputation was slowly restored. However, as was seen in previous chapters, Shimmin's uncritical support soon ended when instances of police violence towards members of the public were brought to his attention. The *Porcupine* became, in the late 1860s and through much of the 1870s, Major Greig's strongest critic and constantly poked fun at the poor quality of the force's recruits and their ill conceived training. By the time of his death in 1879, Shimmin had become an angry exposer of police misdeeds and a critic of their increasingly militaristic behaviour. But all this was in the future, for in 1857 Shimmin was still a firm supporter and was sensitive to the difficulties confronting the beat constable.

The 'Liverpool Life: Police, Prisoners and Prisons' series provides readers with a remarkable documentary account of Shimmin's experience when out on police night shift patrol, with a superintendent as his guide. Although Shimmin is at times moralistic and judgemental in tone, he provides a lively, convincing and authentic account of the Liverpool streets, its brothels and prostitutes, the sailors (both black and white) and the locals, all struggling to survive in their poor and overcrowded neighbourhoods. The 'Liverpool Life' series is the closest a twenty-first-century reader can get to police duty in 1857, not just in Liverpool but in any other major city in the country. Moreover, Shimmin takes us through some of the roughest streets of the town on the busiest police shift, namely Saturday night into Sunday morning, when the pubs disgorged their drunken clientele onto the streets after midnight. We get to see the entire police process, from a verbal warning, then an arrest, through to the incarceration in the local bridewell. Those who know the present system of policing will recognize a great deal of this process. Much of Shimmin's description is self-explanatory, but where he mentions a name or refers to an issue that is not self-evident, I have included a comment in brackets.

XVIII

We are on parade, on a Saturday evening, at Rose-hill Bridewell, and the hour being a quarter to nine o'clock, the eight sections intended for night duty in the northern division of the town begin to pour in so close as to be almost in Indian file, and take their seats as they arrive upon the bench which runs around the large hall. Each man knows his exact place, and all arrive with such admirable punctuality that the stream has no sooner set in than it has fully flowed. The Rose-hill station appears to be constructed on a peculiar acoustic principle, for on occasions of muster there arises a buzz or hum such as will be heard only in a garrison, where, 'with life's elixir sparkling high,' the very air seems inspired with the spirit of youthful vigour and robust health. Taking a walk along the line, 'What sort of a beat is Hatton-garden?' we hear one young officer asking another. He will evidently have to go there for the first time that night. 'Oh, it is very rough,' is the discouraging response. Mr. Ride, divisional superintendent, is in attendance, and the eight inspectors present are first told to 'fall in.' Inspectors, as we have already stated, in addition to their other general duties, have also the special task assigned to them of visiting at stated periods all licensed lodging houses upon their rounds; and having stood up, various communications were read to them, one we remember being to the effect that in consequence of an intimation from Dr Duncan [Liverpool's medical officer of health], it was desired that in the inspection of lodging houses in future two children under seven years of age should be counted as only one, and that a child in arms was not to number at all. The various sections were afterwards paraded in succession, and the number of men to be taken on each beat was assigned. Each officer, somewhat in soldier fashion, had to display his 'kit,' and exhibited a cape swung over the left arm, holding a truncheon, whistle, and rattle in one hand. When mustered, a great variety of notifications of robberies and other special directions were read out to them. One of which we took notice was a personal description, very minute, of a young man who had absconded from Lime-street, and who was 'wanted' on a charge of embezzlement; another was 'Stolen last night from a warehouse in Tithebarn-street, a shawl;' a third, that a lady had that day had her pocket picked of a £5 Bank of England note and of two sovereigns in gold; then there was another charge of embezzlement, with description of party; next, 'Stolen from a man in a brothel, two ten-dollar gold pieces;' a sixth, 'Stolen this morning, a silver lever watch;' and a seventh, that a stable in Pembroke-gardens had been forced open and robbed. The officers were all attentive to these announcements, the reading of which was, however, interrupted by a 'row' amongst some drunken women in Peover-street, adjoining, and two or three men were sent out to quell the viragos who had thus dared to beard the lion in his very den. The great body of the men were then formed into single file, and marched towards the door; about a dozen, however, being kept in reserve. Of these, some had been in court in charge of cases that morning. The superintendent learned how long each had been detained there, and then made him, according to the circumstances of the case, a certain allowance of time. Many of the men, we observed, looked only half satisfied, as if they had expected a greater indulgence than was accorded. Of those going out, some would be allowed to go off at one o'clock in the morning, but the great majority would have to wait till six. One half of those, we were told, going out that night, would come on again next afternoon (Sunday) at three o'clock.

Punctually at nine o'clock the men received the word to 'march,' and then went, accompanied by their inspectors, to be dropped at their beats through all the northern part of the town. No sooner had they gone than the men whom they had relieved began dropping in. As the various sections became filled, an inspector reported them as 'correct,' and the superintendent then formally inspected them, and sent them off. By this system, as will readily be seen, every man is seen between a quarter to nine and twenty minutes after it; and persons who may have complaints to make of incivility or any other improper conduct on the part of an officer are invited to attend during that interval, when they will have the advantage of seeing the whole of the men, and identifying the supposed offender. We were told that the state of the bridewells would soon show the influence of sending out this strong force of 120 men, strengthened, too, by supernumeraries – as it was but natural that when, as up to that hour, there had been only 60 on duty, the weaker force would not be so likely to interfere with disorder, unless it were extreme. Besides, the night was wearing on, and drink would be commencing to produce its too usual effect.

The disturbance in Peover-street was not the only interruption on parade. Three men were brought in by two officers. They all appeared to be drunk. One, a very stout fellow, an Irishman, was in his shirt sleeves; a second, a tall young fellow, had his face all gashed and bleeding. The report was that these two had been fighting near Scotland-road Market, and the third, it appeared, had been a witness to the affray. We went with the superintendent into a little back office to hear the particulars of the complaint preferred. It appeared that a drunken fellow, not one of the three, had been kicking and assaulting everybody that came within his reach, when the two officers went up to arrest him. A crowd immediately pressed round, and cried out that the police were abusing the man – an almost invariable result whenever an apprehension has to be effected in certain districts of the town. The bystanders were doing all that they could to prevent the fellow being taken, and one of the officers who had hold of him was kneeling on the ground, when the rough-looking prisoner in the shirt sleeves, who is employed in the market, either through Irish instinct and love of fight, or because he thought that the officers were actually in danger, rushed into the *mélée*, snatched the truncheon out of the coat pocket of the kneeling officer, used it right and left, and struck amongst others the tall young prisoner with the bleeding face. He appeared much hurt, and the original offender, it appeared, had made his escape in the tumult which ensued. The superintendent having heard all the circumstances, the address of his *sans culotte* assailant was given to the injured man, and the parties, who were very noisy and vituperative, as if they were prepared every moment to burst into violence, were then sent about their business.

We next engaged ourselves in a rapid inspection of the cells at Rose-hill bridewell; but the night being early yet, not many prisoners had been brought in. On visiting the first, we found it occupied by a very rough-looking fellow, who had been brought in not long before for smashing in a jeweller's window in Byrom-street and attempting to steal a watch. On being questioned by the superintendent, he stated that he had been working in a cotton mill in Manchester, but that he had lately been out of work, and that his object was to get into prison, 'the fact being that he did not care what became of him.' 'But would not it have been better to have kept your character good, and have sought relief in a proper way?' 'Oh, no,' he replied, with astounding nonchalance; 'I cannot work, for I have had a paralytic stroke of my right side.' He would appear, however, to have got rid of his alleged paralysis very speedily afterwards, as he never mentioned or exhibited the least signs of it when he was brought up before the magistrates on Monday morning, and it was then stated that there were strong reasons to believe him a ticket-of-leave convict. In the next cell was a wretched-looking female, who said she lived in Crosshall-street, and who had been brought in for stealing a bed-tick [cloth mattress] from a man with whom she had been cohabiting. The prisoner stated in answer to inquiries that she had been nine years in Liverpool, and that she had made her living by going out with the prosecutor gathering 'old clo''; that he used her badly, and tore every 'tack' off her; that she had had no children to the man, and that she meant hereafter to lead a better life. We observed the bridewell keeper gave a very incredulous smile at the last expression. The prisoner also pleaded as a strong point in her favour that she had been apprehended in St. Joseph's chapel while 'attending to her religious duties' before 'Father M'Gra.' The next cell we went to was empty. A man had hung himself in it not very long before. We were told that it was frequently necessary to fasten both hands of a prisoner to one of the rings in the wall, as they often tried to commit suicide, the women especially, the latter by putting the strings of their dresses around their throats. Only three weeks before, a woman, handcuffed by one hand, had taken a string from her pocket, but was frustrated in her attempt by the appearance of the bridewell keeper, not, however, before she had grown quite black in the face. Prisoners confined for drunkenness especially, and who are sure to be suffering more or less, soon after their confinement, from that most gloomy and terrible of all visitations, *mania à potu* [madness brought on by alcoholism], require constant watchfulness on the part of those entrusted with their temporary custody; and yet, with all the care which is undoubtedly exercised, a man has succeeded in hanging himself in a cell in Jordan-street bridewell since these articles were commenced. What a gloomy ending of a dishonourable life!

Before leaving, we observed a Dispensary surgeon in conversation with one of the bridewell keepers; and we know that we are only doing an act of justice when we here render ourselves the medium of acknowledgement, on behalf of the police authorities, of the very great service which the Dispensary surgeons render to the public by their promptitude in attendance in all cases of violence or danger, at whatever hour of the night the police may call them. If not in every case, in the great majority of instances their services are gratuitously rendered, and we have much pleasure in thus directing attention to the unobtrusive labours and self-sacrificing spirit of this deserving class of men. The gentleman who was here appeared to be informing the bridewell keeper of the result of some recent case, in which an indecent assault had been committed upon a little girl. It appeared from his statement that the poor young creature was now suffering from a loathsome ailment, and that it had been communicated to her by her brutal assailant under a superstitious impression which is widely spread amongst the ignorant classes in all this part of the country, that she being pure he should thus be able to rid himself of the consequences entailed upon him by his own vice.

Sick of such painful incidents and stories, we next seek the open air. We are now off on our night rambles, along with the superintendent, through the streets and bridewells at the north end of the town....

It was a glorious summer night, and some of those parts of Liverpool to which we were about to wend our way do not appear to 'shut up' at all in sleep on a Saturday night; but the entire inhabitants empty themselves instead on their doorsteps, and sit there, weather permitting, till two or three o'clock, and many much later, every Sunday morning. And here we may remark a great peculiarity in this respect in some neighbourhoods. Vauxhall-road, with all its adjacent streets, is late; but Marybone, inhabited as would be supposed by a similar class of people, is as quiet as any vicinity up town on a Saturday evening, whilst it is the most uproarious place in Liverpool on a Sunday evening. We are told that this could only be accounted for by the fact that a very great part of the male residents of the streets running out of Marybone are at this season of the year employed in the country, and that they do not reach their homes on a Saturday night, if they come at all before the Sunday, till the public houses and beerhouses are about to close. Vauxhall-road, on the contrary, is largely occupied by dock labourers, carters, and other workmen of the roughest and humblest class, who have got their wages and are eager for the customary debauch. And really when one looks at the dismal dens of court houses where the majority of the poor creatures reside, and the total want of domestic comfort and cleanliness which they generally exhibit, one can scarcely wonder that they should flock out on summer nights in the hope of catching a momentary breath of purer and less stifling air....

It is now past ten o'clock, and Scotland-road is teeming with a moving throng, affording in their varied outward aspects endless materials for observation and speculation. Here is a hard-working mechanic, cleaned up, and going with his wife to 'make the marketing,' and this will be about one of the most pleasing spectacles which meet the eye; for there, are a number of lazy fellows standing grouped at a street corner, in the most dirty and besotted condition, obstructing the thoroughfare, if not insulting all decent passers-by; and here, is a woman who has just slipped out of that gin palace; she has a baby on one arm, a rickety basket, evidently with very little in it, on the other, and she appears to be actually staggering along, her unsteady gait appearing to threaten that she will every moment be letting the child fall. There, are some young girls talking to those rowdy-looking little lads with short pipes in their mouths – girls in years but Cyprians in modesty, and utterly brutal in their appearance, demeanour, and conversation. A further group is made up by a basket woman and her sympathisers; she is treating a policeman to some of the choicest Billingsgate for ordering her to 'move on' and leave the pathway clear. Here, there is a street singer; there, a man selling for a halfpenny details of the last brutal murder or dreadful accident; and yonder, there is a fight. Observe, too, that wretched, barefooted, and ragged little girl, who comes creeping out of the neighbouring pawnshop. (The golden balls are very plentiful in that neighbourhood.) She has been sent to take her father's neckerchief or shirt out of pledge – only to return again on the Monday, when the thirst is found vehement as ever, and the wages are all gone. We peep in at the dark little closeted compartments behind the counter. Those prostitutes there are pledging, perhaps, some trifling, and therefore unsuspected, produce of a robbery; that simple fellow his watch; and that dirty and drunken woman is offering a valueless under garment, which the pawnbroker appears to refuse – treating, indeed, all his customers with a superciliousness so haughty that we cannot but pity the latter, degraded as they are. A momentary glance here reveals a state of things far more suggestive of saddening thoughts than almost any other feature of life in a large city. Not columns upon columns of descriptive writing would exhaust one tithe of the scenes to be witnessed on a Saturday night in this greatest and busiest of all our thoroughfares. It is sufficient, however, to simply indicate what all may observe. We have a different duty assigned us for the present, and must ourselves 'move on.'

XIX

Our first visit on that eventful Saturday night was to a species of minor theatre, situated at the Bevington-hill, and which goes by the name of the 'Nightingale Saloon,' – whether so named in honour of the Swedish songstress [Jenny Lind] or the true-hearted heroine of the Crimea, we are only left open to conjecture. The establishment is one supported exclusively by the working classes, and admission is gained by the payment of threepence at the door, for which, on ordinary week-day nights, those who enter are entitled to a glass of ale, a cigar, a bottle of ginger beer, or other refreshment; but on Saturday evenings the payment is absolutely without this consideration. The building is sufficiently unpretending outside, and the interior is fitted up with a certain air of neatness. A bar runs along one side of the hall, which is also provided with a gallery, but of no very great extent. The stage at the other end is furnished with all the necessary trappings of scenery, etc. The theatre, saloon, or whatever it should be called, was crowded in every part with a very miscellaneous audience, and the character of those assembled naturally formed the first subject of observation. The great majority consisted evidently of hard-working men, many of whom appeared to have just got in from their labour, as could be seen from their unwashed faces and 'unkempt hair,' and several indeed were in their shirt sleeves. Some were really clean and well dressed mechanics, who in many instances had brought their wives or sweethearts along with them; and we shall not be considered too prudish in the remark that we were glad to observe the presence of very few of that class of boys and girls who crowd the galleries of so-called 'respectable' theatres when dramas of the 'Jack Sheppard' [a popular eighteenth-century thief who repeatedly escaped from gaol] school are put upon the stage. There was very little smoking going on, and the demand for drink appeared no greater than a stout, comely, motherly-looking sort of woman was personally able to supply.

The play in progress was a sort of light, running vaudeville (we use the word in its French sense) – all the points in which, musical or otherwise, appeared to hang on the incidents of a matrimonial quarrel; and it was perfectly amusing to observe the heartiness with which every hit on either side was received by the rougher portion of the audience, some of whom kept shouting out in a not very elegant running commentary of their own, as the piece went on. Although we do not pretend that any proof of it was afforded here, it is perfectly idle to suppose that the humbler classes cannot appreciate the beauties of a good theatrical representation; whilst the rich are only sentimentally emotional, the poor, from their life of hardship, are practically and powerfully so; and in view of this fact we could only lament that the moral lesson taught by the piece, if indeed it taught any moral lesson at all, should not have been of a higher and more elevated character. The writer appeared to have had no aim beyond the amusement of the hour, and its only praise was that it contained nothing objectionably gross. We were not, however, altogether unfavourably impressed with our visit to the 'Nightingale Saloon,' for it was suggestive of the support which would be rendered to a better class of entertainment; and it is but justice to its conductors to mention what the superintendent and officers who acted as our cicerones [guides] assured us, that it was a place which gave very little trouble to the police.

The route lay next down Paul-street, a place noted in past times for the number of 'smashers' – that is, coiners and utterers of counterfeit coin – who used to reside in its labyrinth of dirty court houses; but the Mint was a severe prosecutor; transportation on conviction was the almost invariable penalty and this is an offence which for the last few years may be said to have been almost totally rooted out of Liverpool, although moving stories of adventurous forays into this locality can still be related by many old police officers. It was interesting to observe the sensation which the presence of the police produced amongst the residents lounging about their doorways, who appeared to feel a sensible relief as the officers passed, but watched with eagerness as to where their steps were next bent. 'Thank God,' we heard one woman exclaim, 'they are not wanting me *this time*.' We called in on our way at some brothels of the lowest class, kept by white women, and where white girls are kept, but which have the peculiarity of being frequented and supported exclusively by negro sailors frequenting the port. We were too early, however (it was now only about eleven); the women were all out, looking for their sable admirers and patrons, and in each case the house seemed left in charge of a little girl, who answered all inquiries with a certain business air and a conscious cunning which argued no moral misgiving as to any particular impropriety in the scenes of horrible pollution of which she must be the constant witness. We must see, however, a little of the 'fashionable' life of the coloured seamen in Liverpool, and for that purpose attended one of their 'assemblies,' which was held at a beerhouse, let us call it the Kentucky Vaults, in Vauxhall-road. All acquainted with the character of the coloured population of the United States, whether bond or free, are aware of their fondness for the dance, and of their extravagant love of gaudy and showy attire. We were not surprised, therefore, on entrance, to find the counter surrounded by ebony gentlemen, with superfine coats of the 'fastest' cut, linen of snowy whiteness or the most flashy pattern, rings upon their fingers, and shirt studs of the greatest lustre and most enormous size. The lobbies were crowded by them in such numbers that it was almost impossible to get along; but a fiddle and the shuffling of feet were heard overhead; and forcing our way into the kitchen and ascending a rickety staircase, the ballroom, in all its brilliancy (if it had any), burst upon the view. The apartment was small; lighted, if we remember aright, by a single jet from the centre of the ceiling; and the walls were not particularly clean. Orpheus was seated near the window, and the floor was occupied with four sooty individuals, well dressed, but with countenances of the very ugliest African type, and four young white girls, engaged in figuring in none of your vulgar dances, but ... in dancing – a quadrille. The music stopped soon after our entrance, on the sight of certain uniform (blue, in all these parts, is a most unpopular colour); but learning that the visit had not a hostile meaning, 'Come, let us have another set,' said one of the girls, and the dance went on, but under an evident restraint, and with none of that abandon which we should doubtless under other circumstances have seen. The time for closing soon afterwards came, and the landlord, jealous either for the honour of his house or wishing to stand well in the eye of the police with respect to the future probabilities of a license, soon afterwards sent up a message which caused an abrupt termination of the ball by an extinguishment of the light. 'A negro has a soul, ain't please your honour,' said Corporal Trim, doubtingly. Having none of the honest corporal's doubts, we only wish that some better recreation, or at least some congenial entertainment in a less objectionable place and neighbourhood, could be found for the numbers of poor negro seamen continually visiting the port. Even in England a certain prejudice will ever keep them more or less socially apart from the rest of the community; but from this prejudice it appears there are some females who are entirely free – nay who from, we will not say depravity, but some eccentricity of taste, actually prefer a black to a white one. This peculiar class is more numerous in Liverpool than would be imagined, the superintendent assured us. The girls whom we observed dancing were evidently not of the vicious kind; they were generally clean and tidy, and one was actually more than ordinarily pretty. All we can say is, that we left a little less shocked than a Yankee would have been.

Our way lay next up Eldon-street, which partakes of all the general characteristics of the highways and byways in that neighbourhood. Visiting one house of illfame, a very young boy and girl came down stairs, and these appeared to be the only parties in. 'Hilloa! Are you here?' said the superintendent to the lad, 'what are you doing now?' 'Me! I am a sailor,' was the reply. 'Nay, nay.' 'Yes, I am a *turnpike sailor* [highway robber],' said the lad, with a look of the most daring hardihood and bravado. We were told on leaving that he was one of a class who go about with 'the girls,' to receive from them and run off with watches or money which they may have stolen. A considerable crowd gathered to see what was 'the row,' and it was with difficulty that some of them could be kept back – so keen was the curiosity of the women especially – from forcing their way into the houses into which we subsequently went. A few doors from the last, we entered a cellar kept by an old Irishwoman, who was asked how many girls she had now, when she said she had none at present except her own two daughters! Two stout fellows were in, one of them very drunk; and the other, seeing an officer, appealed to him for protection from the old crone, who held in her hand a piece of iron, in form something between a poker and an axe, and who was uttering against them, with frightful oaths, the most horrible of threats. His statement was that the other 'boy,' the one who was drunk, had come only the other day from Cork, and had found his way or been inveigled into this cellar; that, being acquainted with him, he had gone to get him out, but that the old woman had positively refused to let either of them go. Her object, doubtless, was robbery, as soon as the bullies could be summoned for the purpose; and it really appeared as if she had effectually cowed them both. The police liberated them from their dangerous durance, the woman fairly screaming with rage as they left, such curses as we hope it will never again be our fate to hear. 'Now, you would not have struck them with that,' said the superintendent, soothingly. 'Would I not, by —; what did God Almighty give me the strength for but to strike, and take my own part?'

It was a relief to find ourselves once more in the comparatively open air of Scotland-road, although the throng which had crowded it an hour before, instead of diminishing, appeared to have increased. As belonging to the pleasures, practices, and pastimes of the people, of course we cannot pass without observing the swing-boats and 'merry-go-rounds' located on a piece of vacant land, far up towards Kirkdale, and which have become quite an institution in that part of the town. They had, however, just ceased their operations for the night, and the disorderly juveniles whom they cause to congregate were about dispersing themselves, not to go home, apparently, [but] to annoy other neighbourhoods with their noisy presence. The police, if we are rightly informed, have not the power totally to prohibit this kind of public nuisance, at least so far from the centre of the town. At all events, it has been found better to make a sort of compromise with the proprietors of the machines, and induce them to close at ten o'clock each night, except Saturdays, when the privilege is extended to eleven; and so far the fellows have kept faith. They need watching, however. Should the police for a short time be absent, they snatch the opportunity, if they can, of introducing gaming tables, which meet a ready patronage. Now and then a foray on the gamesters has to be quietly organised and rapidly executed; and one trophy of these raids we observed a few minutes afterwards in the shape of a *rouge-et-noir* bank, lying amongst some other curious lumber in the Athol-street bridewell. On our way down to that place we observed a policeman leading gently along by the hand a lost child, which he was passing on to the next beat, and around which were several sympathising women, who were trying in vain to make out from the little thing where it lived. It could talk well, but gave as the place of its residence the name of a street which no one appeared to know and which certainly has no place in the Directory. In case no parent appeared to claim it, it would be passed, we understood, to the Bellman's in Greek-street (a very curious *hospice des enfans trouvés* [foundling hospice]), which we purpose hereafter to visit), and then finally, no claimant appearing, would be taken to the workhouse, and make its entrance upon the great stage of life with all the disadvantage of a pauper *prestige* and training. The Athol-street bridewell is one of the new and better class of such establishments, and at the time of our visit contained only one prisoner. He was, we were told, a man of very violent character, and had separated from his wife, who had lived, however, in constant terror of him. She was sheltered and fed by the kindly-hearted women with whom they had previously lodged, but the visits which he was in the habit of making were so dangerous and annoying that he had been complained of at the central police office. A watch had consequently been put upon the place, and he had been captured that night in the very act of demolishing the poor woman's windows.

Leaving the bridewell, we had not gone far till 'the drowsy ear of night' was 'vexed' by a terrible commotion in a neighbouring court yard. A big rough-looking fellow was standing at the door of one of the houses, and had been making vehement attempts to assault a neighbour living opposite. A policeman had been watching him for some time, but had been unable to capture him, as, whenever he approached, the offender fled into his house and fastened the door. The dispute appeared to have originated with the wives of the two parties, who had been accusing each other, of course in the very choicest terms, of the foulest conduct. 'Well, why don't you leave the neighbourhood?' said the superintendent to the complaining party. 'Well, I mean to do so,' said the man, 'if I could only have peace till Monday; for it is not only ourselves that suffer, but he is a terror to the whole neighbourhood.' It was said that he had been out flourishing a knife. Another policeman was summoned to the spot; the two were instructed to hide themselves at the end of the court, and if he made his appearance out of doors again, to rush upon and take him off to bridewell. We left the two officers standing there, we confess not without some little nervous timidity on our own part for their safety. If they overpowered and seized the ruffian, they would have to drag him through a district where every prisoner, no matter what the charge, would have a hundred of active sympathisers. Those who are continually crying out against, and those who weigh in such dainty scales and punish so heavily any shade of 'unnecessary' violence, real or apparent, on the part of a poor policeman, should have been with us on the occasion – the leading incidents of which we know that, however faithfully, we are so imperfectly describing.

XX

We next visited the Collingwood Dock station to attend a midnight parade, and saw three sections of men muster for the purpose of relieving others along the northern line of docks. This is one of the best and most commodious stations in the possession of the force. It is built of granite and has that massiveness, strength, and finish which characterise all the work which Mr. Hartley [architect and builder] puts from his hands....

We found only three prisoners in the cells. One was a woman for attempting to steal a pair of trousers; the second was a man detained on the charge of passing a base half-crown; and the third was a simple case of drunkenness; but we shall never forget the horrible look of the latter prisoner, as he lay, with blotched face, parched lips, and swollen veins, stretched full length and in an uneasy slumber, on his back upon the form. The pillow had rolled away from him, if it had ever been used, so that the head was the same height as his heels, and he appeared like a demon coaxing a stroke of apoplexy or congestion of the brain.

Besides serving for parade and ordinary police purposes, the Collingwood dock station is also a receiving-house for the resuscitation of persons apparently drowned. A boiler for feeding a large bath is kept constantly heated, day and night. So soon as a body is recovered from the river, or any of the neighbouring docks, it is brought here with the least possible delay, and instantly placed in a warm bath. A messenger is then despatched in a car to the Dispensary,

Vauxhall-road, for a surgeon, and during the time that he is away the bridewell-keeper on duty takes the necessary means for the restoration of life, acting on the printed instructions of the Humane Society; and that he is successful in a great majority of the cases a glance at the register which he keeps most satisfactorily proves. This receiving-house was only opened in January, 1853, and yet it has been the means already of saving hundreds of lives. There is a like one, as is well known, at the Prince's dock station, whilst the Southern Hospital answers as a third for that end of the docks where it is placed.

When we left the station, all the public houses and beerhouses had been shut up – they had disgorged their customers into the street; but although it was now the Sabbath, this is precisely the most disorderly and troublesome hour for the police. Some 'won't go home till morning;' some cannot if they would; and unless the officers are active, thieves fasten upon the latter, and strip them of everything which they have about them. Nor are they always very grateful for the protection thus afforded them. Elated by John Barleycorn, they look upon all interference to urge them home as a deadly insult, and the policeman is too often rewarded for his benevolent advice by a brutal blow. A trying life indeed is that of a police-officer, and no class of men have so much of the discipline of patience.

Our route lay next up over Chisenhale Bridge into the street of the same name. This bridge and its immediate approaches have long been a favourite haunt for that gang of ruffians who accomplish their robberies by violence; and should their victim be able to resist with any energy the attempt to plunder, in many cases he has been heaved into the canal. It would certainly not be safe for any stranger, however stout or stout-hearted, to attempt to make his way alone at this hour by this route from the docks into Vauxhall-road, and yet it is the most direct thoroughfare. Emigrants, consequently are frequently directed along it, not always from design; and much praise as we have already felt bound to accord to the police authorities, we cannot but feel that it is an opprobrium to the very town that any district whatever acknowledged to be dangerous should be allowed for one moment to continue in that condition. We know that it is the duty of the Watch Committee to take the initiative in respect to orders. Let them, if need be, place even a Bude light upon the bridge, and run a close line of lamps – those excellent sentinels – along the street. The vicious residents of the quarter could not endure such an unwelcome flood of light; the danger would at once vanish, or be placed within manageable bounds.

As we approach, the sound of revelry and strife falls upon the ear; and although it is now nearly one o'clock in the morning, the street seems alive with its human swarm. Immediately after passing over the bridge a noise was heard in a house of bad character, kept by a fat drowsy-looking woman. The police entered, and found two men there – married men, Irish labourers. On inquiring the reason of the commotion, the landlady, putting on a pitiable whine, said the noise was not there; she was a 'poor lone woman;' that the two 'boys' and she had been coming over the bridge together when they were attacked and followed by some 'roughs,' and that they had just escaped, and taken refuge in her house. Our party, with a smile, passed on; but a few steps further on a terrible 'row' was heard in one of the courts. There had been a fight between the tenant of one of the houses at the end of the court and some coloured men who were at a brothel in one of the houses up the passage. We found an officer stationed at the end of the entry to prevent any further collision. The fellow who lived at the end house appeared several times at the door in his shirt sleeves; he was drunk, and appeared anxious to renew the fight, but was dragged back each time by his wife and other women, whom he did his best to repel by pushes and by blows. We accompanied the superintendent to the brothel up the court, and found it filled with negroes and prostitutes. The latter were mostly in a semi-nude condition, having only a petticoat and bedgown on, the latter flying open at the breast. On the floor stood one of the coloured men – a stout, noble-looking, well-dressed fellow, his wide nostrils fairly expanded with rage, a living type of what we may suppose Touseaint L'Ouverture [leader of the slave revolt in Haiti] to have been, and we could not help thinking of the terrible retribution, supposing many of the slaves to be like him, which that down-trodden race may some day, on the other side of the Atlantic, have it in their power to inflict. Looking at his majestic form and his evident physical strength, we should have thought that he would have been the last man in the world that any one, even in this roughest of neighbourhoods, would have ventured to attack; but on inquiring into the reason of the disturbance we were told by the landlady the 'gentleman' [had] come in a car, and on getting out at the entry end he was set upon and his hat knocked off and stolen. The superintendent succeeded in pacifying him by telling him they were a bad lot, and that a gentleman like him had better put up with such a trifling loss than go out amongst them again. It also appeared from what the bystanders said of the desperate character of the fellow outside that there would be a danger of the knife. The inmates of the house were particularly civil to our official attendant, who related to us afterwards a strange scene which he had once alighted upon there. On his entrance on the occasion in question he found one of the young women, almost entirely undressed, reading the Bible to an absorbed circle of darkies sitting around! We looked in before leaving the court at another house of the same description, kept by a notorious character, the wife of a man who was transported for a highway robbery a year or two ago. In passing up the street, the whole inhabitants seemed to be out upon their doorsteps, and it was evident from the excitement that more rows than one were brewing. Extra strength was therefore ordered upon the best [*sic*; probably 'beat' was intended], the instructions to the men being, as the first preliminary of any hope of peace, to do their utmost to get the people to retire into their own homes.

After leaving this stormy neighbourhood, and reaching Vauxhall-road itself, that leading thoroughfare appeared in a state of almost profound repose, but there were symptoms of disorder and disquiet in nearly all the narrow side streets on either side of the way. An officer came up, and touching his hat in salute to the superintendent, said 'That fight, sir, is to take place on the Muck Quay, between seven and eight o'clock in the morning.' The Muck Quay – what a Philippi! On inquiring into the particulars of the appointed battle, we learned that the 'difficulty,' as an American would say, was between two neighbours – at least, if those can come up to the definition of neighbours who live in the same street, and in pretty close contiguity to each other – and it had arisen from an attack upon each other with pokers, which had led to cross summonses before the magistrates, whose decision, however, would appear to have been unsatisfactory to both of the belligerents. The fight had been arranged to come off on the previous Sunday morning, and the parties actually had met, accompanied by their respective sympathisers, to the number of nearly 200; but the police had had intimation of the affray, and spoiled that sport, as they do so many others, by their interference, greatly to the disgust of all the enlightened individuals who were present. We are told, however, that, in despite of what the police may do to prevent these disgraceful exhibitions, prize fights occasionally take place on Sunday morning in all that region, the North Shore being a favourite battle ground; and any one who has a taste in that way and chooses to rise about four or five o'clock may enjoy the spectacle of two brutes battering each other almost to death. And the chances are great that he will not have gone out to see a single set-to, for the excitement of combat is infectious; disputes are sure to break out between the partisans of the 'bruisers' on each side, and a dispute in such an arena has no arbitrement but that of blows.

Pursuing our route, we had a curious illustration of the varied duties of policemen, in a decent-looking elderly woman coming up to complain that a man had taken away a child from her daughter. An officer was instructed to inquire into the circumstances, but we did not stop to learn the particulars. Marybone-street was profoundly tranquil, as we had been led to expect; but at the corner of Hodson and Fontenoy streets a group of women was gathered at the door. One, quite a young creature, had a child in her arms, and was crying; her husband had come home drunk, abused her, and turned her out. She told us, with sobs, that he was in the habit of coming home that way 'nearly every hour of the night.' The female sympathisers around wished to carry her off to sleep elsewhere. She, however, wanted to go into her own home, and solicited this interposition of the officers, but was told that it was not a case with which they could interfere, as in the majority of cases such a step only made the matter worse. Our attention was called to the singular conformation of the child's head, which was perfectly elongated in shape, 'like a penny loaf,' as one of the officers irreverently said. What effect must such scenes have upon the future character of the child? Next, in Great Crosshall-street, a riotous crowd was gathered about 'a halfpenny shaving shop,' which it would appear does such a roaring business that on the occasion in question at least it had been kept open till nearly half-past one o'clock on the Sunday morning. The proprietor, his son, and wife, were at the door, and they complained that a rabble of boys and girls had been throwing stones at the door and window. Those they pointed out as the active participators in the affray were driven off; but as neither party appeared inclined to tell the cause of the disturbance remained wrapped up in mystery. A little higher up the street, a woman came and complained that a female had gone into her back premises, and would persist, in spite of all that could be done, in sleeping in her petty. The superintendent promised to send an officer to drive her out and inquire into the case, of which we shall learn more hereafter. We were now on our way to Vauxhall bridewell. In all our lengthy round it was in this street that we for the first time heard the question asked of 'Where were the police?' and found that the officers were actually absent from the beat. The superintendent assured us with confidence that they must have gone to Vauxhall bridewell to book prisoners, and it is but an act of justice to say on reaching there we found this to be the fact.

XXI

If any one would see the nearest approach to a pandemonium on earth, he should pay a visit, as we did, to the Vauxhall and the Main bridewells at an early hour on Sunday morning. The first of these enjoys a bad eminence among all the other district bridewells in the town for the rough and disorderly class of prisoners usually received there. The charges are nearly all for drunkenness, disorder, and assaults. It was about half-past one when we visited the place, and the business was then only just beginning to be brisk. A crowd of women was congregated about the door, consisting of the friends of the parties who had just been taken in, and who were evidently waiting to see whether the charges would be taken, or the accused released. Many of them were drunk, some of them were crying, and so eager was the curiosity of all that they could only be kept from forcing their way into the office by the presence of an officer and his threats to clap them in custody unless they immediately dispersed. On our entrance, the case under investigation was that of a woman whose husband had already been sent below, and she was endeavouring to mislead as to her identity by denying her true name. She called herself M'Taag, whilst her husband had been booked in the name of Nicholson. The charge against them was that of creating an uproar by quarrelling in the streets. 'Why did not you give your right name?' asked the superintendent. 'I did tell him my own name, why would I give *his*? We have not been married long.' 'Now, you know very well that your husband's name is your name.' 'Well, sir,' she answered, 'we were just having a little falling out, *as every married body has.*' We give this information for the benefit of all our bachelor readers. Matrimony would certainly not be a very inviting undertaking if Mrs. 'M'Taag' makes anything like an approximation to the truth. Perhaps this is as good an opportunity as any to state that all prisoners are searched before being locked up in their cells, the contents of their pockets now duly entered in a ledger kept for the purpose, and the search takes place in the presence of the officer in charge of the case, who is required to verify the result by signing the book. Female prisoners are searched generally by the wives of the bridewell keepers, who receive some small annual allowance for that service. The property is returned when the prisoner is discharged. The searching is necessary, not only for the security of what property may be on the prisoner, but especially to take away firearms, knives, or dangerous weapons.

We first made an inspection of the 'rough-room,' in which there were three men, all of whom had been brought in on charges of drunkenness and fighting. They were certainly brutal looking objects. One of them – who appeared quite to enjoy his plight, his spirits being as yet sustained by the drink – had a battered face and two black eyes; indeed, if we recollect rightly, the whole three had more or less of the latter decoration. One of them was dirty and all wet, as if he had been rolling in the gutter. He told us that he had fallen into the canal; and he appeared, from his appeals to the superintendent, as if he were particularly anxious to go home and change his dress. He was urging some such suit when the door was shut upon him. In two or three hours he would be transferred to the main bridewell, where he would be kept till Monday morning, and then, if he had not the means, when brought before Mr. Mansfield [stipendiary magistrate], to pay the inevitable fine, his first opportunity probably of a change of attire would be after the enjoyment of a much-needed bath, in gaol. In an adjoining cell there was also a man who had been brought in for fighting, and who had been so violent that he had to be secured to the wall by one hand, for the prisoner's own safety and that of others in the cell. The bridewell keeper said that they had his wife in another room. The prisoner (indignantly): 'No, no; I am a single man.' It would appear as if it was considered the safest course here to deny anything like a matrimonial alliance. The third cell to which we were conducted contained six women, who had all been brought in on charges of drunken and disorderly conduct. One was a very curious-looking old woman, with gray hair and red pimpled face, who, we afterwards learned, had been no fewer than *ninety-three* times committed, occasionally for felony, but generally for simple drunkenness. Here was a case of incorrigibility for a prison theorist to experiment upon. What system of discipline should be applied to such a hopeless and abandoned case as this? The five other females in the cell were all young women. One of them only was decently attired. They all bore signs of devotion to the cup; and one came up laughing, as if she regarded her present position as almost too exquisite a joke to be thought about. 'Why,' she said, all smiles, 'I never was in prison in my life; you surely would not lock me up.' Like the man in the stocks, she was locked up. In a cell upstairs there was a man confined by himself. The charge in this case also was that of being drunk and disorderly. He said, in answer to inquiries that he lived in Paul-street. The bridewell keeper finished the biography. 'He is a labourer,' he said, 'who works a little at times: he thieves the remainder. He is what may be called a *half-and-half* man.' The prisoner: 'I work always. My missis was bringing a piece of meat down the street, when a man knocked it out of her hand. I went up to resist, and they took me away. Look here,' he said, as if he was now going to strike a chord which would be sure to elicit an approving sympathy, 'a policeman cannot walk Paul-street for those prigs.'

Waiting in the office above whilst the superintendent made an entry of his visit, the woman who 'would sleep in a petty' was brought in by the officer who had been despatched to effect her removal. She was crying bitterly. The officer said that he knew her, and that she was a prostitute. Superintendent: 'Where does she live?' Officer: 'She did live at old Mother Skinner's; but she seems to have no place now.' Superintendent: 'How long has she been a prostitute?' The Officer: 'To my knowledge, about six months. When she first came under our notice, about six months ago, she had only been upon the streets two or three weeks. She was well dressed then, and on being released took a car and went up to the house of her sister, a respectable woman, living in Brunswick-road. She has been a married woman herself, but her husband is dead.' The prisoner fairly sobbed during this narrative, and rose up several times as if to interpolate some statement, but either fell or was pushed back upon her seat. She was evidently affected with liquor, and would consequently be detained till Monday morning. What an instructive history in little is that of this poor Magdalen. Destruction, sooner or later, awaits all in her vicious line of life; but with what frightful rapidity she appears to have run and completed her course. An evident wreck in health, a wreck in character, hungry, houseless – her only refuge now a workhouse or a gaol.

Every one is familiar with the external aspect at least of the gloomy building, with its sooty façade of rusticated masonry, which stands in Exchange-street West. This is the main bridewell; and here all the prisoners are sent each morning, between four and six o'clock, from the various district bridewells in the town, preparatory to their appearance before the magistrates in the Sessions House, with which it is connected by a subterranean passage opening into both courts. Many prisoners, however, are taken direct to the main bridewell; and at the time of our visit, before the vans had gone off for the outsiders, we found no fewer than thirty-five persons already in custody there. The governor said it was a 'poor night;' by which he meant not only that the number was less than the average, but that the cases lacked interest – at least, that they were devoid of any extraordinary features in the eyes of those whose constant occupation it is to deal with the criminal class, and who, we should suppose, suffer *ennui* more than any other class of men from the dreary uniformity with which in eternal cycles the old features of crime are ever coming round. The clerks in the office were engaged in booking a charge against a young, well-dressed lad, but who was evidently tipsy, and who, from the manner in which his shirt was crushed and pulled out at the breast, appeared as if he had been resisting apprehension as far as his tiny strength would admit. The officers stated that the prisoner and another lad had gone up to an old woman's stall under the Goree Piazzas and had sixpennyworth of coffee and bread, but when she asked for payment they had abused her, and then ran away. The officer had followed, but had only been able to catch this one. He was ordered to be locked up, and his pockets were searched, when a deal of silver was turned out; so that, taking him to be the decent lad which his appearance would promise, his conduct in the affair seems to be altogether inexplicable, unless on the interpretation that he had been misguided by the drink. As it was, he would be kept in confinement all that night, all Sunday, and on Monday be fined at least 9s 6d, so that he would certainly pay dear for the coffee of which he had tried so dishonestly to partake. In this bridewell there is some little attempt at the classification of prisoners brought in: for instance, those brought in drunk and simply booked for safety are placed in one cell; those who have been drunk and disorderly in another; assaults and male felonies in a third; and the female prisoners are classified in a somewhat similar manner, with this difference, however, in their case, that the married ones are generally kept apart from the single. In the main bridewell a prisoner is rarely put in confinement alone, the fear of suicide always occurring, though visited every quarter or half hour by the keeper and by the superior officers of the force.

In the first 'rough room' we counted about a dozen wretched and generally dirty-looking fellows. 'This man,' said the bridewell keeper, laying his hand on the shoulder of a brawny fellow in a blouse stained with blood upon the arms, and who had the appearance of a brewer's drayman, 'was brought in for being drunk and assaulting an officer. He also *bit* a piece out of another officer's hand.' The Prisoner: '*I* bite him! Ah, what a foolish man you must be.' 'This one,' continued the bridewell keeper, next directing attention to a negro prisoner, who was very flashily dressed, 'was brought in for exposing his person to a widow woman; and that young man for attempting to drown himself.' There were no cases of interest! We took a glance at the poor would-be suicide. He appeared quite calm, and there was nothing whatever in his demeanour betraying consciousness of the dreadful position from which he had been saved, or that he had, but one short hour before, been trembling on the verge of eternity. We were told that he was a billposter. It appeared that he had been observed running towards the river in an excited state, by an officer. He had got over the chains at the Prince's pier, and was just making his spring to leap into the river, when the officer that very moment reached the spot, and caught him before he fell. He would give no explanation of his motives except that 'he must;' and indeed the matter was too solemn for intrusive inquiry. In the same cell we were pointed out a master joiner who had been brought in on a charge of felony. In a second and smaller rough room, at the back part of the premises, six boys were confined, all on charges of felony. Some had a look of dogged hardihood, but they were all so comparatively young as to raise a feeling of compassion for their position – a feeling, however, which we must confess was somewhat dashed when on inquiring into the offence of the youngest-looking and apparently most innocent of the lot, we were told that 'he was only in for stealing a shirt *this time*, but that he had been ten times previously committed.' Three of the others had also been six or seven times committed. In the women's ward we found eleven prisoners. Two of them had been so violent that they had been handcuffed to rings in the wall. Whenever this is done an entry is made in the memorandum book, giving the reason why, and the time they are so kept. One of these fairly shouted with entreaty to be put into a room by herself, as the other prisoners had been mocking and annoying her. The second one under restraint, we were told, had been assaulting the other prisoners. She was a bad character in other respects, and had been at least *thirty* times committed. Most of the females had been brought in on charges of drunkenness; but one was pointed out as having robbed a man of 20s, and the money had been found in her bosom. On returning to the office upstairs we found the clerks entering a very curious charge against a jolly-looking gentlemanly fellow who had just been brought in, in a state of *Bacchi plenus* [drunk] certainly. It was stated that he had been stopping at a public house at no great distance, and that when twelve o'clock, the hour for closing, came, he had positively refused either to go to bed or to go out, and would give no reason whatever for his conduct. He even now refused to explain, though told that unless he did they would have to find him lodgings where he then was. There is one quite superior apartment in this main bridewell, to which we have not yet referred, but which is worthy of at least a passing notion. It is termed 'the lodge room,' and only that the massive bars which fence the windows speak too plainly of restraint, it is a spacious, well lighted, well ventilated, and on the whole a rather cheerful room. Five curious high and straight-backed wooden chairs composed the furniture, and but that they would certainly be somewhat hard seemed well enough calculated for a doze. This, we were told, was the place where *respectable prisoners* were generally put.

XXII

.... It was now about two o'clock on Sunday morning; our route lay along Dale-street and up London-road; and although there were numerous stragglers to be met with at that hour, an air of quietude reigned which was quite startling in its contrast with the noisiness and disorder of the streets where the last few hours had been spent. It seemed (we could not help the thought) as if the part of the town which we had now entered upon must be inhabited by an entirely different race. And so it was: it was occupied by the decent citizens who lead a regular life, whose duties and pleasures terminate with the day – not by haggard revellers, but by 'men who sleep o'nights.' Yet it could not be said that there was absolute quiet; scattered individuals were here and there to be seen, and we must give at least one instance, showing that peace did not reign in every bosom. A young woman, sobbing, stepped up to the officers, and complained that her husband was in a brothel in Preston-street, and she invoked their assistance to bring him out. They could not interfere. The officer on the beat, who came up at this time, stated that he had gone into the house pointed out to satisfy her, but the man was not there. The young woman added that she had since learned from a woman at the foot of the street, and who knew him, that she had seen him enter. She was left, however, to her own remedy and sorrow. England is so free that adultery is only a moral offence, and with all our legal reforms no penal consequence yet attach to that worst of iniquities.

During our round we had been struck with the uniformity and promptitude with which the policemen on their respective beats every where came up, almost instantly, as it were, on the tap of the superintendent's stick, touched their hats, reported 'all right,' and then went off again, the only break being in Great Crosshall-street, where, as it will be remembered, the officers' absence, as shown in our last article, was satisfactorily explained. Mentioning our admiration of the perfectness of the police machinery and discipline which this appeared to argue, the superintendent said he would give a signal which would show us, supposing a robbery to be committed there and then, the strength and efficiency of the assistance which could immediately be brought to hand. In all former cases a single tap of the stick had been given; the whistle of the officer was heard to response, and he was then seen walking up. Now a double or treble tap was given, or other signal, which we had perhaps best not particularise, and instantly almost we heard a clattering of feet, and three or four policemen came *running* to the spot. Out of breath, they eyed your humble servant most suspiciously, and looked as if they expected an immediate order to take him off. No explanation was given to them; they reported 'all right,' and were then dismissed. 'You should not do that often,' we observed to the superintendent, 'or you may find yourself some day in the position of the boy who cried "wolf".' 'Oh, no,' was his reply, 'it is necessary for me often to do so, in order that I may ascertain the state of discipline in which the men actually are.'

On reaching the neighbourhood of the monument in London-road, the officer on duty was asked as to the state of the walk confided to his care, when he answered, 'Oh, they are all as rough as bears yonder yet.' It was then about half-past two o'clock in the morning. We were surprised to hear this statement, as the front street appeared perfectly quiet. We crossed the way, and were instantly introduced to quite a different scene, in some little dirty back streets, of whose existence and character the stranger passing down London-road would have not the slightest conception; and yet we were told that for concentrated vice, 'boozing dens,' and brothels, this for its size was one of the very worst districts in the whole town. When we say that we entered at Oakes-street and came out at Norman-street, the topography of the place will be pretty well understood.

Precisely as we had seen in Chisenhale-street, not one half of the people appeared to be in bed. The doors were open in many cases, but no one was in the houses; and where the people could have gone to – for surely all the public houses were then closed – remains with us a mystery to the present time. In one instance, a young idle woman was sitting upon the steps, and when asked why she did not go in her answer was that she could not, as 'mother' was out, who had the key. The whole place appeared to swarm with females of loose character, from the old brutal-looking harridan, with bloated figure and dirty and ragged clothing, down to quite little girls, whose sad and vicious course of life, begun so early, had not yet bereft them of all traces of beauty, although it had extinguished their modesty and happiness for ever. Now and then we could observe men come along with women round the corner, and slip quietly into the houses. One young fellow hung his head, and could scarcely be got along with all the blandishments lavished by his companion. He walked slowly and appeared haunted with doubt and dread. Perhaps he was thinking of home, perhaps of some pure spirit elsewhere; but at last he crossed the fatal threshold. Another and more willing victim was a gentleman, evidently drunk – we mean by 'gentleman,' of course, that he was well dressed, using the ordinary parlance of the world. One man stood so suspiciously at the corner of an entry, popping in and out, that the officers felt it their duty to go up and see who he was. He proved to be a fellow who had brought a charge only a week or so before against an officer for using 'unnecessary violence' in the arrest of a prisoner; he had been listened to patiently in the police court, and his evidence treated as if he was one of the most respectable of men.

But hark – there is a sound of singing in one of the houses. Surely there is some one living here, who, however low in circumstances, has yet the blessing of religion; it must be a hymn hailing the advent of the Sabbath day. We draw near, and the pleasing delusion is dispelled. The voice comes from a cellar, and it is that of a young woman singing in not the best of voice the song of 'Alice Gray.' A man, who from his appearance is a shoemaker, is standing on the cellar steps at the door, smoking a pipe, and evidently in a state of considerable elevation from drink; and on asking him the meaning of such an uproar at such an hour, he said at first (as if he thought that a most conclusive apology) that it was 'a wake.' The superintendent descended the steps, and the fellow at first seemed inclined to dispute the passage; but seeing with whom he had to contend, he became suddenly civil, and invited him into the house to take share of a quart of ale which he had upon the table – a piece of hospitality which was respectfully refused. He had told a lie; it was no 'wake.' He then said the young woman who was singing, and who had a baby upon her knee, had 'just been confined,' and they were having a jollification on that account. 'But she should not sing at this hour; you know it is Sunday,' said the superintend-ent. 'Oh, yes,' answered the son of St. Crispin [the shoemaker]; 'but you see it is not me; it is the woman, and there is no controlling *them*.' He added, 'I am going to hear Hugh Stowell Brown [a popular contemporary preacher] in the afternoon.' We hope he did, and that some of the solid shot of the reverend gentleman against intemperance and other vice would reach him, be carried home, and bear fruit. He did not seem a bad-hearted fellow; but oh, the effect which the surrounding pollution must have upon the character of all within its influence and range. Think what a place this would be to rear a family in – then cease to wonder at the number of juvenile offenders, a class whose existence as such is one of the bitterest reproaches to the civilisation of the age. It is well always, if possible, to link cause with effect; and we cannot leave the neighbourhood without adding, it was Sunday, certainly, but a brewery in the neighbourhood was lighted up, although all other establishments were closed.

We next peeped in at Prescot-street bridewell; but the 'drunken carters,' for which it is more especially remarkable, must have been very well behaved that night, as there was but one prisoner, a female. The charge against her was that of attempting to steal a shawl from a pawnbroker's shop in Brownlow-hill. Although she had a baby with her at the breast, it appeared that she was drunk when brought in, and had been so violent at first that she had to be restrained. This is one of the stations at which a fire engine is kept, and two firemen were waiting with all in readiness to turn out at a moment's notice. We here took leave of the official guide who had so kindly accompanied us. Our night ramble was at an end – we had seen in four or five hours all those melancholy but instructive aspects of Liverpool Life with which the police have to deal, and which it has taken us twice that number of weeks to picture to the reader.

Between four and six o'clock each morning, all the prisoners who may have been lodged in the various district bridewells are removed in closed vans kept for that purpose to the main bridewell. There are two of these conveyances, one for the north and one for the south district, and they are furnished and 'worked,' we believe, by the governor of the main bridewell, under contract with the corporation. It appears also that the same vans are used each afternoon for the conveyance of prisoners to the borough gaol at Walton. As the distance to the latter place is some four or five miles, and there is a railroad which goes almost to the gaol door, we were at first surprised to hear to the latter arrangement, but it appears to be the cheapest, safest, and most advantageous which could be made. It is not to be supposed that ordinary railway passengers would like to travel in the same carriage with felons and other misdemeanants, and to have a special carriage for prisoners would be attended with a serious expense. When the vans get freighted at the various outlying bridewells with their guilty and miserable load, they are locked and otherwise secured, but it is not the custom to handcuff the prisoners, unless, indeed, their violence be such as to call for that restraint. The reception of prisoners at the main bridewell each morning forms one of the most extraordinary scenes which life in Liverpool presents. They are delivered in groups, in the rough, unclassified, unassorted, drunk and sober, young and old, and remain together until the various charges, with other particulars, are entered in the books, when they are taken off and locked in the respective cells.

At the main bridewell we were particularly struck with the complete and systematic style of bookkeeping pursued. The staff of that establishment consists of the governor, five turnkeys or searchers, three booking clerks, two description clerks, and one chief clerk or cashier; and these have so much night duty that their offices are certainly no sinecure. The books which have to be kept are as numerous as those of our first-class mercantile houses, and the entries embrace every minutia. There is first a 'rough book', where all charges are entered, ruled into many columns for the name, age, instruction, country, and offence of every prisoner, with a statement of what property may be found upon him, what officer presents the case, with all necessary general remarks. Then there is a 'felon's ledger' for males, a felon's ledger for females, with an index book to each; two rough description books, a mark book [to record tattoos], a special prostitutes' description book and ledger; then for each sex a 'disorderly book,' a record book to be laid before the magistrate in the morning and two copies at least of which have to be made, one for the magistrates' clerks and another for the governor of the bridewell. Besides all these there is a general fine book, a daily cash book, a petty cash book, in which the cost of food supplied to destitute prisoners is entered, and we do not know how many others. One of the most laborious branches of the system of book-keeping is that connected with the identification of prisoners, with the view of ascertaining whether they have been in custody before, and if so how often, what were the offences charged, and did the charges result in a conviction at the sessions. All prisoners charged with felony and all prostitutes are measured (not weighed), with a view to their identification; but still the task is both difficult and delicate, and one of great responsibility. 'You have a megsman [card-sharper] in one day,' observed one of the clerks to us, 'with a pair of fine bushy whiskers on; the next time he comes his face is very likely as smooth as a parson's.' Then nearly all prisoners are in the habit, whenever they think they can do so with impunity, of giving false names and addresses; and thus it is that we find in every criminal calendar such an extraordinary number of aliases. 'The Macs and the Joneses are greatest trouble to us,' said the clerk; 'there are so many long columns to be gone through, and thieves seem to know it, and give those names accordingly. It is amusing, too, how often the scoundrels will give the name of the stipendiary magistrate, the governor of the bridewell, or other well-known public officials. There are no Rushtons now, but many Mansfields.' The possible motive for this is a curious subject for speculation; they probably imagine that by some good patrician name their offences will be more leniently dealt with. If there is reason to suspect a party of having been there before, the books are searched back for five years, with the view of tracing the former entry. They are asked all at once a variety of questions, with the view of throwing them off their guard. On giving their own name, they are interrogated instantly as to their mother's Christian name, or if they have a stepfather, &c., and every name given is rapidly noted; so that, as their powers of invention are scarcely quick enough to give off-hand a list of names all fictitious, under one or other of those which they have given (and as often under one as the other), as a general rule, they can easily be found. 'Here is one,' said the clerk, 'Ellen Gray, brought here on the 17th of June for stealing a watch; she has several different *aliases*, and as the names were all so different we could make nothing out by the book; but I was so confident of having seen her before, that I wrote to the schoolmistress of the gaol, asking if she did not recognise her; when she answered that she did, and had good occasion to know her again' – for the woman had persisted, it seems on a former imprisonment, that she had given a gold pencil case to that functionary, although it was a wicked and gross fabrication. 'She has now,' added our informant, 'been six times committed.' The work of identification, which commences about six or seven o'clock in the morning, has to be gone through with great rapidity, in order that it may be completed in time for the opening of the court; and those who may doubt the necessity for a new and more commodious bridewell ought to see the little dingy closet in which that operation has to be performed. But, indeed, photography has now become such a cheap and facile process that we do not see why it should not be brought in as an auxiliary. What a gallery of forbidding countenances the police authorities would then soon be possessed of! And yet there is no doubt that it would prove a very valuable aid to justice....

Notes

Chapter 1

1 *Liverpool Mercury* (henceforth *LM*), 4 January 1878, Mr Raffles, Liverpool's stipendiary magistrate, speaking to the assembled guests at the opening of the cocoa rooms at 13 Williamson Square, owned by the British Workmen Public House Company.

2 The National Archives (henceforth TNA), HO 73/5 pt 2, Home Office papers: returns to Constabulary Commission, 1839, reply from Kirkdale. British parliamentary papers (henceforth BPP), 1839, XIX, *First Report of the Commissioners Appointed to Inquire as to the Best Means of Establishing an Efficient Constabulary Force*. For a fuller discussion of the Long Gang, see J. E. Archer, 'Poaching gangs and violence: the urban–rural divide in nineteenth-century Lancashire', *British Journal of Criminology*, vol. 39(1), 1999, pp. 25–38, and '"A reckless spirit of enterprise": game preserving and poaching in nineteenth-century Lancashire', in D. W. Howell and K. O. Morgan (eds), *Crime, Protest and Police in British Society* (Cardiff: University of Wales Press, 1999), pp. 149–75. Forty policemen had to protect the hangman outside Kirkdale gaol from a hostile crowd of 30,000 at the execution of John Roberts in 1844 for the murder of Lord Derby's head keeper in November 1843; see *Preston Chronicle*, 27 January 1844. See also *PC*, 22 February and 29 March 1851, for armed robberies at Knowsley and Simonswood.

3 *Morning Chronicle*, 21 September 1860.

4 *Porcupine*, 8 August 1874. A fuller discussion of the Tithebarn Street murder appears in chapter 7.

5 *Pall Mall Gazette* (henceforth *PMG*), 23 September 1874. The Tithebarn Street murder attracted enormous national and local press coverage at the time of the killing and later in the year during the trial. *Times*, 24 September 1874, 25 December 1874, 7 January 1875; *LM*, 28 December 1874.

6 For comments and reports on the 1874 summer assizes see *LM*, 6 and 14 August and 1 September 1874; *Times*, 11 August 1874; *Punch*, 6 February 1875.

7 *Punch*, 16 and 30 January 1875.

8 *PMG*, 26 December 1874.

9 Liverpool Record Office (henceforth LvRO), A. Hume, *Condition of Liverpool: Religious and Social* (Liverpool: printed by Brakell, 1858); *Liverpool Echo*, 16 March 2001, 'Yob Map Targets Streets of Crime'. My thanks to Laurie Feehan for drawing my attention to this article.

10 *Manchester Weekly Post* (henceforth *MWP*), 14 February 1880; *Manchester Courier* (henceforth *MC*), 4 November 1880.

11 *LM*, 24 August 1900; *MC*, 12 January 1875.

12 V. A. C. Gatrell and T. B. Hadden, 'Criminal statistics and their interpretation', in

E. A. Wrigley (ed.), *Nineteenth-Century Society: Essays in the Use of Quantitative Methods for the Study of Social Data* (Cambridge: Cambridge University Press, 1972), pp. 336–96.

13 H. Taylor, 'Rationing crime: the political economy of criminal statistics since the 1850s', *Economic History Review*, vol. 51(3), 1998, pp. 569–90; see also R. M. Morris, 'Lies, damned lies and criminal statistics in England and Wales', *Crime, History and Societies*, vol. 5(2), 2001, pp. 5–26. For a fuller study of mysterious deaths and possible missing homicides, see J. E. Archer, 'Mysterious and suspicious deaths: missing homicides in north-west England 1850–1990', *Crime, History and Societies*, vol. 12(1), 2008, pp. 45–63.

14 E. H. Monkkonen, 'Diverging homicide rates: England and the United States 1850–1875', in T. R. Gurr (ed.), *Violence in America. Vol. I: The History of Crime* (Newbury Park, CA: Sage, 1989), pp. 80–101; and E. H. Monkkonen, *Murder in New York City* (Berkeley, CA: University of California Press, 2001).

15 See head constable's report to the Liverpool watch committee for 1867/68. These reports are bound in the annual *Proceedings of the Council*, LvRO, H352 cou; see chapter 8 for a fuller discussion of infanticide in Liverpool.

16 *LM*, 8 January 1866.

17 BPP, 1877, XI, *Third Report of the Select Committee of the House of Lords on Intemperance*, Qu. 8216, p. 22.

18 J. I. Jones, *The Slain in Liverpool During 1864 by Drink* (Liverpool: printed by Howell, 1865), p. 18.

19 LvRO, H352 cou, Head constable's annual report, 1868/69, p. 486.

20 LvRO, H352 cou, Head constable's annual report, 1874/75, p. 435; LvRO, 352 POL 2/1–19, Head constable's report to the Liverpool watch committee, 1906, p. 21.

21 *MC*, 5 October 1869.

Chapter 2

1 P. J. Waller, *Democracy and Sectarianism: A Political and Social History 1868–1939* (Liverpool: Liverpool University Press, 1981), p. 24, note 37.

2 *LM*, 14 October 1876, Mr Raper, secretary of the United Kingdom Alliance (temperance movement).

3 J. Sharples, *Liverpool* (Pevsner Architectural Guides: City Guides) (New Haven, CT: Yale University Press, 2004) is the best guide to the historic architecture of Liverpool.

4 See J. Belchem (ed.), *Liverpool 800. Culture, Character and History* (Liverpool: Liverpool University Press, 2006) for a brief history of the different groups which settled in the port. See also the BPP *Censuses* between 1841 and 1901 for population figures.

5 *LM*, 25 December 1882.

6 *Morning Chronicle*, 27 May 1850; *LM*, 25 December 1882. The *Mercury* has a number of articles about 'Life at the Docks' by 'a dock labourer'.

7 *LM*, 25 December 1882.

8 *Porcupine*, 7 September 1861. The *Porcupine* contains many excellent descriptions of the slums and courts. Some examples and extracts can be found in J. K. Walton and A. Wilcox, *Low Life and Moral Improvement in Mid-Victorian England: Liverpool Through the Journalism of Hugh Shimmin* (Leicester: Leicester University Press, 1991), and H. Shimmin's journalism was reproduced in *Liverpool Life: Its Pleasures, Practices and Pastimes* (Liverpool, 1857) and *Liverpool Sketches* (Liverpool, 1862).

9 LvRO, 352 POL 2/1–19, Head constable's report, 1903, p. 15.

10 *LM*, 23 April 1850 for Lace Street; 11 November 1857 for Banastre Street; BPP, 1877,

XI, *Third Report of the Select Committee of the House of Lords on Intemperance*, evidence of Father Nugent, p. 22; T. J. Madden, 'The Black Spot on the Mersey.' *The Story of a Great Social Reform* (Westminster: Church of England Temperance Society, 1905), p. 5.

11 *LM*, 18 August 1876.
12 See F. Neal, *Sectarian Violence: The Liverpool Experience 1819–1914* (Manchester: Manchester University Press, 1988), p. 14, and his article 'A criminal profile of the Liverpool Irish', *Transactions of the Historic Society of Lancashire and Cheshire*, vol. 140, 1991, pp. 161–99.
13 *Porcupine*, 28 February 1874 and 7 September 1861.
14 *Porcupine*, 8 November 1873; *LM*, 28 April 1868.
15 *LM*, 21 and 25 March 1895.
16 *Porcupine*, 29 August 1874; *Liverpool Review* (henceforth *LR*), 27 July 1889.
17 Madden, 'The Black Spot on the Mersey', p. 5. Original emphasis.
18 *Porcupine*, 2 May 1874.
19 W. Booth, *In Darkest England and the Way Out* (London: Salvation Army, 1890), p. 48.
20 BPP, 1877, XI, *Third Report of the Select Committee of the House of Lords on Intemperance*, evidence provided by Father Nugent, p. 22; Waller, *Democracy and Sectarianism*, pp. 23–24; *LM*, 5 and 13 March 1895.
21 *Porcupine*, 22 May 1875; for prosecutions for drunkenness see LvRO, H352 cou, head constable's annual reports and the 1872/73 head constable's annual report for details of the changes in the opening hours for licensed premises, pp. 448–50.
22 BPP, 1877, XI, *Third Report of the Select Committee of the House of Lords on Intemperance*, p. 21; Madden, 'The Black Spot on the Mersey', pp. 4–5; *LM*, 28 January 1870.

Chapter 3

1 LvRO, H352cou, Head constable's annual report, 1899, p. 4. See also the brief chapter by W. R. Cockcroft, 'The Liverpool police force 1836–1902', in S. P. Bell (ed.), *Victorian Lancashire* (Newton Abbot: David and Charles, 1974), pp. 150–68.
2 BPP, 1839, XIX, *First Report of the Commissioners*, appendix, John Holmes, 2 March 1836, p. 215.
3 LvRO, H352cou, Head constable's annual report, 1899. This report carried a history of the Liverpool force from its inception in 1836, p. 4. The old stories concerning the inefficiency of the 'old police' were continued in this brief history.
4 *LM*, 29 June 1857. Further details on Hugh Shimmin appear in the appendix.
5 *LM*, 29 June 1857.
6 *LM*, 29 June 1857, original emphasis. See also chapter 5 for more detail on the riots in the 1850s.
7 *LM*, 13 July 1857.
8 *LM*, 13 July 1857; LvRO, H352 cou, Head constable's annual report, 1899, p. 10.
9 LvRO, 352 POL 2/3, Head constable's report, 1 May 1865.
10 *LM*, 13 July 1857.
11 LvRO, H352 cou, Head constable's annual report, 1899, p. 9.
12 See W. J. Lowe, 'The Lancashire constabulary, 1845–1870: the social and occupational function of a Victorian police force', *Criminal Justice History*, vol. 4, 1983, pp. 41–62, for a detailed analysis of the county's recruits.
13 *LM*, 6 July 1857.
14 T. Baines, *Liverpool in 1859* (London, 1859), p. 109.
15 The information for the organizational structure comes from Shimmin, *LM*, 6 July 1857.

16 *LM*, 6 July 1857.
17 The dock police, originally formed in 1815, were incorporated into the main borough force in 1841. In 1857 fire engines were kept at the central station in Temple Court, the north end of Prince's Dock, Lightbody Street and Prescot Street. See Cockcroft, 'The Liverpool police force', p. 151, and *LM*, 6 July 1857, as well as Shimmin, *Liverpool Life*, ch. 15, 'Police, prisoners, and prisons'.
18 LvRO, H352 cou, Head constable's annual report, 1899, p. 5.
19 LvRO, H352 cou, Head constable's annual report, 1857, pp. 4–5; Shimmin attempts to explain the complicated shift system in his article in the *LM*, 6 July 1857. 'Landsharks' were criminals who defrauded newly arrived immigrants and those migrating on to America.
20 *LM*, 13 July 1857.
21 *LM*, 13 July 1857.

Chapter 4

1 *Porcupine*, 2 February 1867.
2 F. Engels, *The Condition of the Working Class in England in 1844* (Frogmore, St Albans: Panther edition, 1969), p. 253.
3 Of the books and articles which examine police–community relations, most deal with community reactions to the 'new police'. See R. D. Storch, 'The plague of blue locusts: police reform and popular resistance in northern England, 1840–57', *International Review of Social History*, vol. 20, 1975, pp. 61–90, and his 'The policeman as domestic missionary: urban discipline and popular culture in northern England, 1850–1880', *Journal of Social History*, vol. 9, 1976, pp. 481–509; C. Emsley, '"The thump of wood on a swede turnip": police violence in nineteenth-century England', *Criminal Justice History*, vol. 6, 1985, pp. 125–49, and his *Hard Men: Violence in England Since 1750* (London: Hambledon and London, 2005), ch. 8, pp. 131–46; D. Taylor, *The New Police in Nineteenth-Century England: Crime, Conflict and Control* (Manchester: Manchester University Press, 1997), chs 4 and 5. For a study of the Liverpool police in the twentieth century see M. Brogden, *On the Mersey Beat: Policing Liverpool Between the Wars* (Oxford: Oxford University Press, 1991).
4 PC John Barrow retired after 32 years service, 22 of which were spent working on Scotland Road; *LM*, 11 October 1881.
5 D. Taylor, 'Violence, the police and the public in modern England', *Memoria y Civilización*, vol. 2, 1999, pp. 141–70.
6 *LM*, 2 April 1850. Also see chapter 5 for tensions between the Irish community and the police.
7 TNA, PL 27/13, part 2, Palatinate of Lancaster: crown court depositions, 8 July 1852.
8 *LM*, 7 December 1852.
9 LvRO, 352 POL 3/1, Order issued by the head constable, Head constable's special order book, 14 December 1852.
10 LvRO, 352 POL 3/1, 22 December 1852.
11 LvRO, 352 POL 3/1, 24 December 1852
12 *LM*, 6 March 1855.
13 *LM*, 5 December 1866.
14 *LM*, 13 August 1867.
15 *LM*, 23 September 1871.
16 *Porcupine*, 1 August 1863 and 8 October 1867; *LM*, 9 August 1864.
17 *LM*, 27 February 1861.
18 *Porcupine*, 17 July and 30 October 1869; *MC*, 22 October 1869, reported on the 'forthcoming' formation of the Metropolitan Police Vigilance Association, one

objective of which was to provide some supervision of police conduct on London streets in order to provide evidence of officers' violence towards members of the public.

19 *Porcupine*, 17 July 1869.
20 *Porcupine*, 17 July 1869; *LM*, 17 October 1877.
21 *Porcupine*, 9 September 1876 and 27 January 1877.
22 *Porcupine*, 27 January 1877; *LM*, 16 August 1876 and 8 February 1898; LvRO, 352 POL 2/1, Head constable's report, 1 December 1859. Mills was fined £5 and the head constable recommended that he should not be reinstated.
23 *LM*, 20 December 1870.
24 *Porcupine*, 18 December 1869; *LM*, 27 April 1876.
25 *LM*, 11 October 1879; *Liberal Review*, 30 March 1878.
26 LvRO, 352 POL 2/1, Head constable's report, 17 September 1859.
27 *LM*, 19 August 1876.
28 *LM*, 28 June 1853.
29 *LM*, 5 July 1860.
30 *LM*, 15 November 1873 and 14 February 1851.
31 *LM*, 24 August 1876. See Emsley, *Hard Men*, pp. 133–37, for other cases of combining issues of masculinity, policing and fighting.
32 *MC*, 5 October 1865.
33 *LM*, 12 February 1875.
34 *Manchester City News*, 1 January 1881.
35 *LM*, 3 January 1862.
36 See the article headed 'A police trick' in the *Porcupine*, 26 July 1879.
37 *Porcupine*, 11 May 1878.
38 *LM*, 5 May 1856 and 7 November 1872.
39 For Murphy, see *LM*, 14 November 1855; for the Croppers, *LM*, 9 April 1850.
40 *LM*, 18 February 1851.
41 *LM*, 23 and 24 August 1876.
42 *LM*, 22 and 25 February 1862.
43 For the football case, see *LM*, 27 November 1894; for street trading, *LM*, 19 March 1895; and for pitch and toss, *LM*, 9 March 1894.
44 *LM*, 9 June 1868.
45 *LM*, 9 August 1892 and 9 February 1893.
46 *LM*, 25 March 1862.
47 For Sunderland, see *LM*, 4 November 1853; for Tinker, *Manchester Guardian*, 30 June 1855, and Neal, *Sectarian Violence*, p. 143; and for Burns, *LM*, 29 October 1866, and *Porcupine*, 2 February 1867.
48 *LM*, 17 March 1854.
49 *LM*, 15 March 1850.
50 *LM*, 30 March 1855, 19 and 26 November 1860.
51 *LM*, 4 October 1875.
52 For the M'Carroll case, see *LM*, 20 October 1854; for the Melling case, *LM*, 6 October 1863; and for the Huskisson case, *LM*, 15 February 1856.
53 *LM*, 1 March 1870 and 8 November 1869.
54 *LM*, 11, 12, 15 September and 30, 31 October 1871; see *Illustrated Police News* (henceforth *IPN*), 23 September 1871, for a report and the illustration. The whole case was a travesty of justice and can be regarded as a face-saving exercise for both the police and the army.
55 See Taylor, *The New Police*, pp. 108–27. Taylor writes that 'begrudging acquiescence more accurately sums up the popular response'.

Chapter 5

1 BPP, 1854–55, XIII, *Select Committee on Poor Removals*, answer 4954, p. 359, opinion of the Reverend A. Campbell.

2 A. R. Forward, Liverpool Conservative councillor, 1893, quoted in Waller, *Democracy and Sectarianism*, p. 141.

3 For good discussions on the sectarian divide within the town, see Neal, *Sectarian Violence*; and J. Belchem, *Irish, Catholic and Scouse: The History of the Liverpool-Irish, 1800–1939* (Liverpool: Liverpool University Press, 2007). The latter suggests (p. 8) that Protestant migrants accounted for about a quarter of those who arrived from Ireland.

4 The theme has attracted considerable interest; the following works form a select but representative sample: Neal, 'A criminal profile of the Liverpool Irish'; R. Swift, 'Crime and the Irish in nineteenth-century Britain', in R. Swift and S. Gilley (eds), *The Irish in Britain, 1815–1939* (London: Barnes and Noble, 1989), pp. 163–82; R. Swift, 'Heroes or villains? The Irish, crime and disorder in Victorian England', *Albion*, vol. 29(3), 1997, pp. 399–421; J. K. Walton, M. Blinkhorn, C. Pooley, D. Tidswell and M. J. Winstanley, 'Crime, migration and social change in north-west England and the Basque country, c.1870–1930', *British Journal of Criminology*, vol. 39, 1999, pp. 90–112.

5 Swift, 'Crime and the Irish'; Swift, 'Heroes or villains?'; Neal, 'A criminal profile'.

6 Neal, 'A criminal profile'; Swift, 'Crime and the Irish'; *LM*, 17 February 1898 and 13 August 1890.

7 These figures were calculated using the head constable's annual reports to the Liverpool watch committee, LvRO, H352 cou.

8 *Porcupine*, 29 May 1875; *LM*, 29 May 1875.

9 *LM*, 30 July 1850; Neal, *Sectarian Violence*, pp. 129–30 and 147–48.

10 See Neal, *Sectarian Violence*, pp. 133–42, for a full description of the 1851 incidents; *LM*, 15, 18, 22 and 29 July 1851.

11 *LM*, 2 March 1852; Neal, *Sectarian Violence*, pp. 144–46.

12 *LM*, 2 March 1852; *Porcupine*, 19 July 1873.

13 *LM*, 20 February 1855, quote from *Liverpool Courier* taken from Neal, *Sectarian Violence*, p. 165.

14 *LM*, 13 July 1860, 15 July 1864, 19 and 20 March 1895.

15 *LM*, 19 March 1850; *Porcupine*, 12 December 1868; *LM*, 26 July 1860.

16 *LM*, 2 July 1889 and 28 April 1868.

17 *LM*, 20 July 1864.

18 *LM*, 16 and 26 March 1870.

19 *LM*, 27 December 1882 and 10 October 1865. For comments on Fenianism see Belchem, *Irish, Catholic and Scouse*, pp. 164–81; Neal, *Sectarian Violence*, pp. 179–81.

20 *Manchester Times*, 22 December 1866; *LM*, 13 and 14 December 1866; LvRO, 352 POL 2/4, letter, 22 September 1866. The pub at 62 Richmond Row, run by Austin Gibbons, was where the Fenians allegedly met in Liverpool; see LvRO, 352 POL 2/4–7, Minutes of the Liverpool watch committee, 22 September 1866.

21 See LvRO, 352 POL 2, Head constable's annual report to the Liverpool watch committee, 1867/68; *LM*, 5 October and 22 October 1867.

22 Neal, *Sectarian Violence*, pp. 180–81; *LM*, 9, 13 and 14 December 1867.

23 *LM*, 25 and 26 July 1881, 3 August 1881 and 27 December 1882; Sir W. B. Forwood, *Recollections of a Busy Life; Being the Reminiscences of a Liverpool Merchant 1840–1910* (Liverpool: Lee and Nightingale, 1910), pp. 88–92; Belchem, *Irish, Catholic and Scouse*, pp. 178–80.

24 *LM*, 19 June 1877, 6 May 1878, 5, 10 and 11 September 1878.

Chapter 6

1 *LM*, 5 August 1875; also see M. Macilwee, *The Gangs of Liverpool* (Wrea Green: Milo Books, 2006), pp. 97–100.

2 *LM*, 10 August 1875.

3 *LM*, 17 August 1875.

4 On the concept of the 'fair fight' and Victorian attitudes to fighting, see J. E. Archer, '"Men behaving badly"? Masculinity and the uses of violence, 1850–1900', in S. D'Cruze (ed.), *Everyday Violence in Britain, 1850–1950* (Harlow: Longman, 2000), pp. 43–44; C. A. Conley, *The Unwritten Law: Criminal Justice in Victorian Kent* (Oxford: Oxford University Press, 1991), ch. 2; Emsley, *Hard Men*; J. C. Wood, *Violence and Crime in Nineteenth-Century England: The Shadow of Our Refinement* (London: Routledge, 2004).

5 *LM*, 10 and 12 April 1876.

6 P. King, 'Punishing assault: the transformation of attitudes in the English courts', *Journal of Interdisciplinary History*, vol. 27(1), 1996, pp. 43–74; M. J. Wiener, *Men of Blood: Violence, Manliness and Criminal Justice in Victorian England* (Cambridge: Cambridge University Press, 2006); A. E. Sampson, 'Dandelions on the field of honor: duelling, the middle classes, and the law in nineteenth-century England', *Criminal Justice History*, vol. 9, 1988, pp. 99–155.

7 *LR*, 27 February 1868; *Porcupine*, 16 March 1861.

8 See the following chapter on roughs and cornermen; see also Wood, *Violence and Crime*, ch. 4.

9 *LM*, 6, 7, 10, 17 and 28 July 1896; LvRO, M347 COR/L/10, Liverpool coroner's court newspaper cuttings, 1892.

10 *LM*, 3 March 1870, 12 May 1856 and 23 December 1874.

11 *MC*, 18 September 1866.

12 *LM*, 26 March 1870.

13 *MC*, 29 June 1887; LvRO, H352 cou, Head constable's annual report, 1862/63, p. 452. See also *LM*, 11 October 1865, for a report on the frequent acts of prosecuted and unprosecuted violence which took place on ships bound for America.

14 *MC*, 27 May 1889.

15 *LM*, 6 August 1890. For a detailed investigation of knife fighting in the Mediterranean region, see T. W. Gallant, 'Honor, masculinity and ritual knife fighting in nineteenth-century Greece', *American Historical Review*, vol. 105(2), 2000, pp. 359–82.

16 *LM*, 23 May 1856. See also *MC*, 26 March 1894, for Judge Day's comments on the shocking fact that so many of the Liverpool population armed themselves with knives.

17 *LM*, 28 February 1854.

18 *MC*, 5 January 1864; for the 'Liverpool cut' case, see *LM*, 13 July 1870.

19 *LM*, 14 August 1874; *Porcupine*, 4 April 1874 and 15 August 1874; *PMG*, 17 December 1874, which carried an editorial on the use of the boot.

20 *LM*, 25 December 1874 and 9 January 1872. Many publicans became increasingly wary of serving drinks to already drunken customers, as their licences would have been placed in jeopardy at the annual brewster sessions.

21 *LM*, 7, 12 and 19 February 1898; *LM*, 5 and 26 May 1892.

22 For the Brien case, see *LM*, 16 February 1893; for Hanlon, *LM*, 12 November 1855; for the life-preserver case, *LM*, 17 March 1874; for Francis, *LM*, 21 September 1859; for Houston, *LM*, 8 August 1874.

23 *LM*, 5, 17 and 27 May 1892.

24 *LM*, 25 July 1871.

25 *LM*, 26 April 1876 and 16 December 1870.

26 *LM*, 1, 2 and 3 November and 19 December 1866.
27 *LM*, 27 February 1856.
28 *LM*, 23 and 27 March 1855 and 26 August 1857.
29 *LM*, 4 October and 11 November 1879.
30 *LM*, 2 April 1858.
31 Wiener, *Men of Blood*, pp. 52–53.

Chapter 7

1 From an article headed 'Liverpool Man-Hawks', by 'A Working Man', *Porcupine*, 24
   October 1874. For a modern view on a similar group of people, note the comments
   of Christopher Grayling, the then shadow Works and Pensions Secretary: 'They lack
   social skills and a sense of responsibility. They hang around on street corners, and get
   sucked into crime and antisocial behaviour. They struggle to find worthwhile work,
   if they are looking for work at all.' *Guardian*, 11 February 2008.
2 The Tithebarn Street murder is dealt with in detail by Macilwee, *The Gangs of
   Liverpool*, pp. 13–81. See also *LM*, 5 August 1874; *Porcupine*, 8 August 1874. The
   Liverpool Mercury and all other Liverpool papers carried daily reports of the murder
   and its aftermath in the days which followed 4 August. A brother and a sister of the
   two condemned men were later themselves found guilty of killing a man in 1877: see
   LM, 18 September and 3 November 1877. It was thought the incident was related to
   the Tithebarn Street murder.
3 LvRO, 352 POL 2/6, Head constable's report, 11 August 1874.
4 *Porcupine*, 22 August 1874.
5 *PMG*, 17 December 1874.
6 *All the Year Round*, 10 October 1868.
7 *All the Year Round*, 5 September 1874.
8 *LM*, 17 April 1865.
9 *LM*, 21 and 23 February 1871.
10 *LM*, 7 and 21 September 1878. See also *LM*, 26 March 1895, for the case of John
    Berry, who was arrested for wounding John Thompson. It was alleged that Berry
    attempted to take some chips out of Thompson's bag on a Saturday night.
11 *LM*, 18 November 1872.
12 *Porcupine*, 24 October 1874. Such stories may well have been apocryphal.
13 *LM*, 4 November 1872.
14 J. J. Tobias, *Crime and Industrial Society in the Nineteenth Century* (1967;
    Harmondsworth: Pelican edition, 1972), p. 14.
15 H. Mayhew, *London Labour and the London Poor* (1851; Ware: Wordsworth edition,
    2008). Mayhew identified many different gradations of the criminal class, from the
    'skilled' to the 'unskilled', which represented a kind of reversed mirror image of
    'normal' society.
16 Quoted in the *Times*, 24 September 1874.
17 *Porcupine*, 9 January 1875.
18 *Porcupine*, 8 August 1874; *LM*, 7 August 1874.
19 *Times*, 11 January 1875.
20 *Porcupine*, 9 January 1875.
21 LvRO, 352 POL 2/6, Head constable's report, 11 August 1874.
22 *MC*, 12 January 1875; LvRO, 352 POL 2/6, Head constable's report, 4 January 1875.
23 Storch, 'The plague of blue locusts'.
24 *LM*, 2, 3, 9, 16 and 23 April 1884. See chapter 11 (pp. 183–86) for details of these
    killings.

25 *LM*, 12 October 1877.
26 A. M. Davies, *The Gangs of Manchester* (Wrea Green: Milo Books, 2008).
27 *LM*, 30 November 1878 and 15 July 1869.
28 W. Nott-Bower, *Fifty-Two Years a Policeman* (London: Edward Arnold, 1926), pp. 148–53; LvRO, 352 POL 2/10, Head constable's reports, 19 October and 27 October 1886.
29 For more detail on these gangs see R. Sindall, *Street Violence in the Nineteenth Century* (Leicester: Leicester University Press, 1990), pp. 66–70, 117–22; Macilwee, *The Gangs of Liverpool*, covers the entire period of the gang's existence and brings to the fore the *Liverpool Daily Post*'s and *Liverpool Echo*'s coverage of the gang phenomenon.
30 *LM*, 13 February 1885.
31 *LM*, 8 and 20 April, 2 May and 5 August 1885.
32 *LM*, 5 August and 9 and 10 November 1886. There were a number of other incidents of assault implicating the gang.
33 *LM*, 1 September 1886; see also Macilwee, *The Gangs of Liverpool*, ch. 14.
34 The assize cases appeared in *LM*, 9, 12 and 20 November 1886. See also Nott-Bower, *Fifty-Two Years a Policeman*, pp. 149–51. Mr Justice Day became known as 'Judgement Day' because of his harsh sentencing.
35 *LM*, 21 December 1886.
36 *LM*, 21 May 1887.
37 *LM*, 18 March 1887.
38 *LR*, 28 August and 9 October 1886. The *Liverpool Daily Post* and *Echo* were firm believers in the gang's existence and were equally critical of the police.
39 *LR*, 3 March 1887. See Davies, *The Gangs of Manchester*, for a detailed account of the Scuttlers.
40 *LM*, 13 May 1892 and 22 December 1893; and for the strike-related incident see *LM*, 8 April 1890.
41 Sindall, *Street Violence*, pp. 45–78.
42 *LM*, 28 September 1869.
43 See *Cornhill Magazine*, 'The science of garrotting and housebreaking', vol. 7, January 1863. Present-day readers would regard garrotting as mugging. In nineteenth-century Liverpool many street robberies involved the use of women as a distraction before the victim was attacked.
44 *LM*, 13 November 1873. The murder referred to is considered at length at the start of chapter 10.
45 *LM*, 7 and 17 June 1853. See also chapter 2 on the canal bridge.
46 *LM*, 14 June 1853, 15 August 1892, and 21 and 25 March 1895. The bridge was, in effect, a toll bridge for unsuspecting pedestrians new to the area.
47 For the Higgins case, see *LM*, 21 March 1854; for Farley, *LM*, 2 November 1855; and for Fairhurst, *LM*, 29 May 1872.
48 *LM*, 13 March 1894.

Chapter 8

1 M. E. Owen, 'Criminal women', *Cornhill Magazine*, vol. 14, 1866, p. 153.
2 *LM*, 27 August 1874 and 15 October 1867.
3 L. Zedner, *Women, Crime, and Custody in Victorian England* (Oxford: Clarendon Press, 1991); M. Feeley and D. Little, 'The vanishing female: the decline of women in the criminal process 1687–1912', *Law and Society Review*, vol. 25, 1991, pp. 719–57. Liverpool percentages calculated from LvRO, H352 cou, Head constable's annual

reports to the Liverpool watch committee for the second half of the nineteenth century. See *LM*, 8 April 1897, for the seventy-seventh court appearance of Esther Savage of Bootle.

4 Harold Furniss (ed.), *Famous Crimes*, vol. 7(86), undated, pp. 114–20. The full story of Flanagan and Higgins (her sister and conspirator) appears in A. Brabin, *The Black Widows of Liverpool* (Lancaster: Palatine Books, 2003), and is discussed in detail on pp. 130–32. See also K. Watson, *Poisoned Lives: English Poisoners and Their Victims* (Hambledon: London, 2004).

5 Of the many studies of infanticide, there in particular may be recommended here: A. R. Higginbotham, '"Sin of the age": infanticide and illegitimacy in Victorian London', *Victorian Studies*, spring, 1989, pp. 319–37; M. Jackson, *New-Born Child Murder: Women, Illegitimacy and the Courts in 18th-Century England* (Manchester: Manchester University Press, 1996); L. Rose, *Massacre of the Innocents: Infanticide in Great Britain 1800–1939* (London: Routledge and Kegan Paul, 1986).

6 LvRO, 347 COR1, Liverpool coroner's courts records, register of inquests, 1852–65.

7 Quoted in Walton and Wilcox, *Low Life and Moral Improvement*, pp. 134–45.

8 F. W. Lowndes, *Infanticide in Liverpool* (National Association for Promotion of Social Sciences, 1872–73), pp. 397–412.

9 *LM*, 26 November 1873.

10 *LM*, 16 December 1868; Rose, *Massacre of the Innocents*, p. 131.

11 LvRO, H352 cou, Head constable's annual report, 1867/68, p. 465; *LM*, 14 April 1868.

12 *LM*, 18 May 1878.

13 For Brough, see *LM*, 24 November 1894; for Quinn, see *LM*, 4 February, and 23 and 25 March 1893. Bed irons were part of the bed frame.

14 *LM*, 14 and 26 October 1865.

15 *LM*, 21 October 1865 and 19 December 1868.

16 *LM*, 8 and 23 March 1870.

17 *LM*, 21 and 29 December 1893, and 22 March 1894.

18 For examples of newly born babies disposed of in privies, see *LM*, 13 and 16 November 1857; head injuries, *LM*, 19 November 1873; in the canal, *LM*, 3 September 1856, 9 October 1875, 14 October 1881 and 28 February 1883; for live infants, *LM*, 19 July 1850, 28 May 1856 and 8 June 1868.

19 *LM*, 2 and 19 August 1853.

20 The case was brought to public notice in *LM*, 10, 12 and 26 January 1876 and the trial was reported in *LM*, 29 March 1876.

21 This case was considered notorious at the time; see *LM*, 1, 5, 6, 12 and 23 February 1877.

22 For examples of bodies in the canal, see *LM*, 3 September 1856 and 28 February 1883; for Devitt, see *LM*, 21 August 1857; for Cochrane, *LM*, 24 August 1857.

23 *LM*, 1 May and 15 August 1866.

24 *Times*, 21 and 24 November 1879. See the case of 'Murder by a baby farmer', *LM*, 28 July 1877.

25 *LM*, 1, 2, 16, 29 and 30 October 1879.

26 *Times*, 21 November 1879.

27 *LM*, 16 and 29 December 1870.

28 *LM*, 1 September 1874.

29 The sample of cases was taken from the three-monthly random sample of the *Liverpool Mercury* between 1850 and 1900. The defendants outnumber the victims on account of two people being tried for the killing of one individual.

30 *LM*, 19 August 1853.

31 *LM*, 1 May and 3 August 1899.

32 *LM*, 21 and 28 June 1895.

33 *LM*, 14 December 1870.

34 *LM*, 14 and 24 August and 1 September 1874.

35 Brabin's *The Black Widows of Liverpool* is an excellent detailed account of the whole case. Brabin raises the possibility that other women may have been involved in similar crimes. See any of the Liverpool newspapers for the arrests, trial and execution of the two women. See also the *Times*, which closely followed the case, and the *Illustrated Police News*, which carried a number of interesting illustrations of the defendants and details of the case, 23 February and 1 and 8 March 1884. Especially useful articles include: for the inquest, *Birmingham Daily Post*, 19 November 1883; for the magistrates' hearing, *Lloyd's Weekly Newspaper*, 16 December 1883; for the trial, *LM*, 15, 16 and 18 February 1884; and for the execution, *LM*, 4 March 1884.

36 *LM*, 6 June 1877.

37 *LM*, 16 December 1868, 10 January 1873, 20 February 1856 and 27 August 1874. The last news item was headed 'Female Savages in Circus-Street'.

38 *LM*, 18 November 1872, and 19 and 4 October 1865.

39 *LM*, 3 September 1869 and 4 April 1882.

40 *LM*, 5 and 6 April 1865, and 27 July 1869. See *LM*, 21 January 1873, for a case where lodgers attacked a landlady after being given notice to quit.

41 *LM*, 21 May 1892; one wonders if the report of 800% is correct. See also Liverpool Statistical Society, *How the Casual Labourer Lives* (1909), p. xvi.

42 *LM*, 21 January 1873. See also *LM*, 15 June and 15 August 1861 for the case of Mary Jane O'Connor, who stabbed Jane Fisher in Christian Street.

43 See chapter 10 (pp. 164–67) for details of this case, and *LM*, 27 November 1873.

44 *LM*, 11 February 1856, 9 December 1874 and 4 April 1882.

45 *LM*, 17 and 18 August 1876.

46 *LM*, 21 July 1896 and 12 October 1875. Back-street distilling was very much a hidden social crime in the borough.

47 *LM*, 20 and 23 February 1855. 'Females of the lowest class' were heavily involved, filling their aprons with flour. Of the first batch of prisoners tried in court, 11 out of 18 were women. See also chapter 5, p. 71.

48 *LM*, 11 April 1893 and 11 September 1878.

49 Father Nugent's comments were reported in LvRO, H352 cou, Head constable's annual report, 1876/77, p. 556. For examples of women assaulting staff with glasses etc., see *LM*, 5 July 1860, 3 November 1860 and 16 November 1872.

50 *Manchester Weekly Post*, 16 March 1889; *LM*, 24 July 1885.

Chapter 9

1 F. P. Cobbe, 'Wife torture in England', *Contemporary Review*, vol. 32, April 1878, p. 59–60, quoting Mr Serjeant Pulling in 1876.

2 Cobbe, 'Wife torture', p. 60.

3 *LM*, 27 December 1867.

4 *Porcupine*, 4 January 1868.

5 *LM*, 3 April 1868.

6 For studies on marital violence and the law, see M. E. Doggett, *Marriage, Wife-Beating and the Law in Victorian England* (Columbia, SC: University of South Carolina Press, 1993); E. Foyster, *Marital Violence: An English Family History, 1660–1857* (Cambridge: Cambridge University Press, 2005); Wiener, *Men of Blood*; S. D'Cruze, *Crimes of Outrage: Sex, Violence and Victorian Working Women* (London: UCL Press, 1998); A. Clark, 'Domesticity and the problem of wifebeating in nineteenth-century Britain: working-class culture, law and politics', in S. D'Cruze (ed.), *Everyday Violence in Britain, 1850–1950* (Harlow: Longman, 2000), pp. 27–40.

7 *LM*, 2 August 1853.
8 For the Roche case, see *LM*, 20 July 1855; for threats, *LM*, 28 February 1854; for the Doran case, *LM*, 27 July 1870 (and the same case is discussed here in a different context on p. 155); for the Lewis case, *LM*, 6 July 1871; and for witness wives' failure to appear in court, *LM*, 22 October 1867.
9 *LM*, 4 December 1875 and 28 July 1885.
10 *LM*, 14 April 1865.
11 *LM*, 19 and 26 October 1875.
12 *Punch*, 30 January 1875, p. 50.
13 For the Heath case, see *LM*, 13 September 1869; for the Farrell case, *LM*, 21 February 1882; for the Ireland case, *LM*, 18 January 1873.
14 *LM*, 3 and 10 July 1855.
15 *LM*, 10 September 1856 and 21 April 1865.
16 *LM*, 22 June 1868.
17 *LM*, 28 August 1867.
18 *LM*, 3 and 4 September 1895.
19 *LM*, 25 and 28 April 1898.
20 *LM*, 9 March 1855.
21 For the Tulley case, see *LM*, 1 January 1872; for the Metcalfe case, see *LM*, 2 March 1874; and for the Hickey case, *LM*, 10 February 1882.
22 *LM*, 1 February 1881 and 1 August 1876.
23 *LM*, 17 December 1874.
24 *LM*, 5 January 1875.
25 For examples of police reactions to domestic incidents, see *LM*, 7 May 1878, 15 December 1868, 29 March 1870 and 9 September 1871.
26 *LM*, 24 August 1857. For more information on possible homicides which escaped prosecution see Archer, 'Mysterious and suspicious deaths'.
27 *LM*, 5 and 6 August 1867.
28 For the Dabbs case, see *LM*, 5 December 1866; for defenestration by Fairclough, *LM*, 8 August 1876, by Lopez, *LM*, 28 March 1876 and *IPN*, 26 February 1876, for the illustration.
29 For Robertson, see *LM*, 8 and 13 November 1894.
30 For an excellent study of the portrayal of women victims, see Wiener, *Men of Blood*, especially chs 5 and 6.
31 *LM*, 27 July 1870. (See also p. 146 on the Doran case.)
32 For Dunn, see *LM*, 19 December 1870; and for Nolan *LM*, 31 March 1870. Both men received six months with hard labour.
33 *LM*, 10 February 1883, and 3 and 10 September 1856.
34 *LM*, 25 October 1865.
35 *LM*, 23 and 25 March 1895.
36 *LM*, 24 and 26 November and 18 December 1890.
37 *LM*, 3 February and 20 March 1893.
38 *LM*, 7 September 1869.
39 For McLean, see *LM*, 27, 28 and 29 September 1871; for Davies, *LM*, 17 August 1857.
40 *LM*, 13 August 1874.
41 Nott-Bower, *Fifty-Two Years a Policeman*, ch. 10; Zedner, *Women, Crime, and Custody*, ch. 1.
42 These figures were based upon the numbers in LvRO, H352 cou, Head constable's annual reports to the Liverpool watch committee. Twelve rape cases were pending.
43 *LM*, 21 November 1855; *LM*, 25 August 1864.
44 *LM*, 15 November 1860.
45 *LM*, 21 November 1855; *LM*, 20 and 21 October and 5 November 1863.
46 *LM*, 26 April 1853 and 4 June 1861.

47 *LM*, 5 and 6 June 1861 and 29 May 1878.
48 *LM*, 4 November 1890.
49 *LM*, 16 December 1867.
50 *LM*, 3 June 1868. In 1864, 'respectably-attired' Samuel Higgins was found guilty of being drunk and exposing himself to 'several young ladies in the employ of Mr Blakey, boot and shoe manufacturer'. *LM*, 5 July 1864.

Chapter 10

1 *LM*, 3, 4, 5 November and 17 December 1873. See *IPN*, 8 November 1873, for the depiction of Corrigan 'dancing' on his mother (reproduced here on p. 165) and a detailed account of the killing. The murder was widely reported, for example in the *Times*, 4 November 1873, and *Birmingham Daily Post*, 3 and 4 November 1873.
2 *Porcupine*, 8 November 1873.
3 *LM*, 4 November 1873. Thomas Corrigan's execution was reported in the same paper on 6 January 1874.
4 *LM*, 31 August 1857 and 29 March 1870.
5 *LM*, 11 November 1879.
6 *LM*, 2, 3, 4 and 11 January and 17 March 1896.
7 *LM*, 13 March 1874.
8 For the Johnson case, see *LM*, 28 April 1868; for the Shepherd case, see *LM*, 6 July 1864; and for the Knowlson case, see *LM*, 18 December 1874.
9 *LM*, 19 November 1872 and 4 March 1874.
10 *LM*, 18 August 1874.
11 *LM*, 5 April 1858.
12 For the Valaley case, see *LM*, 3 August 1857; and for the Keating case, see *LM*, 4 March 1874.
13 *LM*, 12 September 1851.
14 *LM*, 9 March 1855.
15 *LM*, 3 July and 6 August 1896.
16 *LM*, 8, 9 April and 12 August 1863.
17 *LM*, 15 and 24 April 1897.
18 *LM*, 9 December 1875. She was, it was reported, astounded by the sentence.

Chapter 11

1 *Times*, 12 August 1861.
2 For a brief discussion on children and the law, see A. W. G. Kean, 'The history of the criminal liability of children', *Law Quarterly Review*, vol. 211, July 1937, pp. 364–70.
3 P. Wilson, *Children Who Kill* (London: Michael Joseph, 1973); G. Sereny, *The Case of Mary Bell: A Portrait of a Child Who Murdered* (London: Pimlico, 1995); D. J. Smith, *The Sleep of Reason: The James Bulger Case* (London: Arrow, 1994); K. Summerscale, *The Suspicions of Mr Whicher: Or the Murder at Road Hill House* (London: Bloomsbury, 2008).
4 *LM*, 16, 19 and 25 February 1886; *LR*, 20 and 27 February 1886.
5 TNA, PL 27/13, part 2, Palatinate of Lancaster: crown court depositions, 21 July 1855; *LM*, 24 July 1855; *Liverpool Daily Post*, 21 and 23 July 1855. A 'brickfield' was where bricks were moulded and fired.
6 *LM*, 12, 14, 15, 16 and 24 September 1891.

7 *PMG*, 24 September 1891.

8 *LM*, 28 September 1891.

9 *Times*, 11 December 1891; *Birmingham Daily Post*, 11 December 1891; *PMG*, 10 December 1891.

10 *LM*, 5 August 1853, 14 August 1874, 1 July and 3 August 1896, 16 May 1872 and 11 December 1875.

11 For evidence concerning Stokes, see *LM*, 3 February 1875; for the Gibbons case, see *Manchester Guardian*, 11 May 1860, and *LM*, 14 August 1860; see also *LM*, 16 October 1877, for a case in which a shoeblack was stabbed by another shoeblack.

12 *LM*, 28 September 1895.

13 *LM*, 9 April 1884.

14 See *LM*, 26 November 1878. Some 15-year-old drunks were fighting in Derby Road, Bootle. For the cocoa room incident, see *LM*, 20 February 1877.

15 John Travis, with three previous convictions, was discharged – see *LM*, 3 March 1854; for the Murphy case, see *LM*, 17 and 28 February 1898; for the Reeves case, see *LM*, 30 August 1876. For a case in which a 13-year-old stabbed an 8-year-old during a game of football, see *LM*, 12 and 14 August 1876.

16 Reports of earthenware insulators on telegraph poles being damaged by stones thrown at them appear in LvRO, 352 POL 1/13, Orders of the Liverpool watch committee to the head constable, 13 October 1874, and *LM*, 29 November 1890.

17 For Ebans, see *LM*, 23 November 1857; for Morris, see *LM*, 7 November 1872; for the Roby break-ins, see *LM*, 14 August 1879. A 16-year-old was arrested on the ferry to Dublin for firing a revolver, *LM*, 21 August 1879.

18 For pistol gangs, see *LM*, 7 June 1897; see also G. Pearson, *Hooligan: A History of Respectable Fears* (London: Macmillan, 1983), pp. 102–5. For Caligari and O'Brien, see *LM*, 30 June and 7 July 1897.

19 For the cricket incident, see *LM*, 6 July 1896; for the 'peggy' case, see *LM*, 14 May 1872; for the pushing into the canal, see *LM*, 26 October 1875.

20 For the chimney incident, see *LM*, 1 December 1874; for a 'trade war' incident, see *LM*, 13 June 1877; for a work-related argument, see *LM*, 14 December 1868; for resisting arrest, *LM*, 4 September 1871; and for protecting a brother, *LM*, 19 September 1894.

21 *Birmingham Daily Post*, 13 November 1891, and *LM*, 5 December 1891.

22 For studies of teenage gangs in Victorian England, see: Davies, *The Gangs of Manchester*; Macilwee, *The Gangs of Liverpool*; Pearson, *Hooligan*.

23 *LM*, 3 April 1875.

24 The death of Burns was examined in the BBC's Radio 4 programme *The Long View*, broadcast on 24 February 2009. The case was reported in *LM*, 28, 29 December 1883 and 12 February 1884 and the *Liverpool Echo*, 11 February 1884.

25 *Liverpool Echo*, 12 February 1884. For the Blackstone Street murder, see *LM*, 7, 8 and 9 January 1884.

26 See *LM*, 29 July 1885, 10 May 1886 and 31 May 1887, for some reports on the boys' brigade and the Gordon Working-Lads Institute.

27 LvRO, POL 1/13, Orders of the Liverpool watch committee to the head constable, 1 September 1874.

28 LvRO, H352 cou, Head constable's annual report, 1906, p. 26.

Chapter 12

1 *LM*, 26 December 1882, taken from an article headed 'The dock labourers' little ones'.

2 For histories of the establishment of the LSPCC and NSPCC, see, respectively,

A. Brack, *All They Need Is Love* (Neston: Gallery Press, 1983), and G. K. Behlmer, *Child Abuse and Moral Reform in England 1870–1908* (Stanford, CA: Stanford University Press, 1982).

3 *LM*, 12 January 1883.

4 For the Mansfield comment, see *LM*, 2 March 1852; the two headlines cited appear in *LM*, 23 September 1851 and 28 September 1859.

5 For more discussion and further reading on childhood in Victorian Britain, see H. Hendrick, *Children, Childhood and English Society 1880–1990* (New Studies in Economic and Social History) (Cambridge: Cambridge University Press, 1997), especially ch. 2.

6 For the M'Fee case, see *LM*, 16 November 1855; for the Reed case, see *LM*, 3 August 1857; for the Burns case, see *LM*, 13 July 1855.

7 For the Hanwell case, see *LM*, 15 November 1860; for the Tranter case, see *LM*, 9 and 16 November 1872.

8 For the Clarke case, see *LM*, 25 July 1864; for the Fairclough case, see *LM*, 22 June 1895.

9 For the Doran case, see *LM*, 4 February 1898; for the Bolton case, see *LM*, 18 June 1861.

10 *LM*, 1 April 1865.

11 For the Sherridan case, see *LM*, 28 February 1862; for the M'Donald case, see *LM*, 30 March and 1 April 1863.

12 *LM*, 16, 18 and 23 November 1857.

13 *LM*, 29 April 1858.

14 For the Gore case, see *LM*, 7 July 1870; for the 'rough music', see *LM*, 5 August 1867; for the Roughsedge case, see *LM*, 2 and 4 December 1875.

15 For the Lawson case, see *LM*, 10 December 1868; for the lime incident, see *LM*, 27 November 1866; and the children pushed into the canal, see *LM*, 28 March 1874 and 24 June 1895.

16 *LM*, 14 October 1879.

17 For the Jacques case, see *LM*, 3 June 1853; for the Hall case, see *LM*, 18 November 1873; for the Knight case, see *LM*, 11 May 1878; for the St Helens case, see *LM*, 16 April 1897. The *Liverpool Mercury* also had a longer article on school punishment, 14 October 1879.

18 A lengthy report of the town meeting which founded the LSPCC can be found in *LM*, 20 April 1883.

19 Hendrick, *Children, Childhood and English Society*, pp. 45–47; Behlmer, *Child Abuse and Moral Reform*.

20 LvRO, 179 CRU 13/1, Liverpool Society for the Prevention of Cruelty to Children annual reports, case 153, 1883, p. 10, case 292, 1884, p. 10, case 761, 1886, p. 5, case 1675, 1886, p. 8.

21 *Birmingham Daily Post*, 12 June 1891. The sad story of Fanny Adams has bequeathed to us the phrase 'sweet FA', or 'sweet Fanny Adams'. It was claimed this phrase came about when the murder coincided with the introduction of tinned meat to the Royal Navy. When asked what the contents tasted like, some sailors replied that it was like 'sweet FA'. The meaning of the letters in the phrase has altered over the years. The murder and trial of her killer, Frederick Baker, was reported in the *Liverpool Mercury* and most other national and regional papers: see *LM*, 27 and 28 August, and 7 December 1867.

22 *Times*, 27 May 1891.

23 *Times*, 22, 23, 27, 29 and 30 May, 5, 6 June and 3 August 1891. The murder was reported on daily by the *Liverpool Mercury* from 20 May up until the report of the execution that appeared on 21 August 1891.

24 *Daily Post*, 25 May 1891; *LM*, 21 August 1891. The press hinted, when the news of

the murder first broke, that there may have been a sexual motive but this was laid to rest at the inquest.

25 The Blackburn murder was covered almost daily by the *Liverpool Mercury* and other local papers between March and July 1876.

26 *LM*, 2 and 4 March 1874.

27 For cases in which defendants were found not guilty because of the delay in reporting the crime, see *LM*, 14 August 1857 and 3 June 1853.

28 L. A. Jackson, *Child Sexual Abuse in Victorian England* (London: Routledge, 2000), pp. 18–22.

29 *LM*, 17 November 1896.

30 For the Thompson case, see *LM*, 9 March 1870; for the Tearney case, see *LM*, 30 March 1852.

31 *LM*, 24 September 1869.

32 For the Knotty Ash case, see *LM*, 15 December 1866; for the Tearnon case, see *LM*, 16 September 1891.

33 For the Thom case, see *LM*, 21 June 1877; for the Cannell case, see *LM*, 23 June 1879; on the drunk, see *LM*, 5 September 1878; for the Mount Gardens case, see *LM*, 18 April 1863; for the Atkinson case, see *LM*, 3 July 1896.

34 *LM*, 8 November 1869.

35 *LM*, 14 August 1857.

36 *LM*, 29 March 1876 and 15 December 1866.

37 *LM*, 31 August 1880.

38 *LM*, 28 November 1855.

39 *LM*, 24 August 1864.

40 *LM*, 22 April, and 14 and 15 May 1890.

41 For the Hanly case, see *LM*, 12 April 1865; for the Cassidy case, see *LM*, 29 March 1870.

42 *LM*, 10 July 1855. In a case which involved confronting the alleged abuser, see *LM*, 2 November 1866; John Finlay of West Derby was found guilty and sentenced to 12 months' hard labour.

43 *LM*, 20 December 1870.

44 *LM*, 24 April 1876.

Chapter 13

1 *LM*, 4 January 1875.

2 *LM*, 4 January 1875.

3 Mr Raffles, the stipendiary magistrate, was aware of the difference between the reporting on crime in Liverpool by national and local newspapers; see *LM*, 4 January 1878.

4 *Maidstone and Kentish Journal*, 29 November 1875. My thanks to Carolyn Conley for giving me this reference.

5 W. L. Clay, *The Prison Chaplain: A Memoir of the Rev. John Clay, BD. Late Chaplain of the Preston Gaol* (London: Macmillan, 1861), pp. 517–18. Original emphasis.

6 *LM*, 13 March 1895.

7 *IPN*, 23 March 1895. Women in the late nineteenth century were not considered 'respectable' if they ventured outside without either a hat or a shawl over the head.

8 *LM*, 20 and 23 September 1895.

9 *LM*, 30 September 1895.

10 *Hampshire Telegraph*, 1 December 1877.

11 LvRO, A. Hume, *Condition of Liverpool: Religious and Social* (Liverpool: printed by Brakell, 1858).

12 *PMG*, 17 December 1874, which also quotes the *Telegraph*.

13 *LM*, 23 and 25 March 1895.

14 *LM*, 5 December 1891; *Western Mail*, 5 December 1891.

15 *Birmingham Daily Post*, 19 October 1891. See also *Birmingham Daily Post*, 5 November 1890.

16 The decrease in crimes of violence in Liverpool cited by the head constable appear in LvRO, H352 cou, Head constable's annual report, 1900. Quote taken from the *Criminal Registrar's Report 1899*, pp. 36–37, quoted in V. A. C. Gatrell, 'The decline of theft and violence in Victorian and Edwardian England', in V. A. C. Gatrell, B. Lenman and G. Parker (eds), *Crime and the Law: A Social History of Crime in Western Europe Since 1500* (London: Europa Publications, 1980), p. 241.

17 See Jackson, *Child Sexual Abuse*, for further details on ostracism and the punishment of abusers.

18 See for example *Guardian*, 25 May 2010.

19 See Wood, *Violence and Crime*.

20 Indeed, Wood concluded that the period between 1820 and 1870 was not 'a decisive leap into "modernity"'. Wood, *Violence and Crime*, p. 138. Wiener, *Men of Blood*, passim.

21 *LM*, 1 August 1896. Had this occurred in the 1850s, for example, a short prison sentence would have been the norm.

22 For the Boyle case, see *LM*, 28 March 1895; for the Gilboy case, see *LM*, 16 and 24 September 1895; and for the Regan case, see *LM*, 24 January 1896.

23 For comments on Hopwood, see Nott-Bower, *Fifty-Two Years a Policeman*, pp. 151–52, and *LM*, 21 September 1895. See Wiener's *Men of Blood* for his arguments on the diminishing tolerance of male violence, especially against women, in the nineteenth century.

24 LvRO, H352 cou, Head constable's annual report, 1903, p. 15.

25 LvRO, H352 cou, Head constable's annual report, 1899, p. 14. Original emphasis.

Appendix

1 For fuller details of Shimmin's life and work see Walton and Wilcox, *Low Life and Moral Improvement*, pp. 1–37, and the *Oxford Dictionary of National Biography* entry by the same authors (www.oxforddnb.com).

2 *LM*, 13 July 1857, original emphasis. I am indebted to Laurie Feehan for introducing me to the articles reprinted here.

Bibliography

Victorian newspapers and periodicals

All the Year Round
Birmingham Daily Post
Contemporary Review
Cornhill Magazine
Daily Post
Famous Lives
Hampshire Telegraph
Illustrated Police News
Liberal Review
Liverpool Albion
Liverpool Courier
Liverpool Daily Post
Liverpool Echo
Liverpool Mercury (LM)
Liverpool Review (LR)
Lloyd's Weekly Newspaper
Maidstone and Kentish Journal
Manchester City News
Manchester Courier (MC)
Manchester Guardian
Manchester Times
Manchester Weekly Post
Morning Chronicle
Pall Mall Gazette (PMG)
Porcupine
Preston Chronicle
Punch
Times
Western Mail

The National Archives, Kew (TNA)

ASSI 52/4, 6, 7, 8, 10, Assize papers: northern assize circuit, trial depositions, 1884 and 1886.
HO 45/3634, Home Office papers: Liverpool police armed with revolvers to be put on equal terms with robbers, 1851.
HO 73/5, part 2, Home Office papers: returns to Constabulary Commission, 1839.
PL 27/13, part 2, Palatinate of Lancaster: crown court depositions, 1851–55.
PL 27/14, Palatinate of Lancaster: crown court depositions, 1856–58.
PL 27/17, parts 1–2, Palatinate of Lancaster: crown court depositions, 1865–67.

Liverpool Record Office (LvRO)

179 CRU 2/1, Executive Committee minute book, 1883–1906.
179 CRU 11/1, 1896–97, Newspaper cuttings relating to the Liverpool Society for the Prevention of Cruelty to Children.
179 CRU 13/1–2, Liverpool Society for the Prevention of Cruelty to Children, annual reports, 1883–1900.
347 COR1, Liverpool coroner's courts records, register of inquests, 1852–65.
352 POL 1/1–37, Orders of the Liverpool watch committee to the head constable, 1836–1915.
352 POL 2/1–19, Head constable's reports to the Liverpool watch committee, 1852–1905.
352 POL 3/1, Head constable's special order book, 1852–62.
352 POL 4/27, Minutes of the Liverpool watch committee.
H352 cou, *Proceedings of the Council*, 1857–1905, in which the Liverpool head constable's annual reports to the Liverpool watch committee are bound.
M347 COR/L/10, Liverpool coroner's court newspaper cuttings, 1892.
Sir W. B. Forwood, *Some Recollections of a Busy Life; The Reminiscences of a Liverpool Merchant, 1840–1910* (Liverpool: Lee and Nightingale, 1910).
A. Hume, *Condition of Liverpool: Religious and Social* (Liverpool: printed by Brakell, 1858).
W. Lewin, *Clarke Aspinall: A Biography* (London: Allen, 1893).

Merseyside Police Museum (headquarters)

Daily report book 1, 1889–91.
Constabulary force daily report book (discipline), 1891–96.

British parliamentary papers (BPP)

1839, XIX, *First Report of the Commissioners Appointed to Inquire as to the Best Means of Establishing an Efficient Constabulary Force.*
1841–1901, *Censuses.*
1854–55, XIII, *Select Committee on Poor Removals.*
1875, LXI, *Reports to the Secretary of State for the Home Department on the State of the Law Relating to Brutal Assaults.*
1877, XI, *Reports of the Select Committee of the House of Lords on Intemperance.*
1901, LXXXIX, *Criminal Statistics for 1899* (Cd 659).

Contemporary publications

Baines, T., *Liverpool in 1859* (London, 1859).

Booth, William, *In Darkest England and the Way Out* (London: Salvation Army, 1890) (http://www1.salvantionarmy.org.uk).

Clay, W. L., *The Prison Chaplain: A Memoir of the Rev. John Clay, BD. Late Chaplain of the Preston Gaol* (London: Macmillan, 1861).

Cobbe, F. P., 'Wife torture in England', *Contemporary Review*, vol. 32, April 1878, pp. 55–87.

Engels, Friedrich, *The Condition of the Working Class in England in 1844* (Frogmore, St Albans: Panther edition, 1969).

Forwood , Sir W. B., *Recollections of a Busy Life; Being the Reminiscences of a Liverpool Merchant 1840–1910* (Liverpool: Lee and Nightingale, 1910).

Furniss, H. (ed.), *Famous Crimes*, vol. 7(86), undated, pp. 114–20.

Jones, Rev. J. I., *The Slain in Liverpool During 1864 by Drink* (Liverpool: printed by Howell, 1865).

Liverpool Statistical Society, *How the Casual Labourer Lives. Report of the Liverpool Joint Research Committee on the Domestic Condition and Expenditure of the Families of Certain Liverpool Labourers* (Liverpool, 1909).

Lowndes, F. W., *Infanticide in Liverpool* (National Association for Promotion of Social Sciences, 1872–73), pp. 397–412.

Madden, T. J., '*The Black Spot on the Mersey*'. *The Story of a Great Social Reform* (Westminster: Church of England Temperance Society, 1905).

Mayhew, Henry, *London Labour and the London Poor* (1851; Ware: Wordsworth edition, 2008).

Owen, M. E., 'Criminal women', *Cornhill Magazine*, vol. 14, 1866, p. 153.

Pike, L. O., *History of Crime in England* (London, 1876, reprinted Montclair, NJ: Patterson Smith, 1968).

Shimmin, Hugh, *Liverpool Life: Its Pleasures, Practices and Pastimes* (Liverpool: Egerton Smith, 1857, reprinted New York: Garland, 1985).

Shimmin, Hugh, *Liverpool Sketches* (Liverpool, 1862).

Taylor, Dr W. C., 'Moral economy of large towns. Liverpool', *Bentley's Miscellany*, vol. 8, 1840, pp. 129–36.

Books and articles

Archer, John E., 'Poaching gangs and violence: the urban–rural divide in nineteenth-century Lancashire', *British Journal of Criminology*, vol. 39(1), 1999, pp. 25–38.

Archer, John E., '"A reckless spirit of enterprise": game preserving and poaching in nineteenth-century Lancashire', in David W. Howell and Kenneth O. Morgan (eds), *Crime, Protest and Police in British Society* (Cardiff: University of Wales Press, 1999), pp. 149–75.

Archer, John E., '"Men behaving badly"? Masculinity and the uses of violence, 1850–1900', in Shani D'Cruze (ed.), *Everyday Violence in Britain, 1850–1950* (Harlow: Longman, 2000), pp. 41–54.

Archer, John E., 'Mysterious and suspicious deaths: missing homicides in north-west England 1850–1900', *Crime, History and Societies*, vol. 12(1), 2008, pp. 45–63.

Archer, John E. and Jo Jones, 'Headlines from history: violence in the press, 1850–1914', in E. A. Stanko (ed.), *The Meanings of Violence* (London: Routledge, 2003).

Bean, R., 'Aspects of "new" unionism in Liverpool, 1889–91', in Harold R. Hikins (ed.), *Building the Union. Studies on the Growth of the Workers' Movement: Merseyside, 1756–1967* (Liverpool: Toulouse Press, 1973).

Behlmer, G. K., *Child Abuse and Moral Reform in England 1870–1908* (Stanford, CA: Stanford University Press, 1982).

Belchem, John (ed.), *Liverpool 800. Culture, Character and History* (Liverpool: Liverpool University Press, 2006).

Belchem, John, *Irish, Catholic and Scouse: The History of the Liverpool-Irish, 1800–1939* (Liverpool: Liverpool University Press, 2007).

Bickerton, T. H., *A Medical History of Liverpool* (London: John Murray, 1936).

Brabin, Angela, *The Black Widows of Liverpool* (Lancaster: Palatine Books, 2003).

Brack, A., *All They Need Is Love* (Neston: Gallery Press, 1983).

Brogden, M., *On the Mersey Beat: Policing Liverpool Between the Wars* (Oxford: Oxford University Press, 1991).

Campbell, J. and P. Laxton, *Homicide and Manslaughter in Victorian Liverpool: A Research Report* (University of Liverpool, Geography Department, 1997).

Clark, Anna, 'Domesticity and the problem of wifebeating in nineteenth-century Britain: working-class culture, law and politics', in Shani D'Cruze (ed.), *Everyday Violence in Britain, 1850–1950* (Harlow: Longman, 2000), pp. 27–40.

Cockcroft, W. R., 'The Liverpool police force 1836–1902', in S. P. Bell (ed.), *Victorian Lancashire* (Newton Abbot: David and Charles, 1974), pp. 150–68.

Conley, Carolyn A., *The Unwritten Law: Criminal Justice in Victorian Kent* (Oxford: Oxford University Press, 1991).

Costello, R., *Black Liverpool: The Early History of Britain's Oldest Black Community 1730–1918* (Liverpool: Picton Press 2001).

Davies, Andrew M., 'Youth gangs, masculinity and violence in late Victorian Manchester and Salford', *Journal of Social History*, 1998, vol. 32, pp. 349–69.

Davies, Andrew M., '"These viragoes are no less cruel than the lads": young women, gangs and violence in late-Victorian Manchester and Salford', *British Journal of Criminology*, vol. 39(1), 1999, pp. 72–89.

Davies, Andrew M., 'Youth gangs, gender and violence 1870–1900', in Shani D'Cruze (ed.), *Everyday Violence in Britain, 1850–1950* (Harlow: Longman, 2000), pp. 70–85.

Davies, Andrew M., *The Gangs of Manchester* (Wrea Green: Milo Books, 2008).

Davin, Anna, 'What is a child?', in Anthony Fletcher and Stephen Hussey (eds), *Childhood in Question: Children, Parents and the State* (Manchester: Manchester University Press, 1999), pp. 15–36.

D'Cruze, Shani, *Crimes of Outrage: Sex, Violence and Victorian Working Women* (London: UCL Press, 1998).

D'Cruze, Shani (ed.), *Everyday Violence in Britain, 1850–1950* (Harlow: Longman, 2000).

Dexter, W. (ed.), *The Nonesuch Dickens. The Letters of Charles Dickens. Vol. 3, 1858–1870* (London: Bloomsbury, 1938).

Doggett, Maeve E., *Marriage, Wife-Beating and the Law in Victorian England* (Columbia, SC: University of South Carolina Press, 1993).

Edwards, P. D., 'Angus Bethune Reach', *Oxford Dictionary of National Biography*, article 23213 online (www.oxforddnb.com).

Emsley, Clive, '"The thump of wood on a swede turnip": police violence in nineteenth-century England', *Criminal Justice History*, vol. 6, 1985, pp. 125–49.

Emsley, Clive, *Crime and Society 1750–1900* (2nd edition) (London: Longman, 1996).

Emsley, Clive, *Hard Men: Violence in England Since 1750* (London: Hambledon and London, 2005).

Feeley, Malcolm and Deborah Little, 'The vanishing female: the decline of women in the criminal process 1687–1912', *Law and Society Review*, vol. 25, 1991, pp. 719–57.

Foyster, Elizabeth, *Marital Violence: An English Family History, 1660–1857* (Cambridge: Cambridge University Press, 2005).

Gallant, Thomas W., 'Honor, masculinity and ritual knife fighting in nineteenth-century Greece', *American Historical* Review, vol. 105(2), 2000, pp. 359–82.

Gatrell, V. A. C., 'The decline of theft and violence in Victorian and Edwardian England', in V. A. C. Gatrell, B. Lenman and G. Parker (eds), *Crime and the Law: A Social History of Crime in Western Europe Since 1500* (London: Europa Publications, 1980), pp. 238–347.

Gatrell, V. A. C. and T. B. Hadden, 'Criminal statistics and their interpretation', in E. A. Wrigley (ed.), *Nineteenth- Century Society: Essays in the Use of Quantitative Methods for the Study of Social Data* (Cambridge: Cambridge University Press, 1972), pp. 336–96.

Hammerton, A. James, *Cruelty and Companionship: Conflict in Nineteenth-Century Married Life* (London: Routledge, 1992).

Harrison, Brian, *Drink and the Victorians: The Temperance Question in England 1815–1872* (2nd edition) (Keele University: Keele University Press, 1994).

Hendrick, Harry, *Children, Childhood and English Society 1880–1990* (New Studies in Economic and Social History) (Cambridge, Cambridge University Press, 1997).

Higginbotham, Ann R., '"Sin of the age": infanticide and illegitimacy in Victorian London', *Victorian Studies*, spring, 1989, pp. 319–37.

Howell, David W. and Kenneth O. Morgan (eds), *Crime, Protest and Police in British Society* (Cardiff: University of Wales Press, 1999).

Jackson, Louise A., 'Family, community and the regulation of child sexual abuse: London, 1870–1914', in A. Fletcher and S. Hussey (eds), *Childhood in Question* (Manchester: Manchester University Press, 1999), pp. 133–51.

Jackson, Louise A., *Child Sexual Abuse in Victorian England* (London: Routledge, 2000).

Jackson, Mark, 'Suspicious infant deaths: the statute of 1624 and medical evidence at coroners' inquests', in M. Clark and C. Crawford (eds), *Legal Medicine in History* (Cambridge: Cambridge University Press, 1994).

Jackson, Mark, *New-Born Child Murder: Women, Illegitimacy and the Courts in 18th-Century England* (Manchester: Manchester University Press, 1996).

Kean, A. W. G., 'The history of the criminal liability of children', *Law Quarterly Review*, vol. 211, July 1937, pp. 364–70.

King, Peter, 'Punishing assault: the transformation of attitudes in the English courts', *Journal of Interdisciplinary History*, vol. 27(1), 1996, pp. 43–74.

Knelman, Judith, *Twisting in the Wind: The Murderess and the English Press* (Toronto: University of Toronto Press, 1998).

Lowe, W. J., 'The Lancashire constabulary, 1845–1870: the social and occupational function of a Victorian police force', *Criminal Justice History*, vol. 4, 1983, pp. 41–62.

Macilwee, Michael, *The Gangs of Liverpool* (Wrea Green: Milo Books, 2006).

Mather, F. C., *Public Order in the Age of the Chartists* (Manchester, 1959; reprinted Westport, CT: Greenwood Press, 1984).

Monkkonen, Eric H., 'Diverging homicide rates: England and the United States 1850–1875', in Ted Robert Gurr (ed.), *Violence in America. Vol. 1: The History of Crime* (Newbury Park, CA: Sage, 1989), pp. 80–101.

Monkkonen, Eric H., *Murder in New York City* (Berkeley, CA: University of California Press, 2001).

Morris, R. M., 'Lies, damned lies and criminal statistics in England and Wales', *Crime, History and Societies*, vol. 5(2), 2001, pp. 5–26.

Neal, Frank, *Sectarian Violence: The Liverpool Experience 1819–1914* (Manchester: Manchester University Press, 1988).

Neal, Frank, 'A criminal profile of the Liverpool Irish', *Transactions of the Historic Society of Lancashire and Cheshire*, vol. 140, 1991, pp. 161–99.

Nott-Bower, William, *Fifty-Two Years a Policeman* (London: Edward Arnold, 1926).

Pearson, Geoffrey, *Hooligan: A History of Respectable Fears* (London: Macmillan, 1983).

Rose, Lionel, *Massacre of the Innocents: Infanticide in Great Britain 1800–1939* (London: Routledge and Kegan Paul, 1986).

Ross, Ellen, '"Fierce questions and taunts": married life in working-class London, 1870–1914', *Feminist Studies*, vol. 8, 1982, pp. 575–602.

Sampson, A. E., 'Dandelions on the field of honor: duelling, the middle classes, and the law in nineteenth-century England', *Criminal Justice History*, vol. 9, 1988, pp. 99–155.

Scraton, Phil, Ann Jemphrey and Sheila Coleman, *No Last Rights: The Denial of Justice and the Promotion of Myth in the Aftermath of the Hillsborough Disaster* (Liverpool: Liverpool City Council, 1995).

Sereny, Gitta, *The Case of Mary Bell: A Portrait of a Child Who Murdered* (London: Pimlico, 1995).

Sharples, Joseph, *Liverpool* (Pevsner Architectural Guides: City Guides) (New Haven, CT: Yale University Press, 2004).

Sindall, Rob, *Street Violence in the Nineteenth Century* (Leicester: Leicester University Press, 1990).

Smith, David J., *The Sleep of Reason: The James Bulger Case* (London: Arrow, 1994).

Storch, Robert D., 'The plague of blue locusts: police reform and popular resistance in northern England, 1840–57', *International Review of Social History*, vol. 20, 1975, pp. 61–90.

Storch, Robert D., 'The policeman as domestic missionary: urban discipline and popular culure in northern England, 1850–1880', *Journal of Social History*, vol. 9, 1976, pp. 481–509.

Summerscale, Kate, *The Suspicions of Mr Whicher: Or the Murder at Road Hill House* (London: Bloomsbury, 2008).

Swift, Roger, 'Crime and the Irish in nineteenth-century Britain', in R. Swift and S. Gilley (eds), *The Irish in Britain, 1815–1939* (London: Barnes and Noble, 1989), pp. 163–82.

Swift, Roger, 'Heroes or villains? The Irish, crime, and disorder in Victorian England', *Albion*, vol. 29(3), 1997, pp. 399–421.

Taylor, David, *The New Police in Nineteenth-Century England: Crime, Conflict and Control* (Manchester: Manchester University Press, 1997).

Taylor, David, 'Violence, the police and the public in modern England', *Memoria y Civilización*, vol. 2, 1999, pp. 141–70.

Taylor, Howard, 'Rationing crime: the political economy of criminal statistics since the 1850s', *Economic History Review*, vol. 51(3), 1998, pp. 569–90.

Tobias, J. J., *Crime and Industrial Society in the Nineteenth Century* (1967; Harmondsworth: Pelican, 1972).

Tomes, Nancy, 'A torrent of abuse: crimes of violence between working-class men and women in London, 1840–1875', *Journal of Social History*, vol. 11, 1978, pp. 328–45.

Waller, P. J., *Democracy and Sectarianism: A Political and Social History 1868–1939* (Liverpool: Liverpool University Press, 1981).

Walton, John K., Martin Blinkhorn, Colin Pooley, David Tidswell and Michael J. Winstanley, 'Crime, migration and social change in north-west England and the Basque country, c.1870–1930', *British Journal of Criminology*, vol. 39, 1999, pp. 90–112.

Walton, J. K. and A. Wilcox (eds), *Low Life and Moral Improvement in Mid-Victorian England: Liverpool Through the Journalism of Hugh Shimmin* (Leicester: Leicester University Press, 1991).

Walton, J. K. and A. Wilcox, 'Hugh Shimmin', *Oxford Dictionary of National Biography*, article 50352 online (www.oxforddnb.com).

Watson, Katherine, *Poisoned Lives: English Poisoners and Their Victims* (Hambledon: London, 2004).

Wiener, Martin J., *Reconstructing the Criminal: Culture, Law and Policy in England, 1830–1914* (Cambridge: Cambridge University Press, 1990).

Wiener, Martin J., *Men of Blood: Violence, Manliness, and Criminal Justice in Victorian England* (Cambridge: Cambridge University Press, 2006).

Wilson, P., *Children Who Kill* (London: Michael Joseph, 1973).

Wood, J. Carter, *Violence and Crime in Nineteenth-Century England: The Shadow of Our Refinement* (London: Routledge, 2004).

Zedner, Lucia, *Women, Crime, and Custody in Victorian England* (Oxford: Clarendon Press, 1991).

General index

Index of people

I have followed the Victorian spelling – M' – for some of the surnames beginning with Mc or Mac.

Burns, Thomas, PC 57
Butler, William, PC 41–2
Butt, Justice 185
Byrne, Patrick 74

Cain, Robert 24
Caine, Mr, magistrate 141
Caligari, James 181
Callinson, John 50
Calton, William 206
Campbell, Dr 121
Campbell, George 183
Campbell, John and Mrs 48–9
Campbell, Peter 93–4
Campbell, Susan 129
Canavan, James 164–5
Cannell, Charles 207
Cannell, Edward 157
Cannell, Richard 135
Cannon, Sabina 138
Carlisle, detective 122
Carnes, sergeant 54
Carnes, Thomas 159
Carroll, Michael 113
Carson, PC 46–7
Cassidy, David 210
Charnley, Caroline 135–6
Chatfield, Ann 189
Clark, James 151
Clarke, George 182
Clarke, John and Mary Ann 192
Clarke, Thomas 60
Clay, John, Reverend 213
Clingan, PC 44
Clough, Mr, magistrate 48
Cobbe, Frances Power 140, 144
Cochrane, Bridget 125
Cochrane, Theresa 135
Connolly, William 104
Connor, Ann 135
Connor, Elizabeth 220
Connor, Ellen and Michael 148–9
Connor, William 179
Conway, John (alias Brown, Conally, Hooper, O'Donnell) 201–2
Copeland, 57
Corduroy, Sarah (alias Lyons) 171
Corrie, Herbert 178
Corrigan, James 147
Corrigan, Mary 136, 164–7
Corrigan, Patrick 166
Corrigan, Thomas 136, 164–7

Costigan, Daniel 87
Cotton, Henry 44
Coyle, John 77
Crawford, Robina 193–4
Crawford, Samuel 176–8
Cregan, Michael 181
Cropper, Mr and Mrs 54
Cullen, James 41–2
Cunningham, Hugh 106
Cunningham, John 178–9
Curran, Annie 135
Curry, Mr, coroner 120
Cutler, PC 151

Dabbs, Ann 154
Daley, Bridget 129
Daly, William 197
Davies, Andrew, historian 114
Davies, James 158
Davies, Mrs 193
Davy, Michael 107
Day, Justice 107–8, 252 n.34
De Morce, George 90
Dempsey, William 185
Devine, Robert 220
Devitt, Catherine 125
Dickens, Charles 96, 97, 222
Dickson, George Washington 91
Digman, Mary 129
Disraeli, Benjamin 3
Dixon, John 178
Donnolly, John 220
Doolan, Mary 67
Doran, James 192
Doran, Patrick 146, 155
Douglas, Mary Ann 133
Douglass, Thomas 72
Dowling, Francis (Joey) 182
Dowling, Mathew, head constable (1845–52) 39, 69, 70
Duckett, John 98
Duckworth, Mrs 195
Duffy, William 179
Duggan, Patrick 185
Duncan, Dr 17
Dunn, Alfred 156
Dunning, Leonard, head constable (1902–12) 138, 187
Duxbury, James 81–2, 219

Ebans, William 181
Eccles, Betty 128

Index of street names and places